THE VOICE OF MUSIC

THE VOICE OF MUSIC

Conversations with composers of our time

ANDERS BEYER

edited and translated
by Jean Christensen and Anders Beyer

Ashgate

Aldershot • Burlington USA • Singapore • Sydney

The Voice of Music
Conversations with Composers of Our Time
by Anders Beyer

Edited and translated by Anders Beyer and Jean Christensen

Layout: Hans Mathiasen

Published by
Ashgate Publishing Limited
Gower House
Croft Road, Aldershot
Hants GU11 3HR
England

Ashgate Publishing Company
131 Main Street
Burlington, Vermont 05401-5600
USA

British Library Cataloguing in Publication data

The voice of music:conversations with composers of our time
   1. Composers – Scandinavia – Interviews 2. Music –
   Scandinavia – 20th century – History and criticism
   I. Beyer, Anders
   780.922

Library of Congress Card Number: 00-109128

ISBN 1 84014 230 8

Printed on acid-free paper

Printed and bound in Great Britain by MPG Books Ltd, Bodmin, Cornwall

Contents

Acknowledgements

This book owes its existence to the initiative of Professor Jean Christensen, University of Louisville, Kentucky, USA. My collaboration with Professor Christensen in the editing and translation of selected articles from the 1989–1999 issues of *Dansk Musik Tidsskrift* has been an intense and stimulating process, and without her endurance and patience the book would never have come to fruition.

Jean Christensen and I have been fortunate in having particularly able advisers and critical observers who have followed and commented on the work throughout all its phases: Jesper Christensen (University of Louisville), Maura Eaton (Music Officer of the Arts Council of Ireland) and Rachel Lynch (Editor at Ashgate Publishing). We thank them for their invaluable help.

On several occasions the Danish painter Per Kirkeby has generously made works available for use in connection with my projects. For this book Kirkeby has painted a new work which graces the front cover. I am very grateful to Per Kirkeby for his unfailing support in general, and his kindness in creating a new work of art for this book in particular.

A number of benevolent funds, institutions and individuals have provided moral and financial support for the publication, expressing their confidence that the book will make a contribution to the greater understanding of the main directions of twentieth-century musical composition. We would like to thank them for this trust. The contributors are mentioned here in no particular order: Gunilla Hellman (Culture Fund of the Nordic Council of Ministers); Foreningen Norden; Research Council, University of Louisville, Kentucky; the Foundation for the Promotion of Finnish Music (LUSES); Jostein Simble (Director of the Norwegian Music Information Centre); Thorvald Stoltenberg (former Norwegian Ambassador in Copenhagen); Pekka Hako (Director of the Finnish Music Information Centre); Roland Sandberg (Director of the Swedish Music Information Centre); Finn Andersen (Secretary-General of the Danish Cultural Institute); Trevor Davies (former Chairman of the Cultural Fund of the Danish Ministry of Culture).

Most importantly I would like to thank the composers for their kindness and willingness to talk about their music. It is their art which has been both the source and the inspiration for this publication.

Anders Beyer, Copenhagen, May 2000

INTRODUCTION

By *Jean Christensen*

In my essay about *Dansk Musik Tidsskrift* (Danish Music Review) in the handbook of *International Music Journals* (1990), I drew attention to the extensive and generously illustrated interviews as a distinctive feature of the publication. The interviews have long been a characteristic of the periodical and the lively reporting in these 'conversations' with influential composers both in and outside the Nordic countries has stimulated the thinking of Danish composers to the benefit of Danish musical life. These excellent interviews are conducted by well-informed Danes, trained professional musicians and experienced writers on music, who work on assignment and commission and prepare carefully for the task of interviewing. They interview each subject in the subject's own language or one with which he or she is comfortable, a procedure that avoids problems inherent in translations and brings a notable immediacy to the report. Consequently, these interviews are a valuable resource, and it is unfortunate that access is limited simply because they are published in Danish.

It has often occurred to me that a good translation of a number of interviews would be useful, and especially so if the selection represented the broad diversity of composers active in the present-day musical world. As a step in that direction Anders Beyer and I have edited and translated a selection of interviews he has conducted. Most of them were published in *Dansk Musik Tidsskrift* between 1989 and 1999. In order to highlight the Nordic viewpoint we have chosen to favour interviews with composers whose works are less well-known outside of Scandinavia than they should be. The goal has been to represent Nordic interests and to capture obliquely a Nordic view of international subjects. It seems germane to start by interviewing the interviewer who is also editor of *Dansk Musik Tidsskrift*.

Dansk Musik Tidsskrift *has been published since 1925. The changes that it has experienced over the years reflect the changes in editorship as well as those in professional musical standards. Through its history it has been very strongly influenced by Danish composers, and somewhat less so by musicologists and critics. Being editor-in-chief of a highly respected, long-lived and spirited journal must be a challenge for such a young person. Can you talk about your editorship? What it was like when you took over? What you have tried to do? What have been your objectives?*

It was a practical problem, a historically unique situation, that led me to become involved. In the late 1980s *Dansk Musik Tidsskrift* was still being published by Det Unge Tonekunstner Selskab (The Young Composer's Society). 'DUT', as it's called, was actually an agency that produced concerts of new music and it occurred to the composers that publishing *Dansk Musik Tidsskrift* themselves was a conflict of interest. So we had a 'divorce of convenience'; DUT would continue alone and *Dansk Musik Tidsskrift* would become independent. At that time I was a member of DUT's board of directors. The then editor decided that he couldn't continue publishing the journal under the terms stipulated by the new editorial board.

Suddenly the journal had no editor. So we went up to the old Macintosh Plus in *Dansk Musik Tidsskrift*'s office and stared at it. It was one of the first Macs in Denmark. The former editor had paid a fortune for it, but it was an ingenious move because he could *see* that desk-top publishing would be the future of journals in Denmark. We sat down in front of it. We had no manual or handbook and no familiarity with the technology at all. We just practised until we came to the point when we realized that we could actually produce an issue of the journal, miraculously. It was a fantastic time.

Since there was no financial support for the journal, we worked without any pay for the first couple of years. The contributors who wrote for the magazine received nothing either; it was truly a matter of survival. All of us had the feeling that the periodical had to be saved for it had existed since 1925 and if you look back through the pages you can read the history of Danish music, or for that matter, the music history of other countries. *Dansk Musik Tidsskrift* has been used as a resource, and for some books and articles it is the only source. We believed we simply had to do it. And if we could just do it well enough, then the funding agencies, the State Music Council and the Ministry of Culture, could see that we were able to continue in an orderly manner and perhaps would contribute to the endeavour.

Our subscribers followed us even though they had previously received the journal free as part of their membership in DUT. Now they had to pay for subscriptions as well as paying for their membership. But the number of subscriptions increased and eventually we were able to purchase newer computer equipment enabling us to design a more professional lay-out. We built up our computer equipment and made it fit our editorial policies; we have contributors from many different places—not only Denmark—with contacts over the whole world. And the State, that is, the Ministry of Culture through the Music Council, supports *Dansk Musik Tidsskrift*; it is one of the few journals in Denmark that gets substantial support. Thus we have tried to continue the tradition that reaches all the way back to the beginning of the periodical—that is to be an independent, critical and essential journal for the professional music world.

*Where do the interviews fit into the editorial policy? And, have you noticed any-
thing particular in the time you have been involved?*

We have continued the tradition of composer interviews that began in the
1960s. I have noticed that since the start of my involvement in 1987, we have
had quite a number of interviews with composers from the former Soviet
Union. After the fall of the Eastern bloc, we had the opportunity to see and
hear composers who had been obscure in the 1970s and 1980s. We have printed
interviews with Khrennikov, Gubaidulina, Schnittke and Denisov so this book
of interviews also mirrors certain aspects of important music history over the
last ten years.

The present selection has focused on a core of Nordic composers with the
hope that such a perspective might encourage a debate about recurring issues. We have put the Nordic composers in a wider context by including
them with what I might call 'international names', representatives from the
USA, central Europe and from the former Soviet Union.

*Can you describe your method of preparing for interviews? It is apparent that once
you have decided to interview someone, you prepare thoroughly for the occasion. This
has been a distinctive ingredient of these interviews. What do you do?*

It depends a bit on the situation. There have been occasions when I have had
a unique opportunity to interview someone I did not expect to meet. For
example, I was attending the ISCM World Music Days in Switzerland in
1991 and the little ISCM bus with ISCM participants drove out to a country
village in order to attend a concert. It happened that a masterclass in composition was being held at the same time and the Soviet composer Edison
Denisov was the guest teacher. I had no opportunity to prepare at all. He
only spoke French and I knew very little about him. There was nothing else
to do but to set the microphone up and hope that something interesting
would come out of it.

With other composers, for example with Ligeti, I had ample opportunity
to prepare. I knew that he was about to celebrate a birthday and I had thought
about interviewing him for several years. I had taught a course at the University in which I discussed his music: I had heard everything he had composed
and read everything that had been written about him. So I went down to
Hamburg to visit him and could pose a different kind of question from those
I asked Denisov.

*Have you noticed any particular themes running through the interviews you have
published over the last ten years? Any international currents?*

Reading all of these interviews one after another in a short space of time has enabled me to juxtapose them in my mind, and certain things about them do stand out. One can see that there are names that run through all of them — like shadows or 'invisible monsters' (laughter) and these names are Schoenberg and Adorno. They have been so incredibly significant and still are today. Even now composers can't just say they are not interested in these two any more. They have to figure out 'Where do I stand in relation to Schoenberg'? 'Where do I stand in relation to Adorno'? One can see that some of them distance themselves from Adorno, notably, and from the whole Frankfurt School, or from Darmstadt. But it is interesting that even in the 1990s composers have not been able to cast off the historical thinking expressed in the *Philosophy of Modern Music* and the complex issue of modernism. The concerns expressed by composers today are the same as they were about fifty years ago, like the possibility of 'absolute renewal' in music, or the question of using quotations. It is the music that was created at the beginning of the century, the music of Schoenberg, that is still the 'guiding light'.

Do you think composers understand Schoenberg any better now than when he was alive?

When you look at how composers and scholars interpret Adorno or Schoenberg now, there isn't much evidence of a broader understanding of their work. Unfortunately. Often details of their thought are taken out of context and used as proof of some kind of self-evident truth. In the case of Adorno, there is his famous lecture about the 'historical necessity' imposed by the musical materials and then in the case of Schoenberg there is that myth of the 'completely incomprehensible works that will never be played because there isn't anyone who wants to listen to them'. And on and on and on. There is still an unbelievable degree of prejudice with respect to these ideas; over the course of time they have become undifferentiated and have lost their multi-faceted implications. As time has gone on they have been compressed into something like bouillon cubes about which someone says, 'This here, this is Schoenberg', or 'This one here, this is Adorno'. The wider perspective has been lost. It has also been striking to realize how much earlier perspectives tend to become simplified.

Where is Stravinsky in this?

I think that for Danish or Nordic composers, Stravinsky is central. Stravinsky greatly influenced the pluralism that emerged in the 1960s and 1980s when a number of composers could allow themselves to write triads and make music with broad reference to many different forms of music: 'music about music about music', as someone said. It was a style that was largely influenced by Stravinsky's tendency to think in layers. So I think of Stravinsky when I think of composers like Poul Ruders, Karl Aage Rasmussen, also Per Nørgård, or Hans Gefors, just to mention some who have been interviewed in this book: these people really know their Stravinsky.

Do you think there is any way to characterize the music of Nordic composers ?

Do you mean common traits?

Common traits or traits that are not shared. Either one.

In terms of trying to isolate a Nordic sound or distinguish Nordic character-istics, I think Hans Gefors expressed something relevant in his interview: whatever has been shared in the last ten years has been on an institutional level. For me, as editor of a periodical, if I need some information about someone in the Nordic countries, I am never in doubt that I can get what I need. I know everyone in the Nordic region because the information net-work here is unique. Nordic musical life is organized to the highest degree, and operates extensively inside the Nordic boundaries. We have a Nordic Council of Ministers, Nordic prizes in literature and music; there is a web of ties between the Nordic countries. Our periodical, *Nordic Sounds*, serves all five countries. This is essential if Nordic countries are to make a mark in the world and be able to compete with a Europe that is getting stronger by the minute. There is pressure for a common currency in Europe, and a unified approach to politics, military operations and economics. France and Ger-many want to expand, and it is happening—with East Germany. The Nordic consciousness has been reinforced over the past ten years because we realize that in the cultural arena we have been trodden under foot in this century by the French and Germans. I don't think that people notice Denmark very much, but SCANDINAVIA is recognized the world over. When I go abroad and discover that many people think that Denmark is the capital city of Sweden and so on, then I realize that only as a bastion can the north get things done as a cultural entity, that is, unified against the superpowers. I think it is prag-matic cooperation rooted in the realization that together we can achieve some-thing. We are efficient when we fly in formation: think of the Nordic symbol, the flag with swans flying in formation. There is a cultural bond between us. Norway and part of Sweden belonged to Denmark at one time. Our cultural, religious and psychological ties are quite obvious. If I meet a Norwegian somewhere outside of Nothern Europe, we instantly have something to talk about; we share perceptions and fields of interest. We have welfare systems based on common ideas about human values and cultural identities that have deep roots in folk traditions, popular movements that go far back and contacts that are worth developing. It makes sense to work together. But within the artists' own circles there isn't much exchange. Composers know what their colleagues in the other Nordic countries are doing. They keep up with each other, trade commentary in journals, travel to festivals, and so on. But there is no artistic cooperation.

To return to your own interviews. How does it feel to have interviewed someone like Stockhausen on several occasions over a period of time? Having reviewed them is there anything that has struck you in these interviews that you might not have noticed otherwise? Or Nørgård, for example? Have these composers changed over time? Or have you changed?

As far as composers like Nørgård or Stockhausen are concerned, it seems to me that these two make a virtue of the fact that there has really never been anything new in their thinking because actually they have thought the same way since they were children! (laughter) Truly. They explain new directions or ideas as going back to a development that started when they were very young. So that Stockhausen, for example, says that the new *'Formula thinking'* of the *Licht* project is a refinement of the serial technique that he invented in the 1950s. In the same way, Nørgård says about his new technique in which he also uses the *infinite row*, that now the *infinite row* is just one part of an even larger project. I think it would be fair to say that some significant composers have a tendency to want to see in their own work a long continuous thread that ties everything together. When I ask them about various issues, these composers—not only the well-known ones, but also others—I have a clear feeling about what kind of answer I am going to get. I want to say that almost all interviews are set up to engender dialogue—a creative dialogue, a stimulating conversation. That is to say that I have no intention of going in and asking such uncomfortable questions that the conversation goes to pieces. The objective has been more to open up a dialogue.

On the other hand, because I've had the opportunity to speak with some of the composers several times over this ten-year period, I think that I can say that they are all concerned with renewing themselves and that they are taken up with what they are working on at that very minute. That is what interests them and that is what is exciting for them to explain. I always find it stimulating to interview a composer several times because I can see, in spite of everything, that even though they have certain patterns or ways of working, they constantly have their antennae out. They are perhaps the most sensitive people one could come into contact with because they are sensing the world around them all the time through their bodies. I spoke with a composer just recently and he refused to let me play a new CD I had with me because he was just then working on a new piece and he didn't want to be influenced by it. I think it is very exciting to follow a composer's development over a ten year period and yes, it is certainly possible to observe a change, and at the same time acknowledge something unchangeable in the composer's mental constitution—a balance between stability and change.

Especially since you interviewed them when they were younger. Have you ever been really surprised by an answer?

I can't think of an obvious example right now. There have been situations where I have found out something that I didn't know in advance. That sounds very presumptuous, but when I prepare the interviews, I ask questions that I have some idea about what the answer will be. I also try to steer an interview in a certain direction. Although I didn't ask him directly when I spoke with Schnittke at Huddersfield (1990), it was apparent that he could foresee what was going to happen with the Soviet Union. I came to think later that he had an almost prophetic ability. In that way artists have a sensitivity that makes it possible for them to see what others can't.

Then there was the interview where I couldn't understand the answers at all. When I spoke with Sofia Gubaidulina in Stockholm I asked questions in German because she understands German, but she wanted to answer in Russian which was a strange experience because I don't understand that language. It was interesting for me then to come home and have the interview translated for I really understood very little of what she said during the interview. So there have indeed been some situations where I have been surprised.

The integration of public institutions and art in Nordic countries comes out in the interviews. There is an institutionalization, a political element in art that has no counterpart anywhere else, at least not in the USA. What do you think about that?

What has always surprised me is that the ground-breaking experiments, these avant-garde assaults on norms that impact on everything—the new art—all these provocations take place within the arts. These new things happen *within* the established framework. Not from the outside. I can't think of an exception. One may ask, is that good or bad? But it's a question I would rather avoid. We could hope that the system allows as much as possible to come in from outside. I think that this is the way the artistic world functions today in Nordic countries and, as far as I know, might function in some other European countries. What this means is that there is scope for the most extended forms of culture to have a massive impact on the cultural scene, to be seriously scrutinized within the system and evaluated as to whether they work or not. In this way the system holds unique new possibilities for artists, at least here in Denmark with stipends and grants available for projects, and with the entire public supportive of the arts. I believe this isn't so in the USA.

Can you explain why FLUXUS had such a lasting impact here? It was not long-lived in the USA nor did it make a deep impression, but it is still an 'issue' in Denmark. It started out beyond the political norms in the USA, but was absorbed into the norms here, and quickly. Also, why is the average Danish musician familiar with detailed aspects of American avant-garde music—from early John Cage onward—that musicians in the USA ignore?

I think that Denmark is such a small country that artists have had to be international in outlook, and particularly since 1960 there has been a determination to orientate oneself to Europe and the USA, and yes, to the East: Bali, Japan, China. Musicians felt a necessity to think globally more than locally. For Danish composers, and Nordic composers generally, this became crucially important in order to understand themselves. Take Icelandic composers. The first thing they did was to go to Central Europe. That was characteristic of the first half of the century and those composers born in the fifties have also been to the USA or elsewhere to study. This is also true of the other Nordic composers. It is important for them to get out. In the end they come back. An example might be Magnus Lindberg who was at IRCAM in Paris, but has now returned to Finland. I think this openness is characteristic of Nordic composers.

We also avoid 'schools', 'composer-oriented schools', 'epigones' and discourage any tendency of teachers in the conservatories to produce a group of clones. Composers like Heinimen at the Sibelius Academy, or Olav Anton Thommessen at the Music School in Oslo, or, for that matter, Per Nørgård or Karl Aage Rasmussen in Denmark, are teachers and composers who have no desire to create copies of themselves. There is no tradition for that.

Is that why Danish musicians have focused more on clearly individual Americans, Morton Feldman, Nam June Paik, well, Cage, but also Charlie Morrow, people who have attracted much more attention in Denmark than they have, relatively speaking, in American music.

In the case of Feldman and Cage, it is their thinking that has been more influential than their music.

Cage is a special case. Feldman might be a better example; he isn't as widely known or studied in the USA.

Morton Feldman is a bit of a special case in Denmark because of Ivar Frounberg. Ivar was in the USA and studied with Feldman. He came back all enthusiastic about him, wrote an article about him in *Dansk Musik Tidsskrift*, and we had to wonder about a man who had composed a string quartet that lasted four hours. My goodness! Karl Aage Rasmussen has been very taken up with Cage's thinking and music for many years, and Poul Ruders has been highly preoccupied with Stravinsky. Other composers in turn have had to figure out their own relationship to these people.

There it is again, good communication between Danish composers. Any current threads? What about the fact that modernism keeps coming back?

Two things occur to me. I asked Holmboe in a very early interview to think about which composers would survive the twentieth century. He said Bartók and Stravinsky. That was his generation. Later generations would more likely have said Schoenberg and Stravinsky. Modernism and the discussion of it keeps coming back like the waves of the sea, but one can see that even though there is development among composers, there is also a movement away from the fixation on the absolute demand for innovation. Oh, there is still that concern for rigorous structure. That remains a requirement like a big bright sign in the back of one's head: 'It is no good if I repeat myself'. And if one looks at the generation of composers born in the 1950s, even in the 1960s, then the concern for music that communicates on its own terms without any outside reference rises to the surface again; this approach to the treatment of the musical idea goes back to Schoenberg.

György Ligeti

AN ART WITHOUT IDEOLOGY

You were born in a part of the world (now Romania) that became forbidding and insecure early in your lifetime. Recently unrest has flared up again. What were the early years of your life like and what do you think about the recent reports of terrible things in your former homeland?

It shouldn't be forgotten that because of the rearrangement of the states and borders after World War I the 1920s were a difficult time for the whole of Europe. There was social chaos everywhere, culminating in the great crisis of 1929–30. It didn't matter whether one lived in Hungary, Romania or Poland. The perception of Romania under the Ceauşescu regime and communist dictatorship was not a reality in my childhood. My mother tongue is Hungarian. Transylvania belonged to Hungary for a long time and because of inter-marriages, Hungary belonged to Austria from the 15th century on. In Transylvania it was possible to speak of Romanian, Hungarian and German folk heritages co-existing in the same region. They were not integrated; the three completely different cultures existed separately.

For Hungarians it was a shock to have to submit to Romania after World War I. The authorities were Romanian and Romanian became the official language. Hungarians who were the minority naturally didn't care for that. But on the other hand one has to remember that the Romanian people in Transylvania were subjects of Hungary for several hundred years. One can conclude, looking at the current catastrophe in Yugoslavia, that any form of nationalism is an abomination and totally crazy injustice.

We all wish to live in a free and democratic world, no matter who has authority. One should be free to speak whatever language one wants. Until the outbreak of World War II my childhood was happy enough. There was adequate welfare and Romania was a completely normal country to live in — a very corrupt kingdom, but one could live freely. It has been forty-four years since I was in Romania, and that was during the Soviet-type dictatorship of Gheorghin-Dej. But what came after, under Ceauşescu, was worse. Since 1989, with the fall of Ceauşescu, the political situation has changed somewhat, but poverty and hopelessness still prevail.

Though I grew up in Hungarian culture, I greatly admire the Romanian language, which is a beautiful romance language closely related to Italian with mixed Latin, Slavic and Greek vocabulary. Its rich literature is scarcely known in the West.

Your closest family suffered terribly in the last war because they were Jews: your father died in Bergen Belsen, your younger brother was murdered in Mauthausen and your mother survived Auschwitz only because she was a camp doctor. How were you able to survive that hell?

I was not taken to the concentration camp, but instead was called into the work service in the Hungarian military. It was a terrible period in my life. Before, I was attending the conservatory in Cluj (Kolozsvár), but suddenly in mid January 1944 I was put in a work camp. By the end of May 1944 my whole family had been deported to Auschwitz. From 800,000 Jews in Hungary 600,000 were deported, and the majority died or were killed. It was a shock to realize that we were to be exterminated.

How was it possible for you to go to Germany after the war (that is, after the Hungarian Revolution, in 1956, ed.), work as a composer and, in the first few years, also be a shrewd observer of the problems and developments in new music? You left the country that you have called your 'sounding board'. Was it difficult to survive as a human being and retain your personal integrity when you had cut all ties to the past?

That did not have much to do with Hungary, but rather with the communist system. The Hungarian regime was allied with Nazi Germany in the war, but wanted to withdraw from the alliance in 1944. As a result, on 19 March 1944 the German army occupied Hungary, the members of the government were imprisoned and Nazi rule was established. The deportation of the Jews followed. Naturally there were many Hungarians who collaborated with Hitler. In other places there was much more opposition, for instance, in Denmark, Holland and Norway. But after the war I felt completely at home in Budapest. We were hopeful, yes, we didn't suspect that the Soviets would create a new dictatorship. Between October 1945 and end of 1947 there was a freely-elected government that was orientated to the left with a very positive attitude toward artists and intellectuals. But this turned out to be a fake. The police was in the hands of the communists, and behind the stage the Stalinist dictatorship was introduced, step by step, in a shrewd way.

From 1945 to 1948 there was a shortage of food, and eighty per cent of the houses in Budapest had been destroyed. As a student I lived for a long time in a suburb that had not been completely destroyed. My home was a mattress of two square metres in the kitchen. There was no blanket or quilt, nor any heat. Russian soldiers lived in the house. My food was left-overs from their meals. There was no transportation; we walked everywhere. At the music academy all students received food once a day from American and Scandinavian aid organizations.

We lived a miserable life. There was no soap to be had; we washed once a month at most. Try to imagine that for a couple of years there wasn't one window to be found in Budapest. It was an improvised life. Apparently many people live like that in Russia today. But at that time we were happy that the terrible war was over and that the vile Nazi dictatorship was finished.

After three years, everything was more or less in order. When winter arrived we had windows, sometimes even heat. In the course of those three years wonderful literature, music and visual art sprang up. During 1948 the communist dictatorship was formed. The deputies who didn't submit to the communists in the parliament were arrested. Those who would not cooperate with the party disappeared. Some, whose lives were at stake, tried to escape over the border. But people didn't have passports and the border was mined. In December 1948 the communists firmly held the power and the mass arrests began. We young intellectuals didn't know what to do; we were dazed. It was as though we were drugged. We had experienced the Nazi dictatorship, but didn't know the rules of the game with the new Stalinist dictatorship. Myself, I did not read newspapers, but practised the piano. I did my assignments and composed in the library of the Music Academy, which was usually even heated.

During the Nazi dictatorship I was an idealistic, very left-wing socialist. But towards the Soviet Union I was suspicious. We had very contradictory information. In September 1945 some friends and teachers asked me to join the Communist Party. I had a shaky feeling, I refused. But I remained a believer in 'socialism'. Being a naïve socialist, I composed a cantata. It was for my final examination as a twenty-five -year-old at the music academy (Franz Liszt Academy) in 1948. I had been asked for a cantata for four soloists, chorus and orchestra as a final project. In the next year, 1949, a World Youth Festival was planned 'for freedom, against imperial oppression' where the work was to be performed. I actually believed these socialist slogans and began to compose the cantata in the summer of 1948 together with my friend Peter Kuczka, who wrote a text on freedom for all people. When I began the work, I was completely sincere and honest; I believed in the cause. But when I finished the work in the spring of 1949, it made me sick to my stomach. I was nauseated by the degree to which these socialist ideas were used for a filthy purpose in the worst possible police regime, with mass arrests and executions.

You can hardly imagine how horrible daily life was; spies were everywhere. One did not dare say anything, and one had to be careful not to be betrayed. People who worked in an office or in a factory had to check in half an hour early in order to listen collectively to the reading of the Communist Party newspaper. The following day the workers were examined on the previous day's reading. All daily life was regimented. The concept of freedom no longer existed. We constantly had to take part in assemblies and pretend that we were happy and satisfied; we lived in a tight labyrinth of lies. In reality we were bitter—bitter, sorrowful and totally desperate. Every aspect of private life was ruined in this collective. If I had been an opportunist, I would have been able to say 'yes' to all of this and would have become an official composer for the party. I could have had a big career but I could not do it. I would not have done that even under duress.

One day in February 1949 I was encouraged by the Hungarian KGB (AVO) to become an informant and to betray some Catholic friends. The following Tuesday I was to go and report compromising details. I didn't go and therefore expected them to come and arrest me. That didn't happen—they made do with putting me under observation.

After the premiere of the above-mentioned cantata in August 1949 (I was thoroughly unhappy about the performance, but couldn't prevent it) I was criticized by the composers' union (all composers were forced to join the composers' union). The criticism was that there was a fugue in the work which was considered 'clerical' and 'reactionary'. I was asked to compose a new cantata on a new text that praised Rákosi. Mátyás Rákosi was the Hungarian dictator at the time, 'Stalin's most faithful pupil'. I could not publicly refuse because that would mean being thrown in jail, so I asked for time to think about it for a few days. Earlier I had received an invitation to travel on a scholarship to Romania to study folk music. I even got a passport (valid only for Romania) and a visa. I left Hungary as quickly as possible to avoid having to respond to the request for the Rákosi cantata. I was in Romania for almost a year, and thankfully the Rákosi cantata was forgotten in the meantime.

When you lived in Budapest you made many arrangements of Hungarian folk music. Was it to oblige a political system that wanted music 'rooted in the people', as opposed to 'formalist' music?

My 'genuine' compositions—for example, the First String Quartet, the solo Cello Sonata, *Musica Ricercata*, the woodwind quintet *(Bagatelles)*—were all barred. I rejected all the officially approved communist texts based on socialist realism, but to be involved in arranging folk music was no compromise for me. I knew the Hungarian and Romanian folk music traditions quite well. Kodály and Bartók were my models. It was partly a compromise—and yet—ultimately, a little one, for my 'own' compositions couldn't be performed. But some of those choral works based on folk music were played on the radio and sung in

Photo: Györgi Ligeti. (Schott Archiv / Peter Andersen 1989)

concerts. I have never compromised politically and I was always careful with the texts of the folk music, so that they could not be interpreted politically. These things were tolerated, however, and a few works were even published.

It is difficult for me to explain this. I would like to have Lutosławski sitting here next to us; as a matter of fact, he has lived through the same thing. He also wrote 'real' compositions for himself, and pedagogical works and folk music arrangements—not for the regime—but as pieces that were intended to be performed. A composer must also have performances; it is important. I had to 'camouflage' myself and my works. When, for example, I composed that first string quartet which was forbidden, I had to cover up my activity by writing other works that could be performed. Otherwise they could have said that I was finished as a composer and could have told me to go to work in a factory. You have to see my thoughts and feelings in the context of the feelings of the whole people (with the exception of fools, fanatics and shrewd opportunists). In October 1956 the Revolution broke out, a spontaneous, outburst of desperation by 10 million Hungarians. (Later it happened everywhere, no social system can be based on perpetual lies.) In December 1956 I left Hungary—together with 200,000 people. I could not live anymore under this repression and hopelessness.

In the former West Germany you met, among others, Herbert Eimert, Gottfried Michael Koenig and Karlheinz Stockhausen. You started to work in the Studio for Electronic Music in Cologne and took part in the Summer Courses at Darmstadt. In unusually insightful articles published in Darmstädter Beiträge *and other journals, you took part in the aesthetic and theoretical discussions of the time with critical contributions on, among other things, electronic music and serial music. Why did you confront these musical forms? And then, looking ahead: have the new technological advances late in the century given you the desire to try out those ideas about musical materials that you chose to avoid earlier?*

I don't think of it exactly like that. I didn't distance myself from electronic and serial music because I was opposed to these forms. I criticized the music from the *inside*, so to speak. For example, I composed electronic music myself. I accepted fully and completely the aesthetic and theory of serial music that Boulez and Stockhausen derived from Webern and from Messiaen's *Mode de Valeurs et d'Intensités*, but I developed these ideas further. That's what became the static, micropolyphonic forms. These forms have their origins in serial and electronic music. In *Apparitions, Atmosphères* and *Volumina*, for example, I composed for instruments as if I were composing electronic music. What I learned in the electronic studio I applied to instrumental and vocal music. I was not against serial music, but critical of certain aspects of the style of serial composition, which became 'dry' for me too quickly. I wanted 'living' music.

That I later went back to technology with great interest, for instance computer technology, is actually due to the fact that I *never* lost interest in these things. It would be better to talk about a continuity. However, I have to say that electronic music as practised in Cologne at the end of the 1950s was far too primitive. A true Fourier synthesis (additive synthesis, *ed.*) couldn't be achieved; it was only possible to copy several (not too many) individual layers on top of one another. It was a 'manual' studio—there were no synthesizers. We could only produce sine tones, we could only filter regions of 'white noise', and we had manually to cut and splice pieces of tape together. In this, Gottfried Michael Koenig was the greatest master. I regard his work, *Essay*, as the most significant electronic piece that was made using this manual montage-technique.

In the electronic music studio I learned a lot about acoustical illusions and acoustical possibilities in general, that I subsequently 'translated' into instrumental music. The reason that I didn't continue to work in the electronic studio after 1958 was that I couldn't get satisfying results. Much later, with computer-generated sound, we had unimaginable possibilities. I have had many compositional ideas that originated in computer generated forms and sounds, but finally I realized them with traditional instruments, not with computer generated sounds. When I still refer to acoustic instruments, it is because their sound is more 'noble' according to my aesthetic criteria.

And fractals are only one of the fascinating areas in the computer world?

Simply one among many. Fractals have meant a lot to me since the time that I saw Peitgen's and Richter's first computer generated pictures in 1984.

I have the distinct impression that you drop an idea the moment it becomes established and develops into the ideology of a school. In the latest issue of Neue Zeitschrift für Musik *you say that your project is to establish an ideology-free style. This attitude was probably also the reason that your success with micropolyphonic works developed into a crisis for you, one that, as I see it, took on existential dimensions. There were a number of years before the Horn Trio when you composed nothing. You have mentioned that it wasn't a crisis for you alone, but it was also—or should have been—a crisis for all of twentieth-century musical composition. What did you mean by that and how did you work your way out of the crisis?*

In the four years before the composition of the Horn Trio I didn't finish a single work. I had hundreds of sketches for my Piano Concerto, but I couldn't get any further. It was rooted in specific musical problems that crystallized into two directions: one that preserved the avant-garde concept formulated in the 1950s in Darmstadt by Stockhausen and Boulez; and another that led to the minimal music of Terry Riley and Steve Reich, and to continually expanding postmodern tendencies in neo-tonal directions.

I had a composition class here in Hamburg. Many of my students accepted tonal music completely. Some of them had pop music as a point of departure. Their idols were no longer Beethoven, Webern and Stockhausen, but Bob Dylan, for example.

I had realized earlier that avant-garde music is too 'dry', too academic, but I couldn't stand the postmodern tonal-modal kitsch either. Therefore I tentatively tried a different direction. The Horn Trio has postmodern features. It is not a postmodern work, but it is my ironical *flirtation* with postmodernism. I perceived that I could neither use the expression of the avant garde nor the postmodern sounds, but had to find a completely different third way. The way out was, when it comes down to it, the first six Piano Etudes (the first cycle) from 1985.

You have said that one can't be sure that it is the best music that survives or that composers get their deserved place in music history. You have referred to Mendelssohn, who discovered Bach. When it comes to twentieth-century music, I think of a composer like Giacinto Scelsi, who was discovered by Jürg Wyttenbach and Francis Marie Uitti. Do you think that we are confused by misplaced criteria to such a degree that a lot of high quality music is suppressed?

Yes, I am afraid of that. It's been that way with all the arts. Giacinto Scelsi is a very good example. And a thoroughly original American composer like Harry Partch is virtually unknown in Europe. The most extreme example is Conlon Nancarrow. In 1972 I was invited to Mexico City by the Goethe Institute. There I met Mexican composers, old as well as young. Nancarrow wasn't mentioned once. Later quite by accident I came upon Nancarrow's music and found out that he lives and works in Mexico City.

There are composers who are good at promoting themselves, but there are also those who work in silence and have no sense of self-promotion. In these cases it is pure chance that decides whether they become known or not.

There were different destinies back in time. In the late middle ages, in the fourteenth century the names of the composers who survived were those who lived the longest. Guillaume de Machaut lived seventy-seven years (ca. 1300–1377) and, thank heavens, survived the plague. If he had succumbed in the great plague of 1348, he would not have existed as far as music history is concerned. That one man, Machaut, turned the history of music in a new direction. Another reason that he survived was that he carefully ordered copies of his works—in beautifully illuminated manuscripts. Machaut was narcissistic with a propensity for 'self-stylization' in the manner of today's film stars. He was the *star* of music and poetry in France during his time. Through Machaut's music Philippe de

Vitry's way of thinking about mensural notation was developed further. Another example is Guillaume Dufay who was born in 1400 precisely one hundred years after Machaut. He also lived a long time—seventy-four years—and eventually made a highly significant mark on the music of his time. Dufay, who had learned a lot from Dunstable, became the central figure in Franco-Flemish music. Without Dufay all of European music would have been different because composers like Ockeghem and Obrecht based their music on Dufay's work.

Very important composers of the generations between Machaut and Dufay have, only accidentally, been recognized in our time. Ciconia is one of them. If the American medieval-renaissance expert, Thomas Binkley, had not made a recording of the composer's chansons on EMI at the beginning of the 1970s then we would not know of Ciconia today.

Gesualdo was also unknown for many years. He is one of the most original composers of all times. I like to compare Gesualdo from about 1600 with Hugo Wolf from the end of the last century. They were both great masters of chromaticism who had an unbelieveable intuition when it came to expressing a text in music. Hugo Wolf is known because he worked for a time in Vienna. Gesualdo was known in his own time in Ferrara, but then his tradition was broken. The centre of music was moved to Venice, and Ferrara became an insignificant place. When I was a student, Gesualdo was simply one of 500 names one might have know casually, by chance.

There are so many examples: Senleches, Solage, Hasprois, de Caserta—lots of names. Most people don't know these composers at all. But their works existed. The musicologist Willi Apel transcribed the French Chantilly Codex from old to modern notation. It was published in the 1960s and included these totally unknown composers. Since then different English consorts have performed and recorded some of this music. Suddenly we discover that Senleches and Solage were unbelievably great composers—on a level with Machaut, Dufay and Ockeghem. With his completely unusual way of harmonizing, Solage was the Stravinsky of the late middle ages.

Is the musical world poised to move toward the same conditions as those of the world of visual arts—toward a situation where money drives art? I think, among others, of the case of Górecki, who is now bound hand and foot by his publisher as a result of the financial success of the Third Symphony. Adorno's fear of the smothering hand of the culture industry is more relevant now than it ever was. All the hysteria about who has the most numerous and the most prestigious premieres point in that direction.

I utterly hate the superficial and mendacious consumer culture. Visual art is almost totally corrupted by commerce. Music is also corrupted, but only in part. The biggest corruption here focuses on star conductors, star singers, star instrumentalists. Some of these stars are, however, very good musicians.

9

Jessye Norman is a star, but still one of the greatest singers. Star culture and consumer terrorism is at its worst in the case of conductors. Karajan was a big sinner in this regard given his connections with the business world—however, he could be an excellent conductor, when he took the necessary rehearsing time.

The danger with respect to this century's composition is far less. The case of Górecki is a minor, grotesque and amusing episode. The same could happen to any composer who is sufficiently close to tonality or modality and uses some trendy 'new age' or other religious text. It could just as well happen with John Adams or Arvo Pärt. It is purely accidental that it was Górecki. It is just as irrational as a virus; suddenly a new mutant of the influenza virus emerges and everyone gets sick.

The serious part of composition is not threatened by business- or consumer-terrorism because there are no 'wares'; it can't be sold. The prestige surrounding premieres is quite a risable and sleazy affair unfortunately. In comparison with visual art and the enormous production of a Karajan or a Bernstein, it's pretty small change we are talking about. I have been associated with the big business world only once, namely with the film *2001* by Stanley Kubrick. My music was used without my permission and I wasn't paid for it. I finally had to get a lawyer and have a compromise arrangement with Metro-Goldwyn-Mayer.

You have just been in the USA. There, new music has apparently been affected by market forces. What happens in the USA often happens a decade later in Europe. Just look at composers like Adams and Corigliano and their dependence on commercialism. Previously you have been affectionately critical of American minimalism— in the work Selfportait with Reich and Riley. *Minimalism, at its worse, is consumed as pure entertainment music and the genre attracts more and more fans in Europe. As for European art music what do you think about the possibilities of maintaining a meaningful discussion of aesthetic criteria while retaining the concept of authenticity?*

I have a very clear position in that regard. I am convinced that a group of composers can stay free of market dictatorship. In your question you take as a starting point the idea that marketing is much stronger in the USA than in Europe. I see no difference between a work's destiny in the USA and in Europe. In all the industrialized countries the market and consumer demands are the same in the deepest sense. The notion that what happens in the USA happens ten years later in Europe was true in the 1950s and 1960s, but no more. The difference has been levelled out.

Beware: a composer also has to live, it is necessary to earn money. We shouldn't create the false impression that it is necessary to be poor in order to create art. Paul Cézanne was wealthy and didn't have to sell one single paint-ing. It is a beautiful example of money creating independence.

I detest those of my colleagues who want to sell themselves, to get to know the right people, to make the right connections with a recording com-pany, and to join the right circles. You quite rightly emphasize the problems with authenticity. Surrendering to commercialism, and insisting on authen-ticity at the same time is impossible.

Are you moving farther and farther away from the concept of the avant-garde? I'm thinking of your burning interest in ethnic music, in cultures far from the one we know in Europe, in the rhythmic complexity of African music that comes to the surface in the Piano Etudes and the Piano Concerto, among other works.

The concept of the avant-garde has had many political connotations since the time it was connected with socialist utopian thinking about another and bet-ter society. That was the avant-garde movement's programme circa World War I. I'm thinking, for example, of Russian futurism, constructivism and suprematism in the poetry of Mayakovsky and the art of Malevitch and in the music of the young Shostakovich, Mossolov and many others. That deeply conservative man, Stravinsky, never considered himself to be avant-garde. He always said, 'I am a conservative classical composer'.

I see a clear connection between the avant garde and socialism. The excep-tions are, for example, Schoenberg and Webern who were conservative and deeply rooted in their tradition. But the whole avant-garde ideology cannot be separated from a belief in the dream of a better future for mankind. As a result of the collapse of 'real' world socialism—which I prefer to call 'surreal' socialism—a large question mark now hangs over socialist ideology: is it at all possible? Personally, I am, as I always have been, in favour of greater jus-tice and a society without oppression. But I have become sceptical about the possibilities after all that has happened, and will continue to happen. The 'real' socialism—that which doesn't function anymore—created the worst pos-sible nationalism with war, suppression, religious and racial hatred. I see no end to all of that. What each of us can do morally is to act decently and refuse to believe in crazy ideologies.

Given that, you can understand that I have distanced myself from the avant garde, the artistic directions that were derived from Marcel Duchamp: Cage, the 'happenings' at the end of the 1950s, political theatre, and Fluxus in the 1960s. Danish cultural life was also influenced to a great extent by these im-portant movements. Cage's importance cannot be overestimated, the anar-chic concept of art where everything is allowed and everything is possible, was a great liberation. But it was only possible for a short period; these ideas were quickly used up. For me the concept of the avant-garde as an ideology, a utopia, a project, is old-fashioned after all; it is too academic. When I hear composers today who compose as they did in Darmstadt 30 years ago, I say to myself: 'Well but the world has completely changed since then!' On the other hand, the kitschy world that we have spoken about—fashion design in rose, purple and turquoise from Milan, hi-tech advertising on glossy paper, postmodern architecture—is just about unbearable. I detest it; it's false, lies, a façade, bad theatre.

When everything is said and done, the direction that the French call *retro*, this postmodern glance backward, is false and kitsch. On the other hand, the avant-garde has become professorial. But between these extremes there are so many new possibilities.

When one listens to your work one can hardly avoid noticing the humour. Alongside an unusual self-critical and serious attitude, humour has a strong presence in your musical universe. I'm thinking, for example, of the lecture 'The Future of Music', or the metronome piece, passages in the opera Le Grand Macabre, *or parts of the* Aventures *pieces. In the archives of Danish Radio there is a TV broadcast from the beginning of the 1960s where you pedagogically draw on a board at the same time as your electronic piece,* Articulation, *is being played. It is highly humourous, but the humour slides imperceptibly into seriousness. The metronome piece is more than a provocation; it is incredibly refined, a many-layered polyphonic creation. As I see it, it becomes human and accessible. It is as if your music often says: 'This piece is not what it pretends to be on the surface'. Can you explain this?*

I have never heard anyone sum it up as beautifully as you have in your question. I cannot add anything: I don't compose consciously. I cannot talk about my intentions with respect to humour, seriousness, depth and irony in my music. I can only write music. I agree with you and can only be happy that you have formulated it in this way.

As for extreme exaggeration as a means of expression, painters and authors like Breughel, Bosch, Jarry, Vian, Kafka, have all fascinated you and inspired your art. Does your fascination with these artists lie in their representation of something unreal, as though these extremes turn into their opposites and express something generally human?

Yes, I believe so, but I wouldn't call it unreal. For example, in Kafka and Bosch you have people or objects from real life. They are presented in a dream-like context. And often much more concentrated than in everyday reality. For that reason I feel a strong affinity with these painters and writers—and with many others, for instance, Cézanne and Goya. The latter's series of copper etchings, *Los Desastres de la Guerra* (The Disasters of War, ca. 1819, *ed.*), contains the most unbelievable criticism of military war crimes.

I should mention Sándor Weöres from Hungary. He was a kind of Mozart of Hungarian poetry; with an unbelieveable lightness and virtuosity, he uses understatement to express very deep thoughts about life. He was a writer who opposed 'importance'. In *Az undor angyala* (The Angel of Nausea, trans.) he says, 'Don't be pompous'. This has become a kind of motto for me: to work against arrogance and pretence.

In Denmark we have had the chance to hear the first nine Etudes for Piano, the Violin Concerto and the Piano Concerto. From your pen has also come Nonsense Madrigals, *and Irvine Arditti talks about new string quartets from you and Stockhausen. How does your compositional landscape look right now? You have already spoken about microtonality. What are the current problems for you since the beginning of the 1990s?*

So far (1999) I have composed seventeen piano studies and have finished a Horn concerto. Currently I am working on a song cycle (poetry by Sándor Weöres in Hungarian) with percussion accompaniment. When these works are finished I want to devote myself to an old dream, a theatrical fantasy: Lewis Carroll's *Alice in Wonderland* and *Through the Looking-glass*. This work will take 2–3 years. After that, I have promised the Arditti String Quartet a new quartet.

Do you mean a new opera based on Carroll?

No, it won't be an opera. The cast will be a small one because the new harmonic possibilities with micro-tonal intervals can only be realized with soloists. Alice will be played by an actress since no singer would be able to be on stage the whole time. It has to be a young actress who can also sing. The rest will be singers. I will use Carroll's mathematics, nonsense poems and much more. Lewis Carroll's world is as close to me as that of Bosch, Breughel and Kafka; all of them look at reality in a completely individual, somewhat 'crazy' way. It can't be an opera, it'll be a musical or a revue with acrobats and stage machinery. In addition to singers and acrobats, there will be dancers, pantomimes and a little orchestra of 20–25 players, each of whom will be used as soloists.

Between the traditional and modern. The statement is almost a cliché, but it still says something important about your music; it is radical and traditional, it reworks the surviving material into something new. One finds tradition everywhere in your music. Can you describe very concretely how you work with—and possibly also against—tradition in a particular piece? Take for example, one of the Piano Etudes.

Let's take the Sixth Piano Etude, 'Autumn in Warsaw'. What is traditional in that piece? It is a fugue. It's a fugue theme, this lament melody. The theme is partly mirrored and there is stretto. It all depends on the possibility of using the fugal technique of augmentation and diminution. In Bach's work diminution was 2:1. In Machaut's work the ratios of 3:1, 3:2 and 4:3 are also found, because mensural notation provides the possibility of dividing up the *longa*, *brevis* and *semibrevis* into two or three. This tradition became fashionable and took the form of the hemiola which lasted into the nineteenth century (a rhythmic pattern in which the on-going accentuation of 2 x 3 in a 6 beat bar shifts to 3 x 2 before shifting back to 2 x 3). We see it often in Chopin's, Schumann's, Brahms's and Debussy's piano music.

In my piano pieces I have used the hemiola from mensural notation in addition to a similar, but much more complex and ambiguous metrical structure from African music. I want to compare it with the phenomenon that Maurits Escher has called 'convex/concave'. This generates the puzzle pictures in African music.

African rhythm contains not only the possibility of augmentation and diminution in relationships of 2:1 and 3:2, but also of asymmetrical relationships. I have extended this idea with the relationship up to 11:7 and even to 13:11. I use prime numbers most often so that doubles don't result: 3, 4, 5, 7, 11, and 13. Now 4 is not a prime number, but I can use it if I don't use 2, and then I can have the very useful relationships of 4:3, 5:4, 5:3, 7:5, 7:3, 7:4. These are very simple proportions, but not relationships that we can hear. We can figure out triplets against duplets, but septuplets against quintuplets are much harder to hear. Instead, I can produce with these rhythmic relations the illusion of several layers moving simultaneously in different speeds.

It's possible to talk about several traditions in my piano pieces: mensural notation, African music for xylophone and balophone, Bach's fugal technique as a structural means and, pianistically, Chopin's piano works. Chopin composed piano music so that a pianist feels the melodies and the harmonies with his fingers on the piano keys. His piano movements are set so that the hand's anatomy 'fits' the mechanism of the piano. His inventions are quite tactile. This can be found to a great extent in my works. It's also found in the music of Schumann and Scarlatti. In my music, acoustical, optical and tactile elements are melted for the virtuoso; it's music that is rooted in a sensual relationship to the act of performing the music.

It is well-known that you have no message for mankind, that you say 'no thanks' to having your music interpreted within a conceptual framework encompassing utopias and ideologies. Is this pressimism à la Beckett? Don't you believe in progress? Don't you have a dream or a hope in your best hours? If so, have you ever had the desire to reflect this in your music?

I don't consciously wish to reflect anything in music. If a message can be interpreted in the music, then it's fine but I don't know anything about that.

I wish to be a decent person, nothing else, and so I am suspicious about *all* ideologies and messages. My experiences with horrible political systems like national socialism and communism have taught me to avoid any kind of 'great system' and belief.

In response to your question about hope and progress, I'd like to say that I don't share the Beckett-inspired pessimism. Even though he was a great author, I find his position artificial and mannered. After a while it became a cliché in Germany and western Europe—not in the USA and England—to follow him. It was fashionable to see everything as 'tragic'. Terrible things are happening all the time, after all. We can read about it every day in the news- papers. Five hundred years ago, one couldn't read about it simply because there were no newspapers. In 1915 part of the nationalist Turkish military killed about one million Armenians; that was the first act of what later be- came Auschwitz, and Stalin's mass murder in the Soviet Union. And Mao, and Pol Pot, and so on. At the time, no-one knew that the extermination of the Armenians in Turkey had happened as it wasn't in the newspapers. Auschwitz, also, was kept a secret. If Hitler had won the war, there would not have been any report of the mass eradication of six million Jews and hundreds of thousands of gypsies.

Hope? yes—but on a completely different level for I don't believe in any religion or ideology. However, I believe in the rational sciences, especially natural sciences, and also social sciences—but when, and only when, it is prac- tised with intelligence and honour. By that I mean that one has to start with facts, set up a hypothesis, then prove it, or try to disprove it and only thereaf- ter initiate a provisional theory. This is Popper's central idea, and I consider it as the soundest 'philosophy' of all possible 'philosophies'. Ideologies are sys- tems that profess to explain *everything*. True science will not explain every- thing, only small parts of the whole. I entertain great hope for science and technology. The average life-span in Japan after the war was sixty years; now it is seventy-nine years. I call that progress.

'En ideologifri kunst: Et interview med komponisten György Ligeti', *Dansk Musik Tidsskrift* 67, 8 (1992/93): 254–263.

Karl Aage Rasmussen

THE POETRY OF OPPOSITION

'To see is a matter of selection, memory and interest. And using your eyes, of course. But he who sees the best, doesn't always see the most'.

Thus writes the short-sighted composer, Karl Aage Rasmussen, in the entry on 'Sight' in Brøndum's Encyclopedia. *Vision depends on the eye that sees and even a person with impaired vision can see a great deal, possibly more than others. Seeing is a matter of perception, viewing is merely registration.*

So, here we have a near-sighted artist writing about sight. Things are not what they seem to be—everything is turned upside-down. Karl Aage Rasmussen you have always been interested in things, thoughts and phenomena that could be turned upside-down. When did you first see that you would be a creative artist?

I didn't *see* it at all. It is lost in utter darkness. After all it's not a decision you make, certainly not when you start as young as I did. My first scribbles and my first attempts to compose something go back to when I was seven or eight years old.

My parents were what we call 'workers' nowadays. My mother was a needle-work teacher and my father was a typesetter. Rather by accident we got a piano and my mother insisted that I take lessons if it was going to take up space in the living room. I remember that very early on—God only knows why—I tried to write music down. And that *was* strange because there was precious little tradition of art and certainly no musical tradition in my family.

I hated piano lessons and stopped hating them only when my indefatigable mother discovered Edmund Hansen—a colourful man nicknamed 'Toscanini' and given to drink. He directed the local semi-professional City Orchestra which gave performances only a couple of times every year. He had been trained at the Royal Danish Academy of Music though, and he taught violin and piano. When I lamented my ignorance, he also gave me lessons in orchestration. So at twelve or thirteen years of age I actually worked on orchestration exercises.

Perhaps you imagine that I was immersed in Stockhausen, Ligeti and so on, but I didn't know the music of the avant-garde at all. Actually, in my youth I believed that all composers were dead. Svend S. Schultz was a revelation to me. I devoured Svend Erik Tarp's Sonatina and at secondary school I arranged several concerts at which I played—or whatever you want to call it—things like Niels Viggo Bentzon's *Træsnit (Woodcuts)*, much to the amazement of my classmates.

Most of us experience a similar development. We start in a corner with something we like and end up in an entirely different corner. I still remember hearing Carl Nielsen's Violin Concerto when I was thirteen years old. To me the introduction to the first movement seemed utterly meaningless and incomprehensible, something which was of course reflected in the music I composed myself. My first compositions, written when I was ten, were endless variations on the first movement of the 'Moonlight Sonata'. Then there was a heroic ballade about King Agner for which I wrote both music and a text stuffed with alliteration and old Norse poetic devices. Later came a period where my so-called compositions were mostly modelled on a few bars of Hindemith. When did I become a composer? When I left secondary school before passing my last exam in order to enter the Music Academy, I suppose I must have felt something pointing in that direction.

Tage Nielsen, who was Director of The Royal Academy of Music, Aarhus, at the time you were a composition student, told me that you were also a good violinist. And I have read that as a fifteen-year-old you played Grieg's Piano Concerto in Norway. That practical grasp of things, that is, the ability to both perform and compose, must have been an important aspect of your development.

It's been neither important nor unimportant. It's just the way it has been. Two sides of the same thing. Playing led to thinking about compositional procedures and that led to writing something down. At times musical thoughts had to be performed in order to be clarified as thoughts. I could never be a composer who composes at his desk.

I remember Emil Telmányi (the Hungarian violinist who became Carl Nielsen's son-in-law, *ed.*), a unique individual who was my violin teacher, with great respect. Frankly you could learn more about music in one hour with him than in a month studying so-called music theory, and I think that experience made a lasting impression on me: music without a corporeal aspect, music not involving musicians is, essentially, not of interest to me.

Tage Nielsen, whom I mentioned above, also said that you were actually good at almost everything, that you wanted to excel in everything and hated getting wrong anything in which you were involved. You also made no secret of the fact that you wanted to be knowledgeable in a number of areas. You have done a lot of debating and writing over the years, and often with weight and a conciseness that doesn't exactly invite contradiction. If one slurs 'Karl Aage' (Rasmussen's first names by which he is known, ed.) together, it sounds like 'Kloge' (meaning 'a clever guy' in

Danish, trans.). You don't show uncertainty in public, but I assume that as an artist you are always insecure. Somewhere you have written that your opinions are calculated more to invite discussion than to seek acceptance. What has it been like throughout the years to have to live up to the role of an omniscient author, sharp debater and a virtuoso in verbal fencing? I ask because it has been difficult for me to find what's at the heart of Karl Aage Rasmussen, the man. Not that I want to intrude on his private life, not at all. But I have the feeling that sometimes he could be hiding behind words, perhaps also behind music.

You raise a cloud of issues there, but let's begin with the picture you draw of a public person whom I hardly recognize. I feel a bit like Chaplin in the film where he plays a mass-murderer. Every time the judge reads a new charge Chaplin looks over his shoulder in order to see just who *this* defendant is. Can you be self-assured and resist opposition, and at the same time invite discussion?

I have a reputation for being fond of discussion. It may be that I think best when I am conversing. It's not that my head is empty when I am on my own, but there is not nearly as much going on of that which we usually call *thinking*. However if you imply that, for instance, my writing has focused on pegging out directions or passing judgments, then you must be talking about someone else. Most of my writings offer personal ideas about music and musicians, about things that interest me. I presume that the personality emerges in the selection, in the writing, in the *style*.

Currently my publisher Gyldendal is preparing a collection of my essays for publication so I have recently read and re-read lots of Rasmussen without finding much verbal fencing. Perhaps there is a bit of mythology here: when people begin referring to someone as 'clever', the myth becomes self-fulfilling. Besides there is a psychological aspect involved. Of course I know what insecurity is. I am actually rather inward-directed, so discussions and conversations may act as defence mechanisms. As may humour, for that matter.

The image of me as a kind of 'musical executioner' or whatever seems to me completely distorted. I haven't been heavily involved in public debate, for one thing. Once in a great while—like a miniature Holger Danske (the legendary Danish king who wakes up from his perpetual slumber only when the country desperately needs him, *ed.*)—I have been involved in polemics, but God knows, I have never been addicted to debating like, say, Niels Viggo Bentzon. I have no wish to be remembered as a mass producer of opinions. I have always wanted to contribute to new agendas, however. Possibly this also has something to do with my being and remaining a Jutlander, instinctively opposing the idea of Copenhagen as a 'centre'. We have a long tradition for challenging the cultural balance between the province and the capital city.

In a conversation with Stockhausen during his visit to Copenhagen in 1996 you asked him about believing in something. In 1982 you also asked Nørgård and Gud-mundsen-Holmgreen about their belief 'in a wider context, in a guiding power'. Now I'm going to put the same question to you: What do you believe in?

To answer that question you must choose a specific angle. I don't have any religion in the more involved sense of the term. My belief is that it's worth searching for a belief, taking the old view that what matters is not the goal, but the road to it. Like happiness. It's not a final destination, happiness is what you experience on the way. If faith means arriving somewhere where everything is tranquil and harmonious, and where you know how it all fits together, then I don't know what faith is.

I am more inclined to establish a temporary belief. For example, an artist has to believe that what he is doing is meaningful. A composer makes hundreds of choices every single minute. This presupposes a belief that every choice is the right one at that moment. Belief in *that* sense may come closer to a word like attitude. When I feel a solidarity with composers whose music barely resembles my own, it is because I am influenced by their *attitude*. For example I have often been fascinated by John Cage. And everyone who has been involved with Cage knows how his opinions may develop into something that looks a lot like faith—because you believe that it can be fruitful to behave the way Cage suggests—that in freeing yourself from your likes and dislikes you will be more aware of what is actually happening here and now. I have often recommended—to myself and to others—that one should be less deeply involved with the past and a little less fixated on the future so that there is room for the present.

To be inclined towards something means that you wonder about things, something you have in common with John Cage. Among the many composers to whom you have paid close attention, Cage is probably the one who in all his activities has influenced you the most. Correct me if I am mistaken.

It is somewhat characteristic that there are many composers who have 'influenced me the most'. For example, I came to Cage via Charles Ives. My relationship with Ives has become paradoxical: how can the most important composer in your life be one whose music you never hear? I hardly ever listen to Ives' music, but nevertheless, it is an ever-present impulse. That seems to indicate that there are aspects of the very nature of music which, for want of a better term and in a particular sense, may be called 'spiritual'—something which is absolutely central for me.

Photo: Karl Aage Rasmussen (Marianne Grøndahl).

You once wrote: 'Even if John Cage's music should be forgotten one day, his mind models will remain among the most influential of the century'. I understand that rather than his music, it's more his attitude, his way of viewing the world that inspires you.

There is a concept in that quote which is not mine, but one that I may have introduced in our latitudes, the anthropological term 'mind model'. Apparently our brain tends to work on the basis of habitual mental circuits. It is impossible to think about everything all at once and so we devise methods of fixing specific ideas in our mind, fitting them together in habitual 'models'.

For example, we have music on one side and notation on the other. Initially notation was used only to help us remember music, but at some point it turned over and began influencing the way in which we *think* about music. We began thinking about music as something which is notated before it actually sounds. This entirely changes our conception of music. I am disinclined to use moderate words like *attitude*, but would rather take a broader view. Let's just call it our concept about music, our ideas about what music is by and large.

Let me recall one of my favorite stories. Ives' father, George, was a bandmaster in a little provincial town in Connecticut. Ives writes in his essays about a young man whose 'musicality was limited after three years of intense study at Boston University'. He heard George Ives' church choir in which there was a certain Mr. Bell, who was bawling ridiculously out-of-tune. 'You can't have Mr. Bell in the choir, he ruins everything', said the nice young man from Boston. George Ives answered, 'Well, but look at his *face* when he sings. Don't pay too much attention to the sounds, or you may miss the music. You won't get a wild, heroic ride to heaven on some pretty little sounds!' That story is a mind-opener for me, and it relates closely to something that Ives said himself, something which sums up the entire matter: 'My God, what has sound to do with music? What it sounds like may not be what it *is*'.

This is crucial but difficult to explain because it concerns the transcendental in Ives, that which transgresses boundaries, the simple fact that music is so much more than something we listen to. It is the present absence of this awareness that has led me to say that we live in an unmusical world submerged in music. Because as a spiritual and mental phenomenon music can be so infinitely more than that which *sounds*. It lies at the core of my way of thinking and from there it spreads in all possible directions. It has also helped open my ears to all those who have been overlooked and not heard. It isn't enough for me that music is aesthetically satisfying, for instance, or artistically, or stylistically successful. I search for something *behind* music, so to speak.

Can this 'other' that is behind *be articulated? Or is it that 'It can only be referred to negatively, as something absent', like the German philosopher said?*

Here I'll take comfort in the old church father, St Augustine, and paraphrase his comment on time: 'When no one asks me, I know what it is, but if someone asks me, I don't know'. For Ives, it meant the concept of 'strength', of course, the power to transcend boundaries. Valuable music is music which has the power to break down barriers in our heads. Inconsequential music just sounds pretty, and is, in Ives' words, 'an easy-chair for the ears'.

The strength to break down barriers. Give me some examples of music of our time that you feel has this power to break down boundaries.

That is very personal because you are seeking something that can break down boundaries in your *own* head and make you react in an unexpected way. Cage says somewhere that if you rub people the right way, they say 'Ahhh' and if you rub them the wrong way, they say 'Ugh'. It's an incredibly predictable pattern of response, a cultural situation that risks making us into Pavlovian dogs who salivate and bark on artistic command. My own 'transcendental' experiences are rather easily determined by looking at, for example, the list of composers I have written about, talked about, programmed in concerts, etc.

But not to sidestep the question, let me mention a unique individual who might epitomize all those odd, ignored, eccentric individuals. The music of the Italian composer Niccoló Castiglioni is impossible to describe, but that's precisely the reason I find it significant. And that might be a rule of thumb: if the music can be described precisely in words so that you can just about hear it in your mind, then it doesn't contain what I am looking for. In order to have any idea about what Castiglioni's music is, you have to hear it, *Inverno in ver*, for example. And somewhat the same is true for Luigi Nono or Giacinto Scelsi, speaking of Italians.

Nevertheless, I remember that you tried to describe these things in an essay that you wrote about Castiglioni when he was the featured composer at the Lerchenborg Music Days. Talking about this seems just as impossible as it was for the art historian who, when he lectured on the sublime, pointed to a place in a painting and said, 'Here we see the sublime'. Whereupon a member of the audience said, 'Where? I can't see it'. The attempt is just as interesting as it is impossible. And yet we continue to try. So I have to ask you again, aren't you always trying to create the sublime and break down all the barriers?

There is no particular strategy or method that will enable music to transcend borders. That has been a guideline in my life-long show-down with strategies, systems and methods. It *is* very difficult for a modern composer to write music without the support of some kind of methodical thinking. And it is not only hard for the modern composer, but for any composer because all music is related to conceptual models. Of necessity the notes must follow each other in sequence because time passes, and if we can't make it meaningful somehow for one note to follow another, then sooner or later we find ourselves in a vacuum. So we search for strategies.

But transcendence will occur only when methods or systems collide with the unpredictable, when they bump into something incalculable. This happens, for example, in the case of Ligeti who is an extraordinarily methodical, systematic composer. But in an archetypical, profoundly moving way, his methods are pierced by something unforeseeable that creates a universal psychological dimension. That's the source of power in *his* music.

The Polish writer Gombrovitch claimed that modern music is corrupted by mathematics. But is it really any more 'mathematical' than, for instance, Bach's music? Bach isn't different from Ligeti; both count and count, but suddenly all the numbers disappear in the experience of a spiritual or downright physical response to the music itself.

The peaks in my own experience of listening to music are when these boundary-breaking moments occur. Music *is* mathematics, tones are measured frequencies, and just about everything we calculate or work with in music depends on numbers. There is a wonderfully thought-provoking line by Leibnitz, the German philosopher. He writes that music is a mathematical exercise for the soul, but *the soul doesn't realize that it's counting*. And who dares to suggest that he knows what the soul can hear or how it counts?

Long ago I abandoned my youthful and overly sensitive scepticism about numbers. They have come to play an increasingly large role in my music in the last ten or fifteen years. Again this was rooted in my personal history, for given my temperament as you described earlier, that is, a kind of habitual anti-feeling, it was clear to me that if there was one thing I would not do, it was to go along with Central European modernism, which was at that time a cloud of numbers.

You said before that one note must follow another because time passes. We will return to that in a minute. So far you have described what it was that you didn't concern yourself with at first.

One of the first writers who commented on your music was Jørgen I. Jensen. In the article in Dansk Musik Tidsskrift, *'Nye, aldrig før hørte sammenhænge' ('New connections, never heard before') from 1969 he wrote about two orchestral works,* Repriser, fristelser og eventyr *(Recapitulations, Temptations and Fairytales) from 1968, and* Symfoni for unge elskende *(Symphony for Young Lovers) from 1967. He describes the music as a 'musical kleptomania that goes beyond anything anyone has seen before'. Can you look back at your earliest days as a composer and tell us how that stylistic individuality developed.*

Once in the 1960s I heard—in a lecture dealing with something completely different—about a wild man from the prairies who composed music with quotes from all possible sources. I immediately tuned in to Ives, because I had always been interested in working with material that already existed. In French aesthetics it is known as *objets trouvés*, that is, you find existing things and put them together. It meant a lot to me to be invited to the centennial conference on Ives in New York (1974) where I met composers such as Lou Harrison, Elliott Carter, the pianist John Kirkpatrick and many others who had known Ives for 25–30 years.

To this day it would never occur to me to think of myself as an expert on Ives. I have been interested in Ives for personal reasons, not as an object of study. I have taken what was important and thought-provoking for me and that's what I have written about, and used in radio programmes, performances, and so on. The most important thing for me at that time was the discovery of a composer who took what he needed, without any scruples. He was exposing the expressive power in all kinds of musical material—without asking whether it was something he or someone else had originated.

It was nothing polemical. It wasn't directed against the great Western European *Erfindungskultur*, the old notion of having to be original, of using material that must be *nie erhört*—previously never heard (in Stockhausen's famous words). It was just natural for me to work in that way. That is how I started out as a young boy. And remember also that this was the time when Mahler's music suddenly became fashionable.

The title of Jørgen I. Jensen's article was of course aimed polemically at Stockhausen's 'previously never-heard sounds'. It emphasized the fact that I wasn't a composer who said, 'I can't invent anything myself, so I snatch what I need from somebody else', but that it was simply a way of doing something totally different.

Now, you mention Mahler, who composed a song that he used again in a symphony, that Luciano Berio used, and that you re-used in your work, Berio Mask. *Why do you think that a certain expressivity, which was valid in Mahler's time, must now be understood, in some sense, as being used up? A recurring defence of recycled music is that in new surroundings it may carry a new expression, as it were. Let's revisit that piece where you work with the recycling of material that has itself been recycled twice. You call it a 'palimpsest'. . .*

To explain that, we have to go back a number of years. In the beginning of the 1970s I composed pieces that might still be interesting simply because they are so odd. The prototype perhaps is *Genklang (*Echo or Resonance), for piano four-hands, prepared piano, out-of-tune piano (that is, a honky-tonk piano), and celeste. In short, it captured a gradual distortion of the refined sound of the grand piano, a kind of time perspective where a sound is stretched out in an echoing space, or in a hall of mirrors if you like.

Genklang is characteristic of what I was doing at that time because it consists of an infinite series of tiny musical modules. I tried to figure out just exactly how few notes were necessary to be able to identify a particular musical style, for example, a Rheinland polka. Sometimes I felt that just four semi-quavers were enough. And that became a tiny patch that I could sew to another patch taken from completely different music. But since that was also reduced to a very few notes the whole didn't seem like a ridiculously fast film with cuts from thousands of films. On the contrary, the very tight editing technique made it possible to hear something similar to directional cohesion.

Also it had something to do with thinking about music, something to do with Ives, something to do with everything but sound itself. It also had philosophical overtones. Having just read Thomas Mann's *Dr. Faustus* I imagined trying to do what his unfortunate main character, the composer Leverkühn wanted to do—albeit aware of the tragic costs that he had to pay—namely, to actually create a 'new' musical language. I thought that was a fantastically interesting idea: a new musical language that consisted exclusively of old ones.

But I quickly realized that my great vision was doomed to failure. There were problems of form and development that seemed insoluble. We hear an immensely tight montage, but how on earth does one phrase lead on to another in such a montage? How do you establish a beginning and an end? I finally decided to compose a work embracing this problem even in its title.

Writing a big piece on the impossibility of writing a big piece suited the spirit of the times. The work was called *Anfang und Ende* (Beginning and End), the story of a beginning and an end that can't be. It became a farewell to the hope for a new *meta*-language, and I began to search for other means to accomplish something similar. Since the problem was one of form it was clear that the next step had to go beyond recycling tiny modules by 'recycling' a larger formal shape.

This attempt was already partly evident in *Genklang* in so far as a famous slow movement by Mahler is actually hidden in the formal framework of the piece. In the piece called *Berio Mask* there is, to an even greater degree, a pre-existing form: a movement by Mahler that he himself had developed further and that Berio had re-composed.

It was a kind of conversation between the different historic layers. This is something that has never ceased to fascinate me: the history of history, the history of what it is we mean when we say 'history', that is, history as a phenomenon in time, as a manifestation of different times, as something that also expresses itself in the form of different tempi. The composer Hans Gefors compared *Anfang und Ende* with the Italian painter Arcimboldo who painted faces out of fruits or vegetables. It looks like a face, but in reality it is an assemblage of fruit. My work looks like a symphony, but it really is nothing but tiny quotations.

I have had several opportunities to listen to Genklang. *The work is a perfect example of historical perspective. Let's go deeper into the work. The sound of the piano is like—if you'll excuse the continuing use of the fruit metaphor—a fallen fruit, or rather, a really rotten piece of fruit. You use an out-of-tune piano and distort the ideal sound that other composers have previously used very successfully. What composer's sound did you have in mind?*

The out-of-tune piano mainly represents Mahler's music: the Adagietto from his Fifth Symphony was in vogue at that time as the theme music of Visconti's screen version of Thomas Mann's *Death in Venice*. Here it represents a myth of cultural decay. The idea of this music as a huge romantic gesture and, at the same time, as cultural refuse, prompted me to fit it into an ironic, but also a clearly fermenting, crumbling context. The out-of-tune piano refers to decadence but at the same time to yellowed album-leaves of music—the Viennese waltz, small barcaroles, salon music and so on. It is like a truly romantic world that turns into a sunken cultural treasure as you listen.

I loved and still love this Adagietto, but obviously I couldn't use it at face-value because of the romantic *Schwung*. Exposed to the out-of-tune piano it loses its persuasive romanticism. However, it still possesses a stirring, universal and human profundity because romanticism isn't confined to a past epoch. The 'romantic' experience is a discovery containing universal human dimensions.

It has been said that the characteristic aspect of your music from that time is that it is open to expression, that the listener gets to the point where a large cleared field can be surveyed as a whole so that new relationships and patterns appear. That sounds very poetic, but wasn't that way of composing a way of welcoming a substitute for burned-out serialism rather than a music and a technique that would be fruitful in the long run?

I think that I have answered that. There was an element of rebellion in it, but it wasn't a terribly informed revolt because I didn't know very much about Central European serialism. It is senseless to stage me as somebody representing a confrontation with serialism. The fact is that I simply discovered my own voice as a composer.

I ask because you said that you knew in any case what it should not be. Having said that it shouldn't be European modernism, then in a certain sense it must also have been a reaction against something at the same time that it was a deep fascination with Ives?

I believe that a lot of art arises from a strong feeling of what something should *not* be rather than from a clear idea of what something *should* be. Take for example the film *Vinterbillede* (Winter Picture) where the great Danish painter Per Kirkeby paints his biggest canvas ever. It is a film about how artistic conception sometimes takes place *after* birth. First the picture is born and *then* it is conceived. The film is almost scary: the painter paints what looks like a fantastic painting, but he goes on reworking it, changing it, over and over again, and at some point the terrifying artist pours a can of paint over the very best part of the canvas!

He doesn't just paint a painting that already exists in his mind. He starts by doing something that sets him thinking about what it is he wants to avoid. I once described this pattern of reaction in the Danish composer Pelle Gudmundsen-Holmgreen as 'the poetry of opposition', and maybe it is also pertinent to Kirkeby. It certainly also hits the mark with me—the realization that poetry arises when one tries to avoid something, when something seems *too* much one thing or another, *too* sentimental, *too* powerful, expressive, simple, what have you. The friction that comes from trying to avoid something is a better incentive for me than the energy others get from knowing what they want.

During the making of Winter Picture *there are stages when you think that it is really beautiful, that the painting could very well be complete. However the artist doesn't stop, but goes on because a physical restlessness tells him that something isn't as it should be. Towards the end of the film, the artist actually becomes ill. He can feel that the painting is now almost as it should be. Is that also true for you? Do you know precisely when a piece is finished?*

One of the most difficult decisions for an artist is to decide when to stop. This is where gut feelings, experience and technical insights are maybe most needed. Morton Feldman told a story about a painter who was always slightly drunk and always spent too long on his pictures. When he went down to get another bottle of whiskey, his colleagues working in the same atelier took the painting off his easel and put up a fresh canvas in its place. When he came back he looked confused for a moment and then began to paint a new picture.

All artists know that a work can be ruined by working on it for too long. The real artist is one who knows when to stop, not necessarily one who has a clear idea in advance of how everything should end. Feldman said that his extremely long pieces just died of old age. I have known that feeling now and then—the work dies because of a kind of psychological debilitation that you yourself experience in your relation to it.

It doesn't mean that I say, 'Now it is perfect', or 'Now it is finished'. But it means that there is a moment when there isn't anything more I can offer to the work. Then it is best to begin something else. Composers in earlier times had a number of technical means by which to finish off a piece. We do not have that in the same way. Perhaps the very concept of 'finished' doesn't make the same kind of sense any longer.

There was a period when you worked with a stylistic idea that is now either abandoned or further developed. You worked with collage music, quotations and with analytical studies. At that time you said that 'the experience of the well-known in a strange context and of the unknown in a familiar one calls forth new meanings and forms and consequently new ways to listen'. But the available musical resources weren't enough for you to be able to sustain this stylistic basis.

It can hardly be called a 'stylistic basis', but it is correct to say that a new way of listening concurs with my thoughts on sound. If sound is what defines the phenomenology of music then it implies that our ears know how to handle it. And if we are exposed to a sound that our ears don't know how to handle we have to ask, 'Is this music'? and, 'What actually is music'? Therefore attempting to redirect the ears, so to speak, has always interested me, as well as opening our ears to things that otherwise might be screened out by conceptual models. All of us know that we usually listen in a certain way and that consequently there might be something else that we completely ignore.

Someone had the idea of playing Beethoven to pygmies in New Guinea to see how they would react. But they didn't react at all. After a few minutes of being amazed at the noise over the loudspeakers they tolerated it and acted as if they heard nothing. Perhaps Beethoven for them is what static noise on loudspeakers is for us. That's what I mean by 'mind models'. In order to hear anything at all, our ears—and our head—have to be tuned to certain wavelengths. And the structure of our thought will determine what we hear. It seems obvious to me that the broader our mind models, the greater the range of our experiences.

At the end of the 1970s I considered various means by which to handle my 'non-style'. I was kind of redeemed when I started writing musical drama. I did it for much the same reason that Webern started writing songs—he also had a problem with form. When you have to work with a text, and particularly with a text with a well-defined dramaturgical plan, then you have the formal shape in advance. Just as I had used a pre-existing shape in advance, so to speak, by building music inside a movement by Mahler.

Besides, musical drama makes the stylistic element—still the favourite metaphor in the aesthetic debate—less important. It is self-evident that in music drama the music doesn't always represent a specific aesthetic stance but is subject to the dramatic situation. Even Schoenberg used quotation-like material in his operas. So here you have something like a neutral position where the importance of style as a means of personal expression is no longer of top priority. A less *committed* position, you might say. That's how it worked for me.

I wrote two works quite quickly, one right after the other, first the opera *Jephta*, commissioned by Jutland Opera, and after that, the first in a series of works related to an unorthodox, maybe rather naïve attempt to create a personal alternative to established music theatre institutions, namely, the 'scenic concert piece' *Majakovski*.

Once you asked Per Nørgård and Pelle Gudmundsen-Holmgreen how they felt about their earlier works. To judge by concert programmes, your earlier music no longer arouses a great deal of interest, something that is also true for two composers who worked with related methods, namely, Poul Ruders and Bo Holten. Like yours, their earlier works are not performed very often. You all worked with recycling. Do you have an intimate relationship with your early works or are you sceptical about the works of the young Rasmussen?

Why should you look sceptically at something you have done with honesty and integrity at an earlier point in your life? *Je ne regrette rien* as Edith Piaf used to sing—'I don't regret anything.' But the question is whether I still *have* any relationship with them at all. The question is whether I have any relationship with the work that I finished a month ago. I perceive everything to a very, very high degree, like Kierkegaard says, as stages on life's path, and therefore, as things to which you really cannot return. When I hear my earlier works, I feel a bit like when I accidentally meet a girl I once knew intimately. I may find it difficult to understand what on earth we once shared. But of course I don't regret anything, and probably someone else likes her now . . . .

In one place you write, 'Personally, I have to pinch myself in order to comprehend that I was the same person then as I am now'!

I believe everyone recognizes that experience, but an artist recognizes it in a particularly intense way. We are confronted most inescapably with our past when we sit in a concert hall and listen to a piece that is twenty years old. I don't know what to do with it other than feeling a slightly touching recognition that, 'My goodness, that was once me! Was I really interested in that sort of thing then? Did I really think that was the right way to handle a musical or an artistic problem'? At the same time I have to say, 'Yes, that's apparently what I did'. But to do as some do and proof-read one's earlier work from a later perspective seems pointless and plainly dishonest to me.

Now that we are here talking with 'grand gestures' it is tempting to talk about who is dead and what has died. There are those famous quotes like 'Schoenberg is Dead' or 'Is stylistic pluralism dead?' Almost all of you have abandoned unequivocal references to any given model.

If I have abandoned anything, it must be multiple references. There are very, very few unequivocal references in my music, because among other things, the so-called quotations that I used were so short and so anonymous that they can rarely be heard as referring to a specific piece of existing music.

But I have frequently used Berio Mask *in my seminars and can contradict that, since the listeners were able to hear at least Mahler, if not Luciano Berio.*

True, there are a few—let's call them—'exceptions', but they are exceptions of a special order. The most obvious example is Beethoven's *Hammerklavier Fugue* which I de-composed in my work *Fugue*. There are in fact only three pure examples of decomposition in my output and we have not mentioned the main one, namely, my cello concerto with the title 'Concerto in G minor for Cello and Orchestra by Georg Matthias Monn freely re-composed by Arnold Schoenberg and further developed in the Style of Stravinsky by . . . me'. It sounds like a joke and so it is, in a way. You may just as well call it my Cello Concerto. As a matter of fact, the piece has a real title, *Contrafactum*, meaning not just 'against that which exists', but Latin for 'forgery'.

That is probably the work in which the question of authenticity is most urgent, and also the work that has had the most difficult existence. It has only been performed a few times and hardly anyone has shown interest in it afterwards. It is a very special piece, unique for me, because it is the *style* itself that is being decomposed. It is a complete work by Schoenberg, a reworking of an early classical piece that I took just as Schoenberg left it. But I reworked it the way I imagine Stravinsky might have. The *sound* of this piece isn't necessarily all it is about. It is music that challenges concepts like 'authenticity', 'history' and so on, and sets thoughts in motion in the minds of people who think about such matters. Which, apparently, not very many do.

You have talked about the time around 1970, when your music—on one level—treated the problem of composing. Your Second Symphony which you mentioned earlier, Anfang und Ende, is a good example of that. You referred to Hans Gefors' interpretation. At one point Gefors wrote, 'Karl Aage Rasmussen's music [is] a battle between the will to express itself and the oppression of the cliché. This is part of the realisation that today's musical language is based on music that once emerged from the vital minds of the composers of our culture but now is reduced to clichés. Such a musical language is in conflict with that of its dead ancestors'. What do you think of this description?

That it hits the spot. This set of problems played a role in that whole period of my life when I was preoccupied with researching new or over-looked expressive possibilities in pre-existing musical material. According to the classical

European avant-garde tradition (Schoenberg, serialism, etc.), that which pre-exists has already become a cliché. From that perspective expressing oneself truly becomes a battle against the weight of clichés, as Gefors says. But it's not a hopeless battle because there is a means of expression that *doesn't* rely on the material as such. The Dane Gudmundsen-Holmgreen has shown, and often with great simplicity, that poetry and expressivity can be found almost anywhere—in a discarded jazz chord or in a cast-off piece of cultural refuse—and be quite independent of where the material originated.

But as mentioned earlier, I gradually moved in other directions even though my interest in the idea of 'history' continued to burn. I began to experience the sequence of historical epochs as a metaphor for something that had to do with both time and tempo. And gradually it turned into a more direct interest in the experience of time, and in the mark of time on the artistic material, on the music.

I would like to return to the question of time which has occupied you in your later works. The 1970s interest me, not least because you were one of the first to realize that it is important to discuss the perception *of music. That was something to which little attention was being paid.*

The article, 'Oplevelse, analyse og pædagogik' ('Perception, Analysis and Teaching'), concerns the 'biology of the musical experience'. In the introduction you wrote, 'In the debate concerning music teaching . . . there is not much discussion of "perception". It is something that is taken for granted'. As is well-known, the problem of perception-orientated pedagogy and musical thinking was readdressed with an abundance of materials later. You write in this article about the wall between the 'personal' way of dealing with music as 'a means of spiritual influence' and the pedagogical side of dealing with music as 'a means of consciousness, analysis and teaching'. If I understand it correctly, the main influences on your spritual development have been the works of Ives, Cage, Ligeti, Nørgård.

Among others.

Are there other composers whom you would like to include in this regard?

Oh yes indeed, mentioning in no particular order, Stravinsky, Satie, Busoni, Nancarrow, Hauer and others. There is a long list of composers who have meant something to me. Just look at the composers I have written about. It's a very long list.

At different points in my life composers have interested me for two reasons. Either they offer me some new possibilities, let's call them 'technical' in the broadest sense of the word. My interest in time and tempo quite naturally led me to Conlon Nancarrow, for whom tempo is in itself a dimension worthy of investigation. This didn't turn me into a grovelling Nancarrow fan like

Ligeti, who calls Nancarrow the 'Bach of our time'. But Nancarrow's techniques have been of vital interest to me.

Or, composers may change my mind models. I have been concerned with Stravinsky throughout most of my adult life. I was attracted by Busoni's theories of music. I am attracted by Satie, again, as a 'thinker' because in the case of Satie we may question to what extent the music is music at all, if maybe it might just as well be read or perhaps should be perceived in a third way, beyond plain listening. What happens in his pieces is not always terribly interesting to *hear*. And yet Satie's importance for Cage, for example, is enormous, so there must be something going on here, there *is* something behind the music.

My interest in Scelsi and Nono also has to do with the feeling that this music is something more than sound as sound. It is sound turned into pure spirit, so to speak, it is sound that becomes and creates a spiritual awareness in our heads. And perhaps we approach a pivotal point in our conversation here, for I imagine that the misconception of me as some kind of 'superintellectual' partly reflects my enduring conviction that, as it enters our ears music is fused with something that I, for want of a better word, have to call 'thinking'.

That may sound as if I say that the merry and enjoyable art we call music is only interesting—even physically—when it can be experienced as something philosophical or intellectual. But that would be a colossal distortion of my concerns, for obviously music remains present as sound, and I, too, listen to it and relish it as sound. I simply want it also to create a *spiritual* perspective in the broadest sense. Yes, that does sound a bit lofty but we don't have very many good words for it.

What do aesthetic descriptions mean to you? Ones like, individuality, craftmanship, interference, concentration, simplicity, emotional strength?

Some of them I recognize as something I have often returned to. I have often recommended that we substitute the word 'individual' for the boring half-German, philosophical word 'original', because, all of a sudden, it becomes something quite plain. Each of us has his own way of appearing, of walking, moving and so on. Altogether it's what we could readily call our individuality. Everything that is specific without being premeditated. That kind of individuality doesn't have to be construed as 'originality', it is something almost unavoidable. But when Stockhausen goes to great pains trying to avoid doing what someone has done before, I don't see what that has to do with individuality. It's something which is, to use his own language, *ausgedacht*, thought out, it seems to me.

If an artist loses touch with his own individuality then it's probably due to exposure to some form of thought-terrorism or group-pressure, some mind-control police who tell him what he should not do and what he ought to do. Therefore it is also important for me—even though I don't think I have previously mentioned it in public—to consider my own roots. My particular history, my background when I began to compose has actually marked the whole course of my composing career. Not as a result of some intellectual stance with respect to cultural or political things, but as a simple expression of 'my way'. And when I realized that this was what made composing fun and interesting for me, I continued in that spirit. Perhaps you can say that I am still trying to find new ways of using that specific potential.

I don't really know what 'craft' is. As a teacher of composers for many years though, I think I know that craftmanship means something. If I didn't believe that there was something that could be learned, it would be meaningless to teach. But it would never occur to me to say that I could *teach* someone to compose. I will say that at most I can possibly teach someone to think as a composer.

What that means is having an expanded and finely-tuned awareness of how *difficult* it is to compose, instead of thinking that it's like a cow giving milk. This, I think, is an important condition if an artist is to gain perspective. This is not to say that those blessed by God to give milk are insignificant; sometimes they are the most significant of all. However, composers apply to conservatories of their own free will, so they obviously wish to be influenced in some way. Often they only wish for—what shall we say—a coach who stands there on the sidelines and can see a little better from a slightly different angle. Composers have intentions and the craft is the ability to realize these intentions without relying on others. What were the other words?

Interference.

Interference is a word that reminds me of a long discussion I began with Per Nørgård some time back; we call it our 'eternal' discussion. We imagine ourselves as two different types of composers. There are those who seek to discover where a particular music is moving. They proceed 'ecologically'; they don't wish to interfere with the material more than is necessary. Mozart is an example. Or Morton Feldman, who said somewhere that 'every time I try to manipulate my work, for what I think is a terrific idea, I know that in a minute I'd hear my music screaming "Help"'! These composers experience their music as something with its own life, like a woman who has a child in her belly. There isn't any point in her working energetically to make it into a girl or a boy or a genius. The best she can do is to have a healthy life-style and take some long walks so the child will be strong and well.

Then you have another type of artist who thinks that interesting things happen precisely when they *interfere*. At this point we have to abandon the embryo image. I'm not speaking of genetic engineering but about the kind of art where you establish something and then react to it. Examples? Haydn, Stravinsky, naturally also Kirkeby, whom we mentioned above.

It is characteristic of my own temperament that I react. I said earlier that I think best when I'm talking with someone, or when I am in a discussion, because it gives me the opportunity to relate to something. My creative instincts work in the same way and that explains the countless works—if more rare now—in my output where I start with something extant that I develop further.

Concentration.

The creative process is essentially one of concentration. A composer said that he always writes with ink because 'As soon as I begin to cross out, I'm not concentrating any more'? To which he added, 'If I get inspired, I go for a walk', implying that when you are inspired you can no longer concentrate because you will lose control. You have to write the notes that you really mean to write at each single moment. Some composers work with a rubber, and it is obviously their right. However, it is always better to work in a concentrated way for five minutes than to sit and push notes around aimlessly for many hours.

Simplicity.

I don't know what that is.

Emotional strength.

Nor that either.

Those six categories are the chapter titles in what you called 'My Catechism' (Dansk Musik Tidsskrift, *1978, ed.). It seems that you don't have anything to add today— or do you? But evidently, you do have something to strike out.*

Well, yes . . . that is twenty years ago, right? Or something like that.

Yes . . . nearly twenty years.

Well, anyway I'll 'stand by' simplicity as a somewhat banal category. If you want to say something then say it as simply as possible. I hope that those who read my writings will agree that I try to do this. I try to write simply, even on complex issues. Don't make things more complicated than necessary. That's what I understand by the word, simplicity.

But emotional strength is simply so completely tied up with experience that it is a private thing. Kierkegaard used a brilliant distinction between the things you can only do first hand and the things you can do second hand. If I were to write an article on Italian foreign policy, I could ask a friend to go to Italy for me, gather material, possibly interview some politicians, and so on. Based on that I could write the article. It is something I can do second hand. But I can't attend a concert second hand. I can't send you in there to hear the concert for me. I can't ask you to date my sweetheart for a few months because I am away on a trip. These are things I can only do first hand. Someday when Death knocks at my door, I won't be able to ask my neighbour to deal with him.

Emotional strength is something a listener can experience only first hand, and therefore it's not something the composer can put into his work. I can't imagine a method that would assure a composer that his work acquires emotional strength. If he insists on trying, the risk is that the work becomes sentimental which is something completely different. So when I say that I don't know what emotional strength is, I mean that I only know what it is when nobody asks me. I haven't struck it from the list, I have just become a bit wiser, maybe, about where it belongs.

In the 1980s you wanted to 'make a music that wonders . . . or makes people wonder'. In the 1990s I detect a new poetic dimension to your expression, something that extends further toward the listener. I have the feeling that you are no longer satisfied with making people wonder?

That's probably true. I think there was a phase in the 1980s when my instinctive critical attitude was particularly strong and today I find that the least interesting phase in my output. While I have some nostalgia for the works of the 1970s there is a period in the 1980s that honestly doesn't interest me very much to-day. Perhaps I let myself be overpowered by cultural politics, ideology and non-musical notions. I have lived so much of my life as an animator and teacher—it's hardly surprising if these activities at one time or another impact on my creativity in a negative way.

It doesn't surprise me that it could happen, but rather that it lasted for some time. When I look back on my work I usually see clear lines, not in the sense of causal relationships but simply natural movements in different directions as my interests slowly shift and change course.

It doesn't seem wholly unreasonable to see a break with the 1970s aesthetic in your work A Symphony in Time (1982). Jørgen I. Jensen described it as a harbinger of 'an important widening of horizons, not only in the composer's own development, but also in the larger picture of today's musical and cultural climate'. That is a grand statement! What happened then?

The important junctions in my life appear when I come to a point where I can't figure out how to go on the next day. Usually this sets off some kind of analytic activity, sometimes involving the work of other composers. It happened in 1982 or 1983, not least as the result of annoyance with the way in which cultural politics, writing for the media, and pedagogical concerns began to preoccupy my mind. This led me to reconsider a number of things—particularly Stravinsky.

I began to look at Stravinsky to find out what it was that was going on in certain works that made them particularly fascinating to me while others paled. I couldn't figure out what my favourite works had in common. For example, what connects the *Symphonies of Wind Instruments* and the *Fairy's Kiss*, despite their obvious stylistic differences? As I became more and more engrossed in this music, I discovered what the similarities are: not just the stereotypical Stravinsky-style cubism of forms and building blocks, but the experience of time itself and the perception of movement.

We tend to think that music moves, but at the same time we have a feeling that it is a metaphor. For how could it actually do that? Classical tonality has certain built-in driving forces. Harmonic tension and release produce an illusion of movement. And the history of modern music is, among other things, the history about searching high and low for something to replace this worn-out engine.

But Stravinsky didn't use functional harmony. I did a radio programme where I found certain time-proportions in Stravinsky, some precise durational relations between adjacent musical segments, or between segments that are repeated at separate points in the course of the piece. In the *Symphonies of Wind Instruments* I found incredibly precise relationships between the duration of the individual segments, in other words a very meticulously planned pattern of proportions. And I imagined that this was the key to the kinetic energy of this seemingly static music.

This was the starting point for *A Symphony in Time*. I expanded this idea of ambiguity, identity and time from a one-movement time-span like Stravinsky's *Symphonies* into a larger symphonic form. I imagined that we were in a circle with all four movements in a symphony surrounding us. Elliott Carter has a work with a title that resembles mine—*A Symphony of Three Orchestras*—in which each of four small orchestras simultaneously plays its own symphony. The thought of taking time apart captivated me. We hear four movements one after the other, but we also hear four movements each one of which, at any given moment, could be one of the *other* movements. That was my line of thinking and I started to work with Stravinsky's discovery that proportions of time can create an illusion of movement. I worked very matter-of-factly with very simple material and this resulted in a work that became an important new beginning for me.

How much do you demand from the listeners with this work? I wonder whether, after having heard the four movements, you are supposed to be able to put them together mentally. Or is it so that you can listen to them in isolation from each other? Do you get another and more legitimate experience if you can perceive them together as a whole?

I don't know. I'm reluctant to give recipes for the best way to experience something because I know that most often when I find my own way into something, I get the most out of it. I have rarely derived pleasure from listening-recipes myself. When it pertains to works by others I may act as an 'interpreter' because sometimes I can help with opening up a door. But when it pertains to my own music, I don't like doing it. I assume that you can hear the piece as four regular movements without suspecting any special relationship between them.

Let me give you an example. Dennis Potter's masterpiece is the fantastic TV drama called *The Singing Detective*. Here something happens that is strikingly similar to what happens in *A Symphony in Time*. We find ourselves in a kind of time continuum, we never know exactly where we are—whether we are before or after, whether we are in a hospital with the main character, whether we are in his childhood or whether we are at a much later time. I believe that Dennis Potter would feel equally at a loss if you were to ask him 'How should I view this piece'? You should simply *see* it because you can't avoid noticing that time behaves in a peculiar way. I am not at all sure that you can get more out of my symphony by having it explained that one movement is inside another movement, and so on. But you hear a symphony behaving quite differently from most, while, at the same time, it behaves exactly like it should because it has an allegro, an adagio, a scherzo and a finale.

But earlier you were considering the question of how to justify the fact that one note follows another. Your reflections concerning time and your analyses of Stravinsky have made it possible for you to continue along that path. When one reads your articles and essays there is one element that runs throughout. To quote, you say, 'To want to search after time is like searching after dark with a candle in your hand'. Time has preoccupied you, but to what extent has there been a corelation between your theoretical explorations of the phenomenon of time and the actual music that you have created on the basis of these theoretical considerations? To what extent can these meta-reflections on time be heard in your music?

Presumably not at all, because that's not how it works. The way time enters the work—if the experience of time *can* be in the foreground at all—is in the form of a music that has some special time-related features.

Where is the experience of time actually strongest in music? Probably, in the tempo. In many languages the word for 'time' and the word for 'tempo' is actually the same. But the tempo is a very difficult thing to isolate because tempo is a kind of conveyor for everything else. It wouldn't make much sense after having heard a piece to ask, 'Now, what did you really think about the tempo'? Well, if it is a performance of a well-known work then you can discuss whether or not the performance found the proper tempo. But if you heard a piece for the first time and the composer came out all excited and asked if you had experienced the *tempo*, I think most people would be baffled. For the tempo *is* there, it is impossible to imagine music without some kind of tempo; time has to pass.

How can you focus on the tempo as such? When I ask myself that question—and answer it quite unscientifically from my own experience—I find that it happens when the tempo isn't linear, regular, or constant, so to speak. The experience of tempo is strongest when the tempo is in a state of change, when it gets faster or slower or perhaps swings in and out as it does, for example, in a Chopin-*rubato*.

If the experience of tempo is particularly strong when the tempo is in a state of change, wouldn't it be exciting to imagine music that is constantly accelerating or constantly slowing down? Probably, but here I stumble on a technical problem: when the Russians sing their well-known 'Ka-lin-ka, Ka-lin-ka' the tempo accelerates so rapidly in a short space of time that the music soon becomes meaningless. Consequently, I have to find a musical strategy—and here you see the connection between thinking and numbers—enabling the tempo to increase or decrease endlessly. And here I get no support whatsoever from philosophies of time, astrophysics or anything like that.

Here I am left with my own theoretical and technical knowledge, and my imagination. And so music may result that either shows that the idea does not work, or perhaps shows that it works up to a point—or maybe that there is a long way to go before it works with great clarity. But who knows, perhaps it isn't really important whether it works with great 'clarity'.

In 1979 I wrote that in the 1980s time will be *in*. And that may be the closest I ever came to being a prophet. It became almost stylish in Danish music to be a pursuer of time and to see the experience of time as a central concern. We must have felt that this was a virgin area where the experience of time, the concept of time and new time-horizons established not only a new conceptual basis but a direct starting point for the creation of new mind models. And as so often, Per Nørgård had already taken the first important steps.

A series of new mind models emerged, and most important for many and certainly for me, probably, were the so-called 'fractals'. When you begin to think about infinity not as something scary out there in space, but as something down-to-earth—like that cute drawing on a familiar oatmeal box of a little boy who runs with a packet of oatmeal that has a drawing on the oatmeal box of a boy who runs with a packet of oatmeal that has, and so on—then infinity is no longer frightening, but something almost touching. And when all of a sudden it works as a background for new thoughts, I am precisely where I want to be as a composer or artist.

That is where the technical, the audible, the analytical and the conceptual meet in an area which makes room for exploration, stimulates the intellect and, at the same time, offers new shades of meaning that may give rise to new emotions. You use yourself as a kind of test case, I suppose. And perhaps you discover, as you said, some new psychological and poetic dimensions without precisely knowing what they are or where they come from. I don't think that there are any specific tools other than personal experience. When you test a long series of possibilities, sooner or later you will be able to cope with them and maybe even express something with them.

We have to round this off. I would like to explore the poetic dimension further. I believe that somebody—perhaps myself—has written that when you (by 'you' I mean, for example, you and Poul Ruders) threw out collage and style-references, your works became more elevated. I recently heard a piece by you at Tivoli played by the violinist, Rebecca Hirsch. It made a profound impression on me, precisely because there was a poetic dimension in the work.

It is difficult to talk about this in a general way, because each single work has its own background, history and problems. The piece you refer to actually has an unusually long, poetic title. It is called *Sinking Through the Dream Mirror*. And I am in a slightly uncomfortable situation because I can't really explain what it means. The dream mirror *is* something I have dreamt, or so I believe. I imagined that dreams and reality meet in a 'mirror' akin to the surface of water.

The piece uses 'fractal' melodic lines, that is to say, identical lines that form a veritable Chinese box of tempi, both very fast and very slow, endlessly intertwined and fitting into each other like a huge network. When such a melodic line falls, sooner or later it will flatten out. If a very fast melody falls in terms of pitch, and a very slow identical melody fits into it—well, it's clear that the slow melody cannot fall nearly as fast as the fast one can. Thus sooner or later the slow one will make the fast one level out. And this 'level' I came to perceive as the water-mirror—a mirror that the melody can break through only when the composer 'interferes'.

This shows again how theoretical thought inevitably pervades even purely expressive realms. And this simple symbolic idea actually gave the piece its title. But it belongs to the story that it was composed just before I embarked on the opera, *The Sinking of the Titanic*, and that it is likely to be a premonition of the Doomsday mood that prevails in the opera.

I can't explain why the work has such a prevailingly melancholy mood, though. You can't, as I said earlier, wilfully put something like that into a work. In my recent orchestra work, *Scherzo with Bells*, something ordered and systematic collides with something irrational: a rushing scherzo collides with tolling bells—for me a simple symbol of fate and death. In this case the psychological dimension is easier to explain but for that very reason it may also be less profound. However, if this psychological dimension is what you call the 'poetic dimension', then I agree.

You feel particularly at ease in Rome—at one time you increased the number of your trips, and started living there for extended periods. Do these voluntary exiles mean that you simply work best there? Was it the crisis that you experienced in the 1980s, or were you bored to death by the Danish music scene?

The latter certainly is not very pertinent. I am neither bored by the Danish music scene, nor especially charmed by it. The main reason why I began escaping to other skies was quite plainly that I wanted to work where fewer people were likely to disturb me.

Rome as a cultural centre has attracted many Danes throughout the centuries. But I see now that there are some simple, almost musical reasons that meant Rome was the place for me. I'm thinking about the city's very special soundscape. If you were to say that to an Italian, he would be startled because he recognizes only one version of the sounds of Rome and that is a hellish din. But that isn't the only Rome. The historical Rome that I ramble around is not particularly polluted by noise. On the contrary, there are squares, small streets and alleys that empty out onto smaller squares that again expand to larger squares, and so on. That results in a constantly changing soundscape, which, in one way or another, keeps the sense of hearing unusually awake.

I thought about that when I walked over here with a friend for the meeting with you today: how difficult it is to have a conversation in the soundscape of Copenhagen. As soon as you enter one of the many main thoroughfares you almost have to shout at each other. It's stressful, acoustically speaking. In Rome the heavy traffic is kept out of the narrow streets and you travel on a kind of sound stage that changes height and character in a very unexpected and fascinating way.

This soundscape has become my way of staying fond of the city, for the city is, in a strange way, both the theme and the trauma of my life. Since I was about twenty I have lived on a lonely isolated farm in mid-Jutland and I don't think I'll change that until they carry me away from there in a box. But like most people, I have a need for something other than peace and quiet. Rome became the place where I could live a completely different life. If I travel alone to Rome and stay there for a month there are very few demands on me— other than the ones I make on myself. I can determine my own social calendar and mostly direct my life in the way in which I find it most fun to live.

This interview was published in two parts: 'Modviljens poesi: Samtale med komponisten Karl Aage Rasmussen', *Dansk Musik Tidsskrift* 72, 1 and 2 (1997/98): 2–10, 46–54.

Sofia Gubaidulina

INTO THE LABYRINTH OF THE SOUL

Composer Sofia Gubaidulina sits across from me in her hotel room in Stockholm. I ask questions in German and she answers in Russian. She understands me; I don't understand her. But her body language is so strong that I can't fail to grasp part of the content in her answer in spite of the language barriers. She does not hide her Tartar heritage and Russian upbringing — the sharp lines of her face and the excited verbal outbursts reveal all. Her music is, naturally, similarly revealing. She wears all her music and her culture in her facial expressions: unfathomable melancholy, religious dedication, ironic distance, threatening energy. The eyes can express holy piety and murderous fury in one and the same look.

Gubaidulina's music cannot be shaken off once it has taken hold. It does not fade away, but resonates in the senses — the kind of impressions that one could not possibly erase. Perhaps this is because the music's dark illusive apocryphal nature is so compelling. It never reveals its innermost secrets: it is never absolute music for there is almost always something that points beyond the purely musical elements. It can be a text, a ritual, the act of picking up an instrument, a Christian symbol. One symphonic work, for example, culminates in silence: Stimmen . . . verstummen . . . . Only the conductor moves. He conducts and beats time in the emptiness so that the silence vibrates in one's inner being.

To compose in this way is more than a profession, more than a craft. Viewed as a vocation, says Gubaidulina, it is demanding work that requires strong spiritual powers. She is just as uncompromising, both as a person and as an artist, as that other great Russian woman: Galina Ustwolskaja.

In Gubaidulina's works, 'sacrifice' as an image keeps returning like a canonic motif, as a general subject, and as an autobiographical element. In the Russian music journal, Sovetskaja Musyka, she is quoted as saying, with evident biblical undertones, 'When I think of how difficult and complicated my life has been, of the burdens I bear, I say to myself, "I have not asked for any other destiny. I have quite simply got more than I asked for. That's my good fortune"'

Gubaidulina describes herself as a believer for whom religion in practice means the re-creation of the wholeness that has been lost in 'the staccato of life'. With this attitude to life, composing becomes a religious act and each work a new path to the core of faith. The demand for renewal of material is unyielding, but not as a consequence of a central-European modernist aesthetic. In the context of Gubaidulina's music the word 'modern' sounds irrelevant and carries an unusual meaning. At a time when new music lacks a common goal, Gubaidulina has her own clear path to follow, an overriding project anchored in religious belief:

Though I am probably undergoing some form of technical development, my way of perceiving form remains the same. I go deeper and deeper into the labyrinth of my soul and I always find something new. Naturally I have learned a few things along the way, but on the whole I am still following the same path.

Concerning the experiment

One does not have to listen to much of Gubaidulina's music in order to detect the lack of unity in her output; each new work explores new possibilities. It is pointless to arrange the works in large groups; it makes more sense to talk about pairs of works. Experimentation is both part of the process and the result. Gubaidulina's endeavour is apparently to come up with something new in each work that is a 'reply' to something in the previous one. For example in 1983 she composed Perception *where the decisive words were 'Voices. Silenced'. Then to these key words, in her own formulation she added: 'Voices, listen, see—where do words come from? From the inside or from the outside . . . life, tones . . . silence'. She felt that the theme was not completely used up, that there was something left that she had to answer. So a whole symphony, the next work, was called* Stimmen . . . verstummen . . . (Voices . . . silence . . .).*

Gubaidulina says that occasionally it is simply impossible to use up all the possibilities that arise from one work. In* Sovetskaja Musyka 2 *she remarked to a Soviet journalist:*

Those who think that constructive and rigorously intellectual work can have artistic results are wrong because these qualities do not lead to a real experience for the listeners. It may be that the composer has experienced something but it just doesn't reverberate in the listener. There has also to be something extraordinary. However, those who believe that one can just work intuitively, can fantasize about sounds and let them flow out onto the paper, are also wrong, because this kind of art is too emotional and lacks balance or resistance. Good music is only made when the two positions are brought together; the approach to formal elements has to be rigorous, consciously determined and accompanied by strong inner experiences.

She continues with a comment on the modern in music:

I believe that the term 'modern' applies to a work in which a mental state is expressed in musical material. Musical material is a living organism which has its own history, its own development. We don't invent it; it is like the soil, like nature or like a child. It demands something, it wants something, something that is indispensible. If one tries to examine this scientifically it is feasible, under favourable circumstances, to separate and formulate what it is that the musical material demands. But the artistic consciousness responds intuitively or intellectually to the condition of the material. And the modern artist is one who uses only strictly personal resources to react independently to these demands. But a modern work is not necessarily good, and one that isn't modern is not necessarily bad. I believe that such preconceptions spoil analytical thought. They set boundaries and give a tendentious character to evaluations. On the other hand, one should not avoid evaluation. For if that happens difficulties with the material will be overlooked.

CONVERSATION

In 1990 Gubaidulina and Alfred Schnittke were the featured composers at the Huddersfield Festival in Northern England. When Schnittke spoke at the festival about the future of the Soviet Union he was quite pessimistic. The fear and hopelessness that he expressed were almost prophetic: just a few years later things headed in a catastrophic direction. Currently, the situation in Russia is so tense that it isn't an exaggeration to call it a 'time bomb'.

Gubaidulina now lives in Germany and has to look at the depressed situation from the sidelines.

In Russian musical circles the tendency toward dissolution is clear; Moscow's proud Tschaikowsky Conservatory hasn't enough money to repair the buildings and instruments. Everything is falling apart. People don't feel safe on the streets; this insecurity is ruinous for the arts. This is clear to everyone who visits Moscow. How do you feel about the situation in your country?

The conductor Gennady Rozjdestvenskij and I were recently interviewed on Swedish Radio. He expressed exactly what I feel about the situation. He said that he felt as if his skin had been torn to shreds. That is exactly how I feel. It's the same whether we are at home or abroad: it's as if we have been skinned. Whether in Moscow or abroad, we are existentially shaken by what is happening to our country. It is the first time in history that we have experienced such a situation. Earlier, Russia had some similarly horrible periods, as, for example, in the times of Ivan the Terrible and Peter the Great. But the ideological breakdown that we are experiencing now has no historical precedent.

We have an enormous arsenal of extraordinarily dangerous weapons in the Ukraine. Earlier this century people suffered from the arms race, but the country preserved its integrity. Now we are seeing a kind of disarmament of the whole of civilization. Obviously we have feared for a long time that this would happen. Three years ago we were afraid of what could happen, but we

couldn't change the situation. I remember after Stalin's death, twenty years ago, how the intelligentsia gathered around in order to analyse their position. What we are now experiencing is not simply a breakdown after a period of about ten years; what is happening now is the culmination of seventy years of history, namely, the period since the October Revolution in 1917.

During the World Music Days in Zurich in 1991, Dansk Musik Tidsskrift *(Danish Music Review) spoke with Edison Denisov about the fatal developments in the former Soviet Union at the time when the best leaders were emigrating. The institutions that were left behind were without adequate teachers to show the way for the younger generation. Denisov was bitter about the artists and intellectuals who were leaving their own country and settling in the West. It was his opinion that these people should stay and fight against unfair conditions. Why did you leave Russia?*

It was a question of principles. The Russian intelligentsia has an important role to play in today's world. We have to fight to preserve this, for it did not just blossom overnight, but is the result of a development that reaches right back to the tenth century. It took a thousand years to create this phenomenon. Today this phenomenon is being destroyed in Russia. It is crucial to consider how it can be saved. In any case I completely disagree with Denisov. For a person like me to stay in Russia now would mean disintegration. I felt it strongly when the finance minister Pavlov began his reforms in 1990. It was deeply humiliating to be a witness to the great misery it produced. I was deeply insulted on behalf of the people. I went out on the street and talked to people. They believed that they could live with it, that it didn't mean annihilation. It was clear to me that the intellectuals are weaker, not stronger, than the people. What should I do then when I am about to die from this humiliation? I can survive the material difficulties, but under these conditions, I cannot create, I cannot work. After a month I felt that it was not just me who was in danger, but the whole of the intelligentsia. I thought at that time that one should stay and try to help with improving the miserable condition of life. And while the 'brains' flowed out of Russia, I tried to resist following them.

I believe that my answer to the question is more appropriate than Denisov's. He isn't, like me, a weak person, but a very strong one. People with my mental constitution are simply destroyed and must take that into consideration if they love the Russian people. That's why I live just outside of Hamburg and not in my apartment in Moscow. But I have not abandoned my apartment in the strict sense, I am only living in Hamburg—as a foreigner, for a period. It is important for me to preserve my ability to work. I cannot work under the present conditions in Moscow. But my life ultimately belongs to my people.

Photo: Sofia Gubaidulina (Marianne Grøndahl).

If one talks with a person like the former general secretary of the composers' union, Tichon Khrennikov, then one gets the opposite viewpoint: he is of the opinion that there are now really good opportunities for Russian composers as a result of perestroika and the opening up of Russia to the West. He also thinks that the frequent performances of music by Schnittke and Gubaidulina in the West are merely a fashion. Do you see this attitude as an expression of envy? Or is it a problem that one should take seriously?

I don't believe that his opinion is dictated by envy. I believe that he means what he says. He does not rate certain artistic works very highly according to his criteria, and he thinks therefore that they will be forgotten in the future. The same question can be asked about any composer. Yes, what will eventually survive into the future? My composition teacher, Nikolaj Pejko, told me something that he read concerning Chopin, whose music everyone wanted to hear at that time. Once Chopin was invited to a party and he sat and played in room adjoining the room where the party was gathered and no one listened to his playing. It happens at every time, everywhere, and even with the most talented artists. It is our destiny and we have to realize that. Only the future will show what has lasting value. Some composers are temporarily in the foreground, but then slide out to the sidelines. Personally, I am at peace. I often find that at one moment people listen to my music, and in the next don't listen at all. But perhaps it will be listened to consistently in the future. It depends also on historical and social circumstances.

Let's turn to more concrete aspects of your music and talk about the extra-musical elements in it. When I heard the work Stufen, *I thought about the number mysticism of earlier times. The number seven is important in this work. Karlheinz Stockhausen also works with number symbolism; he speaks about 'holy numbers'. Your work with numerical relationships could be compared to the late medieval square number cult. What does the number seven mean to* Stufen, *in particular, and numerical relationships to your works in general?*

I think that number mysticism is a challenge to our times. I have observed that many composers—not only myself—are working with these ideas. I am talking about composers who love numbers. We aren't simply continuing a medieval tradition, but a Pythagorean one. I love this number mysticism, which has been a source of inspiration to me since 1983. When I composed *The Seven Words of Christ* I began to work with the number seven. For me it was a symbolic number, a holy number. Now I'm working intensively with musical form, and the numbers mean more than I can say. For me they are not as important in themselves as for the inherent relationships and proportions they embrace. To become aware of the inherent proportions between bodies of sounds has become highly significant to me, an important challenge that helps create the specific form of a piece. It becomes apparent that this approach brings out hundreds of interesting constructions, and that different combinations of various types of constructions in distinct layers of a musical work lead to collisions that we can perceive as culminating moments charged with suspense. These various number relationships in different layers give me a wealth of ideas, so many that I am forced to discard some. You may call them holy numbers, but for the time being, it is just an experiment. Only the future will show if the experiment is successful. At the moment I feel I am just starting out. For me it is a kind of sacred process.

I hear an epic quality, a narrative character, in your music. There are meaningful elements deliberately encoded in the music. Your fellow countryman, Boris Asafjev, wrote a book that was somewhat important to the development of hermeneutic musicology: Musical Form as Process. *To what extent does your music correspond to Asafjev's thinking? For example, what about his theory of intonation?*

These theories do not concern me much. There is nothing in them that inspires me. The idea of musical form as process is in accordance with my philosophy, but Asafjev's thinking as such has not been a determinant for me.

In your music one occasionally notices a phenomenon that can be described as a Schein des Bekannten, *something that might be a citation from works of an earlier age. I'm thinking for example of the Prelude to Wagner's* Lohengrin *as heard in your work* Stimmen . . . verstummen *that was played at one of the concerts at the Stockholm New Music Festival. Even though you don't use tonality in the same way, there are clear references to Wagner in your music. It seems that you reuse ideas from the past.*

That's a good observation. The musical ideas in *Lohengrin* and *Parsifal* are close to me, and for a time I was very taken with them. I am also fascinated by the philosophical ideas of Wagner's epic cycle. I am happy to be inspired by him.

Two important tracks in your music often run parallel: the serious, even deeply serious, and side by side with this, ironic or parodistic elements. Shostakovich was a master of parody. One can also hear this in your work, for example in the choral piece Hommage à Marina Tsvetajeva. *Seriousness is sometimes closely associated with irony in your work. Could you elaborate?*

It's true that one can find these elements in my music. In the work you mentioned there is, however, only one movement of the five that can be called a parody. It is strategically placed to lead up to the culmination in the fifth movement. The preceding movement closes with the word 'splendid'. I needed a kind of scherzo in this work and the word was actually used in a mocking way, exactly at the moment where everything collapses. It sounds very relevant, even more so today than when I composed the work. It reflects the way I feel about the world these days. The movement in question is both 'splendid' and optimistic while everything around it is collapsing.

I would like to return to the inherent meaning in the music that we spoke of. Several years ago when I heard The Seven Words of Christ *for orchestra, cello and bayan (a concertina), I could not help but think that the two solo instruments were kind of personifications, that possibly they told a certain story without words, or, in light of the title, one might rather say, a drama. Naturally you must have had certain pictures in your head while you composed the work. But did you also have a specific characteristic in mind?*

For me the idea of the Trinity was at the centre. So I chose instruments that to a certain extent could represent this idea, not in the form of an image, but as the essence of the idea. The cello has a particularly high degree of expressivity, which suits the characterization of Christ. The *bayan* personifies the anger of the Father and the string ensemble is well-suited to portray the Holy Ghost. When I wrote this work, these personifications were related to individual moments only. I felt Christ particularly strongly in the sixth movement, when the bayan plays clusters while the strings play in the highest register and the cello plays on the C string and then plays *sul ponticello* in order to mark the Crucifixion. There is nothing to suggest a picture; it's only an instrumental symbol.

Your works often have liturgical titles: Offertorium, Introitus, De Profundis, The Seven Words of Christ. *But you are also frequently inspired by literature, T.S. Eliot, for example. Is there some general schema behind your choice of titles and texts? Do you have a title before the work is composed? Does it come after it is completed, or while it is in progress?*

It is very difficult for me to separate these stages from each other. Once I have finished a piece I cannot remember exactly how it was composed. In the first phase the sound comes to me, often in a form I have trouble breaking up into its component parts. It seems to be built up vertically, so I begin to guess what this sound could eventually mean. When I have gauged its meaning, a formal idea emerges that I will justify with a label, a name that points to the idea of the form. That's all I can come up with when I try to analyse my experience of composing. I rearrange the sound from a vertical to a horizontal shape, so to speak, and with that the form comes into being. My titles are often related to aspects of liturgy, but that includes various and ancient forms.

The title has immeasurable significance for me. I like to associate it closely with the formal idea.

Looking at the formal aspects of your music in relation to your fascination with T.S. Eliot's poetry, the issue of time in music is an important determinant of form.

The act of creating form in music is a kind of reconciliation with time. In this concept there is not only an element of sacrifice but also of transformation. This is the essential concept. Form is a kind of alteration, a transformation, a reconciliation with time, so that reconciliation and transformation merge into one concept. In this there is also a kind of purification.

There is, so to speak, a conversion of time from past-present-future into something that is timeless. Eliot's concept of time runs perfectly parallel with mine. I became completely convinced of that when I began to work with the problem of time in the piece *Hommage à T.S. Eliot*.

Let us go a bit farther back in your development. In the beginning Shostakovich and Webern were the main stars in your musical firmament. I would very much like to know something about how you found your own completely personal musical language.

First I studied all the standard technical forms. I had to penetrate the technical forms and styles of the old masters. I was especially interested in the strict style of the 16th century and was very taken with the composers of that time. But I actually began with the German classics that my teacher indicated I should study: Haydn, Mozart, Beethoven, Bach. During my whole life, Bach has been central to my work. After that I began to go through all the different styles in music, paying particular attention to the Russian school. But when I was 19 or 20, I was completely taken with Wagner. I was also interested in the Second Viennese School, and then Shostakovich in the Russian school, and subsequently the composers from my own generation. When I look back on my path in music, the names of Bach and Webern lie at the centre.

In the West we talk about the three major composers from Moscow: Schnittke, Denisov and Gubaidulina. There are many talents—both new and old—in your country, that are just becoming known. Is it also a part of your work to promote the younger generation, so that these three don't stand alone in the spotlight?

I think that there are many young talented Russian composers who follow us in being experimental. Several come to mind: Alexander Knaifel, Juri Butsko, Victor Suslin, Alexander Vustin. From the younger generation I would name Vjatsjeslav Sjut, Jan Jekimovskij, Juri Kasparov, Jelena Firsova. The latter has created strikingly good works. There are also a number of people in the various republics who are now kind of foreigners to us, but in any case are good friends, for example, Farad Karajev from Baku. In Armenia there is a whole list of stars. Thinking about it, I have reason to be very pleased.

'Ind i sjælens labyrint: Et møde med russiske komponist, Sofia Gubaidulina', *Dansk Musik Tidsskrift* 68, 5 (1993/94): 158–164.

Þorkell Sigurbjörnsson

COMPOSER AND OPTIMIST

You were born in 1938 and have been a central figure in Icelandic music for more than forty years. How would you describe the musical establishment of which you have gradually become a part? How did it look at the beginning of the 1940s?

I can only remember back to the middle of the 1940s. Musical life was good and active then. As one of its goals, the Reykjavík Music Society, founded in 1930, wanted to establish a music school. That became the Reykjavík Music School, the oldest one in the country. The Music Society also promoted the establishment of an orchestra. Of course they intended the music school to teach young musicians so that we could have a real orchestra in this country. In addition, the Music Society organized a concert series with foreign soloists and chamber musicians. That was during the war when a number of artists travelled to America. On their way they had to make a stop-over here in Iceland; people like Serkin and Busch, great international stars, gave some concerts here. It wasn't easy to fly in one day and out the next, so they usually had a lengthy stay here in Reykjavík.

Relatively late Jón Leifs took the initiative to set up STEF—the performing rights organization. How well-established was the musical milieu in Iceland in the 1940s?

In 1944 Iceland became a Republic and only then did we have the basis for setting up new institutions. The Composers Union and STEF were founded fifty years ago. The National Theatre opened its doors in 1950 and became the permanent home of The Iceland Symphony Orchestra. So the music establishment here is relatively young.

The international outlook one finds here is a comparatively recent development. Although traditionally Icelandic composers travelled, especially to Central Europe, one could probably say that it wasn't until the 1950s that Iceland embraced the outside world.

We benefited greatly from the fantastic teachers who came as refugees from Austria and Germany, such as Dr. Robert Abraham Ottosson, Dr. Heinz Edelstein and Dr. Victor Urbancic. Urbancic was an immigrant from Austria, an opera conductor and composer. The contribution of these men was like a vitamin shot for music at that time. Robert Ottosson had studied with Bruno Walter and was also a very fine pianist. Urbancic was the organist at the Catholic church. Edelstein was a cellist from Freiburg. He developed a new method for teaching, specialized in teaching children and taught solfège. I was fortunate to be one of his first students in preparatory school for the Reykjavík academy of music.

You entered the Music School as an instrumentalist, not as a composer.

My main instrument was the violin and I also played the piano. The reason that I ended up playing more and more piano was that my teacher at the Music School, Wilhelm Lanzky-Otto—the Danish pianist and horn player— encouraged me. His sons, Ib, who is a horn player in the Stockholm Philharmonic, and Per, who is an organist, were my schoolmates. Wilhelm said that Per was so lazy that he never practised, but if we played together it might work out. You might say that it was first and foremost in Wilhelm's own interest to teach me to play the piano. I studied violin in school, but then I had an accident and broke one of the crucial fingers. After that, my instrument was the piano.

While it has been traditional for Icelandic composers, such as Jón Leifs and the artists of today, to travel to Central Europe, your interest was directed toward America. That was where you had your first significant experiences.

I suppose there is something to that. I went to the secondary school in Reykjavík and saw an advertisement in the paper in 1957 for a scholarship to study in America. I had composed music for use in high school—theatre pieces and that sort of thing. When I went to the American Embassy to apply they told me that the grant was primarily meant for people who were interested in science, not music or languages. But I was lucky and my application was accepted. So I went to a small 'liberal arts' college, Hamline University, in St. Paul, Minnesota, in fact, the oldest university in Minnesota, where there were only 1400 students. It was a one-year stipend and that suited me fine. I could learn a little English and continue to study the piano. There was a distinguished old lady who taught piano. The Music Department was very interested in new music, primarily because Ernst Křenek had taught there and some of his former students were now members of the faculty. I did well and when they asked me what I would be doing the following year and if I wanted to study for a degree, I said 'Certainly', and they renewed my grant for another year.

I also studied sociology, philosophy, English and literature. I earned a liberal arts degree, a Bachelor of Arts, and then I continued with music studies at the University of Illinois in Urbana. There was a composition teacher named

Kenneth Gaburo, a student of Petrassi and, as you can imagine, serialism and 12-tone music were the subjects that fascinated me. On top of that the University of Illinois had one of the first electronic music studios and it was accessible to students. Of course it was rather primitive then.

You spent a year and a half in Illinois?

Yes, Lejaren A. Hiller was responsible for electronic music. I also studied musicology with Dr. Alexander Ringer, who is famous in the field. I was married in the USA, came home, and the next summer (1962) I went to Darmstadt and heard lectures by Stockhausen, Ligeti and Maderna.

What did Darmstadt mean to you? Did it enhance your experiences in Illinois?

Yes, you could say that, for there was indeed a very active music scene in Illinois. The University had a really good radio station with good programmes from new music festivals. I had already become familiar with *Le Marteau sans maître* in Minnesota. Webern's music became available while I was there. As a matter of fact a set of four LPs of his music was released almost the day after I arrived in Minnesota. I bought it and listened enthusiastically. You could say that Darmstadt supplemented my experiences, for I was already familiar with a fair amount of new music from my stay in America.

You also composed the first works that you still acknowledge in your worklist. Some composers reject their early works. How do you characterize your early style?

First and foremost I have to say that I have never been dedicated to any particular direction. I have always been very curious and have listened to all kinds of music: ethnic music, music from India, Africa. That doesn't mean that I like all kinds of music, but I have been curious, attended many different concerts and experienced many different attitudes and aesthetic directions. In those days I didn't think of myself as a composer, 'Now I am a composer'. It wasn't like that wonderful little film about Carl Nielsen when as a youth he says goodbye to his mother with the line, 'Now I am going to Copenhagen to become a composer'. I was a musician and I was generally interested in music, in music history. I played the piano and was very curious about new works for my instrument. I played chamber music—preferably new works.

One understands when you describe these periods that the composer in you somehow developed out of practical necessity. You have talked about yourself as a composer using the phrase, 'I compose works to fill out a programme'. The element of utility has been a decisive factor.

There have been many occasions in the Musica Nova Society here in Reykjavík when we have said, 'Our programme is ten minutes too short—what instruments are we using?' And then I have composed something.

You came back from the USA to a situation where Musica Nova was quite new. In Finland they have the Korvat Auki (Open Ears) Society and in Copenhagen there is the Young Composers Society (DUT). Musica Nova is also a group that introduces new music. Can you say something about its role in Iceland?

From the beginning, the group had two goals: first, to present young musicians, that is, to be a kind of forum for newly-educated young musicians, and second, to present newer music. So it promoted not only the latest music, but also the youngest musicians. These young people also wanted to play the masters of our century—that is, Hindemith and Bartók, and so on. And that was fine, too.

THE ENCOUNTER WITH IVES' MUSIC

Moving into the 1960s it is evident that this was a break-through period for new ideas. When you go to the National Gallery in Reykjavík and look at the collection that was purchased at the time, you can see that there was a keen interest in the international avant garde. There was a very strong FLUXUS movement here in Reykjavík. Was it also the case in music that there was an interest in international directions? Did Paik perform in Iceland?

Yes, Paik and Charlotte Moorman were here for a concert. Cage was here, but not as a musician. For many years Iceland Air had a route from New York to Luxembourg; it was the least expensive trip across the Atlantic—with the old-fashioned Skymaster and Cloudmaster. It took twelve hours to fly to New York, with refuelling in Goosebay, Labrador. David Tudor and John Cage, for example, often came here on their way to Europe and stayed while the planes were refuelling—or being repaired. We 'knew' these people and met them. I often happened to meet them by accident as they were on their way from Europe to the USA and stopping over here in Reykjavík. At that time, Iceland Air wasn't out in Keflavík, but here.

So they actually stayed here in the city?

Yes, yes, they visited the city, walked the streets. Reykjavík was a lot smaller then than it is now. Eventually we invited Cage to be the guest of honour at the Reykjavík Festival in 1982.

Photo: Þorkell Sigurbjörnsson (Sóla).

As for the contacts between Iceland and Denmark, you can see—again at the National Gallery—that there must have been a very close association with the Danish artists of the 1950s and 1960s. The entire Cobra Movement is represented at the museum, for example.

Svavar Guðnardson was a member of the Cobra Movement. He was in Denmark for quite a few years, and the sculptor, Sigurjon Olafsson, was also known in Denmark.

That is one side, but generally speaking one gets the impression that after 1944 the relationship with Denmark was not as cordial as it had been.

I never experienced it that way, but I remember that older people from my grandmother's generation in Reykjavík thought that the government in Copenhagen was at the root of all problems. That idea isn't current in my generation. We have had Home Rule since 1918. It was the Second World War that caused Icelanders to travel to the USA instead of Europe. And we have had very good teachers here because fortunately most of the Icelanders who went abroad to study have returned. Gunnar Kvaran studied with Erling Blöndal Bengtsson in Copenhagen and lived in Denmark for some years. Now he has returned home. Hafliði Halgrimsson, who studied in Rome and England, now lives in Edinburgh. He only returns to visit.

You said earlier that you were interested in musicology and the whole range of disciplines that you became familiar with in your first years in the USA. If you put on your musicology hat and look at some of your earlier works can you single out a particular one and describe it objectively?

That is difficult, naturally. As I said before I was never interested in direct imitation—perhaps unconsciously, I don't know. I really did like many different composers—Stravinsky, Ligeti, Penderecki and Schoenberg. And occasionally I was excited by Webern, though only for brief periods. But I was never inclined to say, 'Now that was fantastic, I am going to try to do something like that'. I believe that my first reaction was, 'What can I do with that? How can I react against or with it?'

We could also approach this theme by asking, 'What techniques did you use at that time? What instrumentation did you choose? What expression did you try to achieve? What were your goals and what means did you use to reach them?'

It was very practical. It was music I played myself with my colleagues and I have always been interested in choral music, vocal music. Oh, I forgot to name someone who was a great influence: Charles Ives. It was precisely in those years that I heard the *Concord Sonata*, thanks to Jim Tenney. It was incomprehensible but very exciting. My teachers here had a German education and could easily understand the development or traditions of German music through romanticism, Brahms, Mahler, Schoenberg and Alban Berg. But they could not understand a personality like Charles Ives or Henry Cowell. They could identify the quote from Beethoven's Fifth Symphony in the *Concord Sonata* but they could not fathom the meaning of the music at all. I can remember that I played one of his tone row pieces with a group. Very difficult. The piano part in *Over the Pavement*, that went against everything else, I found very interesting. It is fascinating music that takes place on many simultaneous rhythmic levels.

Did these experiences leave an impression on your own music?

It could be, I can't exclude that. I have always been interested in polyrhythms and controlled aleatory.

As in the Polish School?

Yes. But I had already begun to use that technique before I heard any of those Polish pieces. I believe most of all it was because of what I had heard in works by Charles Ives.

How did you notate the music at that time?

The music was very carefully written out. I have never used graphic notation. Only very, very peripherally. I wrote precisely what every instrument should perform. But exactly *when* was not determined.

Is that what you mean by the concept of controlled aleatory?

Yes. There was a period during which I composed works like *Flökt* that was played at the ISCM Music Days in Amsterdam in 1963. Bruno Maderna conducted. He had Earle Brown's score, *Available Forms*. I met him just before the rehearsal and he asked, 'Do you know Earle Brown'? 'No'. There was a place in *Flökt* that he thought was like Brown's, an aleatoric passage, but that wasn't something that I had been aware of beforehand. Nowadays you could say that it was a kind of *Zeitgeist*.

The next important phase for me was about ten years later, around 1970, when I became interested in Buckminster Fuller who said, 'Do more with less'. I had read some of his books and he lectured at the University of Iceland. What he said conformed a great deal to what I wanted to hear in music. Making larger forms out of less material. Just three or four notes.

How did your fascination with Fuller's ideas of using limited material find expression in your own music?

There was a competition here for the Reykjavík Festival that started in 1970. The entry requirement for the competition was an overture for the festival symphony orchestra to be conducted by Bohdan Wodiczko, a Polish conductor and a very stimulating personality. He was principal conductor here for several years. He was very positive and said to Atli Heimir Sveinsson, Jón Nordal and me: 'Write! Write! It will be performed!' And he encouraged me to take part in the competition. I said that I didn't stand a chance. But then I had some ideas about this 'Do more with less' technique and it turned into a very optimistic overture. I believe only two works were submitted, and by sheer luck my overture won the prize; it has been played once or twice since then. A Finnish conductor said that it is the kind of music where you feel that you cannot change a single note. Everything has its place. So I thought that I had succeeded; that was encouraging.

What is the name of the overture?

Ýs og Þýs—Much Ado About Nothing. It was a very lively piece. *Euridike*, my concerto for flute, is written in the same style. It is based on a motif with a capital M. It is through-composed from the beginning to the end and goes through metamorphoses, transformations. You could say that I was interested in the idea of making everything that happened obvious. You shouldn't have to look at the notes to see: 'Oh, that's what happened'.

You have spoken of your interest in choral music. This implies some limitations in working out complexity. It's necessary to simplify to make it suitable for voices.

That's right, and it has been a great experience for me to compose for youth choirs. What people used to think was very difficult is nowadays perceived as very easy. You can compose very demanding music even for amateurs. The standard is rising and you can write far more difficult choral music than you could thirty years ago.

Is your choral music based on major-minor tonality?

No, it's modal. I have also composed hymns for the hymn book. I think it's important to compose for amateurs and for children. I have written a considerable amount of music for children.

Why is composition for amateurs so central to your work?

I enjoy it. I think of my own childhood. What would it have been like for me to have had the opportunity in school as a nine- or ten-year-old to make music with a grown-up musician or composer? I think it is fun and I have received many letters from people who have found it to be a positive experience.

It has been traditional in your family to study theology. Your father was a bishop and your younger brother is Bishop of Iceland. Has your church music been an expression of your faith?

I have had difficulty establishing a definite faith, but a strong text, for instance a forceful psalm, inspires me. I have the feeling that it should be sung. Not just read. I would rather hear it as music than read it.

Then you don't compose music like Bach did—in glorification of God. Is it more the common humanity in the text that interests you?

I don't have any doubt that God exists—whatever that means—some kind of power over which we have no control and that we will never understand. Whether it is DNA or whatever, I don't know. But you can celebrate that power. And you can call it God, why not? However, I wouldn't like to stand up and profess a faith. My faith is so weak and insignificant. I could never preach. I don't have the strength that it requires.

A FEELING OF COMPLETENESS

When we come to the 1970s we have a better opportunity to study your music because some of it is recorded on CD. I remember the first piece that made an impression on me—a piece for flute performed by Manuela Wiesler. It was called Kalaïs. *This music from 1976 has a eruptive force and sometimes sounds as if it were a notated improvisation.*

Kalaïs was composed for Robert Aitken. We had scheduled a concert with Hafliði Halgrimsson who intended to write a new piece for the three of us, but he wasn't able to finish it. And as the date of the concert got closer I realized, 'My goodness, our programme is ten minutes too short', and I rang Robert Aitken and asked him, 'If I compose a flute piece for you, could you play it at the concert'? And that's how it happened. He is a fantastic virtuoso, so I knew that I could write anything I wanted. I asked him if he had ever tried to play the flute without the head joint. He said, 'No, you can't do that'. At the time I was composing a trio for flute, cello and piano and wanted to have the flautist play without the head joint at the end, shakuhachi-style. Then he tried it and said, 'Yes, it can be done even though it creates a peculiar mood'. But it sounded beautiful, if a little exotic.

What was your thinking behind that piece?

Well, it is flute music and has something to do with air, wind. That's what I had in mind. Someone blows, and it becomes a sound that can change from the most tender expression to the most violent one. Sounds that only a flautist can produce. But it should not be like a catalogue: it should be complete. You should have the feeling of something that begins incredibly quietly and gradually grows with a kind of organic development. The flute is, of course, one of man's oldest instruments; it's almost like an extension of the voice. It is blowing air. And when I had begun to compose the piece this old myth about Kalaïs, the phenomenal musician in Greek mythology, suddenly came to me. He was the son of Boreas—the northern wind—so I thought, 'Why not name this piece for Kalaïs, the son of the wind'? It is a celebration of the flute and the wind, of the techniques of blowing.

Have you composed works that take as their starting points a specific mood inspired by nature like many other Nordic composers? Jón Leifs has used that as a programme.

Yes, possibly. I composed a piece entitled *Mistur*—a light fog that you can see through. I thought that the notes were transparent. I didn't say, 'Now I am going to describe mist', but it suited that kind of mood. And another piece is called *Haflög* (Melodies of the Sea) because there was a lot of movement in it and that reminded me somehow of the sea. Recently I composed a little piece 'Gletcherlied' (Glacier Song), I can show it to you. (He gets the piece.) This is dedicated to my old friend, Vladimir Ashkenazy. I said, 'It's going to be a nocturne'. He said, 'Well I don't mind if it is a nocturne, but there has to be also something Icelandic about it'. So I said, 'Yes, of course. "Night by the Glacier", how about that'?

Are titles important to you? Do they come before the piece is composed or during composition?

Both. Naturally they come after, mid-way. One thinks: it reminds me of one thing or another. Of course it could be called opus 1 or opus 2, but that's so impersonal. I think that the title is like a signature: 'So, now I am finished with this'. That's part of the work.

When I think about it, I don't have the feeling that there has been a steady progression or development. I sit down and compose, compose, compose, and without any problem. Then suddenly there is a moment when you think . . . what now? . . . why? The only thing I work on is not repeating myself. I think a lot before I write a single note—I try to get the whole picture. Something has to come out of the earliest ideas. 'Now', I say to myself, 'I have these three notes. What can I do with them'? But it is also possible that the first idea is a kind of complete thought, an atmosphere. 'So', I then ask, 'how do I make something with this atmosphere'? Suppose I close my eyes and, for example, I assume that I am writing something for orchestra, . . . Now I am sitting in the auditorium, the orchestra is on stage and suddenly the sounds come forth and I have to get involved in this situation at one point or another in time. And how shall I begin to become part of the situation? I don't think abstractly and say, 'I need an A-flat'. What's that? Yes, it is a pitch, but without any expression. For myself I need some kind of meaning or significance. I think it is important that there is enthusiasm. If you create a kind of depressed mood, then you must also feel it like a really deep depression. But mostly I am optimistic.

So, is your music optimistic?

There aren't very many dark chapters.

Here we have the score for 'Nocturne' subtitled 'Gletcherlied'. What is the significance of it? What mood do you want and how do you achieve it? There is a long bass note on G and then we have some triplet figures in the harp.

Nocturnes are romantic, night music. Evening moods. Quiet. But I also wanted it to be a bit cool, a little like ice, as if you are in a tent pitched next to the edge of a glacier. It is fantastic to look at it, but it's not warm, so there is a kind of contradiction. 'Nocturne' is something warm. 'Lied', 'Nightsong' is warm and beautiful. But 'Gletcher', 'glacier', 'jökull' . . . that's something else.

You must have heard about the big eruption of Vatnajökul a few years ago. They say that the power that was unleashed in three days was like 3800 atomic bombs. It was nature's outburst. It's not benign; it's frightening. You could drive to East Iceland and look at it; which is what I did. It was an incredible sight. There were pieces of ice that weighed 20–30 tons, as big as houses, being thrown around like toys.

JÓN LEIFS

Are there others of your generation or among your contemporaries that you feel a connection with and who might even have inspired you?

I don't think that you can be completely independent of what goes on around you. Over the years I have been present at premieres of works by Leifur Þorarinsson, Atli Heimir Sveinsson and others, and there have been many works that I liked and some that I didn't. However, I have never been taken completely by surprise, never been in a position where I have thought, 'Now, I have never heard that before'.

I was surprised when I heard Ligeti's Horn Trio. I had heard his earlier work, *Atmosphères*, but then suddenly tonality returned to his work. I thought, 'After all, this *is* the same composer'!

The period of the Horn Trio was a very critical one for Ligeti—one that he had to work through. Have you had comparable crises in your development where you either experienced a compositional block or you had to revise your way of thinking?

I have had many desperate moments when I have suddenly started to think that nothing is working any more. What has helped me is the fact that I am an optimist and if something goes wrong one day, if there is an accident, I know that it's not always going to be that way. It won't be a crisis for the rest of my life; I have experienced that many times.

Do you have close colleagues with whom you talk about compositional problems?

No, but naturally we talk about things, though not in writing. We don't have a music journal and the only thing about music that is published here is newspaper criticism. Debate about music hardly exists here. But we discuss things. Atli Heimir and I spent a long time recently discussing our colleagues. That happens once in a while and we don't necessarily agree. We don't think in the same way, but that doesn't matter. The occasion was Leifur's burial. We had the feeling that his Second Symphony, which was premiered in the Autumn, was the work of a new Leifur, although we knew that he was terminally ill. So Atli and I were a little depressed and were thinking about the old days. Leifur was sixty-three years old. His symphony was a strong celebration of life and also the music expressed the wild temperament that was a part of his personality.

Now you're speaking of an artistic personality. Soon it will be time to celebrate Jón Leifs' centennial. Can you say something about his significance in the development of music in Iceland? There are aspects of his work that receive very positive evaluation and others that people prefer not to talk about.

He always encouraged me—I don't know why. Everyone knew some of his music, the Requiem and the simple *Icelandic Dances*. I heard the premiere of Leifs' *Saga Symphony* on the radio in 1952 and thought it was incomprehensible. I can remember thinking as a teenager, 'Here is an Icelandic composer who composes a symphony and I understand nothing about it'.

His significance in the development of music in Iceland?

I think that actually his significance for the generation—which doesn't know his works—is mostly in terms of the Composers Union and STEF. He established those organizations. As an organizer and as a campaigner he was significant, but his music didn't speak to me very much. I didn't much like the programmatic aspect. In 1972 we heard his *Saga Symphony* again at a concert by The Iceland Symphony Orchestra, and then again in a new recording made by BIS. It is music that has no development; there is no main thesis or 'argument'. That's my feeling. It's like a landscape. It just stands there. Perhaps I don't understand his time-scale. It is music for geologists, historians and natural scientists.

When you say that there is a lack of development are you thinking about this piece or about his whole output?

Well, if you think about a piece like *Hekla* (the name of a volcano in Iceland, *ed.*) there is a development from quiet calm to violent eruption. But if the piece didn't have a title like *Hekla* and you heard it as a symphonic work, an overture or something like that, you would think, 'Why? What happened here'?

Leifs wrote a book in German entitled Islands künstlerische Anregung *(Iceland's Artistic Mission). It was published in Reykjavík in 1951.*

Yes, it's a strange book that praises a way of thinking that we have since come to question. I don't think that those ideas have had much influence in this country. There were many people who were very enthusiastic about Hitler in the 1930s, but I believe that they soon realized what his real goals were. Typically they were people who had gone to the Olympic Games in Berlin and who had come home enthusiastically saying, 'Wow, Germany! It is fantastic what they can do there'! I also believe there were some adherents in Denmark. But as soon as the rest of the world realized what Nazism really stood for . . .

And as for Leifs himself?

I don't know the details about Jón Leifs, I don't know to what extent he sympathized with the unfortunate movements in Central Europe, but he did live in Germany during the war. After the war he came home to Iceland. Guðmundur Kamban, an Icelandic author who wrote some plays, was killed in Denmark after the war. He wasn't a Nazi, but people suspected him of being one because his plays were performed in Germany in the 1930s and during the war. But those were historical plays about life here in Iceland and in Greenland. Yes, they have Nordic subjects, but Kamban wasn't a Nazi. Some Danish patriots thought simply the fact that his plays were performed in German theatres was unacceptable, so he was shot in the street in Copenhagen. Poor Guðmundur Kamban. Jón Leifs moved to Germany, was educated in Germany, had a career in Germany, married a German woman—his life was in Germany. And then suddenly his world fell apart.

How did he react when he came home? Was he disillusioned? He did have some ideas that were untenable.

He remained an Icelandic nationalist. He thought that with our Icelandic history and literature we had something to give to the rest of the world. He thought that the sagas were something that Icelanders should cultivate and use as a source of inspiration.

Did he like Wagner's music?

I don't think so. It is strange that you mention Wagner, because I remember that once he talked about Wagner. We were eating dinner together on some occasion and Jón Leifs began to talk about Nordic culture, mythology and said, 'Wagner ruined everything for us'.

Because he had constructed his own Nordic mythology that wasn't the real Nordic mythology?

Yes. And Wagner's mythology was accepted and approved—by Hitler, among others. So Jón Leifs thought that Wagner had ruined the possibilities for other Nordic composers and authors.

To what extent have the sagas and Icelandic traditions played a role in your concept of music?

I have never felt that it was necessary to limit myself. I am interested in the world around me; Greek, Roman, Nordic and Indian mythology all interest me. There's a lot that's very good and very interesting about Nordic mythology and the sagas, but what about contemporary literature from Iceland and from other countries? That's also interesting.

THE MUSICOLOGY THAT NEVER WAS

Today's important musical institutions have been established in Iceland during your time. You now have an opera house and royalty collection societies. You also have a Music Information Centre and nowadays we see musicians, for example the Caput Ensemble, who are at least as good as the leading sinfoniettas from the other Nordic countries. How does music in Iceland look to you now?

It's correct to say that there has been a fantastic development in music here. It has been exciting to follow, and each year there are more young musicians who are even better than those who emerged five years earlier. The problem for us is that we are a small country and we have limitations. It is the burning desire and greatest hope of Icelandic musicians to travel abroad. The Caput Ensemble can get together and play concerts, but after that they split up and go to Germany or Holland or other places. If the Ensemble is to survive in the future it is absolutely necessary that they have more opportunities to perform here not just twice a year, in the summer or the autumn, but all year-round. And the Icelandic Symphony Orchestra, for which we are very grateful, has the same problem. But how many concerts can they play here in Reykjavík? There are real practical limits, economic ones. I have close relatives who are fantastic musicians but who cannot get work here in this country.

Couldn't you develop a State Ensemble like those in other places? That doesn't mean, of course, work for 100 people, but it provides the opportunity for a full-time permanent ensemble that could tour Icelandic music.

We have talked about it and have agreed that that's what we should do. Create an ensemble of five to twenty people; it should be possible to find the money here in Iceland to pay salaries and cover some of the travel expenses. That would give an ensemble like the Caput new opportunities. It's been like start-stop traffic on a poor road with too many traffic lights. And now it's become plain—you know that we have about seventy music schools in this country with about 8000 music students. There are perhaps only one per cent who can think about becoming professional musicians in the future, but in any case, that's still quite a few. I know that the music school in Reykjavík is having a hard time just now. Maybe because of the elections for local government that are coming up . . .

Why is there no opportunity to study musicology at the University of Reykjavík?

That's what is stupid. The University of Iceland has not yet accepted musicology as a subject. You can study medicine, law, theology, philosophy, literature and sociology, but not music. Iceland is in many ways very underdeveloped. There is an historical reason for that. You have to remember that until 1918 the University of Copenhagen was our university. No doubt about it, Copenhagen was Iceland's capital city and our university was there. It is only in this century that we have tried to establish these institutions in this country, with a very limited population naturally. But optimism dictates that it will happen one day. Many years ago Henry Cowell came here on a trip.

He gave a lecture at the University and the University President was there. Cowell talked about his own music and new American music from the 1920s and 1930s. Suddenly he stopped and said, 'I have heard that this University has no Music Department. Is it true? What a scandal'! And the people from the Humanities Department were sitting there. We have to maintain our optimism; changes for the better will surely happen some day.

'Komponist og optimist: Interview med den islandske komponist Þorkell Sigurbjörnsson', *Dansk Musik Tidsskrift* 73, 5 (1998/99): 146–153.

Olav Anton Thommessen

A MULTIFACETED SONIC EXPLORER

Let's look back through history in order to understand the development of recent Norwegian music. You once said that national romanticism had been unduly prolonged in Norway and that many famous Norwegian cultural personalities— Hamsun and others—had sympathized with national socialist movements in Southern Europe. What's your view on the cultural legacy in Norway?

That is still a rather controversial subject and it has not been spoken about explicitly enough. Recently in Iceland the film about Jón Leifs, *Tårer af sten* (Tears of Stone), really put that period in perspective. (Leifs was embroiled in national socialist ideology, *ed.*) To do something like that with the Norwegian composers of the time would be very difficult, not least because the relatives of those involved are still living. A number of festering conflicts remain. Many wounds are not yet healed.

No one has told me what *actually* happened. I have had to put the pieces together and make my own interpretation of the details. But it is clear that Norwegian national romanticism went through a very negative development from the time of Norway's independence and liberation (1905) through the 1940s, when nationalistic sentiments continued to prevail and ideas from Italian fascism and Mussolini gained a foothold in Norway. They had slogans like 'You have to fend for yourself', and 'You must purify the national identity', which I believe greatly affected the arts for better or for worse. Think, for example, of the painter Gerhard Munthe, of buildings with medieval-style carvings on them and of everything that was cultivated as something pure and Nordic. Folk music continued to be idealized and some composers continued to gnaw on Grieg's quasi-folklorism—I find the whole thing completely incomprehensible. Composers travelled to France and picked up a few ideas there, or they travelled to Germany and learned some new techniques, but on the whole most of the composers used nationalistic material. The only composer really to break with this trend was Fartein Valen. Valen was born in Madagascar so the Nordic 'tone' was not actually very relevant to him. In many ways I feel a certain kinship with him. I was born in Norway, but I didn't grow up there and even though these Nordic folk melodies are truly charming, they aren't something I am passionate about.

Valen represented something extraordinarily interesting in Norwegian music. He wasn't well received: he represented European culture in the broadest sense and practised a form of neoclassical expressionism. This is a direction that *no-one else* at the time represented in Norway. He came home with a host of ideas that were completely foreign to everyone. If David Monrad Johansen was influenced by French impressionism, or Pauline Hall by neoclassicism, it was on a very superficial and half-hearted level. Valen represented a true internationalism. He was also such a weird person that he was later marginalized and treated like some odd apparition. If there had been a responsive system capable of absorbing him in Norway, its art music would surely have gone in another direction.

Unfortunately, because many people still fostered nationalistic views, some of the artists were led to support the wrong side. The artists who truly had something of an international character in them—Geirr Tveitt, David Monrad Johansen and Olav Kielland—became in some way *non-persons* after the war. They were shunned, and an amateurish generation of self-taught composers came out of the woods to take their place. Professionalism was viewed suspiciously because it had led us into Nazism. For that reason the specialists, those who truly knew something, received no particular recognition. Instead, attention was focused on another type of artist, one considerably less sophisticated, who was, by and large, self-taught and as such unlikely to be contaminated by such international depravity as Nazism.

We have had to struggle with this prejudice ever since. Expertise became discredited because so many experts had become Nazis. It has taken a long time to rebuild the understanding that a certain amount of expertise is actually desirable and far preferable to reinventing the wheel time and again, as some of those homespun artists did.

After the war, there was a precipitous lowering of standards in Norwegian composition. A main reason was that there was nowhere to study composition in the country. You can understand why such a naïve person as Geirr Tveitt became attracted to Nazism: the Nazis planned to build an opera house and conservatories and gave priority to higher education. We still don't have an opera house. The Music High School was only built in 1973 and instruction in composition didn't start until 1980—that is, in the form of a complete course of study and not just a diploma exam. So it has taken its time. Some of the artists who became Nazis may have seen a so-called new era as the possibility for professional advancement. However, when they were discredited, there arose an even better argument for putting off the establishment of the Music High School, the opera and the concert hall—it was fashionable to do without it.

Let's skip ahead and consider those Norwegian composers who recently resigned from the Composer's Union in protest against the new avant-garde. I heard a premiere of a work in Trondheim that was so romantic, it could have been composed in the last century. So the situation that you have described still exists in Norway. I don't see anything like that in either Sweden or Denmark. A branch of Norwegian composers is still devoted to pure and unspoiled—I nearly said uncontaminated—lyricism.

In the Composer's Union there is a small group that is marked by loyalty to such ideals. They are very unappreciated because their aesthetic position is not acknowledged and they embrace an aesthetic that had its day a long time ago. I don't actually know why they compose, since they continue to live with this artistic myth. Most Norwegian composers are interested in current ideas, not least because of the programme at the Music High School and the establishment of NoTam, a new centre for electro-acoustic music. Consequently, most composers are orientated toward today's music, but there is still this little pocket of dissatisfied people who sit and feel that they are being treated unfairly.

A STABILIZING FACTOR

But in your case, you say that because you moved around with your parents you were suddenly put into situations where you had to deal with many new directions. You once used 'Auschwitz'—a powerful word—to describe the various atmospheres of the many boarding schools in which you were enrolled during your turbulent life and the changing circumstances you experienced. Can you describe your upbringing?

If one looks at the children of diplomats as a group, there aren't many who have been successful. Diplomacy is not a particularly child-friendly occupation. On the other hand the children of diplomats have a fantastic opportunity to experience a great number of things. In my case, I had a very active 'inner' life, for the stable ingredient has been music. From the outside, my life must have looked like that of a vagabond. I have gone around and thought—almost half-acoustically—about musical ideas without letting myself be influenced by external changes and this became a way of surviving my itinerant upbringing. But it has also been very positive, because these days I maintain an active inner life.

When did you settle down in Norway after roaming the earth?

In 1969. I took an advanced course in pedagogy in order to be able to teach in Norway. That's how I got into the milieu of the music conservatory in Oslo. Subsequently I was granted permission to teach instrumentation—I took over from Trygve Lindeman. I was also allowed to teach a bit of music education. In addition I travelled to Utrecht and studied sonology there. The funny thing is that my education didn't match the Norwegian curriculum because I had studied composition in America, and they said I was 'overqualified' for many jobs. So the year after my study in Utrecht, when I applied for the position of teaching theory at the newly established Music High School, I got the job.

In Utrecht and in the USA you had several defining experiences. You met Xenakis at Indiana University in Bloomington.

It was a very unsettled time with the student resistance to the Vietnam War, and so on. At the height of all that, it was the students who had to decide everything—we actually need a bit more of that today. We discussed who the composition teachers should be. We talked about Castiglioni and Xenakis. One group opposed Xenakis because the members thought his mathematics was pure charlatanism. Xenakis didn't arrive at the 'truth', rather he arrived at solutions that worked *for him* and inspired him. He said that a glissando is a straight line—which in fact it isn't actually—but for him, it is. And if one builds up one's own system in that way, isn't it a kind of 'truth'? But a number of students said that Xenakis wasn't being consistent. After a number of tug-of-wars, Xenakis arrived. These two years were extremely invigorating. He built up the electro-acoustic music program and the computer centre and began developing his interest in UPIC. He laid out his research during the lectures. His productivity was impressive; during that period, he composed *Nomos Alpha, Eonta, Nuits* and other important works.

Xenakis was really in top form and delivered some fantastic lectures that were inspirational. In addition to that he introduced to us the world around Varèse. This was quite new to me, because everything was very orientated toward Germany, with Hindemith and Schoenberg as central figures. So here comes Xenakis suddenly and talks about the French world of music, which was extremely interesting and completely unknown in mid-western America. Although Varèse was an American he was actually quite unknown at that time. He had died by then, but his music suddenly received a huge amount of attention. Coincidentally Bernstein was beginning to explore Mahler and The Beatles were extremely active. It was a truly exciting time to be a student.

You have been called 'the biggest compromise in Norwegian music'. Is that—looking at it positively—an expression of the pluralism that is also part of your music?

I believe that was a printer's error—or rather, it *was* a printer's error. It's not far from 'compromise' to 'composer' in Norwegian. But it is a kind of Freudian slip. There is something to it, but they got it wrong. There was an article in *Dagbladet* the other day, where it said that I was an advocate of pure music because I had said that I couldn't stand Chick Corea's interpretation of Mozart. I had pointed out that Corea purely and simply cannot play Mozart, but suddenly I was guilty of insisting that my Mozart be pure. The journalist was all in favour of impurity in music, but he can hardly have heard my music because you can barely get more impure music than mine. 'Compromise'? I have heard an awful lot of music and there are some types of music that I don't like. For pure stylistic reasons I don't like country music, and I have difficulty with jazz if it's not inspired. These are the only two styles I have any problems with, otherwise I think all music has something to offer. The other day I heard a Korean opera from the 1300s. I have never heard anything like it before. You discover things all the time that you would never dream someone could have invented. There is always something that you haven't heard. I really like to listen to music.

SONOLOGY

Your willingness to listen is evidence of your pluralistic approach to music: your positive words about Valen and Xenakis; your activities in the school as a professor, where you don't miss an opportunity to travel with your students to the premiere of a Stockhausen opera; your ravenous appetite for film music, etc., etc. How is it that your interest in listening to so many different kinds of music hasn't influenced your own way of thinking about music? What about the pluralism mirrored in your work when you recycle music history?

Together with Lasse Thoresen and others, I worked in an improvisation group called *Symfrones*. We were greatly inspired by Stockhausen when he came to Oslo in 1969 with his group and improvised freely—Kagel, the Kontarsky brothers and Eötvös—that was a star-studded group. They sat on the floor and messed around; it was really 'modern' and they made all kinds of sounds. So we thought that we had to try it as well and we began to play together. That way we got a kind of understanding of what music *is* without defining stylistic criteria and without the constraints of having to play in a specific style.

Thoresen and I gradually discovered a hidden world lying beneath all the styles of music: the real force that makes music acquire the form it has, the sound it is composed of, and the way these sounds function within the whole. As a starting point, we began to work with the theory of sonology, which has been extremely useful for us as a pedagogical tool. It has been well received at the Music High School because many performers have found it useful in deciding the difference between one interpretation and another. It is, after all, useful in comparative musicology. One compares different kinds of styles and finds common tendencies at a deep level—not on a superficial one, but actually on the level of musical impact. We have spent a great deal of time on this and it is one result of this pluralism that you speak of. We attempted to determine comparative criteria. You begin to discover that there is actually something astonishingly stable in music. It has to do with clarity and with the ability to discover the means to formulate things as perceived by the listener.

This was the same time that scholars working in linguistics began to explore . . .

Semiotics . . . and also the thing with Chomsky's 'generative grammar'. We lived through a very exciting time in linguistic research. We found that we could possibly construct an auditive music theory from the principles of the language theories that Saussure developed in 1911. But we were also interested in what the structuralists had done in light of Levi-Strauss' socio-cultural research that identified connections between cultures.

We were inspired to think about whether we could do the same thing in music. For years we tried to publish a book about what we discovered, but it's not so easy—we still work with those old stencils. Perhaps we will get it published someday. It is really strange that our thoughts can't be printed, since it's original research—speculative possibly—but it *is* original and therefore, perhaps, it isn't taken seriously because that's not what the research community is interested in. They would rather take something that is already known and simply shuffle it around. Here we come with something that is completely innovative, but it turns out that it is difficult to get sonology recognized as proper research. It is a tool for discussing music for performers and composers, and is based on what the listener perceives.

Many musicologists have an opinion about both semiotics and sonology. One group is sceptical about the possibility of sonology as a science, possibly because the critics are not adequately informed. Who knows? Is it possible to say briefly what sonology is about? Is it a kind of hermeneutic method that can be used to discover what music is about?

Yes, but to say 'is about' is a bit too strong; it's wrong to imply that it is possible to know what music 'is about'. But it is possible to know what *functions* music has—that is relevant. Rameau discovered something very important, namely that a sound could have a function on the strength of the three chords that he put down. Rameau had great insight—the idea of functional harmony—that is, giving a sound a function. But no-one had taken this idea further. We have tried to do that, and to say that there *have* to be more functions than just three—tonic, subdominant and dominant—and that there have to be more sounds in music that can provide these functions. At this point we start to look at how music plays itself out in time. It is tremendously important to have criteria and concepts that can describe music as an art that takes place in time. There is very little in traditional theory teaching that tells us anything about time; it tells us a certain amount about the elements but not about musical time itself.

Photo: Olav Anton Thommessen (Ines Gellrich).

It has taken Thoresen and me a long while to describe musical time. We have discovered that superimposed layers of time exist simultaneously. There are at least four layers that go at different speeds. And here we begin to talk about speeds in music. We discovered that sonology can often be compared to Adam in the Garden of Paradise. He simply went around and named things, 'tree', 'bird', 'sand'. We have only put *words* on these functions, so we can hold on to them and they don't just escape. That's what sonology is: a tool for trying to describe music without using personal reactions such as, 'It sounds like an insane murderer loose in the woods'— or that kind of fantasy.

We base our theory on something we call 'intersubjectivity', which is the kind of subjectivity that we share that is interesting; it's not pure objectivity. Music theory has possibly been too objective. On the other hand it can get *too* subjective if we can make do with saying 'It sounds like an insane murderer in the woods'. You can't work with that kind of description of music. But if you discover criteria that are common to everyone's experience, then you can work with such a description. For example, if you have repetition— we call them 'fields'—for instance, a strophe, there are certain things that are repeated periodically. Then when this field is closed, something new begins and you have something that you can describe. That is what we have tried to do: make a description of sounding music.

Can it be said that this is a modern 'doctrine of affections'?

No, because it has nothing to do with feelings, it deals only with describing effects. The effects can inspire any kind of emotion; you may say music that sounds happy uses a particular selection of these effects extensively. However, we don't go that far because our theory is not generative: it is exclusively descriptive and analytic. You can't compose with the help of this theory, it is only on the pre-compositional level that the theory can help to organize one's thoughts. It is an auditive-analytic system. This is very important because when I talk to a student, I can pinpoint the specific dimension in the sound image that the student is in the process of constructing. Furthermore, I can see how the student is in the process of developing this dimension and how it will eventually work when it is performed. We use the method as a kind of common reference that helps us to talk to each other about our work.

Are you in touch with research that is going on in Utrecht?

We were, but we aren't any longer. We have had a lot of contact with GRM in Paris, but that is also completely finished. At one time we also had a great deal of contact with England and the research that was going on there. But now it looks very much as though John Paynter's great pioneering work in the schools has fallen apart. At this point we don't have much contact with other places, but we continue with our work. We have a new kind of student who is more interested in the constructive side of music. That is to say, not the affective side that used to be the focus of interest. So new students are working up ideas about music that remind me of the over-constructed music of the 1950s we rebelled against. Such is life.

Do you also use sonology to expose the structure of your own music?

Of course. Sonology is a tool that can be used to analyse all types of composition; that is the best thing about it. Lasse Thoresen has been able to develop graphics to describe these phenomena in music—a kind of score for listening. We get students to make 'listening scores' out of the strangest pieces: from ethnic music and Afghanistan nose flutes to the most crazy electronic music. One student came in with a piece that was almost completely constructed from various components of noise. I thought it was a horrible composition, but his analysis of it was actually completely correct. It *was* an analysis of the sound image.

Indeed any kind of music can be analysed with this tool. It's extremely useful. When you are through, you have a kind of score that you can begin to discuss; you can see how the form is created, and which elements create the form. We are very interested in form, which I think much new music lacks.

In the 1960s Danish music reached a high point in pluralistic thinking. Music from all periods became a part of the matrix and was put to use. For some composers the problem of form became insurmountable. The Dane Karl Aage Rasmussen asked questions such as, how can you create form from heterogeneous material? How can one legitimate the fact that one tone follows another? How can we perceive musical development? How does one know when a piece is finished? The problem of form became overwhelming. In addition to that, music that incorporates music from earlier periods can also create form problems. You used Grieg's Piano Concerto at the beginning of The Glassbead Game, *the large-scale work that has the movement,* 'Through the Prism', *for which you won the Nordic Music Prize in 1990. Could you explain how you use existing works in your own compositions?*

I have composed over 150 works and I think there are twelve that use pre-existing music. A great deal of my music does *not* use it. I have found that the choice of musical material is completely irrelevant. I think there is strong evidence that in the period of national romanticism too much weight was placed on the character of musical material. There had to be a pretty little song, a trumpet signal, or an 'inspiration'. However, if you look at Beethoven (hums the beginning of the Fifth Symphony)—a classical example—there is nothing pretty there, no exciting material. Or if you look at Haydn's symphonies the material is of minimal significance. What is interesting is what is *done* with that material. That is to say, what form it takes. This leads me to believe that you may use anything you want in a work. You may take a work by Grieg or any other piece as the basis, as raw material.

It is important to understand that music originates in something other than in inventing a melodic theme or tune. Wagner's material isn't spectacular (sings Siegfried's motive from the *Ring*). That motive isn't the world's most enchanting idea, and in any case, there is nothing in the sound itself that indicates it represents a sword. The art of composing takes place on another level. I have come to believe it is equally valid to use one thing as another. There are a lot of devices and ideas that you can extract from extant material and use in your own way.

I also like to find the relationship between the musical material and the form. The more one meditates over the raw materials of a work, the more the form tends to emerge from the material itself. You discover that it is like a kind of Chinese box, and that the overarching present form is in the original material.

It's great fun to write large-scale pieces; too much is lost when concerts of contemporary music consist of ten-minute pieces here and five-minute pieces there. One of the consequences of writing longer works is, however, that they are performed only once. The Cello Concerto, *Gjennom Prisme* (Through the Prism) has as yet never been performed at a concert. It has never been played! Think of that. The piece is sixteen years old, it is nine years since it received the Nordic Council Music Prize, and it has never been performed at a concert. Concert managers are terrified by big works. I have circumvented the problem by writing a large-scale piece in 'chapters'—that is, in sections—but some of these sections are so long that they have only been played once. That's the problem with being interested in form; the result is large works. It isn't so much Grieg's small miniature forms that I find interesting; it's the big ones.

Your thoughts on large-scale form are along the lines of both Wagner and Stockhausen. You aim to achieve a physical effect from sound and instruments and you are very sceptical about 'cyberspace' and have been negative about computer music.

Yes, I am very involved with live music. I think that it still has its place, but it is clear that the sound of an orchestra can be translated very well into cyberspace. I am completely aware of that. The sound of an orchestra has a fantastic quality that has taken generations to develop. It matches our desire to listen and our ability to discern sounds. The orchestra comes out fine on loudspeakers with amplification . . . I don't have a problem working with that kind of sound. But what's happening today? One goes to a concert in order to experience what one has experienced before. I think that's a pity, because you can actually gain the same thing by listening to a record.

Wouldn't a large-scale opera be a better framework for your ideas?

I have composed three operas, but they are chamber operas. You don't get a chance to make something big. I'm not going to bother working for years on something that isn't going to be played. I could just as well sit and glare at the TV. You have to be realistic about these things.

Don't you have a decent opera house in Norway?

No, we don't have an opera house—we don't even have a place for chamber opera. So there's a huge problem on a purely physical level. We have musicians who can play new music. Jón Leifs in Iceland composed such huge pieces that it nearly took the entire population of Iceland to play them. That approach to composition is completely unrealistic. We *have* the musicians in Norway and we have the orchestras, but we don't have the spaces. It is so ridiculous. It took us a long time to get the Music High School, and as soon as we started the school attracted 500 students, and now it is too small. It is quite absurd, but that's the way it is. What we lack in Norway is a cultural 'infra-structure'.

FILM MUSIC

It's evident that you are deeply fascinated with some quite special topics. Why are you so fascinated with film music?

The medium of film has given composers the possibility of creating a completely new art music that is different from all its predecessors. Historically many late romantic features and futuristic features were extended in film music. It is still borne of European culture because it was predominantly created by Europeans living in America—and, to a lesser extent, those living in Europe of course. It is laughable for anyone to say that orchestral music ended in 1911, because it has clearly continued in film scores as a late-romantic and futuristic orchestral music. It's actually alive today. At the moment, I am listening to the music for *The Insurrection* by Jerry Goldsmith, which is enormously exciting. There are very few concert composers who write such interesting music. I would much rather listen to something like this than to another pretentious reactionary Norwegian composer with his latest soul-searching song.

They say that film music is fundamentally dishonest because it is about something that was not experienced by the composer. On the contrary, I think that it is honest music because the composer has not mixed his feelings into it; it is completely objective. As a result the work can be concerned with technique and composition.

A film music score may sometimes have three movements that are completely engrossing to listen to, and good enough to be heard in a concert hall. Instead, we hear yet another performance of Mussorgsky's *Pictures at an Exhibition*. I think that it would be infinitely more interesting for the public to hear the music of Franz Waxman for *The Bride of Frankenstein, the Creation of the Female Monster.* It is an enormous piece. Or Jerry Goldsmith's music for *Supergirl* where there is a movement that is called *The Monster Tractor.* It is a dazzlingly virtuoso orchestral piece, and very well composed. When dollar bills are dangled in front of the noses of the musicians, they play their hearts out. You won't *ever* get contemporary music played like that in the concert hall. It's the same with John Corigliano's music for *Altered States.* This is really advanced contemporary music with many purely abstract devices, a lot of electronic expansions of all kinds. The music for *Alien III* by Elliot Goldenthal consists of orchestral pictures that are manifestly excellent. By studying these works one can learn how to develop instrumental music with the help of electronic make-up and all kinds of effects. This is possible because the producers work with big budgets.

There are always two or three films a year with remarkable music—much more interesting than most concert music. I think it is perverse that orchestras don't think of performing this film music when they, at the same time, talk about how orchestras are in crisis and what have you. There is a wealth of exciting music out there, if you only care to get acquainted with it.

There are also composers such as Takemitsu and Schnittke who understand how to use elements from one kind of music to enhance the other.

Yes, and they have learned something about working with both genres of music. Take, for example, Schnittke's Second Cello Concerto based on the film, *Agonia.* It is a fabulously dramatic piece. I think this distinction between popular music and serious music is something that came about after the war. Before the war composers had a popular dialect in their style. They could absorb much more of the musical scene than composers do today. I think it's important that a composer speaks in different styles in each work—in the same way that a speaker can address you in a casual, a didactic and an emotional manner.

Composers also made pleasing music in days gone by. Mozart did, Beethoven did, everyone did up until Schoenberg, who composed cabaret songs. This split is, in fact, something that has happened recently; you purify a position instead of being able to move with it. Right now I am writing a very *flashy* orchestral piece that lots of people will almost certainly think strange: music in casual dress. In a way that is also what is happening in *Makrofantasien*; it is speaking to the public in different ways.

You have just used the word, dialect. Earlier you told me that what composers write today isn't really new music, but dialects of a larger language family. This is a provocative idea because there is still the post-Darmstadt attitude that music should be absolutely new each time, or, in any case, there is a belief that it can be that way. But you don't perceive music as something that should break with everything that has gone before, and consist of something previously unheard?

No, because a break is a kind of continuation. If you do the opposite of something then you are largely doing the same, because you would not have done the exact opposite if it had not been for what had come before. Consequently, it is a kind of continuation. There are very few instances in music history where one can find the beginning of a completely *pure* style. Gabrieli's style was one. The early form of serialism that was heard for a very short time in Darmstadt was a completely pure style, that is, if you want to use the concepts of 'pure' and 'impure'. It is very seldom that this happens in music history and it has happened perhaps on only one or two other occasions. But it isn't anything one can count on when creating new music.

All this talk about a 'new' music—the idea that you should make a completely new kind of music—originated at the beginning of this century. There were several tactics for creating it: one was neo-classicism—the recall of order—where they went back and tried to draw conclusions about what music was, and hence what it could be. Composers drew some general conclusions and created a new style that reflected all the knowledge and experience that had been stored up in musical notation. Next, you have 'the call to order', the twelve-tone music: one invents a principle of order that doesn't necessarily have anything to do with how one listens, but has more to do with music as an intellectual process—a notated music consisting of mechanical variation. And then you have the third direction, where you venture behind the musical substance and try to make music that is an archetypal expression. This third direction is futurism. Take for example, Mosolov's *Iron Foundry*, and that type of primitivism and cultic expression.

These three postulates emerged at the beginning of this century and they suffered different fates. The one that has survived is the serial mode of thought—the computer has suddenly given it a new lease of life. But there is also the archetypal mode of thought and it continues in film music: music as primal effect. That is a tradition that continues today, while neoclassicism has been seemingly tamed into post-modernism in which you merely rework the past from different angles.

Let's continue the focus on the sources of your inspiration. Wagner's music fascinates you. Tell us about it.

Wagner accomplished an amount of work that is downright scary. You can talk about Jesus, but think what Wagner managed to create—in addition to designing a complete theatre with seats and everything. It's a life's work that is simply fantastic and he did all of that in less than seventy years. It says in the Bible that you should reach seventy years and then die; and that's what he did! The instrumentation that took him so long to develop is outrageously interesting; that's where impressionism has its roots. You can hear Debussy when you listen to the second part of the music for the *Venusberg*. It is pure Debussy in sonority—solo strings in octaves, with the most delicate flute lines. Wagner talked about the music of the future and his music, in fact, is this music. His sound is so commercial that it is pure *movie-time*; the scene of the rising sun in *Götterdämmerung* is pure and simple Hollywood. The end of *The Ring* is a Hollywood tear jerker. It is fabulously effective and competent, but he uses almost no material.

The Ring is an enormous variation in which Wagner launched a whole new way of composing. Wagner made the composing process more effective. This is one of the first mechanistic compositional processes that did *not* come from the Leipzig school. Wagner introduced a kind of variation technique that became the precedent for the twelve-tone system. *The Ring* is a genuine variation; these themes can be taken up and woven in wherever they are needed. It provides unbelievable insights into the nature of composition. It took Wagner a very long time to find his way—it is interesting to see how long it actually took. But bang! all of a sudden he realized what he could do to make the compositional process more effective. It is the obsession with automation that emerged at the start of this century. How much of a composition can be automated? I think Wagner found an incredibly interesting answer to that question.

Let us go back to your early childhood, a period of your life that isn't discussed very often. Could you talk about it?

I moved to New York when I was twelve years old and had composed music for as long as I could remember—it's a lot easier to write music than it is to practise the piano. I made compositions that were variations of the music that I had to practise and technically a great deal easier than the pieces I was forced to practise. They were very much à la Grieg and all in A minor. When we arrived in New York my parents were introduced to Vera Zorina and her husband Goddard Lieberson who was the director of Columbia Records. His son Peter Lieberson has become quite a well-known composer in the USA. His father was really kind to me and said that he could help me get some instruction, so I began to study at The Mannes College of Music in New York. My teacher was Carl Schachter—who, himself, became a well-known theorist—and I studied composition with him. The work we did involved imitating various styles of music—I had to write minuets in the style of Haydn, and that sort of thing. It wasn't the kind of composition instruction that I wanted or needed and when I returned to Norway to teach composition with some colleagues, imitating styles wasn't part of what we did. However, that's what composition meant for me as a twelve year-old in New York.

Later I took my portfolio to Indiana University in Bloomington. Bernhard Heiden looked at my helpless imitations and asked: 'What are these neanderthal harmonies'? That was Bernhard Heiden who taught at Indiana University. My initial reaction was that I didn't want to go to a school that rejected my efforts in that way, but later I appreciated his reaction. He taught me to compose in the style of Hindemith—a very liberal kind of teaching that I liked a lot. He taught general principles, and that suited me very well. However, I didn't actually like Hindemith's style; it wasn't what I was after, so I didn't get anything specific from the course that I could build on.

It is interesting to hear that it wasn't contemporary music that inspired you, but older music. I suppose that was due to your upbringing. Is it possible that you only truly heard contemporary music for the first time when Xenakis came to teach at Indiana University?

We had a couple of recordings of music by Arne Nordheim at the Consulate in New York. I think it was *Canzona* and *Epitaffio*, and I first heard them when I was about 14–15 years old. I thought they were really interesting but I didn't know why—the music was so different from everything else I had ever heard. It remained lodged but unused in my brain. Indeed those pieces were inaccessible then and are so still for many people today. Listeners don't know what the music is about, they don't know the parameters. Because they have only clichés to rely on, it *isn't* accessible. And that's the problem, especially for young composers, because they risk becoming imitators of other people's styles, or members of the conservative wing I spoke about earlier—the sort of people who compose trumpet fanfares, fugatos and such things. They are the ones who have not grasped the scope of contemporary music and find themselves too much submerged in obsolete technical aspects of composition. Then suddenly there comes a day when they are too old to change their styles and so they are stuck. I was lucky to go to the right school. It is actually vital which school one goes to because there are so many places where you don't learn enough, and things can go terribly wrong.

Let's hear about your situation at the end of the 1960s, which is when you went to Indiana University. Your encounter with Xenakis and his ideas about music that is without emotion, was decisive for you, even though your music doesn't sound like Xenakis' at all.

His way of looking at music as acoustic architecture, simple and pure physical elements, sculptures that make their way through space, fascinated me. I think that that way of approaching composition is so amazingly physical—you can imagine that you are actually in a building, a three-dimensional space, and that music is the material from which the building is constructed. That was very close to the way that I experienced music. I experience Beethoven in that way, particularly his orchestral music—a very physical medium. Our emotions are fundamental; they concern our ability to respond, whether with sorrow or with joy. The ability to react has something to do with this basic source of emotions. Through our emotions we comprehend our existence as energy, pure and simple. Music is just this. I think of Xenakis' music as pure acoustic energy. He is very clever at measuring precisely how much energy he needs to let out at any given moment.

Xenakis believes that mankind hasn't developed since the time of Greek and Byzantine thought. It's a ridiculously provocative stance to take, but there is something in it, for if you look at these systems of thought that he feels a part of, you can see that they are fundamental models. As far as I can tell he makes a kind of music that has never been heard before; it almost defines a new type of civilization. Xenakis imitates. He thinks about how Greek drama 'really' sounded and then he tries to make his own version of it. Xenakis sees the philosophers of that time as akin to the philosophers of today and he tries to build a bridge across the gap in time between them. He achieves this, in part, by looking at the formal side of things: mathematics. I am profoundly unmathematical; I *cannot* think in that way. But I can find my own way of adopting that kind of thought without being so formally rigid.

Some composers have rejected their earlier works. They no longer recognize themselves in them and they choose not to speak about their juvenalia because it no longer represents what concerns them. How would you describe your style before and after your encounter with Xenakis?

I believe that Xenakis really taught me about polyphony. I had actually never really understood polyphony and simultaneity. That to say, you can work with a form of musical expression where several events take place at the same time, supplementing each other. Xenakis explained it to me like this—he said that a number of universes function simultaneously. You can experience a simultaneity that actually isn't chaotic, rather like society itself, where a great number of things are happening at the same time which may or may not influence each other. He has introduced the notion of interpreting counterpoint as simultaneity in Western music: heterophony. There is very little Western music that really tries to investigate the nature of heterophony, and that is something that he has worked extensively with. These sound masses consist exclusively of heterophonic events. It's incredibly interesting.

I have done nothing as impressive as Xenakis, but the idea of working with the elements of heterophonic sound, merging transitions and polyphony as simultaneous events, fascinates me too. I always compose all the structures in my music simultaneously. I don't just write one layer and then the next; I write the whole thing at the same time, so that I have to hold all of the events in my head. It is a lot easier to make the first layer and then lay another one on top of it, but when you do as I do, you can make sure that they don't contaminate each other, that they are always in complete polarity.

Is that why you call yourself a 'multi-tracked' phenomenon?

That's it. But it also has to do with the fact that when I compose I have to have lots of stimuli around me—three radios and a television turned on and also, if possible, someone I can chat with. Only then can I concentrate on all the layers. I'm Richard Strauss who composed at the kitchen table while his family streamed in and out. It is nice to have distracting things that function as stimulation. It can very easily get too overheated if you concentrate too much. When a composition is at its most complicated, it's very demanding to hold all of one's thoughts in check at all times, at least for me with my limited brain capacity. When the whole orchestral apparatus is activated, I find it incredibly complicated to ascertain where I am. You have to be able to see the layered relationships that emerge and to hear how they will actually sound so that you are not just working on a theoretical premise.

You also have to think about how to get one layer really to stand out. It's a matter of instrumentation but you have to be careful to make sure that it really happens. It's too simple just to say, 'Here is one layer and here is the other', without actually hearing anything. Nørgård showed me his Fourth Symphony and said to me, '*Fascination* is being played here'. One violin plays *Fascination!* It is an amusing idea, but I don't think that anyone hears it. If *Fascination* is an important idea then the composer should probably ensure that it can be heard. People listen differently, but if you have an idea, it stands to reason that it should be heard. As I said, it is all a question of instrumentation. There are many composers who simply have an idea, and don't assure that it's audible. In Xenakis' music you can hear *everything* that he has written. You can *hear* where it goes. Nothing is lost—nothing. If something disappears, it disappears into the heterophonic confusion, but it continues to contribute to the whole so that no-one is left wondering, 'What happened to that idea'? You can *hear* what happened. It is important to be realistic about sound.

TIME IN MUSIC

This brings us to the concept of time in music. Several Nordic composers have written about it and have composed works that play directly on aspects of time: the Swedish composer Anders Hultquist has composed a work that he calls Time and the Bell, *and the Danish composer Ivar Froundberg has written a work with the same title. Another Danish composer, Karl Aage Rasmussen, has written a series of works that dwell on the concept of time. For a Nordic composer like Cecilie Ore, time in music is a recurring theme. There are even books published on the subject. Still, I have a problem with actually hearing work that engages with time in music. Sometimes I wonder whether it is just a theory that physically can't be heard. Or maybe it is a theory that's not meant to be heard in musical sound? To a listener it does seem strange to be told about formal principles in a musical composition and still not be able to hear any of them.*

Music *is* an art that takes place in time. We should think more about time, and about how it unfolds. I find theoretical observations about time very difficult to grapple with, but they can result in interesting music. You can't *hear* the Gregorian song in Perotin's work—it operates in theoretical time. And you can look at composers who have tried to make these stunning, fast, *flickering*-pieces— like Mendelssohn in his age. Despite the fact that his music is incredibly fast you can still make it out. Yet I believe that at the time many people thought his music had reached the limit of what could actually be perceived. It's amazing to think of how original his scherzo movements really are, but then after that, music simply got faster and faster. Composers now put an enormous amount of work into a particular detail that may contain a completely correct row but it is played so quickly that if you blink you'll miss it. What's the point? You could just as well have written a 'grace note' instead.

Take Beethoven. He became deaf, but one of the things he was able to discern was how to stop time. You can hear this in the Overture, op. 124, *Die Weihe des Hauses*. He is *reading* a Handel overture and anticipating what's going to happen on the next page and enjoying the reading. This pleasantly suspended moment is the result. Throughout this weird overture he is reading Handel with his own strange sense of warped time. It is the same in the late string quartets; they are so slow that no-one had composed anything like them before. It wasn't until Beethoven became deaf that he began to work with theoretical time. There is a limit to how far theoretical time can be stretched—you also risk the engine beginning to spin in neutral, at which point it becomes nothing more than an interesting idea. I prefer to stay within the boundaries where I can actually experience time.

It is part of the way we view things in sonology; we are not conservative, but we have criteria. You *have to be* able to hear what you write. Many of our students today think that it is irrelevant and many modernists have thought the same. But in spite of that I, and a number of others, insist that it has to be audible. There is no meaning in writing music if one can't hear the messages. The sceptics think that it's acceptable for music to appeal through its proportions, or just on an analytical level. They take the view that you don't have to hear every single part of the musical concept. For me it is absolutely fundamental that I can hear the ideas—I mean, if it doesn't appeal to the ear then it is not music. How can that be so difficult to understand? I think that it is completely incomprehensible that music should bypass hearing. If you are able to work out an idea that expands the way we hear things, then so be it. But if you make something that is actually an obstacle to listening, then I simply don't see the point of it. At the Music High School we are adamant about this. Indeed we are so strict on this point that we encounter problems with the younger composers. They are no longer interested in the position that we take on this. The pendulum is about to swing again, but I won't abandon my point of view.

In your music aren't there apocryphal references and hidden quotes?

I'm not sophisticated enough for that. I'm not particularly intelligent, if I had been, then maybe. I struggle so hard with composing, and if you can't hear what goes into it then I don't understand why one writes it at all. When you hear a piece for the first time, there is inevitably a lot that you don't understand. You're left saying, 'What on earth?' Then, once you've heard the work a few times you're left feeling 'Yeah, uh-huh, that's what it's all about'. Yet everything was actually present in the work from the beginning. The problem with much orchestral music is that people aren't used to listening to *so* much counterpoint at one time and as a result they think it's just a big mess. But that's not the case. There are some incredible carefully thought-out relationships and a lot going on at the same time. There are many people who think that orchestral music is difficult to listen to. It demands a 'lateral' way of listening.

Polyphony, being multi-layered, is important to you, but sometimes it is perceived as chaotic. It's a terrible situation to be in when you yourself can hear it, but your audience . . .

I hear it, that's why I do it. That's why I have composed a piece called *Please Accept My Ears*, where I ask my audience to consider the notion that there is possibly something wrong with my hearing . . . because *I* do hear all these things. In the viola concerto, *Ved Komethode* (At the Head of the Comet), I tried to make etchings of specific structures—they are not completely 'focused', but the piece I am working on at the moment is *completely* focused. I have called it *Im alten Stil* (In the old style) because it is written in *my* old style that is completely focused. It's like the horn concerto, *Beyond Neon*. But where development takes place in the viola concerto there are smears . . . the placement of the layers is very important, but the elaboration is a bit more diffuse. This is something that I have begun to work with lately. It is more 'out of focus' so that you get less detailed landscapes—sounds that are not quite as sharp and distinct around the edges. It is a style of smears in which I etch these structures instead of focusing them.

In other words a kind of palimpsest where you can see that you have erased the original lines, so the earliest form isn't clear any more?

Yes, as if, for example, you were to make a very clear painting and then take your thumb and smudge it, that's what is presented. It creates a very diffuse and quite exciting atmosphere. There isn't as much structural argumentation as there used to be when you could discern the influence of Hindemith and neoclassicism in music. Now if you smudge that, the argumentation becomes less intrusive and is a little more interesting, not so excessively obvious. That's why in my new orchestral piece I am trying to make a sound that is super clear, just to be able to say that I have now finished with doing that once and for all.

It's interesting that when I tried to compose an opera I had tremendous problems. You hear so many different and new approaches to opera, with *Sprechgesang* techniques and so on, that I decided in my third opera to compose an opera in the way that Wagner did. At the time that he criticized Italian opera he had composed one himself, namely, *Das Liebesverbot*, a pure Donizetti-style opera, in fact. He was familiar with what he criticized, which is important. When I criticize operas and librettos then I feel the need to write one in order to understand what is involved; in order to avoid creating such a thing again.

I did that with my new work. I couldn't stand any more of this kind of super-focused 'tuttelut, tuttelut', so I wrote one final work in this style to get it out of my system. You can't sit and bullshit about a form that you don't actually understand yourself. So *Hertuginnen dør* (The Duchess Dies) is a text-based opera with dialogue and so on. It's a quasi-baroque opera, a meditation on baroque operatic forms, and it actually works quite well. It has set-piece 'numbers', with arias, ensembles—everything. Precisely what I think opera should not be.

And you think that it works well in any case?

On yes, yes. It does. It *always* has. But I think opera should be something else.

What?

I think opera should be more like what Luciano Berio did—a kind of dream world with a mixture of all kinds of arts, dance and what have you, so that realism is completely dispensed with. Instead, one creates a panorama of mental states, the experiences of dreaming. My opera *The Hermaphrodite* is like that—a series of scenic hallucinations. The production could be very interesting, and one could do something interesting with the orchestra as part of the scenario. There is a lot one could do, if only one were allowed to.

I get the impression that a part of your aesthetic goes back to futurism. To what extent does your approach to music find its roots in the movements at the beginning of the century?

There's certainly something in that. It is only recently that people have discovered how many incredibly exciting things happened around 1910. For me it began with finding out about all the music that was created during the French Revolution. I discovered Étienne-Nicolas Mèhul (1763–1817), François-Joseph Gossec (1734–1829) and many others that I had never actually heard of before and who are quite brilliant composers. Suddenly you see Berlioz in another light, and realize that he wasn't as strange as everyone thought.

Beethoven was actually influenced by Mèhul and others who invented the French Revolutionary style. The classical style was developed during the French Revolution. We thought we knew a whole lot about futurism, but I got a recording several years ago where they had reconstructed all of Russolo's machines—the noise generators. Then there appeared a piano transcription of Luigi Grandi's *Aeroduello* from 1935 that I can't remember ever having heard before. Music like *Sacre* is just a part of this movement. Suddenly you find out that this belongs to a huge world of ideas that have since been forgotten! And now Soviet Futurists like Vladimir Deshevov (1998–1955) are being recorded and a recording of Mosolov's Piano Concerto, some of the strangest music I have ever heard, is being released. Then there is someone like Ivan Wyschnegradsky (1893–1979), who composed microtonal string quartets in 1923, and George Antheil—not only his *Ballet Mechanique*, but also his piano and violin sonatas which are completely crazy and which could have been written today!

Now these things are being released on CD we can begin to get a picture of what actually happened at that time. The 1960s are only a kind of shadow of what went on earlier. The 1960s saw a massive movement based on the ideas that were founded in 1910. Now you can truly see what it consisted of. I listened to the *Scythian Suite* by Prokofiev and a number of other astonishing works and realized that they were part of a whole series of compositions from that period. Respighi, whom you don't think of as a Futurist, *was* one in fact.

Film music was the continuation of the Futurist movement. Max Steiner's *King Kong* is futuristic music, heavy orchestral wheels that grind round and round. Likewise Waxmann's *Bride of Frankenstein* which is in precisely that style. You can begin to fill the lacunae in music history. The period before the First World War leading up to the 1920s were extremely significant. There are many ideas that we haven't yet grasped. There was a woman named Louis Fuller who danced an 'electric dance' with phosphorescent lights, and she went to Marie Curie so that she could find out how to apply radium to her costumes in order to create more dramatic effects. The poisonous radium contaminated the audience and everyone died three months later. Here is an artist who left a mark!

Did they die?

Probably. They were certainly contaminated by the radium, and they died of poisoning. They didn't have any idea what it was, only that it shone and was very beautiful. It was a completely crazy time. There is a lot that I read about now, that I didn't know about before. Until now, music history has consisted of Schoenberg, Webern and so on, but that was far from being the whole story. A great many fertile things happened, not least the connection with the Russian Revolution and the freedom that it initially represented. There was an explosion of experimental music. The recordings of Russian piano music of the 1920s are now available, including one by Arthur Lourié (1892–1966), a mind-blowing piano piece that goes beyond Skriabin and his type of tonality. It has become much easier to approach music history from perspectives other than the established conservatory versions that only recognize the imitators of Schoenberg and Webern. There are many other ideas that can be developed and I think it's strange that not more is done about it. There is a mass of ideas simply waiting to be taken further.

NORWEGIAN MUSICAL LIFE

We began this interview talking about the music history of Norway and national romanticism. You went out into the world like Askeladden, possibly to find yourself, and then you came back to Norway. What did it look like? It was undeniably a rather barren musical landscape that needed to be cultivated. How did that happen?

Oslo is the only place where one can study music composition in Norway, so all the compositional 'cases' come to us. It has been really rather cozy. It has been our privilege to have the opportunity of teaching talented young people. We have some very exciting composers in Norway now, it is not as barren as it was. We have made a kind of impact on composing and the composers now talk to one another, not least because of the Music High School. They meet each other as students and that makes the milieu much friendlier than before. There has been a colossal improvement. There are now several generations of composers who are genuinely interested in travelling abroad and they need to do this to get further training. Many travel in order to become familiar with the world of the arts and to find out where they stand.

I am aware that a very fertile milieu has grown up in Oslo in the last twenty years. But before that, when you came home in the 1970s there was no such thing as a degree in composition, nor an institution functioning as a music conservatory.

No, but there were people like Ole Henrik Moe who went unrecognized even though he built up the Henie-Onstad Museum to a level which attracted musicians of international standing. And it was not so long after I came home that we had the visit by Stockhausen and his improvisation group that I mentioned earlier. Kagel came several times because there was enough money to invite these people. It didn't take long to achieve an improvement.

What about Arne Nordheim who had worked at the electronic music studios in Warsaw? Wasn't that significant? As far as I know, you have never composed electro-acoustic music. One usually has some role model either to sympathize with or to revolt against. He must have played a part in all of this?

Of course. He was very kind to me from the beginning. I was invited to visit him early on, indeed I was accepted into the music world very quickly. I was elected to the governing board of the Composer's Union, and as a result I was initiated into all the issues and understood how Arne was trying to organize things. He paved the way for many composers. I sat on the Board of Directors the whole time he was President of the Union. Arne has had a great impact as a cultural leader and as an organizer. Now he has retired somewhat, but at that time he was always there to assist colleagues and was very generous. I don't underestimate that.

He changed styles rapidly. Suddenly in the 1960s he developed a beautiful, relatively mild style. But he had a reputation for being a 'pling-plong' composer for a long time after he stopped composing electronic music. Now he writes music that is in no sense difficult to comprehend. I don't know if he has become a moderate, but he has adapted himself to a situation.

There's an implicit criticism in that last comment . . .

It's difficult to speak about close colleagues, but I think that Arne has found a solution as a composer: he explores familiar formulations. But it's hard to say where the distinction lies between style and that which you quite simply have heard before. To my mind his music lies on the borderline; for example, there is a great deal that I really admire in the Violin Concerto. However, I think that as an organizer he has paved the way for us. There is no doubt about that and we are very grateful to him. Before the war, the artist as an individual had a position in society, he was asked for his opinions and was actually listened to. That role was destroyed by the artists who became associated with Nazism. Every artist who tried to step forward was met with 'No, we'll be damned if we bother to listen to that fascist nonsense'.

That was the attitude that Arne encountered. 'Don't come here with your confounded artist-stuff' or 'pling-plong'. But over the years he has been so consistent in his views that he *has* achieved a moral position. When things take a turn for the worst he is listened to. For example, there was a time when there was a threat to reduce the funding for the Norwegian Music Information Centre. At first I was asked to become President again, but then I didn't hear anything more about it. Eventually I was told 'No, no, too bad, but we have had to ask Arne to do it again, because it's really serious this time'. So I knew that they had really dragged in the big cannon—not the little one—and were taking aim, PANG! They got the big concession right away. I couldn't have done that at all. Arne can be of use in situations of crisis. The position that he has created for himself is really impressive. We have very few like him in Norway. Think about Sweden where they have Bergman, Lidholm and so on, or in Denmark, where you had Poul Borum and several others. In Norway Grieg filled that role, Bjørnson, Ibsen (like Strindberg in Sweden) also filled it, but since Johan Borgen and André Bjerke there has been no-one like it in Norway. Perhaps Odd Nerdrum, but that is all. When, for example, Dag Solstad tried to take a moral stand over a polemic topic everybody screamed 'Damned if we'll listen to an ex-commie'. That's still a cuss word. There are very few who have stood up and said something that society needed to hear. But Arne has been able to do this. He has resurrected the role of the moral artist who is worth listening to. We are grateful to him for that. Others have only become celebrities—harmless, but when Arne says something about Norwegian culture, it gets heard.

A NEW ARTISTIC ROLE

I met you some years ago in Berlin where we talked about East and West. You spoke tongue-in-cheek about the situation earlier in the Eastern countries (O.A.T., carried away: 'Yeah, the good old days'). It was a provocation, or at least, mind-provoking. Are dictatorships good for the arts?

No, not at all. I was really exposed to something very dramatic when I studied in Poland. Let me tell you a crazy story: I got to know an English composer who was really nice, Nigel Osborne. We were students together in Poland in 1970 and became very good friends. Osborne married a Polish woman who worked in The British Council and he tried to get her out. We arranged some improvisation concerts with a group we had formed in Poland together with some Polish composition students. We travelled around performing some chaotic concerts and gathered rather big audiences. The audiences were ready for that sort of thing. Then the authorities began to dislike the fact that we attracted so many young people, so they tried in different ways to discredit us. One evening, they knocked me down and broke my tooth, while Nigel found a uniform in his collective. He said to me, 'I have a uniform lying in the apartment. I don't know where it came from'. I thought that was strange. At that point (1970) we were so afraid that there was going to be a Soviet invasion that I had moved into the Norwegian Embassy. I had telephoned the Norwegian Ambassador and said, 'The Norwegian colony is hereby about to move in', and they said, 'By all means'.

We all sneaked over to the American Embassy and sat and watched Mickey Mouse films in the cellar while we expected the Russians to invade. It was completely insane. But then I mentioned that Nigel had found this uniform. The embassy people said, 'What! This is an obvious provocation. Do you understand what that means'? 'No', I said. 'It means that they probably intend to accuse you of protecting a deserter, a Polish deserter. This means five years in prison. We have to get you out of here this minute'. I realized that this was the time for me to leave, but it took a month and a half for a foreigner just to request permission to leave; it was completely surreal. 'You have to get going right now', said the people at the Embassy, and so the British Embassy was contacted. At the time the matter of the stray uniform was being dealt with by the police a different ministry was taking care of our exit visa. We prayed that there would be no contact between the two. And since the exit permission arrived before the charge was ready, we got out of Poland. There are many such stories; it was a completely crazy, surreal and stressful time, like a black comedy, literally speaking. It was like living in an art work, a surrealist one. The good old days consisted of a work of art, a morbid one. I was there for only one year. It's unbelievable that people could accept such a situation, but they lived with it for forty years. At the end they said, 'We don't have time to dream this dream any more. We have no food, we have nothing. We have to stop!'

Now it is altogether different in Poland—in any case, it does not consist of that surreal dream anymore. But art did have a truly large position in that society, because the society itself was an artwork, so they could use the arts to comment on the artwork. There wasn't much else to do anyway. There were good reasons for art gaining such an important position, precisely like Norway during the war. Nazism was also a kind of surrealistic performance artwork—possibly more brutal, but quite similar. There too, art was of immense significance as a weapon of opposition.

In today's society, aestheticism is misused by being applied to politics and consumption. Instead of applying aesthetics exclusively where they belong—to art. You gain aesthetic experiences from all levels of society, so that art has lost its function as the primary aesthetic object. Instead, *everything* in society has become imbued with aesthetics, for good and bad. It makes it hard to tell whether people still take pleasure in experiencing art. For many, it is no longer interesting—they prefer to experience something else. It's a growing problem. We should think about art as something much more encompassing than simply going to a concert and sitting and listening to someone twang on the piano for four minutes and then having to clap. I think there is a need to do something more drastic with the concert experience.

So we return to your thoughts on a new framework for the arts.

Yes, that the frame itself is thought of as part of the whole, because it is difficult to imagine that anyone would be interested in a simple little piano piece. You confront aesthetics when opening a packet of cornflakes with a design on it and a little doll inside. It is appalling, but aesthetic—an appallingly poor use of aesthetics. And in politics, what with the party logos, yellow and blue to identify the parties. In my opinion, it isn't right to use aesthetics like this. It is too reminiscent of Nazism!

When I asked provocatively if a dictatorship is good for the arts, it was because some soul searching works came from Shostakovitch and from the Polish composers who worked under extremely difficult circumstances. Now, there are some who think that today's composers are downright spoiled and that's why so many toothless works are being created.

Yes, because they don't think of the whole process involved in presenting an artwork. One must try to see how the whole functions within a big framework in order to change it. That's what they did in the French Revolution, I'm sure. When I was in China in the 'good old days' during the Cultural Revolution, the symphony orchestra was actually used as an ideological weapon. It was a metaphor of how people actually could cooperate. They were impressed by seeing a model of cooperation. I am sure that the French Revolution used the symphony orchestras in the same way, to show people how they could work together. The concerto, where the individual has to relate to the group, is a kind of abstract theatre-piece which shows people how such a problem can be resolved. Even if you don't understand the musical structures and developments, you readily recognize the primal situations that emerge in a concerto. The soloist stands in front of the orchestra which gives its support, and which takes over some of the soloist's ideas. All of this is ideological. You need only to think of it on a bigger scale: what does this apparatus actually mean? What is its real function? We need to return to this way of thinking instead of thinking only about construction and all its related problems.

Now you are defining a new role for the artist. You are describing an extroverted approach, away from construction, a role in which the artist must consider his place in a larger context.

I think so. For I think—now being slightly moralistic—since society pays for art, it ought to get something in return, something that the citizen can relate to. The problem is that some artists believe that you have to reach *everybody*. I think that you have to find a point of contact and I am satisfied if I reach the orchestra. Then I feel as though I have achieved a small victory and that I have done my bit when the orchestra doesn't get up, doesn't leave the stage, put wigs on and sabotage everything.

'En flersporet klangrealist' appeared in two parts in *Dansk Musik Tidsskrift* 73, 2 and 3 (1998/99): 38–46, 74–83.

Erik Bergman

A REFINED PRIMITIVE

The first item on the programme when you visit Erik Bergman in his home in Helsinki is a guided tour of his instrument collection. Quite naturally, almost like a ritual, everyone who visits has to see the collection before embarking on the topic of the composer's music. Titicaca, Uzbekistan, Turkey, Macedonia, Africa, Peru—you name it—he's been there. And he's not been there for nothing: an impressive treasure trove of instruments from across the globe hangs from the walls as well as covering the top of everything in the apartment. Erik Bergman and his wife, Solveig von Schoultz, began to travel around the world at the beginning of the 1970s gathering instruments. Their collection has become exceptional—so rare and comprehensive that it is the subject of a musicological dissertation (Anne Bergman, 'Bergman's Instrumental Collection', Åbo Academy, 1979). These strange instruments from so-called primitive cultures don't just lie around and gather dust—they are used in numerous instrumental works and have inspired musical rarities like micro-intervals or new tuning systems. And this is not a recent development either. The composer's interest in the sound world of the Orient can be traced back to the ground-breaking work, Rubaiyat *for baritone, male choir and orchestra, from 1953.*

BACKGROUND

Meeting Finland's senior composer (b. 1911) is fascinating because, by virtue of his age, he is a unique reservoir of historic knowledge and practical experience of his country and its development. When Bergman was born, Finland was a grand duchy of Russia, thus he has witnessed from the start Finland's development into a modern independent country, which, from a Scandinavian perspective, has emerged as a powerful cultural force.

As early as 1931 Bergman began to study composition, piano, violin, organ and voice at the Sibelius Academy, and soon after that he went to study composition abroad. Bergman describes what it was like to be a composer in the 1930s and 1940s, about the climate for new Finnish music and about his first trip abroad.

My *Suite for String Orchestra* and my *Passacaglia for Organ* (Op. 1 and 2) were part of my diploma work at the Sibelius Academy. The works were written in the spirit of Nordic, national romanticism. You had to write in the approved style of the conservatory—nothing with parallel fifths or anything like that.

This inspired me to break the rules and I composed a little piece, a choral work, *Arkaisk Bild* (Archaic Picture, Op. 35c), to a text by Johannes Edfelt, that contained everything that was forbidden. To be able to protest and to write the way I wanted felt like a great release. At that time I was made director of the Academic Choral Society. I was chosen because the chorus wanted to update its repertoire and I was asked to compose something. There were six premieres of my works at the first concert.

Later I began to compose works for speaking choir. No-one knew how to react; it wasn't music at all. I used texts by Christian Morgenstern, notably in the last movement, 'Das grosse Lalula', from *Vier Galgenlieder* (Four Gallow Songs, 1960) for mixed choir, which had counterpoint and everything. When the piece was finished the audience didn't know whether to laugh or cry. Since then it has become something of a hit.

Later in the 1930s Bergman came to a compositional dead end. He had no-one he could really talk to in Finland and sought contact with the musical scene in Central Europe in order to meet composers and musicians. In 1937, Bergman began to study with Heinz Tiessen in Berlin.

Celibidache and I were students at the same time. A lot was happening in the Berlin of the 1930s and 1940s. Karajan began the Sunday matinées in the Berlin Staatsoper and competed with Fürtwängler's Berlin Philharmonic. The climate was tense with 'degenerate' art. Hindemith had to leave the country, and so on. My professor, Heinz Tiessen, couldn't get performances of his work at the large German music festivals because he had a Jewish publisher. It was hard for advanced art to even exist under the 'aryan' laws. Eventually when the war was over, Germany became home to the European avant-garde with the summer courses in Darmstadt, and so on.

In the 1940s I reached a point as a composer, where I was unable to continue in the traditional style, so I had to seek out new areas. This led to compositional techniques that were close to the twelve-tone method. For example, if I had a note that was going to be important as a point of culmination, then I couldn't use it before that point. These experiments didn't come easily—for years I had resisted serialism. When I studied in Berlin in the 1930s, I thought it was too artificial and constructivist. Not until the end of the 1940s when I studied with Wladimir Vogel in Switzerland, did the twelve-tone method become essential for me. It became the means for me to break free from the cult of Sibelius that didn't just dominate Finland, but the whole of Scandinavia.

Photo: Erik Bergman.

Then later I left the orthodox twelve-tone technique behind and sought my own expressive means, in the way that all composers of necessity have to do. A technique should not only benefit art. No matter what technique you use, as a composer you have to delve down to the deepest parts of yourself and ask what it is that you really want to achieve. I have tried to keep away from all the 'isms' and go my own way, but it hasn't always been easy.

These days, pluralism provides a solution for many, and that's OK, but I consider it very important to develop new expressive means. You have to renew yourself all the time, create new solutions to problems when you compose.

ELECTRONIC MUSIC

Due to this basic approach to compositional practice, Bergman always begins a new work from scratch.

I always start from point zero and each time I ask what it is that I want to do with this new work. Then I set out accordingly, just as you have to do in the case of electronic music where you face a thousand possibilities. For each work you have to make a set of decisions and you have to eliminate things so that the idea of the individual work becomes something specific.

With respect to electronic music, I was very taken with it when it came out, so to speak, in Europe. I was in the Italian radio's electronic music studio in Milan at the end of the 1950s where I became very familiar with the ideas of Bruno Maderna and Luciano Berio. Both composers were there at that time and built the studio into a powerful centre. Since then, Cologne and Stockhausen and others have come along. It was interesting to be there, but it was a one-time phenomenon for me; electronic music hasn't left a noticeable trace in my output. It should be said, however, that I gave a series of electronic music seminars as Professor of Composition at the Sibelius Academy. For an entire Spring term, electronic music was a theme, with experts in the field coming in. It is important for young students to have the chance to take a stand with respect to every aspect of composition. I always say, 'Nothing is forbidden, long live freedom'!

Speaking of teaching, there was once a young man who wanted to study with me. I asked him to show me what he had composed. He really wanted to compose *modern* music. What he had with him was not actually modern, and it was very simple. I had to tell him that he had a very long way to go. You can't just hop from something banal to something highly complicated; there has to be an inner process where you become aware of what you are doing. I told him that once he had gathered all the external stimuli then it was important for him to go into his study and decide what he actually wanted. After that he could come to see me again and formulate his goals in words. That's tough! But in that way you may reach an understanding of how each individual person thinks. It means that you can't teach all students in the same way, but must teach them according to their own specific personalities. When students had problems with composition, I shared their problems, sometimes even at night! I found teaching terribly demanding; it is very difficult to guide young composers. When I retired from the Sibelius Academy, I didn't want to have private students, but wanted to concentrate on composing.

SIBELIUS

In Denmark there were a number of composers who had difficulty freeing themselves from the legacy of Carl Nielsen who dominated musical life and thought for many years. Apparently something similar happened to Bergman, only it wasn't with Carl Nielsen, but with Sibelius.

Yes, all of Sibelius's contemporaries and the generation that followed lived in his shadow. After my second composition recital at the end of the 1940s, I was invited by Jean Sibelius to visit him. He had heard some of my music on the radio and wanted to talk with me. During the visit he encouraged me and inspired me to continue. He made a point of saying that he was happy to find young people who dared to do something different and new. On this occasion Sibelius also said that he was considered by the public to be someone who stood in the way of all other composers, forcing them to live in his shadow. He said, 'That's not my fault; I have done nothing to create this situation'. He made it clear that he admired new ideas and he was actually not at all as conventional and old-fashioned as you would think. He declared that at the beginning of the century he was very interested in Schoenberg's music. I don't know if his biographer, Tawatstjerna, knows this and has written about it, but Sibelius was actually very interested in these things. In his Fourth Symphony he extended tonality, but in the Fifth Symphony he fell back and didn't have the strength to continue in that direction.

It's natural that a strong personality—like, for example, Nielsen in Denmark—will dominate. Lately in Denmark, new directions, and good composers who demonstrate completely new approaches, have emerged. That's natural, but the plight of those who are excluded because of certain strong personalities who dominate musical life is also understandable.

Later I received some calls from Sibelius's son-in-law, Jussi Jalas, who was principal conductor of the opera. Jussi phoned and said, 'Now Jean has heard your music again and he particularly likes this and this . . . . He asked me to call you'. The last communication from the family came when Sibelius died. His wife, Aino Sibelius, asked me to come to the graveside and to conduct the two university choruses in 'Mitt hjärtas sång' (Sibelius's op. 18). When the coffin was put into the earth, I conducted that little song as his last farewell.

Erik Bergman: A Refined Primitive

Right from the beginning, the human voice has been an important resource for Bergman. Over a period of more than 50 years he conducted and composed choral music—it represents the greatest part of his output. These works have been significant in terms of stylistic development and, even if they are not key works, they are still very important within the context of post-war European choral music. What is it about the medium that so attracts him?

I was interested in the human voice from my earliest years; as a young student I sang tenor in the Academic Choral Society. But an important inspirational source was my work with the Chamber Speaking Choir from Zurich, the foremost speaking chorus at that time. To celebrate their tenth anniversary they commissioned a piece entitled *Vier Galgenlieder* (Four Gallows Songs). That was how I became familiar with the possibilities inherent in speaking choruses. I cultivated everything that lies between bel canto, whispering, and *Sprechgesang*, the expressive means that lies between speech and song, and so on.

Bergman has also used this technique in his new opera, Det Sjungande Trädet *(The Singing Tree) to a libretto by Bo Karpelan. It was commissioned for the new opera house in Helsinki in 1991. Here he uses* Sprechgesang *in one of the most important roles, that of the fool.*

This fool sees everything and knows beforehand how things are going to turn out. Taking the role of the jester, he voices uncomfortable truths about the king. In order to distinguish his role from all the others, he uses *Sprechgesang*; he neither sings nor speaks. He must perfect a technique similar to that of Schoenberg in *Pierrot Lunaire*. It is used deliberately throughout the opera.

In Bergman's choral music there is an unfailing instinct for the practical. As in the works of the renaissance masters, you feel that the composer himself is a singer. There is an awareness of the possibilities of the voice—the choral writing is completely idiomatic.

You have to have a very clear idea about what the human voice can and cannot do. You should not—as has Heinz Holliger for example—compose as if the choir were an instrument. You should penetrate the mystery of the song and also explore the purely physical aspects. Consider a work like *Lament and Incantation* (for soprano and cello) written for Dorothy Dorow. Here in Finland when old women mourn their dead there are long lamentations. The same thing happens in the first part of the work; the singer should almost weep. In the second part, the *Incantation*, the singer should invoke the evil spirits. This is a song without words that cultivates the suggestive, and expresses rage using highly-charged dynamics.

NEW PATHS

If you look at today's young generation of composers in Finland, you find a wealth of talent that has even attracted international attention: Saariaho, Lindberg, Kaipainen, to name but a few. What do you think of the latest developments in Finnish composition and how do you stand in relation to it?

I have to relate it to the situation in which I found myself when I began to compose for speaking chorus, serial music and God knows what else, and found very little understanding. It was terribly hard to fight for something that was completely new here. We founded a society, Contemporary Music, that later became Finland's representative at the ISCM. We produced concerts of new music, held lectures, made analyses. We tried to cultivate a green field. Hardly anyone came to the concerts; no-one understood a single thing about the music. But in response to the information we provided, steadily more people became interested. This entire development—the rise of new music from an 'embryonic stage' to today's responsive audiences—is there for the benefit of our young composers. The line I stood for has now been continued and I like to say, somewhat roguishly, that now that I can see the positive development of new music, I can die in peace! The new music scene here seethes and bubbles with life with so many young gifted composers like the ones you have named. But let us not forget one who has had a truly great influence in this process: Paavo Heininen. He teaches composition at the Sibelius Academy and gathers youth around him. Through his work as teacher and through his compositions he has been a key figure in the development of new music in Finland.

Another reason for the blossoming new music scene here is the number of gifted conductors who are now becoming internationally-known: Esa-Pekka Salonen, Leif Segerstam, Okku Kamu, Jukka-Pekka Saraste. They are also helping to pave the way for the performance of new music. And a wealth of new music is being composed in Finland as a result of the completely unique grant-system we have. (Twenty to twenty-five Finnish composers receive stipends lasting from one to fifteen years.) These government grants make it possible for composers to completely and utterly concentrate on composition. I know of no other country in the world that has a comparable system of support. Finally, we also have musicologists who have gained recognition: Erik Tawaststjerna, Eero Tarasti and Mikko Heiniö, all researchers who teach at the university in Åbo. In addition they have also begun a programme of research at the Sibelius Academy.

Erik Bergman continues to comment happily on his many years of experience as a central musical personality in Finland and his glowing enthusiasm burns its way into the consciousness of all who meet him. He provides the background and histori-cal roots to the growth in new Finnish music. Bergman is not just a legendary figure, a nostalgic source of anecdotes. Today he is the same listening, searching, innovative person he always has been, as can be heard in his final salvo which is more impatient than resigned:

There is so much to do on earth, one man's life is too short and insignificant. I don't think that I have done enough in life yet. There is so much I haven't been able to achieve!

'Bergman—en forfinet primitivist. Et møde med den finske komponist Erik Bergman', *Musikhøst* 1989 (programme book for the new music festival 'Music Harvest 1989'): 2–5.

Vagn Holmboe

My Unattainable Goal

You came from Jutland to Copenhagen to take the entrance exams for The Royal Danish Academy of Music. Tell us the story.

In 1926 I went to the Director of the Academy, Anton Svendsen. I showed him some compositions, a trio, and some other things and asked him if it was adequate for admission. I knew no theory of any sort and I only knew that a fifth was the fourth finger on the violin. Svendsen said, 'Take private instruction in theory for a year and then you can probably enter'. He said it in a very friendly and kindly way, but when the December exams came I went to take them anyway. I knew very well that it was a bold thing to do, but I had composed a quartet and studied several pieces for violin, among them a Handel Sonata, and I played the Sibelius 'Berceuse' on the piano. I thought that I could justify applying on that basis.

It happened, however, that I wasn't called into the exam itself because one after the other my fellow students went in, played, and came out—in alphabetical order—and 'H' was skipped. When everything was over and I thought that my chance had passed, a little man came out. He had grey hair and was very friendly. I didn't know who he was; only later did I find out who he was—no, yes—I found out that it was Carl Nielsen. He said, 'Let's go into room A so we can look at your things'. That we did, and he asked if I could play, so I played some of the Handel Sonata and some of the Sibelius. I had my quartet with me and he looked at it. When he had looked through it he put his hand on it and said, 'Yes, you can consider yourself admitted'. I was totally surprised and happy, so I took the first train home and woke my mother and father in the morning to tell them that I had been admitted. It meant that my father had to support me for the next three years.

Later you were hired as a teacher in several places, among them, at the Academy.

I had a minor job at the public music school, then I worked at the Institute for the Blind in charge of ear training and as a choral conductor. That helped a bit financially. Then I was hired by the Academy in 1939.

You were a reviewer with the newspaper, Politiken, *but you also wrote reviews in* Dansk Musik Tidsskrift. *They say that the tone can be brusque these days but you could also be tough then. I'm thinking about your discussion of Jørgen Bentzon's* Dickens Symfoni *(Symphony No. 1 in D Major, 1939–40) in* Dansk Musik Tidsskrift.

Yes, I regret it a bit today. I thought that Bentzon could compose better than he had in that work. That was the basis for my criticism. Bentzon wanted to be as popular as Riisager. He was actually jealous of Riisager, because of his popularity. I said, 'Cut it out'! He had composed *En romersk fortælling* (A Roman Story) which was remarkable, but when he composed the *Dickens Symfoni*, I thought he had gone in the wrong direction, that is, against his ability to do something intense.

For how many years were you actually a critic at Politiken?

Seven. That was right after World War II. I remember that when I said, 'I think I should leave the paper', the Editor-in-Chief, Hasager said promptly, 'I can give you twice the salary and completely free licence'. But I realized that if I were to do that I would be tied for the rest of my life, for it would raise my standard of living and I could never find another job at the same level. So I said 'No'. I wasn't a natural newspaper man. It is also a poor combination to be a composer and a reviewer. You can't be free in both positions and you have to be!

FOLK MUSIC

When you first started to compose you were very clearly interested in folk music from the Balkans. Sven Erik Tarp is supposed to have teased you once by saying, 'We all like Vagn Holmboe's Romanian folk rhythms from Horsens' (a town in Jutland, ed.). Tell me about your early years as a composer and how folk music inspired your own music?

I was in Romania in 1933–34 in order to study Romanian folk music. (I also met my wife Meta there—we were married in Romania.) I visited the mountains and listened to the songs of the shepherds and to the different gypsy ensembles that played for Saturday dances in the country villages. When I came home, I was naturally influenced by the whole Balkan region, including Bulgaria, the former Yugoslavia and Greece. What interested me was not the picturesque character of the music, even though it was, of course, very entertaining to listen to the music on the tapes that we had made. The thing is, this music had nothing directly to do with my music. It's simply not possible to plagiarize folk music without making it bad. But I am very interested in the basis of folk music; it's direct and emotional and it combines deep feelings with clear expression. There was something elementary in this music that I had already come into contact with in Copenhagen in the music of the *Neue Sachlichkeit*, namely, to get down to basics and then build from there.

When I came home there was a certain influence from folk music, especially with respect to rhythm. My rhythm became completely free, because every kind of rhythm is found in folk music. Its natural rhythms, be they 13/8 or 7/8, are tied to the dance steps or to the text that is being sung. This interested me and therefore many of my works, especially those in the 1930s and 1940s, are based on specific rhythms. The melodies themselves are influenced by the simplicity of folk music. I go along with Joseph Haydn, who also used folk music in his works—not that I am asking to be compared to Haydn.

What was it like to come back with that inspiration from folk music to a music scene that was dominated by Riisager, Tarp and Koppel, who had a completely different attitude towards creating music? At least one of these composers is considered a writer of divertimenti. Your music must have seemed austere, or sober, with a foreign air about it. What was it like to create music and get it performed in Denmark in the 1930s?

The situation was very difficult in Copenhagen when I and my wife, Meta, were getting established. There was high unemployment and it wasn't possible to get a teaching position. I couldn't get either theory or violin students, and my wife, who was a pianist, couldn't get piano students either. There was almost no opportunity to get works performed. The only possibility was the concert series being produced by Det Unge Tonekunstnerselskab (DUT, or The Society for Young Composers). Here I could, in the course of a year, get two or three works, or, in the best years, four or five, performed. At DUT we composers met with each other and heard each other's works. There was also a bit of help from art exhibitions where our music was played. The situation was actually very difficult.

Musically there were two camps or directions (even though in Denmark we don't go in for having 'camps' as much as they do in Sweden or Germany). One direction was influenced by French music and was represented by Riisager, Tarp and Schultz, and the other was more based more on the *Neue Sachlichkeit* style, but developed further. Amongst the older generation this direction was represented by Jørgen Bentzon and Finn Høffding. Among younger composers, it attracted Syberg, Koppel and myself. There were several others who emerged and disappeared again. We all knew each other and got along well enough but we had different aesthetic perceptions.

In our camp we took things a bit more seriously, we wanted to move on to something new—beyond *Neue Sachlichkeit*, and on to something different. And at the end of the 1930s when the political crises were mounting, something happened, there was an emotional tension. My own music had been based on a certain matter-of-factness, a kind of clarity because I had searched for something elementary, but this increasingly disappeared—not clarity, hopefully—but the goal itself became something else, a spiritual goal that was not least due to the beginning of the war and Nazism's negative impact.

THE SYMPHONY IS DEAD

When you talk about the atmosphere among composers at that time, the two camps, and the easy exchange of ideas, I am reminded of a certain article in Dansk Musik Tidsskrift *from 1940 in which you have a discussion with Knudåge Riisager. Let me read your questioning reply to his statements.*

> You write, 'The symphony is dead', but I have to ask anyway: What is dead? What do we understand today by the concept of a symphony? Do you mean by a symphony a work for orchestra with a cyclical form divided into parts, with a principal movement in the so-called sonata form, with special tempo designations and development, and a more-or-less major-minor tonal melody and harmony, that is, a classic-romantic symphony?

When I read that, I have the feeling that you were at work on your own symphonic development and therefore felt a bit offended that there was suddenly a colleague who was declaring the symphony dead. Was this exchange of ideas part of the development of your own symphonic language?

Yes. The discussion about whether the symphony as a principle was alive or dead was important to me at that time because I was concentrating on the concept of the symphony. I took an interest in Riisager's article. I understood very well that from Riisager's point of view, music was determined by clear norms, and these could not be symphonic in the real understanding of the word. There couldn't be any deep conflict or strong background in this music, though there could be a very nice musical development. Therefore I thought that it was only an aesthetic difference. My view was that the symphony was alive, not in its old form, but in a steadily- and perpetually-renewed form. This is what you can see today, for the young and younger composers are still writing symphonies. So, in that sense one can say that the symphony is still alive.

Can you describe in more detail the difference between your music at that time and the music of Riisager, Tarp and Nielsen?

Photo: Vagn Holmboe (Rúni Brattaberg).

Yes, in just a few words: I am from Jylland (Jutland). You have an entirely different outlook if you have roots in Jylland than if you are from Fyn (Funen) or from Sjælland (Sealand). I very much like both the Sjælland attitude with its fine shades of sentiment as found in the music of Gade, for instance, and the one typical of Fyn, as found in Carl Nielsen's music. The characteristics of Jylland are something different again. One reason is that there is a greater, what shall I say, I won't say 'seriousness' for there is certainly seriousness in Nielsen's and Gade's music, but, in my case, an urge to go beyond what you find in their music.

At that time you were affectionately called the 'Danish Parsifal'. There is something stern and pure about your music and perhaps also your life, meaning your life-style. Do you agree with this characterization?

Well Ok. It is a little bit of a cliché but it is close enough to the truth when you think about it. I actually look for—I looked for, anyway—something very basic on which to build my music. That means I would not, for my life, give up melody as a chief principle. For me, it belongs to the primal core of music. I am well aware that rhythm came before melody—a million years before possibly—but for me music's ability to sing, and to communicate something is decisive. A single tone can be a melody.

FIRST STRING QUARTET

If we look at the formal structure there is no trace of Germanic formal structure, nor Italian, nor for that matter, Russian. I have the feeling that we would need to go to an entirely different place, that is, Arabia. You said once that as a young man you wanted to study Arabic music and that you got in touch with the researcher Gottfried Skjerne. You wanted to learn all the tonalities and the entire background of Arabic music. When I hear, for example, your First String Quartet, I perceive scales that refer to, or somehow recall, the Far East. Can you describe the Arabic element in your music?

For many years, since I was really young—I was interested in the music of the Orient, both the art music and, of course, the folk music. The art music is particularly interesting in certain countries, China, Japan, India and certain Arabic countries and the last was the reason I went to Romania. My goals were not to study Balkan music; I wanted to go via Romania to the Near East, Syria, Lebanon, and on to Egypt, and if I could have afforded to do so, on to Algeria. There were certain forms of music that interested me greatly and that I knew from German phonograph field recordings. I didn't get any farther than Romania because I fell ill with typhus. I survived but I had to turn around and go back home. Therefore I had to make do with the insight that I got from Balkan music.

With respect to the First String Quartet being affected by foreign sounds, maybe that's correct. I haven't thought of it before, but perhaps the sound has something Indian about it. The first movement begins with a long solo that is then developed and corresponds rather closely to the Arabic *taxim*, or sometimes *simbesrim*. These are quite rare forms of instrumental music. The *simbesrim* is found mostly in Algeria, it can last 2-3 hours. A *taxim* is a prelude to a song or a piece of music, or just a prelude to itself, so to speak. The long viola solo in the opening is actually close to the principle of the *taxim*. I hadn't thought about it until now.

I thought of an Indian raga when I heard it. There is a foreign ornamental quality in the melody, and at the same time a search for balance. If a melody goes high, it is balanced with something that descends. It seems to me that two qualities co-exist, an inspiration from foreign melody that I find unique in Danish music and a search for balance. Can you relate to that summation?

It is difficult to comment on one's own music except to say that it comes forth when you dig deep in yourself. Obviously my music has a physical basis, including my knowledge of American, Asiatic and African musics, which is quite comprehensive. This knowledge will of necessity have an impact on me and must collide with my own nature that is neither Asiatic nor American. What makes music worthwhile is the interplay between that which comes out of your soul and those things you hear from the outside — the latter disappear again, but they leave their impact. For all I know, I have very seldom quoted folk music or any other music, except for some really short verses of Gregorian chant and one Croatian folk ballad — only one verse to give just the right character to the appropriate place. Otherwise, the music itself is different.

Would you say that the First String Quartet is an homage to Bartók? Bartók's Sixth String Quartet also begins with a long viola solo.

My First String Quartet is very likely influenced by Bartók's work, for his set of six quartets are, in my opinion, a major monument in the history of the string quartet. As for my quartet I see in my notebook that it is composed *In memoriam Béla Bartók*. However, I see that the dedication doesn't appear in the score.

No, but it is entered in your notes from 1949. Specifically, one hears the reference to Bartók in the uneven metres and rhythms, 3+3+2.

The music does not stem directly from Bartók but it is parallel, you could say, for I was familiar with this kind of expression before I became acquainted with Bartók's music. I knew about the free rhythm and I knew about the free tonality—we may call it modality—and was aware that music couldn't be forced into 4/4 or 3/4 time. A bar in 7/8 can be a liberation, that was what I was looking for, or, to put it better: among other things, in folk music I found a liberation typically based on dance steps. That made it possible for me to be free rhythmically and played a certain role—admittedly a diminishing one—because the melodic element became more and more compelling.

Let's talk about the development of form in the First String Quartet. It is very difficult to fit the work into a classical form—sonata form, or other variation forms we know about. We could call it organic composition: the music develops like a plant that grows, things are derived from each other. This kind of composition results in repetition of material as well as development of material, but it doesn't lead to new, earth-shaking ideas. How do you yourself understand this form of musical development?

It has always been very important to me that music unfolds organically. The music of the classical masters can sometimes be a little four-square because of specific formal criteria. For me it was crucial that music develop independently of what happened tonally, melodically and rhythmically: one aspect should relate directly to the other, positively or negatively. In that way an organic form ought to emerge and I have found this process confirmed in nature innumerable times.

It has been inspiring for me to look at nature and not just say, 'Oh isn't it beautiful', but rather to follow the growth cycles and see how plants live and die, how life comes to an end and how an organism develops. Often it is just simply hard to understand how a little seed can become a huge fir tree; it's beyond our comprehension. Even the special ways in which things grow interest me. I believe that it has influenced me. Not the picturesque, but nature's inner strengths.

When foreigners hear music from Nordic countries they often expect lyricism à la Grieg and Sibelius, and they find this in your music, too. It's difficult to say how this relates to purely musical elements because it's risky to draw those kinds of parallels. But sometimes I hear the austerity that we spoke about as a consequence of your use of fourths. For example the first movement of the Sixth Symphony consists of almost nothing but fourths, and they are also found in the First String Quartet. Brahms's and Strauss's musical world is based on thirds, yours on fourths. This interval introduces a kind of stoic nobility, a dignified music. Could you explain what the interval of the fourth means to you?

It has something of a double meaning. On the one hand I am worried about it, but on the other there is something life-giving about a fourth because it's free; it's independent. A third is dependent and has associations with a triad, but a fourth is so far away from the tonic, that is, it has a freer relationship to its surroundings. The interval of the fourth itself has, at certain times, been immeasurably important to me. It was a major element in the Sixth Symphony. And I don't really know why, only that it took years to sketch that work.

From the end of the 1940s to your most recent works—that is, the choral works—I find consistent use of fourths. What I see and hear is a persistent investigation of a compositional tradition that dismisses the notion of an avant garde rupture. It is one long evolution. Am I right to say that there has been no break in your way of thinking since about the time of the First String Quartet?

As far as I can remember, there has been no 'break' in my music, but during certain periods there have been eruptive developments of one aspect or another. As far as the concept of the interval of the fourth is concerned, it's still important to me today. Although theoretical things don't interest me much, I am just about ready to compose a piece in which the fourth plays an indirect role. Now that we speak about it, I realize that the fourth remains something of a 'mysterium' for me.

APOLLO AND DIONYSUS

Let's go back to the period around 1949-1950, when the First String Quartet was composed. A glance at your worklist reveals that it was a very productive period in your life. There are many new works. In the string quartets one can trace the development, particularly in the rhythm because of your interest in Balkan music. During this period you seem to have found your own voice as a composer. Is it possible to say that with the First String Quartet Holmboe emerged as a composer with his own personality?

Yes, it's hardly a mistake to say that my First String Quartet marked a kind of turning point, or a starting point. I was prepared for it, but suddenly my composing broke free in those years. Yes, it must have been 1949. I composed a number of works all at once, in the course of a short period of time. It was unusual, I normally give myself a fair amount of time to compose a piece. Specific categories of compositions usually require that a set amount of time be devoted to them. For example, it usually takes nine months to compose a symphony. But a quartet, which usually takes about three months, at that point took hardly a month to finish. Speed has nothing to do with the quality of the music or the kind of piece, we are simply talking about a sudden tidal wave that came rushing through.

Your work must have been like some kind of ecstasy then.

Yes that's what it was, and that's what it still is, but it takes longer to compose now. After about half an hour I get out of breath and have to go and rest for about an hour. Then I can get down to it again.

Could you talk a bit about the music scene in those years? It must have been stimulating, since you were able to be so productive. Presumably there were ties to the works from the war years, but it seems as if a whole new Vagn Holmboe emerged about 1949.

I don't think that trends in music played a role at that time because everything was stagnant; even in 1949 things hadn't fully recovered. I think that I was motivated by inner causes. I came to a point in my personal development which made it necessary to write music, and, you could almost say, another kind of music. I had been getting ready for it for a long time.

In 1940 you won a prize for the Second Symphony and you also had the kind of success that led to performances. The inauguration of the Danish Radio Concert Hall in 1945 was celebrated by a premiere of your symphony.

Yes. I composed some symphonies before the quartet. The Second Symphony was premiered in a competition, and the same happened with the next one. It was the Fourth that was premiered for the opening of the Radio Hall after the war. But the real breakthrough came only after the war. One is not even aware of such developments oneself because one experiences music on different levels. One can comprehend it analytically, technically, and formally by analysing it bar for bar; the lowest level is the subliminal one where you have eruptions of the mind. Between the two is the level where these eruptions must be brought within artistic boundaries, which means toning down the excessively wild parts. The mind itself wants to gesticulate too much—like an actor who flails his arms around so that everything turns into a farce. It's the same in music: if you gesticulate too much and lack an apollonian restraint, then it goes awry. There has to be a balance between these three levels. The composer may be indifferent about analysis; it's not inherent to composing and I don't think that composing should start with analysis either. But the other two levels, the wild one—you could call it the dionysian—and the re-straining, or the restrained one—the apollonian—are important.

These are the ideas you wrote about in Mellemspil *(Interlude), your book that was published in 1961. For you, music starts with looking for the balance between the apollonian and the dionysian; the two poles should be balanced at all times.*

The apollonian runs the risk of easily becoming too academic, boring and formally over-correct. The dionysian runs the risk of turning completely wild.

The right balance between the two will force the dionysian to stay within limits and make the apollonian come down off its pedestal. In the best cases, you find a good balance which may swing out into either side.

And then there is the melodic element that you have never deserted. Since you discovered Balkan folk music you use simple, but intensely emotional melodies and contain them within your own framework. Would it be appropriate to describe this as controlled ecstasy?

In certain circumstances you might. Violence can be mastered by the intellect and balance achieved that way. But that balance is as fine as a strand of hair. It can swing up and down—that is, up into the academic and down into the primitive. But between the two lies a wealth of possibilities. It is important for me that melody is allowed a predominant part. Not that there has to be a pretty melody or anything like that—it isn't actual melodies that I am seeking. It is rather that a note should sing from inside the work, and it's unimportant if it is one note, or twenty, or a whole work. It needs to be able to sing. Even in the most technically complex jungle you should be able to tell that the music behind sings and even if no melody stands out, it's there anyway. That's my goal—my unattainable goal!

FLEXIBLE THEMES

Let us look closely at the melodic element in the First String Quartet. The first theme immediately illustrates that themes in your work have two aspects. They may be used in passages that are loud, strong and intense. Molto intensivo, *it says in the score. But the same theme has another side so that it may function in a pianissimo lyrical passage. You can hear this in several places in the First Quartet; the themes are very flexible.*

What has interested me is not so much the melodies, but the melodic quality that allows for both a powerful dynamic development and for motivic material that lends itself to a more pastoral, or softer, character. It is this that makes these themes, or motifs, flexible—so that they can transform themselves and change—with the flow of the music.

In the second movement of the First Quartet, you maintain a mood, almost a Buddhistic emptiness, an attention to nothingness. We are not on the way to any particular place. We might think, 'Now a main theme is about to appear', but it doesn't come. It is like a contemplative, inward-searching, almost meditative experience. Is this the way it was intended?

The second movement of my First Quartet is rather special as it is introduced with a sound image that has a melodic aspect, but doesn't go anywhere. Suddenly it is transformed into a number of variations or variation-like segments, which are very unruly but which are somehow kept under cover, almost deviously so. The movement is quite strange; I cannot analyse it myself, it's not possible. I have the feeling that this is something I never did before and never will do again.

What do you mean?

It means that this special connection won't be repeated again in my work. I mean, this ennobled calm at the beginning, over a deep bass note in the cello, and then, a melodic turn in the upper strings followed by the more rapid and intense parts won't be encountered again. This constellation has a very special formation here but not one that I could imagine doing today.

A survey of your work over the last 25 years reveals a period in which your music enjoyed less favour than it does today. Right now there is a great interest in what's melodic, recognizable and intense. There was, however, a rather long period when the younger generation took over, ca. the 1960s, when younger composers following new trends held new aesthetic points of view. What was it like to observe that developments were taking a different direction from yours?

It seems that when composers are between forty and fifty they are considered derelicts, but they compose all the same. Bach did that, but he was already definitely pushed to the side by Telemann, Matthesson, Stamitz, and so on, because of the advent of a new style. The rococo came forth and pushed aside the old baroque style. It affected music, architecture, everything. The same thing happens in every era. When a composer is a certain age, a new generation comes along and it has just as much right as the older one had.

For my part, it was very clear that in the course of the 1950s the next generation was ready to take over. I couldn't follow where they wanted to go in the 1960s. Well, I could follow, but I couldn't really do anything in that direction and it is clear that at that point my music became less conspicuous in the concert halls, but I have never noticed any lack of attention. I have never felt that I was pushed to the side or stepped on. In any case I have continued to compose and I was just as happy, because for me it was more important to get things composed than it was to get them performed.

The new generation has my full approval; they did the same that we did in the 1930s when we broke with the previous generation. We looked up to them in the beginning but then distanced ourselves from them because we thought that we had to move on. Our students or the next generation have to move, and they will. They have to distance themselves from us, that is, Koppel and me—unfortunately Syberg is no longer alive—and Niels Viggo

Bentzon, he also belongs to our generation. I have always felt it was natural, like when you see a beech tree grow. Everything follows a necessary order and the tree's leaves wither away to make room for the new leaves that will come next year. I am pleased when the younger composers succeed.

Are you thinking of anyone in particular?

I can't remember names very well, but I listen to their music now and then. I don't want to name anybody in particular because I might forget someone who should be mentioned.

Epilogue

You have been a collector throughout your long life; some of your collections have been used in your music. Your transcriptions of street cries, which have been published in book form, seem far removed from your work as a composer.

When I came to Copenhagen, I lived in Østerbro. It was really amusing to write down the street cries there. I took down thirty or forty of them. I was used to transcribing and would really have liked to have been an ethnomusicologist, only I couldn't stop composing. I took the mornings off and cycled around the city as much as possible. Later I cycled from town to town, to Sorø, Slagelse and around Jylland.

Can you remember some of them still?

Yes, let's see if I can remember them — (sings/shouts) 'Cauliflower, cauliflower . . .', 'Straaaaw, here are straaaa', 'cauliflower, cauliflower, cauliflower'. You turn on the interval of the second and on the third — that's central to all music, even in Cambodia, South America and Africa.

What are you working on at the moment?

Just now I am working on a kind of concerto grosso for string quartet and string orchestra. I am having some problems with those famous fourths — I am trying to combine them with trills and such like. In short, this new work is something quite technical, though it doesn't have a technical cause but a musical one. I would really like to have the music shimmer a bit in some places. I am happy that I can still compose.

And in what direction is your music moving just now? Is it a new direction or a continuation of your work in recent years?

I always believe that it will be a continuation. I don't believe in a break because that is just an intellectual exercise. As far as I am concerned, music has always been continuous, something that grows.

'Mit uopnåelige mål: Samtale med Vagn Holmboe', *Dansk Musik Tidsskrift* 71, 2 (1996/97): 219–223.

Per Nørgård

A Composer on Inclined Planes

You once dreamed about a music that didn't exist, something completely different, a vision, a secret that you carried around for many years. It seemed that music was lacking something and you thought there was a need to add to it.

Yes, add, not just a little 'chip', but something with a definite dimension. I had a naïve, yet obviously real feeling that the potential of music was much greater than anyone dreamt. I always reacted against the kind of thinking that defined certain cultural entities and reduced life to a 'nothing but' formula simply because we had entered a post-religious period and were in a rational frame of mind. I felt entirely separate from my contemporaries when it came to accepting the prejudices of our times. I could not subscribe to the nihilism that was taken for granted those days. I had the feeling that there was a potential in music that was unexplored and was wholly fantastic.

So, at an early age I imagined a completely different music—one in which every single note was actually a part of several melodies so that in a way the notes in a large infinite whole created one melody. All melodies actually emerged from the same enormous stream, a kind of illusion of a line that in fact was only a point, but one that continuously showed new facets of itself. I imagined a music woven from one such note that seemed to change frequency. It was a vision I didn't dare to talk about to anyone.

Actually I had a recurring nightmare that left me shaken the morning after. I knew only that *something had happened*. I am in a house high on a mountain, actually a house by Jørn Utzon—at the time I didn't know any of Utzon's buildings, but your description of your stay in the Utzon house on Mallorca reminded me of that one. Deep casings, nothing on the white walls, a glowing light from the sun and the bright blue sky outside. I am alone. There are two rooms and I am in one that is empty. I go into the other and there is a large black grand piano. As I go toward it I know that that is my destiny, and then, it ends. Everything is possible in a dream, so it sounds inconsequential when I describe it. There was a particular *illumination*—some supernatural colours and light. It wasn't ordinary at all, more like some sort of torch. I was fourteen years old. The dream recurred a year later. Exactly the same. The same room. I was there, and went to the adjacent room, and there was the grand piano. I swear that it was like a film clip that was replayed. Not only did the light burn just as strongly, but it was exactly the same dream again! So in one way or another it must have confirmed my belief that I was a composer.

Did you consider it a dream of destiny at the time?

Distinctly . . . you *are* moved by such a thing, and I have not had one like it since. It undoubtedly influenced me to become more self-confident.

But then your vision about the single melody that contains all other melodies might make one think of the 'melody' you later discovered and described as the 'infinite row'. The similarity is striking . . .

That has also occurred to me. It seems that I discovered it in the course of a development that, in fact, can be traced from work to work, starting with *Constellations* (1958), and especially with the *Studies for piano* (1959). This development turned out to be the beginning of the infinite row. That is the 'upshot' of the dream I had as a seventeen-year-old, but it was ridiculously utopian! Any sensible person would have advised me to be quiet and to become a carpenter.

If we were to trace your development from the time you were about seventeen years old and decided to take up music, until about the time of your debut concert, we would notice something that was present from the very beginning: you have always moved about on 'inclined planes'—so to speak—and have described your situation as being on a slippery slope. Just as soon as you have established one style, you break with it and find a new one.

Yes, that's right. On one hand you may say that unlimited irresponsibility is the hallmark of such a person: 'He will never be loyal to anything'. On the other, you might find that it's being faithful to *restlessness* that has driven me.

The former is closer to how we used to think of artists, for example, from the generation before yours. With composers like Holmboe and Koppel, the person was the style. These composers discovered one path and stuck to it.

I thought about music that way when I began to study with Holmboe. He had a huge influence on me. And aside from the man's status as a composer it was a shock for a Nørrebro boy like me—a draper's son—to enter the world of Vagn and Meta in their home in Holstebrogade, but more obviously so in Ramløse. Everything was so much grander than at my parents' home on Greve Strand, which is more like a small-scale merchants' Bellevue. All of Køge Landevej (the area of Greve Strand, *ed.*) is a kind of Klondike. It was already like that. I have a deep respect for the world of the draper, there isn't a hint of irony in what I say. On the contrary, the more perspective I get on my parents' life, the more I admire what they achieved. But at that time it was awfully close to me and it wasn't *my* life. That I had to hold onto. 'You won't try to determine my life'; they didn't either. They accepted the fact that I made my drawings and that I did nothing special at school. But then to encounter Holmboe, Ramløse and the magnificent scenery around Arresø influenced me enormously. It was like coming home in a way. Home to myself. To what I had inside.

It was almost as though you were accepted into Holmboe's family?

Yes, yes. The incredible warmth. It was truly a revelation to me from the start. It confirmed the dream. I showed Holmboe my first piece, which was definitely not in the 'Nordic style'. It was called Concerto in G Major (1949) for piano solo—not for piano and orchestra. I don't know why I gave the piece this swaggering title, but I had an idea about the concept of the 'concerto' and something that 'concerted'. It actually could be a piano solo, yes, why not? Bach's *Italian Concerto* was a shining example for me in my early youth. But after looking at the notes for the Concerto in G Major Holmboe turned his head, looked at me and said, 'I am surprised'. At that moment a connection was made between the serious side of my dream and my play world. Because actually I had just only *played* at being a composer. It was a typical play world. It was as if I was seeking out an older composer—that's what Stravinsky wrote that *he* had done, so then I should do it too, isn't that so? But from the moment that Holmboe recognized that there was something going on in me, it was as though I was seized by the collar. As you can see, it changed my life.

The impact of Holmboe's world and all his seriousness naturally meant that I both started to smoke a pipe like Vagn, and began to appreciate the Nordic light over the hills of Ramløse. It also meant that I was sensitized and felt a connection with Sibelius when I heard Holmboe's *Sinfonia Borealis* (1951–52). Holmboe didn't talk about Sibelius, either positively or negatively. It has struck me many times that no-one talked about Sibelius then. What in the world made me want to study Sibelius' music when I heard Holmboe's *Sinfonia Borealis*? I also wrote to Sibelius about an organic approach to composition. I still believe in composing that way; I don't make non-linear compositions. I have been true to that, so to speak. If you look more closely at that period of my development you will see that I wasn't yet traversing these different planes, but if you look back a little farther I was actually on one *before* I started working with Holmboe. If you look at the pieces that are unpublished—and shall remain so—for example, the Concerto in G Major and the Concertino no. 2 for piano solo (1950) that Elvi Henriksen performed,

then you can see that already there is something special going on. At that time I was preoccupied with reading Uwspenski's *Tertium organum*, which treats time as the fourth dimension and illustrates it with the example of a horse that rears as it comes up over the top of the hill because it is disturbed by a tree that grows in front of it, although we know that this is the effect of perspective, etc. I was preoccupied by the infinite row—which I hadn't yet discovered! For example, all phenomena are sort of porous, vibrating. Vibration is actually the central word for me. When I met Elvi Henriksen—I will never forget it, she is a really pretty woman—she said: 'There is something strange in your music, it's like it has something new to do with time'. You know, that made me think, 'That's just right, now my music is getting somewhere'. And then it wasn't going anywhere at all. Just look at the reviews of my debut concert: 'Mysteriously unclear', wrote Walther Zacharias. 'A lot of notes that don't make sense to the ear', wrote Jørgen Jersild. 'In any case, the young composer has made it impossible for his next work to go backwards', wrote Poul Rovsing Olsen. The only one who really wrote that there was something unusual going on was Frede Schandorff Pedersen from *Politiken*. So that was my beginning.

If you look at my works from that period—let's take the Concertino as an example—you will notice that they are completely foreign to the Danish tradition. It doesn't fit into the Nordic tradition, it's not in a Nordic style at all. It's troublesome music. And entirely unsuccessful. Holmboe noticed my extreme disappointment. It is quite a shock for a young composer—I got shingles on my back the week of the performance. Besides, it turned out later that Elvi Henriksen had also read *Tertium organum*, so it wasn't strange that she talked about 'time' in my music.

Before your debut on the 17th of January 1956 you weren't exactly an unknown quantity. Several of your works had been premiered, not least at the Nordic Music Days, where your suite for flute was on the programme. At that point in time you were absorbed by the Nordic idea: you were a Holmboe-fan, and you had even corresponded with Sibelius.

Sibelius' music was a new discovery for me—something that I haven't got over to this day. You find places in Sibelius, for example in the Seventh Symphony, where it is almost impossible to analyse what actually *is taking place*. There is some form of heterophony that isn't to be found in other composers' works: a tympani part can just suddenly behave completely independently in terms of rhythm. Sibelius' entire relationship to rhythm is very, very lively and unusual.

Photo: Per Nørgård.

Right after your debut in 1956 you got married and travelled to Paris to study with Nadia Boulanger.

I travelled to Paris—and idiot that I am—I didn't supplement my studies with Messiaen's courses at the Conservatoire, but remained with Nadia Boulanger and went to the concerts of the Domaine Musicale. I despised all the superficiality of the fur-clad ladies in dark glasses who embraced each other. Boulez was there too. It made me sick to my stomach. Remember, I was a healthy Nordic fellow! So when Nadia said, 'Mr Nørgård, your horizons are very narrow', I was deeply wounded, but I have been able to see since then that she was absolutely right. But it was an alien world. Listening to the pianist David Tudor knocking on the underside of the grand piano didn't provoke much more than a shrug of the shoulders from me. It was a style I couldn't relate to at all. Paris was considered a centre. Later, as everyone knows, our field of vision expanded so that today we have no world centre, but deal with multiple centres. The North today is just as good a centre as Paris or Vienna. You can't say that what goes on in Paris is 'finer' than that which takes place in the North, even though they still think so in the city of cities. Now we also know more about Vienna at the turn of the century. That was a truly decadent city—beyond all others. The fantastic music that Schoenberg developed there is admirable in its radicalism and its independence from the imperial music that surrounded him, but that was different from the situation in Copenhagen. Why should Copenhagen at that time suddenly produce music like Schoenberg's? That would have been completely absurd. Carl Nielsen's reaction was, yes, in a way, as radical as it could have been, just like Sibelius's reaction in Finland. Why expect everyone to go along with an 'experiment in the collapse of the world' as Karl Kraus described the situation in Vienna? So when I arrived in Paris, the Domaine Musicale didn't interest me at all. I actually kept a distance from Nadia Boulanger's aesthetic. I didn't admire everything she stood for. She had Poulenc and Jean Français in her studio and, although we were on speaking terms, I didn't care for their music. Inwardly I felt like an emigrant. I had a project in Paris, but that project assumed that music should express the Nordic character and the authenticity of the 'Sibelius-experience'.

Did Nadia Boulanger help you to develop further and work with your discovery of Sibelius's music?

No. We discussed Sibelius. I tried to introduce his Sixth Symphony to her, but she was just as far removed from that as I was from Paris. She had quite a cool attitude towards him. She was generally very critical. For example, she couldn´t relate to Boulez. She said, 'Boulez may have a language, but I don't recognize it'. I believe she was plunged into a deep crisis when Stravinsky began to use serialism. At our Wednesday classes we usually sang through different works and then there came the terrible moment when she distributed *Canticum Sacrum* and a young scandalized 'Boulanger-ist' stood up and said, 'Mademoiselle, I have discovered that the melody we have just sung contains twelve tones'. She became very agitated. I don't remember at all how she explained it, but suddenly, everything that she had preached for years about the blessings of diatonic music didn't hold up any more. But that didn't interest me very deeply—this emigrant from the North. What did I compose in Paris? *Sångar från aftonland* (1956) for alto voice and five instruments! To texts by Pär Lagerkvist. That was my main work while I was Paris. So, I don't know . . . I hardly made the most of the situation . . .

If you made something of it then it might have been more in the area of craftsmanship, from a technical point of view. For example, you had to be proficient at the piano?

Yes. It was marvelous to go through the 'hard' school. And Nadia was a marvellous reader of my music. Her ability to point out inconsistencies was unique and impressed me deeply. Her merciless dissection of, for example, the piano piece, *Trifoglio*, made me revise the music totally. She read the piece through and said, 'I'm a little disconcerted'. She said it because she thought that I expressed *goodbye* very beautifully in my music: 'You say a very beautiful goodbye. I find your way of saying goodbye very moving. But you can't go on saying goodbye forever'! Now that is an awful criticism, because it indicates that a piece of music revels in a single mood and never moves out of it. I learned a lot, like simply trying to be concise in a piece of music. However, stylistically it hardly influenced me at all. But to turn back to your idea of 'inclined planes': I can actually point out things that I think have always been part of my music. For a time I worked within the Nordic style with its particular expectations, for example, modality, triadic chords, rhythmic ideas, etc., a whole string of expectations. But I broke with it around 1960. There was an impulse from the beginning, but it was held in check in the Nordic world of the 1950s.

Now that you are back to the issue of 'inclined planes' and your early frustrations, I would like to return to Frede Schandorff Pedersen, Politiken's *reviewer, who wrote about your debut concert in 1959:* '[T]houghtfulness *and* emotions *dominated what is actually said in the pitches. It is as if one should continually recognize a meaning that isn't obviously projected by the composition, from the life of the notes'. And further on: 'His first string quartet demonstrates an even, exceptionally well-founded craftsmanship, a large creative talent. Why does he then strike out to a place where anybody would be out of his depth? His future development perhaps will provide the answer'. Is what Frede Schandorff Pedersen wrote about the twenty-three-year-old Nørgård due to your wish to create a fruitful kind of confusion?*

Yes. It can be said very simply: I want ambiguity. I have come up with an all-purpose, general term for this simply because I haven't found anything better: interference. Interference, or ambiguity in the broadest sense of the word, became apparent even as far back as when I made my *Tecnis* (the composer's home-made comic strips with musical accompaniment, *ed.*). I can remember that I found the right term when I had my brother swear to our goal in life: to confuse as many as possible as much as possible. At that time it was with our Tecnis. My brother wrote the texts and I made the drawings and the music. And there was no denying that we confused the members of the family with these strange worlds. So happenings were a part of my private life—before 'happenings' existed. There is that ambiguity again. To introduce another view into something that someone else believes they 'understand'. That is still my mission. It has never been my intention to compose loose or floating forms. For example, I have never been attracted to impressionism, but rather to very precise forms that *contradict* each other while each is compellingly necessary! I can remember that I was interviewed by Morton Feldman in Holland at a festival in Middleburg in 1986. He apparently didn't know what our topic was to be, but he had read something about my music and the Nordic component and he said, 'I am a New York Jew and this thing here with the Nordic—now that I have met you and can easily see that you actually look very Nordic—could we talk about that?' No, not really, I thought. So I suggested that we could talk about something which he had said and which I had once read and that I found quite wonderful, which was, 'If I work with the notes, trying to do something special with them, and then I hear a weak but clear voice calling, "*Help!*" then I know that I should stop trying'. So I said that for me it is precisely the opposite. 'I work with them at length—until I hear a loud and clear "Help!"' And that is my mission: to create concise forms that provide completely clear suggestions. That was already evident in the piece I wrote as a seventeen-year-old: I create a 'gestalt' but it is somehow refuted by something else. Perhaps there is a bit of Zen Buddhism there. In Zen Buddhism there are three opposing basic principles: stillness, shock and paradox. If you chose paradox as the basic norm, a short-circuit makes it possible for you to enter life for a moment and realize that it is incredibly strange. I have always felt that we undervalue what we are in the middle of and I hate it when someone explains 'what it is we are in the middle of'. There is *always* more to it than we think; that is something I have 'known' from the beginning. Don't ask me how I knew it. I don't know it any more than I know where that dream came from. But I do think that this knowledge is my firm foundation.

Now that I am this old I can *see* these inclined planes and how they developed. It was a long time before I found the word for it—I believe it was after the Wölfli-period. It was also confusing for me: what in the world was happening? I'm thinking about the shift at the time that I ventured into the realm of the psychedelic at the end of the 1960s. I composed *Rejse ind i den gyldne skærm* (Voyage into the Golden Screen, 1968), *Den fortryllede skov* (The Enchanted Forest, 1968), *Grooving* (1967–68), which were the kind of 'psychedelic works' in which you enter some different kinds of infinite patterns. Then, after the Second Symphony it became necessary to find a rhythm that could articulate the infinite melody. The Second Symphony, well, simply flows in motoric quavers. So I followed a sober plan: music that moves in quavers all the time can hardly be the music of the future. But initially, the infinite row had to be expressed in terms of quavers—or, crotchets, minims, etc.—and when I composed *Rejse ind i gyldne skærm* with the first presentation of the infinite row, I thought it sounded so exciting that I had to make a whole symphony out of it. This was the Second Symphony (1970) and that was interesting enough. But I knew as I said before that I couldn't stay in that place. I have always thought in terms of Koestler's open hierarchies where each level is as important as another. I think in terms of whole forms that are themselves enclosed in whole forms of different kinds—and in this context I analytically explored the new possibilities inherent in the proportions of the golden section in order to avoid the persistent motoric movement of the previous works. It was simply necessary to think in new ways, and it may be that the only possible result was the Third Symphony.

So, suddenly I found myself in the hierarchical world of the Third Symphony and it was more appealing to audiences than the Second. Following the success of the Third a friend asked me, 'So now you have arrived at your goal?' to which I answered, 'You have understood nothing'. It was probably then that I started to realize the significance of these inclined planes in my life. Every time I thought to myself that I had arrived at a place from which I could continue, the thought made me kind of claustrophobic. Indeed, you could achieve an endless number of pieces by just moving the 'bricks' of the Third Symphony around. Perhaps even compose another nine symphonies. I suppose at that moment I realized that if I did that, I would give up my basic mission, that is, ambiguity. I am reminded of a time at the Warsaw Autumn Festival when *Luna* was performed—a work that for *me* is full of interference and paradox. It was a success and people came and congratulated me. However, I was bothered by all the friendly remarks about what 'beautiful nocturnal music' it was. So I simply left during the intermission, went to a bar and drank one whiskey after another until I fell into a kind of crystal clear state. Suddenly I realized that I was obviously depressed, because in spite of my efforts my work was apparently still misunderstood: it seemed completely 'comprehensible'. I had to radicalize my musical language!

Let us go back to the transition from the 1950s to the 1960s, to the shift in Danish music that has been described as a radical step in aesthetics and style. For you it didn't really constitute a break in spite of what is frequently claimed. Much has been said about the famous trip to the ISCM World Music Days in Cologne where some of you heard Pli selon pli, Kontakte *and* Anagramma. *Presumably that was a shock for several Danish composers of your generation. But a look at your works shows that the new sounds were not so completely new to you. You were in Rome at the ISCM World Music Days the year before in 1959 and you had composed in a serial style before 1960.*

Yes. In Rome I realized that it wasn't as simple as I had believed it to be when I was in Paris, and I gained many strong impressions, often from the performances of works by completely unknown composers. I could hear that here was something that I couldn't attain with my technique. It was enervating and fascinating. When I got home from Rome I wrote a feuilleton that was published in *Politiken*. This article clearly shows my vacillating position. The older Danish composers and musicians didn't like it. When one heard something like this it was quite normal and 'correct' to be revolted.

Even though Ib Nørholm composed his Tabeltrio *and Pelle Gudmundsen-Holmgreen composed* Chronos *after the trip to Cologne in 1960, the long-term reaction was to adopt an extreme form of simplicity that later became known as the 'new simplicity'. The Danes created a kind of opposition or answer to the complexity that emerged from Darmstadt, among other places.*

Yes. Not many let themselves be caught up in the sounds coming from the south. We were fascinated when Stockhausen produced his new *Zeitmazse* in the 1960s. But it wasn't really what we had been searching for.

But on the other hand, I don't get the impression that you unequivocally separated yourself from that world. You allowed yourself be inspired and consciously took structure into account.

Yes, for us the new ideas worked like a colossal x-ray—almost like an x-ray of the Danish tradition. And we became unpopular, for example, for criticizing the Danish milieu in our reviews. A new piano concerto by Koppel—as stated in my review—was a farewell from the old world. We certainly had the feeling that it couldn't continue like that, but it wasn't that we had come up with a new goal, in imitation—*so ein Ding müssen wir auch haben*—it wasn't that: it was the *soul-searching* that was important.

But that also meant a confrontation with the institutions, which, in your case, meant that you had to give up your position at the The Royal Danish Academy of Music in Copenhagen.

I was employed at both the academies in Copenhagen and Odense. In addition, I was working as a reviewer, which was quite demanding, and I needed to continue composing. But I had been doing this from the end of the 1950s and into the 1960s. What was strangely new was that I attracted the young students, all the composition students. None of them went to the older, established composers who were also composition teachers. I had Fuzzy (Jens Wilhelm Pedersen), Erik Norby, Ingolf Gabold and Svend Nielsen. They all asked for me because they didn't want to work with the older teachers. I realized that the instruction that I had had previously was—to put it politely—incomplete. I mean: to drink tea and sit and chat generally about music—yes, fine. But there should obviously have been *seminars*. Here take this, listen to it, 'What in the world did Schoenberg do?' We heard nothing about him. They maintained a post-Nielsen aesthetic, and if you asked about Webern you were shown a score from which anyone could see that 'there were holes in his head'. So, I wanted to try to get beyond that. It was against this background that the confrontations arose, and with that, the shift of the 1960s. We were no longer willing to accept older people's versions of things. Now we wanted to find out for ourselves. This didn't please the majority of the theory staff, which, aside from me, consisted of older men. Some were more 'quiet' than others, but the more vociferous of them said, for example, 'Damn, now we will have to think things over before we let things like "workshop concerts" get going!' Basic things such as the workshop concerts that I wanted to establish in Copenhagen—and which I started in Århus as soon as I moved my teaching there—were stopped every time by the group. And when figures such as Ligeti or Lutosławski came to Copenhagen, *I* had to hire them—the Academy 'had no money for such things'. My students contributed to paying their costs and we simply arranged private seminars. So the tension was already quite intense when the 'Ole Buck affair' set things off.

By referring to the 'Ole Buck affair' you mean the time when young Ole Buck was not accepted in the Academy although he had already demonstrated unusual talent as a composer.

Buck submitted a piece that was one of the best that had ever been written in the history of Danish music, the *Haiku Songs* for soprano and orchestra. He had received the highest evaluation from the expert staff consisting of Holmboe, Høffding and Tage Nielsen. And then Buck was rejected because he couldn't harmonize a chorale melody correctly! I couldn't possibly accept that. I went through all the applications. You should have seen me that spring. I studied them every day. The staff in the office glared at me, but they couldn't forbid me to read them. I made a note of all those who had received a B+ in their main course of study. Every single one was accepted. And yet the one who had received an A- was not. You may have read *Dansk Musik Tidsskrift* from that time when the problems seeped out into the public arena. Out of consideration for Buck, the Ole Buck affair was referred to as 'Case X'. Riisager, who was Director of the Academy, was deeply unhappy about the situation—he was supposedly *for* new music—but he had to comply with his faculty.

So you left the place.

So I left and everything was up in the air for four days and then Tage Nielsen from The Royal Academy of Music in Århus called and said, 'Have you any interest in coming over and working with us as a composition teacher?'

This was in 1965. After the struggle in Copenhagen you entered a very fertile period in Århus.

All my students 'moved' with me to Århus with the result that Danish music spread and became decentralized. That was one consequence. The students became teachers and active composers in Århus, and, later on, in other places in the provinces. It wasn't very long before I suggested that we should have a new music society in Århus. So AUT (Århus Young Composers Society) was established.

Slowly a whole new music scene developed in Århus. When I mentioned the institutional breakup it was because I wanted to reinforce the image of a whole generation supporting a change which encompassed aesthetics, styles and a new mentality.

Yes, definitely. So what happened was the right thing.

We are getting to the 1970s, and newer Danish music begins to become interesting to people other than Danes. The interest grew slowly—particularly in the English-speaking world. In 1974 came John H. Yoell's book, The Nordic Sound: Explorations into the Music of Denmark, Norway, Sweden. *He writes on p. 50 that 'your unpredictability may lead to . . . vaporization in a cloud of mysticism . . . or, perhaps, the numbing paralysis of an identity crisis'. Yoell closes his characterization as follows (p. 172): 'Possible seepage from the psychedelic and rock subcultures adds further complexity to this composer who seems to run in several directions at once'. Here one could say that your tactic of generating confusion succeeded completely. Yoell seems to have been frustrated in his search for a pigeon-hole into which he can put Nørgård's music. He doesn't understand the concept of 'inclined planes'.*

That's right. Yoell predicts that I will end up with a personality disorder or a neurosis, or that I will stop composing. He has the most promising futures planned for me—and I have disappointed him until now. But from what we were talking about, you can easily see that there is no contradiction between what I did in the 1960s and what I was doing before. I continued to compose works in which I used the infinite row as a technique—that was my form of twelve-tone music, so to speak. But from a deeper perspective there was something else that I was looking for. The infinite row is a result of interference-thinking. And I will never forget what, for me, was possibly the most important thing that happened in the 1960s. When I was making the electronic introduction for *Babel* (1965, rev. 1968), I became more and more fascinated with *interference*, simply and purely, physically. That was the first time I really experienced beat-tones and realized their perspectives. So I composed a work that was called *Den fortryllede skov* that completely depends on interference. It was in turn reworked to become the first movement of *Rejse ind i den gyldne skærm*. From that point on interference became more than a concept and appeared in a physical form. Later I can see that it was then, really for the first time, that I was able to pinpoint my interest: ambiguity, or interference, in the broadest meaning of the word.

Earlier in the conversation we reached the Third Symphony and the encouragements you were given to continue composing in the same style. Now that work was a high point in Danish music. The Third Symphony has been referred to as a symphony that formulates a philosophical outlook on life, like Mahler's symphonies.

A 'philosophy of life' symphony? It is possibly that, on one level or another. But it was rather like working with the elements of the golden proportions at the core of what fascinates me. It wasn't as though I wanted to write a symphony that presented a philosophy of life—God save us! It was more as though something *grew*, and because I began to work with the elements in a certain way, it finally became what you might call a 'philosophy of life symphony'.

These elements come together in an all-embracing symphony, you might say.

Perhaps the concept of the all-embracing work amounts to something that can resemble a 'philosophy'. I didn't start with some melodies and their development; from the beginning it was the sound that was at the centre. Truthfully, it is a deeply rational work. I started with sound, with all the overtone series that 'fall down'. It was deeply fascinating for me to work with several overtone series, with ambiguity. The overtone series is a hierarchical phenomenon! Actually it consists of many overtone rows that can be collected into one, which can be shown to be a part of other overtone series, on and on. In the course of the orchestra rehearsals I became convinced that I had a rich material in my hands. I allowed myself to trust my perception that it was just as important as any other sort of technical apparatus, infinite rows, or other things. My respect for perception had become a decisive factor because of my experience with *Fragment VI*, the work that was a winning composition at the Gaudeamus Festival in 1961. All the remarkable things I put into that score couldn't be *heard*! It was a shock for a composer who had always assumed that one should be able to hear what is in the score. It *looks* unbelievably exciting. And I had made an impressive layout, no doubt about that. The Third Symphony was composed a dozen years after this experience and was influenced by my interest in the powers of gestalt psychology and my study of perception, for example, of interference.

Perhaps one could even say that the 'perpetually falling line' in new Danish music began with the overtone rows in your Third Symphony.

At the beginning of the Third Symphony you hear a very high sound—this seems to be the first time in a composition that someone consciously uses the ears' non-linear properties, in order to create difference tones in the bass by putting many dissonances in the treble. So there is a *bzzz* created inside the ear. You've experienced the phenomenon from hearing a piccolo in a concert hall when the conditions are right and the sound gets going? *Bzzz, bzzz*, it goes, right? I thought that was *exciting* and so I made it happen like that in the Third Symphony. So all of that grandiose talk about this 'philosophy of life symphony' can be viewed as a matter of technique. I mean: you can analyse the whole symphony starting with the very exact, precise observation that in the first movement there is a gigantic growth process involving sound, rhythm, melody and so on, spread in the form of an arch. Finish. After that you enter a garden where *detail* is the focus; that's the second movement. Well, it starts very high with a downward run of a series of subharmonics in the minor; it spirals down, and then a whole number of melodies emerges—melodies that people can hum. The Third Symphony became a work that revealed many dimensions, and—okay—in a way, you may also hear it as a kind of continuation of a work by Mahler. What's wrong with that?

Now I come to your question: the music became too single-minded again. The reason for my life-long aversion to 'single-mindedness' is to be found, I think, in my hatred from early childhood of the male-dominated world I found around me—with its fascism and macho-values. I believe that the drive inside me directed itself towards ambiguity because it was, and is, the only answer to the prevailing tribal mentality with its black and white dichotomies. Towards a human world instead of a man's world. But back to the Symphony! While it is true that in the Third Symphony, there is, for example, one rhythmic layer that uses the golden proportions grouped in two, in four, in eight and so on, the *junctions* are still noticeable. But actually, for a couple of years I composed works with tools I used in the Third Symphony. I believe that that was the most stable period in my life—until I found Wölfli. On the way to the Third Symphony I composed *Sub Rosa* (1970), which is based on melodies from the infinite row in one way or another, and from the Third I composed *Turnering* (1975) and *Twilight* (1976–77). In *Twilight* I tried to create interferences between a large melodic complex that had grown up and a new one that shoved its way in after the other one was already launched. So the work vibrates, and then you hear the new one—all by itself. That way of composing can't be repeated, so if I had not found Wölfli then I would have been forced to 'invent him' because I already had the commission for the Fourth Symphony from Hamburg Radio (NWDR).

You saw an exhibition about Wölfli at the Louisiana Museum of Modern Art in 1979 . . .

Yes. The author Jørgen I. Jensen wrote about my Louisiana-experience in the book that you have edited (*Per Nørgård: Fourteen Interpretive Essays*. Scolar Press, 1996, *ed.*). Jensen was a little upset about my reaction when I saw Wölfli's drawings. Perhaps he believed that I was about to go mad myself because of my preoccupation with Wölfli's 'mad music'. But for my part I wasn't really worried, for I knew that this was a moment of emancipation. I mean *the world* wasn't changed by the Third Symphony. *Twilight* hadn't changed the world either, nor had it changed *me*. There *was* something that did not work. As I said: it was the single-mindedness of the rhythmic idea that didn't work, and to throw off all that hierarchic network was at that point a release. Also, I had simply to admit that if I couldn't compose without that then I'd better stop. So bar by bar I proceeded to write the Fourth Symphony. With the pretext of using Wölfli's idea about an *Indischer Roosengarten* and *Chineesischer Hexensee*, I could say to myself: nobody can pre-determine how such music must be. What was important for me in the longer term was that this freedom provided a number of solutions to the 'problem with rhythm'. By just throwing myself into a chaotic compositional condition I became more and more clear about the burning issue, namely, *rhythm*. As far as I am concerned one of my 'conquests' of the 1980s was the completely new forms of rhythmic worlds which I began to explore, such as eternal accelerandos, the 'squareroot of 2 rhythm'. I last explored other rhythmic depths in the piano concerto *Concerto in due tempi* (1994–95) and in the work for two pianos, *Unendlicher Empfang* (Infinite Acceptance, 1997).

In terms of structure and other things, would it be fair to say that rhythm has given you the opportunity to produce ambiguity where you can have different layers that don't chafe or rub each other. With regard to the rhythmic proportions, do you take care that the layers don't coincide?

You could say that, but it must obviously be in connection with melody and sound, and so forth. There is no denying it, the *gestalt* is inescapable. What is deeply fascinating about rhythmic ideas is that they can attach themselves to melodic forms of great simplicity, combining to produce complex patterns — a 'dynamic wave'.

But — if I may just take up the thread of the conversation from before — even though you abandoned the hierarchical principles and the infinite row, they returned later.

Yes, that's right. It's like the lovely image in an article you published: though I believed that I had burned my bridges, it turned out that apparently I hadn't. Later, when I had a musical problem, perhaps a bridge might come and say 'Don't you need *me* now?' In a sense, the infinite row popped up again as a *tool*; earlier, it had been the celebrated focus of attention, for example, in the Third Symphony, which is a kind of 'celebration' of the infinite row's many layers and hierarchies. But later it becomes an indispensable means for realizing my *rhythmic* visions! Things that are tied to the infinite accelerando aren't possible without using the infinite row as the foundation — to mention one example.

I have sometimes heard you say, 'I don't know how I can go any further. It is completely hopeless and I don't know if I can finish this work'. This kind of frustrated situation arises because you don't compose with a ruler and graph paper marked off in milimetres. The whole time you are unsure where it will all end. Anyway you have always, as far as I know, been fortunate enough to find some 'bridge' ringing at your door . . . Can you say that you are more successful when the idea comes to you than when you have to sit and construe it?

I believe that's correct. I can never work with bars drawn in advance on the next seventeen pages — showing where the tempo is supposed to change and so on. I would never be able to do that. I would probably panic. I composed, for example, the Fourth Symphony and the opera *Nuit des hommes* (1995–96) bar by bar. For the Piano Concerto I had nothing more than [sings a short phrase] — and that's not much to have for a whole piano concerto. I couldn't get beyond that, but I knew that it contained the key to the rest. It was like holding the end of a thread and all I had to do was to keep pulling. That turned out to be correct. So at a certain point I simply began. Up in the flute when it goes [sings the part]. I liked that beginning a lot. The only response I have for young composers who come to me and ask, 'How do you write the music out?' is, 'How did you start?' There was a young composer who put the question to me recently, an unhappy fellow who apparently had set in motion many ideas which he couldn't continue. So I said, 'The only advice I can give you is to consider what you started with, what you wrote down — if you don't believe in it fully, then drop it. But if you really can say that there is something there that continues to fascinate you, then stick to that! What you compose later has to live up to what you started with. You must never drop below that level. That is the touchstone. If the continuation loses altitude, then drop it.

In your case the concern for the ambiguous and the many-layered indicate an interest in something more than so-called professional music. For many years you have been interested in working with amateurs. Then again, look at your varied output: you can compose a hymn like you did for the film Babettes Feast *(1987), as well as music that demands complete attention.*

Well, yes. For example, *Du skal plante et træ* is sung by many Danish choirs. For me the dichotomy is only on the surface. My work has been described as consisting of different 'layers of growth'—which is more complimentary than Yoell's suggestion in 1973 that I struck out in seventeen directions at a time. In everyday-life you invariably stumble around in a great number of 'layers'. But the thing with amateurs and single pieces of music comes from my vision of the fundamental idea that interference doesn't need grand gestures. It can happen with one or two recorders. But each time there is obviously a new tension between whether it *succeeds* or *doesn't succeed*, because each time it depends on the quality of the idea and its ability to endure. These are qualities that don't depend on great complexity or virtuoso display. This is William Blake's 'grain of sand', to see infinity in a grain of sand or sense eternity in a bird's flight . . .

Arne Nordheim

ON ARTICULATING
THE EXISTENTIAL SCREAM

What is a composer's essential motivation? For some the answer is entirely elusive, for others it is crystal clear. Can you remember how you got started in music?

I have been fascinated by all kinds of music since my earliest childhood. I always stopped when there was music nearby and even as a child I listened to the radio a lot. I remember that when I heard Beethoven's Second Symphony, I became somewhat cross when I realized that this wonderful music *had* already been composed. I would liked to have composed that symphony. It began there, without a doubt. At least my general enthusiasm started there in any case. I was simply completely crazy about music; it was the only thing that interested me. A piano was fantastic, a revelation. I had an aunt who had what we Norwegians call a 'hymn-bike' (harmonium, *ed.*) — a little organ you had to work with your feet. The fact that the notes didn't stop — that was unbelievably exciting. So I held down the keys and stamped away to get enough air — and then came the sound. I can still remember the sound of that harmonium. It was a game to enter into the sound. I was around 7–8–9 years old.

My school songbook only had tunes. When I visited my aunt I took the little book with me — *School Songbook*, it was called and I still have it — and then I harmonized the melodies. I always wanted to get into the sounds, be inside them. In our house in Larvik where I grew up, we had a store room with an iron door. I loved that iron door because it made a fantastic sound when you closed it. It just kept on sounding for a long time. That was a great experience and I had the feeling that I got right into the sound. Later I had the same feeling when I worked with electronic music. For example in the studio in Warsaw, where there were excellent opportunities to explore the possibilities of sound, once more I heard the iron door from my childhood. It's there in several of my works.

Was it a big step to go from playing the harmonium to deciding to become an organist?

No, it wasn't. But I didn't really decide to become an organist, it was more like something that developed naturally. My father played the violin and built violins, too. He played all the pretty melodies and loved it. *His* father was a farmer who had never been taught to play the organ, but could play it never the less and really liked it. So when the church organist got sick or couldn't play for some reason, they would send for my grandfather. That was very likely the reason that my father's greatest wish was that I should become an organist. It was actually *his* wish. For my own part, I thought it was deadly boring to play those four-part hymns. So I quickly lost interest. But the decisive moment for me—I can date it exactly, even the actual decision, it was the eighth of February 1949—was when I heard Mahler's Second Symphony, *The Resurrection*. It was the first time I had heard anything by Mahler, and it moved me deeply. But it isn't so much the music that animates me, it is more the existential scream that I am trying to articulate. And I am still working on it.

When you mention Mahler I am reminded of your work, Tenebrae, *for solo cello and orchestra. It begins with a long pedal point in the strings like one of Mahler's symphonies.* Tenebrae *is not a study in the style of Mahler but one notices the inspiration from his tonal poetry. I am also reminded of your early work,* Aftonland. *One of Per Nørgård's early works is also based on Pär Lagerkvist's poem. Was this poem for you what Hans Bethge's* Die Chinesische Flöte *was for Gustav Mahler?*

It is obviously difficult to speculate on another's thoughts, but I would imagine it is the same. Actually that leads to a completely different discussion, for one could find it puzzling that Mahler used this material. There is an unbelievable amount of kitsch in Bethge's translation, both in the language and in the imagery. There is something problematic about it, but musically *Das Lied von der Erde* is overwhelming. It is so strong and that is the principal thing for me. The fact is that Mahler successfully articulates the existential scream. It is like some of Francis Bacon's portraits that I saw in Louisiana (Louisiana Museum of Modern Art, Denmark, *ed.*). They are splendidly Mahleresque—this great cry for help.

Mahler searched our subconscious for some form of collective consciousness. Layers of history are involved and I imagine that you want to connect with that. From what has been written about you, it appears that opposites like light and dark, life and death, are your main concerns. You approach major existential questions by reusing historical musical experiences.

I would say that you can reuse the experiences but you can hardly reuse the articulations. It has to be the experiences that you use again. They have a great recycling value.

You have talked about the primal scream. What is it you want to uncover in your own experience of music? Tell us why you are so fascinated by Mahler's Symphony and why it has affected you so much.

It was very likely Mahler's recognition of that fellowship of loneliness and desperation that you can only find by searching deep in the human mind. In a certain way we are all alike in this respect. At that deep level we are all a part of each other and there are no boundaries with respect to body, soul, clothing, houses and so on. I think those are the depths Mahler reached. Of course he also uses obvious texts and messages, but that's not what is actually important. The most important thing is the emotional strength that he is capable of articulating. That's what engages us at the deeper level. That's Mahler's strength; he attains it with the help of little things, strange things, folklore and sentimentality, the fragmentary development of formal parts, and so on—a procedure for which he was violently criticized in his time. In the reviews of the time he was criticized for using historical material, among other things. He is a great puzzle, an enigma of vast dimensions. He has never ceased to fascinate me.

You use the human voice like Mahler did. Is your use of the human voice also the means by which you reach these deeper levels?

Yes, that's it, for there is the direct connection to the strongest feelings, through the articulation of the voice and the fact that it belongs to a person who steps forth. And if it is very successful it is not even necessary to hear what is being sung, but you *have* to hear that it is a human voice. That a person is trying to reach you. That is important.

Tell us about your texts. They're certainly not simple prose texts. They are the classics, Dante, the Bible, Ovid—great literature. What is it you find in those texts that can satisfy your desire for self-expression?

In this literature I see the sovereign expression of that shared loneliness. That's the most important. And next, it is the need to make a text 'sound'. The sound of human presence is my concern. I also like to work with several languages at the same time. I have a work called *Wirklicher Wald* (The Forest of Reality) for soprano solo, cello solo and choir—actually the voice and the cello are equally important. At one point the soprano sings part of the Book of Job in Hebrew while the chorus sings a text by Rainer Maria Rilke in German. Here you have the dual situation, characteristic of mankind—it happens to many people. The soprano who sings in Hebrew and the chorus that sings the German poems in a chorale-like setting form a configuration with the cello moving between them like some sort of mediator, on one side leading the way towards the choral mass, and on the other, leading away from the choral mass towards the soprano, who then takes the lead.

So what should we call it? It's a multi-layered technique where one layer is put on top of another, over and over. A technique that fascinates me.

ART AND SOCIETY

Speaking of texts in general, I note that you, Olav Anton Thommessen and Rolf Wallin, have all received the Nordic Council Music Prize and that in their acceptance speeches your two colleagues expressed a very unequivocal scepticism about the possibilities for art in a commercialized society. But in your case I don't have the feeling that you would use art as a direct means to criticize society. However, as always with you, there are exceptions. In one work you have a person reading from the Declaration of Human Rights. How do you feel about the possibilities of using art to denounce monstrosities and of applying art directly as a political tool?

As far as music is concerned it is very difficult, if not impossible. But I believe that a composer—and, taken as a whole, all creative artists—only have one thing to do and that is to make their art as good as possible. Poets should write good poetry, composers should compose good music. It is, well, a guide line, but something that is very important for me. And I hold myself to it. Better string quartets: better world!

Allow me to go back to your first works. I am curious to hear you describe what you encountered when you went to Oslo as a young man. What kind of music scene was it?

In the first place, the idea of becoming a composer was so crazy that no-one could conceive of it. It was considered necessary to try to obtain a position in life, something secure that you could fall back on. Then you could compose in your free time. But basically I was never particularly concerned about that. I didn't listen to all the warnings. I *wanted* to compose and I began to compose some string quartets. The first was played in Stockholm, the second in Copenhagen, the third in Oslo and so we come to 1956.

What I am aiming at is that in one way or another the social situation must have limited your creativity. After all, you went abroad.

Yes, that's true. One ran up against a wall everywhere. There was no-one to take this music seriously. We had music, but no-one paid any attention to it. That is, until we established Young Nordic Music (Ung Nordisk Musik). Today it's called UNM, and it continues to be an active organization to which I am greatly indebted. Music was taken seriously there. The first two one-movement quartets that I composed weren't so successful, but the third one in 1956 went really well. It is simply called *Strygekvartet* (String Quartet). Today it is performed in an extraordinary number of places. The quartet has torn itself away from me and I have let it go, but it continues to sell.

You were in Paris early on and studied musique concrète.

Yes, that is half true. It is a story that I have tried to resist for a long time, but it doesn't seem possible to get rid of it. I *was* there and there *was* musique concrète and the great figures were there, Schaeffer and all the others. But there wasn't any sort of course of study; it was more a question of going to concerts, making introductions and analysing works, explanations of how a work was composed. I learned an incredible amount from that, but it wasn't anything like a systematic study. So I have to clarify that bit of history.

One tends to contrast the two movements that came from Paris and Cologne. Did you also find this to be the case?

Yes, there was a real loathing between the two. I was also in Cologne, and Cologne was very tough in one way or another. You took the system as it was, no-one changed anything. But I am a *trial-and-error* composer. I need to change things all the time, all the time make it a bit better: a little rounder on the edge here and a little sharper there. That's the way I have to do it. As a composer I rely on trying things out. In Paris you did nothing but try things out and then throw out the bad. And it all ended up with a long string of tape with numbers on it and a journal with directions on how to make things work. These journals hung on the walls down there. I experienced it even more strongly when I went to Warsaw where they used Polish Radio's equipment. There were real opportunities to get into the world there, a lot farther than in Paris—or than they *wanted to* in Paris. Even then they were a little under Karlheinz's dominance.

You have always been on admiring, but critical terms with Stockhausen and his music. You have spoken positively of Gesang der Jünglinge and Kontakte, classic works made with very simple technology. Gesang der Jünglinge is a work that also uses human voices, and you were working with timbre at that time. What did you learn from that school?

What I learned resulted in the works I made in Warsaw. That was the result. In Warsaw the human voice was used as the starting point in many different ways. The voice that reads the Declaration of Human Rights . . . 'all men are born free' . . . was a commission from the Polish Radio, and I thought that it was an appropriate text. Those were hard times in Poland in the 1960s and 1970s and that text belonged there. You don't hear it, but it is there. First and foremost the voice has many parameters, for example, amplitude, that is the strength of the voice, characteristics of the attack, the building up of the formants that are characteristic of an individual voice. All of this serves to

guide the processes. It is a kind of cannibalism: you consume your own stuff and then feed it through the system.

Now you are already far along the path of what could be called the third direction. You didn't choose Paris, or Cologne, but Warsaw. The first time I went there I met Josef Padkowski. He is a scientist and was also very involved in electronic music at the point in time that you were in Poland. I got the impression that the equipment they had there was some of the best anywhere in Europe. Can you describe the scene when you arrived and explain exactly why it had to be Warsaw?

Studio Experimentalne was a studio that had been built from scratch. Much of the equipment consisted of modified instruments that were normally used for electrical, electronic and acoustical measuring—you had filters and ring modulators of the kind that made it possible, for example, to send several conversations through the same line. At one end the signal was encoded and at the other end it was decoded. But if you didn't decode it you got a result that could be extremely exciting—something we were always looking for. They simply built the equipment that they needed for each task, with old-fashioned soldering and so on, and it was often necessary to lash wire around the apparatus in order to avoid humming and things of that sort. So it was all very lively and inclusive. The Poles had invested so much in it that they had a whole team just to make equipment. There was, for example, a chief of instruments whose only task was to design and build whatever was needed. A very creative and positive environment. And just then Josef Patkowski, the director, commissioned a piece from me. *Pace*, that is, Peace. He had heard *Solitaire*, an earlier work I had composed in the studio, that he liked very much.

Recently the works from this period have been issued on CD: Solitaire, Pace, Warszawa, Poly-poly *and* Colorazione. Poly-poly *was, as far as I can remember, premiered in 1970 at the Osaka World Exposition in the Norwegian pavilion. How did you set to work on it?*

In that work I tried to get an overview of everything that is found in sound. I began by assembling all the material. All human sounds. All sounds from known things, daily situations, kindergarten, everything from children at play to test shooting of new products at a weapons factory. Everything is there, I think. Everything that is representative is there. First I made a list of categories and then we set about the work of assembling the material. We found a lot. There were six sound programmes running at the same time. They all

Photo: Arne Nordheim (Ines Gellrich).

had differently timed cycles of rotation. They also got displaced in relation to each other, like Mars in relation to the earth and the sun, so the paths of the planets are hinted at. That is partly a salute to Kepler, so you could say Johannes Kepler is also included. As all of these programmes were running we had to make some calculations so that it didn't just become a great big thick stew. We had to get some assistance with the calculations from some friendly mathematicians. They contributed a model and we put in all the sounds. Silence was one of the elements of sound, you could say, for silence was just as important as sound. The proportions had to be so that there were ten seconds of sound and seven and a half seconds of silence. Little rules like that were built into the piece. It ended up being a large, slow, simmering soup of associations, like when you look into a pot and see the stew cooking, some places bubble up. So we let it simmer there in Osaka. We figured out that if we used the numerical proportions that we gave to the arithmeticians it would take 102 years, 3 weeks, 4 days, 11 hours and 17 seconds before the layers would fall at the same place again. That means that those who were at the premiere would long be dead when the piece was finally finished. For practical reasons the piece lasted only the six months the exhibit was set up in Osaka, and then the whole thing was no more. But luckily some of it has been saved on the CD you mentioned before so that one can hear how it sounded in Osaka in 1970.

There was also another exhibit in Osaka in 1970, a famous round auditorium where they played Stockhausen's music. Did you visit the German pavilion?

Yes, except that I wasn't there during the opening ceremonies, as I had been working on the preparations and tests in order to get our own exhibit up and running before it opened. When the World Exhibition opened I travelled home, so I didn't get to be in the exhibit itself. But naturally I went around and saw that there were several music installations and Stockhausen's was rumoured to be truly impressive. But in typical fashion there was a sign outside that said *Eintritt am strengsten verboten* (Entrance Strictly Forbidden). So we never did get in. But I know that they were there and that they set up various things. But we didn't make it inside so I didn't experience it at all.

You never experienced electronic music coming from many directions? That was Stockhausen's vision of spatial music even at that time.

No. But you experience it with extraordinary brilliance if you have the opportunity to perform *Kontakte* correctly. It is a spatial piece. And in *Gesang der Jünglinge* he works with five channels. That's a mystery. Why five? It's an old idea that life is ordered by the four directions of heaven, and so there is the fifth . . .

'MEMORABLES'

Around 1970 Stockhausen changed direction aesthetically-speaking. He composed Mantra *in 1970, where he began to notate again after having written intuitive music—well, not* written *intuitive music. There was also a change in your music. There was a soundscape piece like* Floating . . .

Yes, it is a soundscape piece. What I was concerned with in *Floating*—and that I later purified in *Greening*, which I composed for the Los Angeles Philharmonic—was the technique of over-layering. I put one sound on top of another, in fact it's a minimalist idea. For example, large parts with *tutti divisi* in the strings, counterpoint in forty-eight parts, are allowed to unfold. Actually, extreme demands are placed on the listener who has to sort out and make forms from this sea of sound. He has to think himself into the sound and form it himself from within. And motifs reappear again and again, simply because they lie on top of each other. Known materials become new along the way; it is quite fascinating. That's what happens in *Floating* and in some of my later works. I can't see how composers can survive without repetition. It remains a prime constituent of form. Repetition. I have some sort of private terms that I use and I came up with one, 'memorables', meaning motifs or structures with strong enough peculiarities that they keep on being remembered. And the idea is captured in the term.

What you call 'memorables' includes recycling your own things. Do you use a kind of formula that stands up to being used again in other works?

That's right. In the piece called *Greening* I would say that materials from *Floating* aren't recycled, but that the basic idea about over-layering and complex counterpoint is. This is probably a typical example of a place where I reuse things: not note for note, but big segments are recycled.

As we talk about your works from this period I'm starting to think about the Polish school—Penderecki's Trenos—*and Lutosławski . . . and also a little about Xenakis. Not because I would accuse you of plagarism but concepts like aleatoric counterpoint and graphic notation became part of your world. Were you inspired by these composers—and perhaps also by the sound world of Ligeti?*

Yes. I can certainly see your point and you are not far off the mark. For, what happened in Europe while we were, so to say, encumbered by serialism? Was it not precisely a piece like Penderecki's *Trenos*? Wasn't it a shock? A joyful shock with an inherent feeling of freedom to match the violent, strong emotional impact that naturally reflected the work's background. It is a song of lament. He released this huge scream—there it is again—that had been walled up for so long. It didn't seem possible to escape from that and so, as a very young man, he did it. Yes, I can easily recognize myself in it. Lutosławski's idea of controlled aleatory was immeasurably interesting as theory, and it also served him magnificently in practice. So it was no wonder that one was influenced by the significant works that he produced. In addition to its pure emotional strength, his music also showed incomprehensibly elegant crafts-manship. I have to say, I was very impressed by Lutosławski.

THE FUNCTION OF CRITICISM

Then came some works which on an expressive level approach the late romantic sound. I'm thinking of Stormen *(The Tempest)—your music for the ballet. At that time certain writers maintained that your music was influenced by late romanticism and that you fell back on the expressive means of earlier periods. I have heard you reply to that criticism, 'Yes, well, it is just that the listeners have changed, not I'. Is this a polemical statement? Or just how do you look back on it?*

You can certainly consider that to be a polemical statement because obviously I have changed, and obviously the listeners have also changed so that they are no longer aggressive toward the new, but are more open to it than they were be-fore. In a way you can say that we have taken steps towards meeting each other. And if I may say so, it has been a beneficial encounter and has generated a number of works worldwide that I believe we can be happy about today.

Now I would like to ask you about something your colleague Olav Anton Thommessen wrote about after listening to a work of yours from the time of Greening: *'I find a lot of conflict in the balance between the exposition of the material and the composi-tional drive. Because of what I regard as his unwillingness to take a definite position I am often frustrated and so listen with a reduced intensity'. You have said of your critics that you sometimes cannot relate to their criticism because they don't grasp the intention of your music, that they take as their starting point something com-pletely different from that which is built into your music. Can you relate to Thommessen's criticism?*

No, I don't understand it. I see no conflict. I think it is, if I may say so, a typically negative observation from a colleague. So I see nothing other than that I must have disturbed Thommessen and unfortunately weakened his ability to judge (laughs).

In Denmark we are accustomed to thinking that we have a history of frank discus-sion and that ours is an open society with no tradition of creating schools of thought. In Norway are you also openly critical and is there free exchange of experience? For all I know, Lasse Thoresen and Olav Anton Thommessen are adamantly opposed to producing 'clones'. But does Norway today have an open-minded climate that fosters discussion?

No we don't, and we basically never have had one. I don't know the reason why. There is no open forum in Norway of that kind. Whatever comes out comes across as the kind of criticism that you just cited by Thommessen. Critics are uncomfortable with such a forum or they simply don't find it interesting.

So you have not had much criticism, positive or negative, in Norway compared with what you have received abroad. Where and how have you found the motivation to continue to work?

The motivation is there. It comes from one's own impulse. I produce in a regular stream. But in Norway there is no tradition of discussing the issue. Perhaps the spectrum is too narrow so that everyone avoids it—you know—it is often incredibly uncomfortable both to be criticized and to criticize others. The goal is, after all, to move ahead. One must compose better works. The next piece must be very much better than the last, and the next one better still. We each sit on our own mountain top.

But you have the opportunities and the potential to create a tradition of exchange. You yourself have been a newspaper critic. How did you see your role at that time?

I was quite critical then. My columns were probably more concerned with contributing information than advising colleagues. I was concerned with the activity of informing, writing on festivals abroad, selecting phenomena and writing about them. I had the opportunity, that's right. But it was a small pool at that time; everyone knew each other.

Eco

I would like to revive an old topic of discussion. It has been said that modernism has a 'definite project'. You have spoken about the collective loneliness, the primal scream, the forgotten experiences, and about what the Germans call 'declining cultural values'. Does your 'project' comprise something beyond a fascination with these things?

That is a very big question. I have to think a little about that. I do have a project and a need for an acceptable formal shaping of musical actions. They have to fall into place for me. Quite simply, I need to have a project that I feel comfortable with. One is circumscribed by one's own artistic potential and inventiveness. That is what I try to achieve and if I find something in the 'declining values' and feel it is right, then I use it. But I don't follow any school or movement.

Let's try to be a little more specific. Let's take the work, Eco. *It deals with the history of the suffering of mankind. Again we have the opposing elements, from chaos to stillness, from the virtually apocalyptic opening to total quiet. It is your technical means that I am interested in. The way that you realize your thoughts.*

What is there in *Eco?* There is text and a chorus, orchestra and soloist. They cooperate on articulating a text. Again, like a scream. We are back to the cry. That is my project.

Adorno called Schoenberg's music a seismograph of fear. You've turned back to the scream so many times during our conversation that it leads me to think of his description of Schoenberg's music because this includes expressions of decline, loneliness, dissolution. And when I look at what has been written about you there are some notions that crop up again and again—death and loneliness—and also the notion of church bells as something that provides a connection with nature and the past. Could you say something about the things that repeatedly preoccupy you from one work to another?

Let me try, and by a happy coincidence I'd like to refer to *Eco* from 1967, a typical work in many ways. In its delight in the acoustic it is also a typical work of the time, particularly in its circling around my personal and, perhaps, private needs for expression and my longing for contact and handshakes across time, space, the grave and history. Salvatore Quasimodo's poems present us with a large reservoir of allusions that have their sources far back in our cognitive development and it is as though these Italian poems seamlessly slide into David's Psalm 137. This *unnoticeable* literary transition is mirrored in my work by the sounding flow. In an extremely slow process these sound pictures can change colour. By means of constant *overlayering* and *hollowing out* of the sound I obtain a building material that mirrors the poems' primary expression in time and space—blessedly free of the terror of semantics and demand for meaning. *Eco* is therefore one of *my* typical works, and in it I can sometimes detect memories of the music I have never heard.

'At artikulere det eksistentielle skrig: Interview med komponisten Arne Nordheim', *Dansk Musik Tidsskrift* 70, 6 (1998/99): 199–204.

Karlheinz Stockhausen

EVERY DAY BRINGS NEW DISCOVERIES

Looking at your work in the context of the development of music composition in this century, it's obvious that it broke new ground in a number of areas, for example electronic music, pointillist music, serial music, intuitive music, music theatre, right up to the current multi-form formula composition. The closer we come to today's Stockhausen, the more formula thinking comes to the fore. But isn't it now a question of refining the existing technique that you have achieved, producing a kind of concentration of all the compositional techniques and aesthetic experiences that you have collected over the course of your years of experiment in so many areas? How would you describe your music now, at the beginning of the 1990s?

In the first years of the decade I was still composing DIENSTAG AUS LICHT (TUESDAY from the cycle called LIGHT). Towards the middle of the 1990s I will compose FREITAG (FRIDAY) and MITTWOCH (WEDNESDAY) and at the end of the millenium and the beginning of the next I will, God willing, compose SONNTAG AUS LICHT (SUNDAY). Since 1990—without a break—I have been composing and realizing the electronic music for DIENS-TAG at the Electronic Music Studio of the West German Radio. It is finished, but in the process this work led to so many new questions and tasks that I will be kept busy for years perfecting these new discoveries. I am thinking of the OKTOPHONIE (OCTOPHONY), as well as a new musical technique and forming of dynamics. This gives the music a completely refined relief. Furthermore, since 1990 I have continued to develop space music *(Raum-Musik)* beyond octophony to the extent that the actual movements of the instrumentalists and singers through the audience are composed for the first time. Examples of this are found in the second act of DIENSTAG AUS LICHT, which is subtitled INVASION – EXPLOSION mit ABSCHIED (INVASION – EXPLOSION with FAREWELL). In the INVASION a first wave of invasion comes from the left, passes through the audience along three passages and disappears to the right. Next, after an interlude of electronic music, another wave comes from the right and crosses through the hall moving to the left and toward the front. One battling trumpeter falls on the stage in front, and this occasions PIETÀ, a duet for soprano and flugelhorn, performed with electronic music. Then follows a third INVASION that moves from behind

the audience along three passages toward the front. In a theatrical performance the stage is finally blasted open. In a concert performance a choir enters
from the left and right side of the stage; the men come first, then the women.
SYNTHI-FOU, a crazy synthesizer-player—my son, Simon—plays an extraordinarily lively and varied solo along with the electronic music.

I thus composed vertical space music, including all conceivable movements
upwards and downwards, as well as space music played by musicians who move
through the audience in all possible directions. To this is added the composition in completely differentiated dynamics which I have only just started. In
1992, from January through March, I will again be working at the Electronic
Music Studio and for the first time I will be able to work out everything.
That will be a whole new, far from easy, task.

So far I have had the opportunity to attend three parts of the gigantic LICHT, *that
is,* DONNERSTAG (THURSDAY), SAMSTAG (SATURDAY) *and*
MONTAG (MONDAY). *Can you describe those parts of the cycle that have not
yet been performed?*

You mean FREITAG, MITTWOCH and SONNTAG?

Yes.

I call FREITAG AUS LICHT the 'day of temptation'. Here I will represent
archetypal human temptations in music. These are, in the first place, the temptations to use the body as a musical instrument, including, therefore, the variant
of exchanging human bodies. Unusual experiments with the body are significant human temptations. To use the body itself carefully, like a composer
does an instrument.

The other thing which fascinates me is the temptation to transform oneself,
in the course of which therefore, one musical situation—in very gradual degrees—is transformed into another one: vocal into instrumental, instrumental
into electronic, electronic into surrealistic sound, and so on. To this end I will
experiment with the simultaneous realization of several widely divergent *sound
scenes (Tonszenen)* in the same space where they then will be interconnected—
not only musically but also by means of physical bridges whereby the elements
are exchanged, multiplied and so forth. This is a very interesting endeavour,
one that I have never tried before and that I have never experienced anywhere else; it is, in fact, an attempt to realize a truly poly-scenic composition.

In FREITAG the main task will thus be the creation of pumping sound-
reliefs in front of, to the right, left, behind, under and above the audience.
Sounds will not only be simultaneously connected along lines or by layering,
they will also be parts of a sound-wall that pumps forwards and backwards.

For the moment this can be realized with only up to eight components. That's what I will start to experiment with in January, and we will then see how far I can get. That is FREITAG.

Next comes MITTWOCH. I have had sketches ready for all the days in LICHT since 1977/78, and in those for MITTWOCH I explore the idea of a 'heavenly parliament', something I heard and saw in a vision one night. The most important implication of this is that I have to invent a new language because I am convinced that the languages of existing music theatres in all cultures are essentially tied to everyday language. Sure, there already exist— in my own works, too—certain unusual extensions or compressions of time, as well as instances of phonetic imaginary languages, for example, in LUZIFERs TRAUM (LUCIFER'S DREAM) from SAMSTAG aus LICHT. But what I want is a new grammar, a new syntax and, of course, a new rhetoric combined with new words. More than that, a whole new vocabulary. I am going to use many words that are syntheses of various extant human languages, like at the beginning of LUZIFERs TRAUM. For an example, I may construct a word which has three phonetic components that are respectively German, English and French. Furthermore, there will be abstract words that, as yet, do not exist, since a heavenly parliament must of necessity have a new hyper-language that is purely musical in its nature, yet carries meaning. The sense will only be partially perceived, but I believe that that is an interesting problem. It fascinates me, for I have come to realize that all traditional languages are largely dialects of one spiritual language that is common to all human beings. What inspires me now is that, in connection with MITTWOCH, I would like to compose a language that is *not* like Esperanto, in other words, *not* an 'extra-language' but a language that comes from existing languages and additionally from a phonetic nonsense-language to form a composite hyper-language. It is an enticing project and, as you can imagine, one that has its humorous moments. I realize that I will take the idea of the parliament into the absurd, as it is made up of spirits who attempt to shape or organize the world merely by speaking, singing or shouting—doing everything possible with the voice. That is, in fact, what most people do nowadays, and it is generally considered to be real work though it is nothing but phonetic manipulation of what others are supposed to do: a very strange attitude toward human work. Let's have lunch.

[Later]

Within the seven-day LICHT cycle, the theme of SONNTAG is the mystical union of EVA and MICHAEL. Where MITTWOCH is the day of cooperation and mutual understanding, SONNTAG is the day of mystical union. With SONNTAG I have assumed the task of composing a musical planetary system where the proportional lengths of layers of time correspond to the

rotations of the planets around the sun in our solar system. In terms of visual space, this is not an easy job. I will obviously need a very large hall where objects move around each other and around a centre, just like the planets and the moons move around each other and around the sun. They also have to have a large distance between them. All in all, it will look like a large model of our solar system, with the notion that all the planets are inhabited by musical spirits, namely, singers and instrumentalists, and that they are all equipped with windows so that you can travel from one planet to another and maintain contact with each other. In short, it is a mixture of comedy and modern musical temporal composition. As for the musical language, timbre, dynamics and crew of each planet, you can already imagine that I will use these to give each planet its specific character. I have already written extensive sketches, but what I have said may suffice to give you a general idea.

Perhaps you could also expand on the subject of DIENSTAG *because it is going to be premiered in Milan in 1992, and Danish audiences know very little about this portion of* LICHT.

DIENSTAG AUS LICHT was commissioned by La Scala in Milan after the first performance of MONTAG. Now, you say that the work will be premiered in 1992 in Milan, but that has unfortunately been postponed. Some time ago, I received the message from the new general director, Fontana, that DIENS-TAG will not be staged in Milan in 1992, supposedly due to lack of money, although DIENSTAG is far cheaper than those three parts of LICHT premiered earlier by La Scala. But a new opportunity has opened up, and it is likely that DIENSTAG will be given its first performance in Germany in June 1993, and subsequently in Milan in 1994, as a co-production of a German opera house and La Scala. I am not free to reveal the name of the opera house since there is no definite contract, but I think it will come to fruition. Before that, DIENSTAG will receive a number of concert performances.

The first part has already been premiered, in 1988 at the ceremony celebrating the 600 years since the founding of the University of Cologne, at the large Philharmonic Hall of that city. This part, entitled DIENSTAGS-GRUSS (TUESDAY GREETING), or FRIEDENS-GRUSS (PEACE GREETING), is for mixed choir, solo soprano, nine trumpets, nine trombones and two synthesizers. It portrays a musical battle between two large groups. One group consists of sopranos and tenors plus nine trumpeters and one synthesizer player, the other of altos and basses, nine trombonists and one synthesizer player. The groups are positioned at the right and left, behind the audience. The soprano walks around in an effort to bring the strife to an end. This first

Photo: Karlheinz Stockhausen (Kathinka Pasveer).

part of DIENSTAG AUS LICHT lasts twenty-one minutes. It is preceded by yet another brief greeting entitled WILLKOMMEN (WELCOME) for the same instruments that I have just enumerated.

The first act of DIENSTAG AUS LICHT was composed in 1977 and is entitled JAHRESLAUF (COURSE OF THE YEARS). This was the very first part of LICHT, and it was premiered at the National Theatre in Tokyo with the Japanese title, *Hikari*, which means 'light'. It was composed for gagaku ensemble, gagaku dancers and five actors. Based on this I wrote a European version with instruments to correspond to the gagaku instruments; this one has subsequently been performed in concert version a couple of times.

An expanded version of this work—for DIENSTAG AUS LICHT—with two singers (a tenor and a bass as MICHAEL and LUCIFER, respectively) was premiered this year [1991] on September 29th (St. Michael's Day) at the *Alte Oper* in Frankfurt. By then, JAHRESLAUF was integrated as the first act into DIENSTAG AUS LICHT. The instrumental version, that is, without singers, dancers and actors, continues to be presented in concert performances under the title, DER JAHRESLAUF (THE COURSE OF THE YEARS).

JAHRESLAUF, the first act of DIENSTAG, is essentially a dispute about time and timelessness. Within the framework of LICHT, DIENSTAG is the day of strife and war, the day of Mars. Therefore the theme is *Lauf des Jahres (course of the year)*. One group of musicians plays the music of the *Jahrtausend (Millenium)*, which is furthermore personified by a dancer. He moves only *once* during the entire performance (that lasts about an hour when staged and about 50 minutes in a concert version)—for example in 1992—over a giant-sized number ONE that is visibly elevated towards the back of the stage so that it can be easily seen. The *Millenium-Runner* is costumed appropriately in completely neutral white. Behind him sit three musicians each of whom plays a *shô*, a gagaku-orchestra instrument; in their stead, the European orchestra has harmoniums. In the most recent performance three synthesizers replaced the harmoniums and they sounded like harmoniums or the *shô*.

A second group of musicians plays the music of the *Jahrhundert (Century)*. In the gagaku-ensemble they are *ryuteki* players accompanied by a *shoko* drummer and in the European ensemble there are three piccolo players and a percussionist who beats an anvil. The dancer who belongs to this group represents the *Century*. In 1992, his course will be a huge number NINE.

Then there is the *Jahrzehnt (Decade)* group: in Japan, there are three *hichiriki* players and a *kakko* drummer; in the European orchestra, there are three soprano saxophonists together with a bongo drummer. The *hichiriki* sound somewhat like shawms or English horns, but somewhat more shrill. Possibly the Greek *aulos* was a comparable instrument. The soprano saxophones are marvellous counterparts and play perfectly refined glissandi. There is a third dancer embodying the *Decade*. In 1992, this will be illustrated by another number NINE.

The *Century-Runner* runs nine times over his path, back and forth. The *Decade-Runner* doesn't run exactly nine-times-nine courses, that is, not eighty-one; he comes somewhat short of that because there are interruptions during the performances. I think he runs fifty-seven times back and forth; you may check the score. Anyway, he must move faster still.

The runners have appropriate costumes with corresponding colours. As mentioned, the *Millenium-Runner* is white. Then the *Century-Runner* is blue; the *Decade-Runner* is yellow; and the *Year-Runner* is green. This is occasionally done differently, though.

A fourth group of musicians represent the *Jahr (Year)*. The musicians in the gagaku group play *gakuso*, *biwa* and a *taiko* drum; their European counterparts play electric harpsichord, electric guitar and bass drum. The fourth dancer, the *Year-Runner*, must run back and forth across his year course more than 300 times for 1992 in order to make the rhythm of the years explicitly clear.

There are four interruptions called *temptations* in the JAHRESLAUF. LUCIFER, the bass, attempts four times to bring time to a stop by means of enticements, and MICHAEL sets it back in motion each time by *incitements (Anfeuerungen)*. The first temptation is an attempt to prevent the musicians from continuing to play: bouquets of flowers are brought forth much too early, as though the performance is already over; musicians are, quite naturally, receptive to praise. Then, a little angel appears with the request that the audience applaud so that the musicians will continue to play. The audience does applaud, and so those who have come to congratulate the musicians with their premature flower show must withdraw.

The second temptation follows a little later. A cook brings in a large table heaped with marvellous food. Again, this is another temptation for the musicians to interrupt their musical work, a stronger one at that. At the moment when the performers start toward the food, a lion bounces in, runs up and bites the *Year-Runner* and the *Decade-Runner* in their breeches making them instantly return to their positions so that the years can resume their course.

Again, after a lapse of time, a third temptation arrives in the shape of a modern automobile that quickly races across the stage with a monkey behind the wheel. Everybody stops in their tracks to watch in fascination, amazed at the performance of this vehicle. The monkey demonstrates the refinements of some brand-new features of the car. Once again, MICHAEL intervenes in the guise of a child who yells: 'Please play on. Everybody who continues to play will receive 10,000 Marks'! This suffices to make the musicians carry on with the music, because musicians always need money.

So time marches on, until the fourth—and strongest—temptation, namely sex. An exciting naked woman on a platform rolls on stage to the accompaniment of highly suggestive nightclub music. The performers are completely carried away. At that point, MICHAEL has no other solution than to launch a terrific thunderstorm with lightning and thunder-claps, which also turns off all lights. The musicians are shocked, and, thank heavens, play on. At the end, there is a presentation of prizes for the best *runner of the years* and a beautiful procession.

After a pause, Act two begins, but in a more physical mode. This is where an INVASION, which I briefly described at the opening of our conversation, occurs. It is a physical battle between one group with trumpets, percussion and synthesizer, and another with trombones, percussion and synthesizer. The group of trumpeters includes a lieutenant of sorts, who is a tenor. The trombone group is headed by an officer, a bass singer. They conduct a musical fight assuming highly stylized postures and gestures. There is sufficient time for members of the audience to take mental snapshots of distinct tableau because at times the performers freeze in bizarre positions, after which the battle rages on.

The musicians all play from memory. Two play portable synthesizers; two others carry percussion instruments. They also have speakers attached to their bodies. Samplers, special aggregates and cables are carried by assistants. It functions brilliantly. Via *MIDI* equipment they play strange sounds on synthesizers and on imaginative percussion instruments that are equipped with touch-sensitive keyboards projecting electronic sounds.

The scene entitled PIETÀ follows the second INVASION during which a trumpeter is wounded. A soprano holds the trumpeter in her lap, but at the same time, the gigantic spirit of this same trumpeter stands behind her. The two sing and play a moving duet, together with electronic music, that lasts approximately 18 minutes.

Following this, a third INVASION blasts open the wall at the back of the stage. Already in the first INVASION a rock wall, complete with shrubs, climbers, even small trees, is blown up. Behind it, a chrome steel wall becomes visible. In turn, this is blown up at the end of the second INVASION. Behind it now appears a rock crystal wall with sparkling crystals. Finally, after the third INVASION, even this wall is blown to pieces, and behind it one glimpses the beyond. One sees a space of glass, completely transparent. Glass-like beings are singing strangely coded messages. These glass-like beings are evidently engaged in a war-game with ships, tanks and airplanes made of glass. These glass objects roll across a vitreous game board between the players who sit to the right and the ones who sit to the left. The beings in the beyond have croupier-rakes made of glass and push glass soldiers, tanks and airplanes onto a transparent conveyor-belt that carries everything away. The players seem bored. It becomes clear that wars on our planet are only materialized manifestations of war-games played by superior beings. They play war like we do as children with our clay soldiers and other war-toys. The set-up in DIENSTAG resembles a stock exchange. Behind the alien beings, one sees score-boards on the left and on the right with numbers that register how much military equipment has been destroyed by each party.

In DIENSTAGS-ABSCHIED (TUESDAY FAREWELL), a crazy character enters riding a gun-carriage. He has huge green ears, a long red nose, oversized sunglasses and grotesque gloves; he plays in the midst of a battery of synthesizers. The carriage swerves around, turning in circles. The *Synthi-Fou*, as I have named him, plays hot dance-music accompanied by electronic music; however, it's not really human music but something that's oddly stylized, with long phrases, completely weird harmonies, extreme rhythmic durations and virtuoso cascades of sounds that blaze with a fiery inner life.

Now, that's the INVASION—EXPLOSION with FAREWELL from TUESDAY. The glass-like men wave to glass-like women—who are sort of cosmic Red Cross nurses—and the latter join the men on stage. The women stand behind the men (they do not look at each other) and touch only the tips of their fingers; they move in a jerky manner, almost like puppets or robots. In a kind of geometric dance, these creatures of the beyond disappear into the distance until they are no longer audible or visible. This leaves SYNTHI-FOU alone on stage. The point is that even cosmic beings may be distracted or amused by a mad musician, to the extent that they abandon their war-games and listen in astonishment and, eventually, move on to remote regions. However, the penetration of the wall between this world and the one beyond by means of musical *invasions* merely causes these beings to withdraw further into the cosmos. The result is that one already feels the urge to blow up the next wall by means of music. This is DIENSTAG AUS LICHT in condensed form.

In the programme booklet for the concert performance of JAHRESLAUF and INVASION in Frankfurt, September 1991, only these two parts are described. The first complete performance at the Gulbenkian Foundation in Lisbon of the entire DIENSTAG with all of its parts will be on 10, 11 and 12 June [1992]. A year and a half ago we gave a series of fourteen concerts there; we performed SIRIUS three times, then followed that with eleven concerts, each with a different programme. That was fantastic. Nearly 15,000 listeners, mostly young people, searched us out in the beautiful auditorium in Lisbon. That's where we shall give the three presentations of DIENSTAG. We will be travelling there together with the student choir of the Cologne University and all the soloists—I believe there are thirty-one solo singers and instrumentalists—and we will work there for six days: three days of rehearsals and three performances. That will be the first complete performance of DIENSTAG AUS LICHT. Following that, we will travel (on 25 June) to Amsterdam to give another concert performance at the opera house (possibly followed by a second one, 26 June). As mentioned, the first staged performance will likely be at a German opera house in June of 1993, though I believe that it may possibly happen earlier at the end of May. Then DIENSTAG AUS LICHT is ready.

Your description of the whole war machinery in DIENSTAG *leads me to ask if the work itself reflects the contemporary world? Does it mirror actual events you have lived through?*

The history of our own time doesn't interest me very much. The seven themes of the seven parts of LICHT are essentially beyond time and are not tied to events of the twentieth century. Their real meaning is as follows: MONTAG is the day of birth, veneration of the woman, the day of children; DIENSTAG, the day of conflict and war; MITTWOCH the day of cooperation and mutual understanding—that is, of a new shared language and shared visions. DONNERSTAG in LICHT is the day of learning, of the human process. It starts as a child learns language, learns about the world, the relationship between sun, moon, stars, the experiences with parents, including hunting, war, peace, laughter, crying, singing, praying, and the passing over into the world beyond. In the second act, one experiences a journey round the world aboard a rotating planet Earth which makes seven stops in seven different terrestrial cultures. The third act takes place in the celestial residence of MICHAEL, the *Cosmocreator*. FREITAG is the day of temptation, as already described. SAMSTAG is the day of death and resurrection, the latter achieved by the transformation of matter into LIGHT. SONNTAG is the day of the mystical union of MICHAEL and EVA. In this way, MONTAG is the sequel to SONNTAG and starts the eternal cycle over again.

In my view, the wars we have lived through only confirm the existence of a timeless legitimacy. For example, war as a conflict between groups of peoples is really war between spirits that are incarnate on this planet. It is thought-provoking that I composed the INVASION and the EXPLOSION in a period of high international tensions. I finished the work on 14 January 1991, and the following day, on 15 January, I went to Paris to direct a series of performances of my works at the conservatory. I vividly remember getting the morning papers with the headlines proclaiming that the Gulf War had broken out. It struck me as significant that I had finished the work the day before, because that day was followed by months during which the whole world was hypnotized by this blazing conflict in which a great number of people were killed in a very short time and horrible destruction was inflicted on the area. In this sense, I get the impression that my theme for DIENSTAG aus LICHT is relevant to all human beings.

But in a wider sense, everything is music for me—a very important realization. As a child I lived through every day and every night of World War II. For six long years I experienced the fantastic spectacle of warfare in the sky, with air defence and all the different forms of air strikes and different effects of light, and, above all the music that is part of it. During the last six months of the war, as a sixteen-year-old, I was near the western front, in a military hospital where I helped the wounded. The many daily attacks with various types of bombings produced a completely unbelievable music that went on for days and nights. This taught me that all acoustical events are of interest. What you hear in a war, musical statements that arise from a military conflict, is something that you simply can't experience in any other way. In that way I experienced war music as a singular kind of music in the widest sense.

I am interested in everything that can be turned into music. Also the music that is present in nature and that I can change into art music. The quintessential elements are always, after all, matters of tempi, musical energies, dynamic gradations, unique kinds of timbres, polyphonic space, movements in space. Add to that movements in polyphonic spaces. For example, INVASION contains a tremendously complex polyphony of sound objects that are fired off and come zooming down from the ceiling at different speeds like sound bombs. Simultaneously, one hears sound grenades which shoot upwards out of the floor and walls while the sound bombs fall. It is a poly-spatial concept, and a fascinating compositional challenge. It took me months in the Studio for Electronic Music to produce these movements of sound with the new technique of OCTOPHONY.

Speaking of technique, I understand that formula composition allows the freedom to work with highly varied ideas. It seems that this formal system is extremely flexible. But that, in turn, implies that, at the same time, it can be difficult for the listener to grasp the structure and the meaning of the composition. Is it important for you that the listener captures the complexities of the many layers? Or, have you no great expectations of the audience? In an interview with Gisela Gronemeyer you said that art is for anyone who wants art. Does that mean that you are not concerned with clarifying things for the audience, or, do you expect the listener to sit down and study the music?

I have studied music pedagogy and published six volumes of texts with over two thousand pages and graphic examples about my work. In addition, I have published numerous scores that have extensive prefaces with precise directions for performance practice. In other words, I have had countless 'conversations', comparable to this one, and they have been written out and music examples added. You may be familiar with my lecture 'Die Kunst, zu hören' (The art, to listen) from volume five of *Texte zur Musik*, and know that, on the occasion of performances, I have made every attempt to help listeners understand how a work—in this case, IN FREUNDSCHAFT—is composed and how one might listen to it. For twenty-one years I taught annually at the *International Summer Courses for New Music* in Darmstadt where I analysed and explained my works. I am, indeed, greatly concerned that the listener should know how to listen to my music. Still, what you say is also right: I don't impose restrictions on myself to wait until everyone comprehends what I have been doing before I proceed. Rather, I feel completely free to form music just as I think it should be and in a way that fascinates me. I provide what help I can for the listener, but I know perfectly well that very few exert themselves so as to listen repeatedly, study scores and analyse music. So to my mind, everyone is free.

There are almost six billion people on this planet. Nobody knows how many will ever be interested in my work, even in a thousand years. It is therefore meaningless for me as a composer to devote a lot of thought to figuring out how many people are going to keep up with me, or how many are going to analyse my works. You have to compose what you yourself can hear and simply expect that someday others will also be able to hear the same thing. I believe it's best that way. What is typical of our century and largely promoted by the media, is the general belief that everything aired or distributed must be instantly comprehensible. But that's an enormous misconception. It's rooted in the assumption that there exists such a thing as *the* public. We must correct this view and make it clear that people are individuals, each following a unique path toward learning and development, each one free to make personal choices. Let us be less eager to teach and to prescribe rules of conduct, and rather just state: 'If you want to listen, you can; here are the recordings and scores. We give concerts; we will provide information if you are interested and become involved, but it is your own choice'.

We know, of course, that the overwhelming majority of our contemporaries are interested only in very simple, entertaining music. That's maybe the way it has to be. But it is a shame that the current, misdirected interpretation of democratic ideals has led most people to believe that only the taste of the majority has merit, and that an ingenious and very futuristic development of the arts is impossible in our times. This ought not happen, in my opinion, for it means that mankind no longer knows where it is going. Then we will be stuck at our present level. I can not accept that this should be the meaning of life. What is meaningful in life is that one learns something new every day in order to stay alive and not end up spiritually dead. In the short span of a lifetime, one should strain to acquire as much new knowledge as possible and remain wide open to future developments of mankind and constantly develop oneself, sensible to persistent progress toward a higher stage of humanity. To further this goal is a prerogative of art music, provided that it is very carefully composed, innovative and demanding.

Speaking of the dissemination of your music, there is the problem that you work with elite players. Since the music is so demanding, few musicians can adequately perform these pieces. Your son, Markus, performed in Copenhagen recently and demonstrated that it is possible to execute your highly varied tempo changes. It seems unbelievable but when you hear it you realize that it is possible. I know that many musicians are scared of performing your works because they find them extremely difficult. There is

*only one designated group of musicians who travel around performing your music.
Doesn't this set limitations on the wider circulation of your work?*

Probably. However, until now there have also been very few individuals who
have travelled in outer space, but with time there will be more, and that will
bring an important opening up of our planet to the universe. It is the same in
music. There are always those who have to go first and show what is possible.
These pioneers then have students. The performers with whom I collaborate —
instrumentalists, singers, dancer-mimes — now have students. Suzanne
Stephens, for example, has already trained four marvellous students who can
perform HARLEKIN, dancing and playing the clarinet, non-stop for about
45 minutes. And very well, at that! So we see the slow beginning of a completely new chapter in music history. Important developments in history always start small.

Anyhow, the most gifted musicians should know what is possible, set their
standards high, and work with model musicians. In two to three generations
there will then be numerous interpreters who possess comparable qualities.
The beginning of a mutation of mankind takes place very slowly. This transformation is no longer tied to one nationality or one country. I work with musicians of different countries and races who come from widely different educa-
tional backgrounds. I am not worried at all.

The overall problem today is that there is no money available for the kind of
music I compose, including music for the theatre. In Germany, for example,
we have about 100 opera houses that give performances night after night. Many
of these opera houses have annual budgets of 100 million Marks. That's a huge
amount of money. But they play the regular repertory almost exclusively, and
contemporary music theatre only very seldom because they are forced to work
within the rigid structure of their organization. This includes an ensemble of
permanently hired singers, sometimes expanded with two or three guest stars,
and an orchestra. Since the permanently contracted ensemble already is very
costly, it isn't possible to hire more vocalists, instrumentalists and dancers for
solo parts. Many opera houses have something like forty-five singers permanently engaged, as is the case at the Opera in Düsseldorf. A singer is paid in the
region of 2000 Marks per month to sing whatever standard works happen to
be programmed. A work like one of the operas of my LICHT is not the kind
they could quickly learn by heart; in fact, they would have to rehearse it longer
than usual since this is something they were never taught at the conservatory.
So, they would have to be taken out of the regular routine for a significant
length of time (several months, probably) to rehearse that work exclusively.

My works frequently contain directions for physical movements that are more
complex than those that a stage director might improvise; these are notated
with the same precision as the notes. My works also require the kind of instru-

mentalist who is not a member of the orchestras of opera houses as they are. In any case, they have their orchestras sitting in the orchestra pits waiting to be put to use. I do not write for the usual configuration of players in a standard orchestra with a conductor; consequently, my operas are not performed. With the exception of the second and third acts of DONNERSTAG, the operas of LICHT are to be performed on the cover of the closed orchestra pit.

What's more, I need electro-acoustics. That means, for example, eight sets of paired speakers in a ring around the audience, and often more than that because the listeners who sit under a balcony can't hear the sounds from the speakers above the balcony. The architecture of auditoriums in opera houses with balconies and boxes is not well suited to my music since it was conceived for a kind of opera that is seen from a distance with a single source of sound: in front of the audience is a box that looks as diminutive as a TV screen from the seats of most members of the audience, and a Mozart opera, for example, is performed in that box—the singers are far away. Earlier this week, I went to the Cologne Opera and I was astonished to hear how weak the singers sounded from where I was sitting in the thirtieth row. I also heard very little from the orchestra; the sound from the pit reached me only indirectly. That kind of experience is a far cry from the acoustical effect that I want which is that the sound be truly present as a physical sensation, right next to the listener, clearly perceptible, with everything understandable. I have, as yet, no idea about how the situation might be changed. It would take a revolution to alter social structures to such a degree that other sites, beside opera houses and concert halls, could get a share of available funds.

Symphony orchestras don't play my music at all. I have composed thirty-nine works for orchestra and choir with orchestra, and they are never performed. Nothing! And that's the way it has been for forty years, although we have more than 120 very expensive professional orchestras in Germany. Many of them keep in excess of a hundred players on the payroll; they are paid very good monthly salaries. Many orchestra musicians have salaries of 10–12,000 Marks. They don't play my music. Why? Because a performance of one of my works requires at least four days of rehearsals, even as many as ten days in the case of INORI, a work that lasts approximately seventy minutes.

At the moment, programming follows a formula of three or four pieces per concert and an intermission. An overture or symphony opens the first half of the programme, before the intermission there is a piano or violin concerto, and the second half is a symphony. In about ninety percent of all cases, this symphony is by Mahler or Bruckner. The conductors increasingly want works for large forces and the longest pieces on the repertory, so that they can show off their own skills. These conventions leave no room for my works. Yet works like mine exist and there is a need for drastic change in all of those countries where this type of music culture prevails, including Japan which imitates

Europe to the letter, even to the point of largely abandoning its own tradition. So, something radically different will have to replace the current spaces, ensembles, orchestras and opera houses.

If, somehow, there were enough money for the project, how would you then envision the appearance of seven opera houses dedicated to performances of your LICHT *operas?*

On very beautiful, natural terrain you could build seven different, sufficiently spaced auditoriums for LICHT, as well as a complex for storing scenery and props. Each auditorium should be supplied with a circle of loudspeakers in order to project the sound all around the audience. The seating arrangements in these auditoriums should be flexible so that you could open and close scenes around the audience during performances. The audience could also be seated on a platform, as it was at the World Exhibit at Osaka back in 1970. The height of the audience could then be altered by hydraulics. In the case of LICHT, each auditorium should have a production workshop for preparing costumes and props. Each hall would have its own unique features.

For MONTAG, there would be a space with a body of water, giving the sensation of the sea and a sandy beach. The audience should feel as though it was in a modern hotel by the sea, where a rite is performed around the large Eva figure. DIENSTAG would need a spacious open plane surrounded by large areas for the *invasions*, as well as a very deep area in front of the audience (that is to say, the direction in which the audience mostly faces). In the IN-VASION—EXPLOSION act, DIENSTAG requires great amounts of metal. First you see a rock-wall, then a wall of chromium-plated steel, then a crystalline wall. The entire auditorium would be irregular with open areas between blocks of spectators so that performers have room to run back and forth through the audience during the INVASIONS. There ought to be no more than 600 or 700 people in the audience, otherwise the OCTOPHONY cannot be heard properly. The auditorium would also have to be very high so that the vertical movements of the sounds would be perceptible.

Each day of LICHT would pose different demands from the space. If you study the libretti and synopses for the individual days, you will see what materials, colours and spatial layouts are needed in order to hear the works properly. In any case other auditoriums will certainly appear, in which the audiences can hear sounds from every direction: from above, from below, and from all sides, moving around audiences according to the scores—similar to the spheric space at the World Exhibition at Osaka—and with still many more possibilities. These spaces should also have openings, tunnels and adjacent spaces through which performers can enter or leave as needed and into which they could disappear. In this way audiences will truly be engulfed by the sounds, they will feel the sound all around them, and it will be possible to aim the sound projection so that every sound passes close by the listeners or moves around them. This is the future, even if initially it is limited to a few model auditoriums.

Strangely enough, Germany now imports musicals from England and builds new auditoriums especially for them, for example, *Cats* and *Starlight Express* by the English composer Andrew Lloyd Webber. And performances are sold out four years in advance. It boils down to a question of publicity. The underlying idea is the theory of mass production. The contents are quite simple pop songs; it's just a variant of theatre as entertainment. But this could be refined. Some day new auditoriums will be constructed for LICHT as well. That is a given.

Current opera houses are really only built for operas in the traditional repertory, which includes most operas from this century. There are composers today who still perpetuate the patterns of the classic-romantic opera. I recently heard an example of this, a work by composer York Höller from Cologne, with the title *Der Meister und Margarita*. For this opera he received first prize for the best new opera from the last six years. Yet it is perfectly traditional: the singers perform on stage as usual and the orchestra sits in the pit. Four tiny speakers in the hall project a few short, taped recordings, but they are barely noticeable. The work follows familiar conventions, and that determines the result. It is a literary opera, with a lot of Sprechgesang and normal speech. The orchestra delivers a plain musical background to what is sung or spoken on stage. The stage decoration is the real show from the audience's perspective.

Operas from the eighteenth century are, as a matter of fact, thinly scored; they were written for small, unprepossessing theatres. Of course, you can perform them with today's larger orchestras, but then the size of the orchestra is simply increased to provide greater acoustic energy levels for large opera houses. So, you still hear every word that is being sung. The singing voice is not covered, as is largely the case in the operas of Berg and Schoenberg; in their works it is already very difficult to understand the text.

Could these seven buildings be placed right here?

Sure, no problem. Our Foundation would have enough land. But there would be a storm of protest, because the countryside around where I live is protected. It is not even feasible to get permission to add a room to your own house; the law forbids it. Not long ago, I ran into this problem. I wanted to add two rooms to a small house in order to store musical instruments and scores there; my house is really too small. I had the plan drawn by a local architect, and it was merely a matter of a few square metres. But no, the rooms had to be instantly removed. The regulations are disturbingly rigid.

We may envision a cultural revival that transforms chosen spots on this planet into beautiful, artistic parks, but that goes absolutely against common, socialist-leaning attitudes. The authorities might allow a soccer field, an airport, a zoo or a botanical garden, but then only if everything is orderly, with signs that say 'Keep Off the Grass', and so forth.

You won't find the instinctive sensibility to comprehend a new kind of artistic space, like that of a splendid Japanese temple precinct. Such a temple is a complex of several structures within a large terrain that includes a garden that is an artistic creation in itself. Japanese gardens are miraculous by themselves and they are surrounded by carefully cultivated woods. In such an area there may also be a beautiful stage that would be used for Gagaku music or Nô plays. But such things would be inconceivable in today's Europe, certainly in Germany! The predominant view is, 'We have our opera houses, our concert halls for symphony orchestras, our museums, and that's enough'.

One doesn't have to study your scores too closely to realize that structures based on numbers are important in your music. Often musicians will count out loud while playing. It is tempting to compare your numerology with the late medieval cult of the magic square that played a role in Thomas Mann's Doctor Faustus. *How do your numerological principles—or how does constructivism of the whole—relate to your aesthetic, philosophical, even utopian, views?*

Anybody who has worked in a modern electronic music studio knows that one constantly operates with numbers: numbers for sound volume, numbers for durations, numbers for pitches, numbers for constellations of timbres (spectra), numbers for spatial movements. In the programme booklet for the *Frankfurt Feste*, in the text on OCTOPHONY, you can read about the fact that any position in space is nothing other than a configuration of numbers for the volume of sound and sequence of speakers.

Years ago, when I was twenty-two, I started to use numbers in musical analyses to replace names for pitches and Italian terms for volume, from *pianissimo* to *fortissimo*, in order to simplify the descriptions. The same principle can be applied to durations. I used not only traditional note values, but used numbers for all durations that could not be represented in traditional notation. For fractions of a beat I used a decimal point (sometimes followed by complex numbers), which caused Stravinsky to chuckle over this German Professor Stockhausen who wrote, 'MM 63.5'. And he repeated: 'point five'! Well, if he had known what he was talking about he might have realized that not just 'point five' should have been indicated there, but—with a futuristic *Stockhausen-Metronome*—63 point 56778, as, for example, in the case of a tuned pitch on the piano. Naturally, if you want to give a precise numerical indication of the pitches of the tempered scale, then you arrive at complex numbers. Never mind that any child can sing those pitches. The same is true of tempos as well as dynamics.

Last week, while mixing a recording in Hannover, I noticed that even 0.2 or 0.3 of a decibel constitutes an audible difference between different sound sources, if they are to be balanced spatially exactly in the middle. So: you listen until it is correct, and upon seeing what you actually heard you are completely astounded when you learn that the apparatus indeed records a difference of 0.3 of a decibel. Then I write this down. Our ears can be highly discriminating when it comes to spatial orientation. All the characteristics of music can be represented by numbers. When you compose, music comprises numbers, particularly so when you compose with electronic equipment. My son, Simon, selects numbers when he programs his synthesizer. He uses an *Atari* computer which he must also program exclusively by numbers. When measuring sound, there is nothing but numbers. When we push the study of anatomy to its fundamentals, we know that our bodies can be represented by numbers. Who knows what a DNA code is? By the way, in Europe it is often referred to as a DNS code. Do you know what that is?

We call it DNA.

So do I. Crick and Watson provided a new formulation of the DNA code that had already been discovered in the 1930s. The gene, which calls forth life and dictates our physiological form as well as our characteristics, is known to be a numerical sequence of components. Astronomical events are also described in numbers. They must be exact down to a millionth of a second to be valid. All cosmic events, everything that happens on this planet, all has a material exterior that's accessible to touch, smell, hearing, vision. However, what goes on between the sensory system and the brain consists of a transformation into numbers. Only numbers exist in the brain; it translates everything into digits. Our most modern computers are merely limited copies of our brains, for the human brain is, essentially, nothing but a giant computer. The small computers we produce are miniature copies of our brains.

When you look closely at human nature and our natural surroundings, you notice that particular numbers are crucial. This is recognized in the Pythagorean number sequence, 1 plus 2 plus 3 plus 4, from which an entire universe can be developed, all based on the number ten. Two times five fingers, as we can see it on our own hands and two times five toes seen from above, show the Pythagorean system. From this, the entire universe is built— 1 plus 2 plus 3 plus 4. That is a series, and the serial order of these four numbers is the key, for if we place our two hands next to each other with the thumbs toward the outside, we get 3 – 4 – 2 – 1 (the two little fingers in the middle), so that no interval is repeated. The intervals are all different: 3 followed by 4 gives plus 1; 4 followed by 2 gives minus 2; 2 followed by 1 gives minus 1; 3, the first number, following the last, namely 1, gives plus 2. It is important to keep in mind that the intervals between numbers are very significant.

In music, this numerical relationship has been translated into *serialism*. *Formula music* simply takes this further by incorporating even much more than just the durations of notes, pitches of the notes, intensities of the notes, composition of tone spectrums and spatial positions of tones (that is to say the decisions concerning the directions and the velocities of the tones moving around above and below the audience in the auditory space). In addition to all this, a formula includes pre-echoes, echoes, scales, pure pauses, coloured pauses, modulations and improvisations: in short, more qualities of sound. Of course, these qualities of a formula can also be comprehended in terms of numbers. From such a genetic code of music that can be used for composing, it is possible to develop a large organism. That's what I am doing in LICHT. The only difference from earlier projects is that rather than lasting the usual quarter- or half-hour like traditional music, this organism lasts for approximately 24 hours. LICHT is nothing but a galaxy that's derived from a single nuclear formula.

In his *Kunst der Fuge* Johann Sebastian Bach attempted to derive a large work from a single theme by using all the possible manipulations and combinations of that theme. At the end of the twentieth century, this principle is being applied on a far more differentiated and complex level to many more parameters than anybody could have imagined in Bach's time; in fact, to everything whenever possible. It is even applied to the movements of dancers, to costumes, colours, fragrances, spaces—everything. That is an evolutionary fact.

In this sense, formula composition is a refined further development of serialism and incorporates the intermediate phases of aleatoric music and indeterminacy (also known as variable determinism), right up to the latest concepts surrounding parameters that were not even thought about earlier: composition based on the degrees of surprise *(Überraschungsgrad)*, degrees of destruction *(Zerstörungsgrad)*, degrees of renewal *(Erneuerungsgrad)* and so on. Today all these elements are subject to numerical control in musical compositions. It's a typical late twentieth-century phenomenon and it's directly related to modern technology; it's incredibly significant!

Naturally, there are also mysterious relationships involved, as you indicated with your reference to the cosmos. We have not only inherited the Pythagorean system of 1 plus 2 plus 3 plus 4, but also the series of prime numbers have lately become an important factor in music. These are the numbers that are not divisible: 1, then 3, 5, 7, and 11, 13, 17, 23, and so on. Now, traditional music is derived from 1 to 2 to 3 and so forth, where 1 to 2 are the octaves, 2 to 3 are the fifths, 3 to 4 are the fourths, 4 to 5 are major thirds and 5 to 6 are minor thirds. The major and minor thirds and their inversions, the sixths, were considered vulgar and were called the 'imperfect six-three chords' (false parallels). They were supposed to have originated in England where they were initially sung in popular music. (From what I hear, maids in Vienna are about the only ones who indulge in singing parallel thirds.) After thirds and sixths, the major and minor seconds were added, and with them, major and minor sevenths as well as major and minor ninths.

Towards the middle of this century, my electronic work STUDIE II introduced intervals of the 25th square root of 5 into music. The 25th square root of 5 produces intervals that differ significantly from the ordinary division of the octave's twelve tones into eleven equal intervals. STUDIE II excludes octaves, fifths, fourths and major thirds from its scale. In GESANG DER JÜNGLINGE, I used forty-two *different* scales for individual sections. That gives a completely different kind of melody and harmony, as well as a very different rhythm when these scales are used for determining the the durations.

In the last few years I have worked intensively with micro-scales (remind me to give you some scores as a present). That is, micro-scales applied to instrumental music, because I use them for flute, basset-horn and trumpet. I use fingerings that are highly unusual and which must be learned from scratch by the musicians, as they have never encountered them before, no matter how long they have been playing their instruments. New melodic and harmonic structures occur and, above all, new timbres. The evolution of scales into ever finer, unexplored areas is increasingly important.

Apparently, I was the one who first introduced groups of 11 notes and 13 notes into rhythm. It is believed that Brahms introduced groups of 9, that is, three times three. Though Chopin used a group of 17, he used it only as a cadential figure, not systematically as in my GRUPPEN *für 3 Orchester* (1958) or ZEITMASZE (1955) where triplets, quintuplets, septuplets, and groups of 9, 11 and 13 *(Neuntolen, Elftolen, Dreizehntolen)* became just as important as the even-numbered divisions. In later works, particularly of electronic music, there are still much more differentiated rhythms based on irregular and complex numbers. That, in turn, produces other very interesting experiences! Number 7 plays a significant role in my music, as does 11. Everything related to Lucifer is connected with 11 and 13.

Is there a conscious effort to give material presence to the cosmic and the divine within formula thinking?

Well, as I have emphasized repeatedly, formula thinking is not my invention, but is the next step of a planetary development. The millenia-old use of *ragas* and *talas* as formative elements of Indian music, or the variations of primal forms in Chinese music, influenced the musical techniques of Central Europe via Greek music. Working with primal forms like *ragas* and *talas* is an absolutely fundamental technique. The principle resurfaced in late medieval Europe in the form of isorhythms. The monks knew that, and partly from Greek sources learned how to use *color* and *talea*. In Baroque music, we have this extraordinary spiritual phenomenon, Johann Sebastian Bach, who somehow was aware of the primordial rules of construction. In the twentieth century, this knowledge has again been honoured by the twelve-tone techniques of the Viennese School, notably in the revival of isorhythms in Anton Webern's works. Webern wrote a thesis on the subject of Heinrich Isaac's *Choralis Constantinus*, and he studied Isaac's technique of melodic and harmonic development. I learned a little about the subject during my studies in Paris with Olivier Messiaen.

Messiaen accomplished a synthesis. He studied Indian rhythm and melody and related them to the Gregorian use of neumes (which also connect duration, intensity and pitch). Because Messiaen was a church musician he referred his students again and again to the theory of neumes, and he used it himself as a composer. In Cologne I had already studied musicology and therefore knew something about the transcription of neumes into modern notation. So, there again was a connection with the primeval tradition of creating form based on archetypes. Though he later repeatedly maintained that it was unintentional, Messiaen was the first to approach a synthesis of Indian music, Gregorian music, medieval isorhythms and the serial music of the early twentieth-century Viennese School. For my generation, the vision of such a synthesis was an explosive confrontation, and we have brought it to bear on every parameter of music.

In 1953 following my studies in Paris I started work in the Electronic Music Studio of the West German Radio. At the same time, I studied communications theory at the University of Bonn, as well as linguistics including phonetics and phonology. Linguistics is fascinating, but I was not specifically interested in the theory of languages; rather, I was fascinated by phonetics and acoustics, notably the analysis and notation of phonetic phenomena. At that time, Professor Meyer-Eppler taught communications theory and phonetics in Bonn, and through him I became familiar with modern techniques: statistics, chance operations, aleatory and the incipient digital theory. I subsequently applied the conceptual apparatus of these disciplines to music, so that I became chiefly responsible for the introduction of terms like 'parameter', 'serial', 'aleatoric' into German musical vocabulary, terms later adopted by the French. Some of my first articles from 1953–1954 were published by French periodicals, and they contained the various new concepts that arose from my studies of information theory, phonetics, acoustics and communications theory. At the Music Conservatory (*Musikhochschule*) in Cologne I received a pathetically poor education in acoustics from Professor Mies who taught us a bunch of confused nonsense about pendulums and the like in order to explain tone frequencies. Actually, nobody really understood the nature of acoustics. Through my work in the Electronic Music Studio, I eventually learned the empirical and theoretical bases for acoustics, specifically electro-acoustics. I also contributed to the development of the field, an ongoing project.

Consequently, after 1951 music was moved to a completely new level. In this phase, technology and music, acoustics and musical composition, co-existed within the same arena.

Since 1951, then . . .

A completely new level existed compared with the entire tradition that had preceded it. The break with tradition *(Zeitschnitt)* was a result of developments in electronics and the new techniques for storing unlimited amounts of information relative to perception. This started a new technological and cultural era.

Your LICHT *Project seems to be comparable to Wagner in so far as his work expresses an ambition to encompass the past, the present and the future, as well as criticism and visions, art and religion. Does your great heptalogy also end with a Götter-dämmerung, or are you, unlike Wagner, a cultural optimist?*

I have to counter that with another question: what vision of the future is there to be found in Wagner?

It's a fact that his work has been interpreted as possibly indicating ideas about the future.

In what ways?

Well, it possibly points, to a certain degree, toward a new dimension by the force of its giant scope.

No, I mean, what *future* does his work promise? Does it actually point towards a new future?

Some interpreters have emphasized that the Götterdämmerung does not exclude the emergence of a renewed world.

Really?

Yes.

Where is that indicated?

Well, by musicologists and . . .

No, what I am asking is, where in Wagner's work is there such a reference to the future, in the music and in the text? Where?

Well, it would be at the end, the finishing part of the work.

What I want to know is whether Wagner in his work establishes any connection to the future?

That I don't know.

But that's what you just said. You said: 'Wagner's work expresses an ambition to encompass the past, the present and the future'. What future, then?

I was referring to people who have said that the work is not necessarily the end of everything, but could open to something new. I don't know how concrete you want it, but . .

I would like to know concretely whether or not Wagner's work contains any kind of vision of the future.

You find nothing like . . . ?

No. I have always had the impression that his work is exclusively retrospective, a last review of a Germanic ideology, a Germanic world view. Something like a summary or a sentimental return.

Hmm. That would then be the difference between yourself and Wagner?

I think so, yes. My work is not at all concerned with the past, but is based on the idea that the protagonists represent a theory of evolution, a will for evolution. LUCIFER represents a static concept of the cosmos according to which spirit and perfection are forever immanently present. Contrary to MICHAEL, he needs no evolution, since evolution is tied to imperfection, and to the effort to achieve perfection. MICHAEL's view entails misery; it means suffering and death. The LUCIFER of my work LICHT wants none of that.

So, essential principles are at stake. The protagonists are not historical figures, but instead, I insist that whenever my work LICHT is performed, these two spiritual forces manifest as timeless, immanent cosmic spirits: MICHAEL as creator in our local universe and the one who inspires all developmental processes, and LUCIFER as the antagonist who opposes the uniting will of the cosmos. LUCIFER is the no-sayer, whose message is: 'There is no single and unifying will-power or unifying spirit. God is a phantom, and I am just as important as he'. That is LUCIFER's rebellion.

Then there is the third principle in LICHT, EVA. She is the feminine principle in the cosmos, always endeavouring to mediate, in order to beautify and perfect all living beings. She is responsible for new life on the planets. She wants to enable mankind to have more musical and more beautiful children, Sunday-children. That's EVA's mission, and for that reason she always tries to reconcile MICHAEL and LUCIFER. She is enthusiastic and very hopeful.

In this regard it is true that my work is not only concerned with our times; rather, the protagonists are timeless, ever-present. They inspire us, they are the great spiritual forces that motivate us, the guiding principles. They will be present for all the future, just as they existed throughout the past. I assume that this concept is unrelated to any specific epoch in the life of this planet—contrary to Wagner—or to any partial solution or conclusion. What interests me is the outlook, the futuristic dimension and the question, what does this concept contribute to the future development of mankind?

This is also true of the music. Every small scene, every detail, that comes to me day by day, is based on the formula, which is the unifying principle, the skeleton of the whole. I need an uncannily large number of inspired ideas and loads of intuition regarding details to make sure that all these details become integrated in the large genetic process of the work; in that way the larger organism is enriched and keeps growing.

Wagner uses the Leitmotif technique to bind his musical and intellectual universe together. Is your formula approach a comparable principle?

As far as I know, the Leitmotifs are like traffic signals that announce what kind of character is arriving, like signs that say, 'Attention'! In the formula technique for LICHT, the super formula *(Superformel)* is the code for the entire work. Nothing falls outside the formula: the large form, which is a projection of the formula over a long period, and the smaller forms, which reach into the tiniest structures are either expansions or compressions, which stretch or condense the formula, or they are superimpositions, mirrorings and transformations of the formula. It is largely comparable with a genetically coded organism, in which the multiplication of cells leads to the growth of a complete body. Everything is derived from the formula, and there is a radical difference between the use of intermittent signals to announce the arrival of a character and the use of a single germ to develop a great organism with all its various figures and shapes.

True. Talking about the formula, I'd like to read you a relevant comment on this line of thought in an essay by the American composer, Morton Feldman, who says

... the artist has an incredible problem. Especially if they are young and they are growing up because everything is right. Bach is right and his *Kinder* are right. Gluck is right, Palestrina is right, Karlheinz [Stockhausen] is right, everybody is right. The confusion of a young artist growing up is not the confusion that everybody is wrong and I'm right, the confusion is that everybody is right, am I wrong? So, you're intimidated, because every system works, because they set it up so that it does work, and it's the nature of western men to do fantastic things, and so it works. Hegel works, Kierkegaard works. Kierkegaard said, 'It doesn't make any difference, because eventually what is gonna happen to me is that I will be part of his system, he is gonna incorporate me in his system'. So if he doesn't work alone ... then someone else incorporates [him]. This is the formula of Stockhausen, and it is based on a military formula. And the military formula is this: 'You make a small circle to exclude me, I'll make a larger circle to include you'. And essentially, this is a dynamic in history. And then after 300 years we look at it, we refine it and we start all over again.[1]

What would be your response to this?

What is the problem? I think it is stupid to claim this has anything to do with the military, because the military is part of an overriding cosmic force that, for instance, gives coherence to solar systems. It is pointless to get all upset because our solar system does not include all the planets of the universe; that is what other solar systems are for. I fail to see that it is problematic for a young composer to develop his own world. He is free to do that. Like Gluck .... That's fine. Why make a problem out of the fact that one is afraid of others? Anyone who has the desire and the gift to do so should build his own world; it can only be a source of fascination to others. It is so much more interesting to build one's own world than to want one world in common. I certainly don't want to see everything being the same. On the contrary, I want to realize only my music.

Pursuant to our discussion about Wagner, it seems clear that Adorno was not exactly optimistic in his view of culture. He and Jürgen Habermas promoted a certain branch of philosophical history that sees modernism as an unfinished project. Adorno maintains that 'the new' is an important categorical designation, and taking Schoenberg as his chief witness he establishes that negativity is essential in defining moments of truth. Key phrases are, 'historic necessity' and 'the objective tendency of the material'. Today we are inclined to question this school's belief in an 'historic necessity', and rather see this faith in the coercive force of history as a compulsive obsession. Still, these responses to modernism remain focal in debates and function as a counter weight to the postmodern vision of abolishing the concept of an 'historic' time frame. You knew Adorno and discussed his Philosophy of New Music *with him and your own music has been interpreted in the context of the philosophy of history that Adorno put forth. But to what extent do you recognize yourself in his philosophic construction? Have you actually been able to make use of his ideas in your compositions?*

I met Adorno a number of times. On one interesting occasion we were sitting in the Schlosskeller in Darmstadt late one evening after a day full of seminars and concerts, and he said, 'Stockhausen, I am really a musician, a composer'. One of his students sitting next to him (Andreas Razumovsky, a music critic, if I remember rightly) commented, 'But Teddy, you are really a philosopher'! Adorno replied, 'That's unfortunately what I always hear, but truly, I am first and foremost a musician, a composer'.

Now, some of his songs had been performed at the Summer Courses, and they revealed that he was not a very original composer. He always wanted to pass himself off as a pupil of Alban Berg, because Schoenberg had refused to take him as a student. Adorno's problem is characteristic of many intellectuals in the field of music who are devoted music lovers. They always long to be composers of original works, just as the great masters of the past wrote original works. But deep down they realize that they lack the wealth of talent and the mark of genius needed to become original composers. But this longing finds expression in their theories. In particular, such people are enormously negative towards other composers whom they want to sweep aside by the sheer power of their intellects. Adorno was like that, and he made dreadfully mean comments about many composers. Even the world-famous Stravinsky was included in the list, not to mention people like Orff, Egk or Blacher whom he totally annihilated. The only one who was accepted as a representative for new music was Arnold Schoenberg.

Adorno was strongly attracted to my works. He attended several performances and he noticed that they reflect a strong belief in the necessity to discover something new wherever feasible. It is not a simple matter to discover something really new; the process is closely linked to technical evolution. It would not have been possible for me to make so many new discoveries without the development in electronics, the new technology in performance practice and without the general interest in innovation: the exploration of outer space that began around that time, astrophysics, nuclear research, new trends in biology, the development of artificial materials. Since 1950, there has been a veritable explosion in all these fields, and it continues. Every day the electroacoustical industry puts out new equipment. There is no end to it, and it is accelerating. There is no stopping it.

In music, this takes on a particular significance just as Adorno's role takes on significance, because—though a mediocre composer—he argued that the permanent revolution caused by technological discoveries also affects musical performance techniques. To me, that is particularly important in the context of electronics and all the related studio equipment and performance practice. Driven by its own internal dynamics, this force is, as Adorno realized, a reality, whether a composer goes along with it or not.

The thing is, there are still many composers who continue to write one symphony after another, oblivious of the innovations of the twentieth century and the opening up of radically new techniques. They are once again writing series of string quartets, they follow the traditional patterns for orchestral scoring, write their solo concerti, their little operas and Lieder, their orchestra works in four movements, and so on. You'll notice this expressly reactionary tendency everywhere, and it currently calls itself *postmodern*. It's a truly revolting term, for there is no such thing as modern, postmodern, or for that sake, premodern. For a CREATIVE individual, every day is given to new discoveries, new questions and new inventions.

Any person who is obsessed with becoming famous in his field but finds out that he lacks talent, will respond by an attempt to develop his own system; this is also true of musicians. But if his circle is too narrow, as Morton Feldman expresses it, and he becomes afraid of the larger circle which threatens to absorb him, then he becomes angry and starts attacking other composers. Europe is rich in mediocre or incapable people with huge egos. Here, at the end of the twentieth century, because all generally accepted criteria of quality have dissolved, there are plenty of opportunities for such people.

'Inherent historic evolution' is a reality, no matter whether a Stravinsky or an Orff or a Stockhausen goes along with it. Music has its own dynamic. Just like physics, which again is not dependent on the contribution of some physical scientist in, say, Munich. Daily, something new is revealed within physics, space research, astronomy; every day brings new discoveries. Some astronomer in California may pass away, but another will surely notice the next supernova or discover a wholly new region of the universe.

You must acknowledge this inherent evolution and realize that music is not a separate entity but one of the spiritual realms, besides being one of the natural sciences, namely the science of acoustics. Within the scientific study of acoustics, new discoveries are made every day, and it is up to composers whether they make use of these innovations or not. Most of the interesting experiments nowadays are made by pop musicians who are not composers but 'transformers'. They pick up whatever comes along, load it into their samplers—also into their mental samplers—and they blend it in their brains as well as in their computers, until they have a mix that somehow sounds ultra modern. When that mix is projected through modern equipment, it often sounds rather interesting.

These pop musicians are not afraid of modern techniques. They simply take everything that the industry has to offer by way of modern technology and make something different of it, something new. And that's perfectly fine.

No matter what area you are in, you can't possibly carry on as a productive individual, not even for one more day, unless you firmly believe that tomorrow will bring something interesting, not just more of the same. This results in total confusion among musicians because they are scared at the very thought of being modern, since they assume that nothing remains to be invented and discovered. That's a tremendous mistake.

Morton Feldman was, actually, a poor guy. I met him several times and we got along with each other very well. His problem was his eyes. He wore glasses that were almost half an inch thick. On top of that he was an alcoholic and a great gourmand. He loved eating more than composing. Once in a while, his poor eyesight forced him to draw notes the size of eggs on a sheet of paper stuck to the wall. He quite simply couldn't draw anything very complex; tones had to come two seconds apart or more, otherwise he would never have finished a piece. So, he made a virtue of necessity. But he was an intellectual and wanted above all else to become famous, and so he used his intellectual resources to denounce others. He was what he was: That's that! Morton Feldman: 'as slow as possible' and 'as soft as possible'. That is about all. But it constitutes a kind of private style, as in the case of the painter Yves Klein, who one day decided to paint only blue pictures. He became famous for his blue pictures, blue objects and blue happenings. One may paint only squares, like Josef Albers, or only write 'as slow as possible', like Morton Feldman. That's the way of 'style-composers'. They look for some very narrow, tiny little circles that circumscribe their self-identities and allow others to recognize them. That is the stuff polemics and congresses are made of. There has to be some theory too, and some philosophical statements about the 'circle of the nothing', the 'border of silence', or the 'void of muteness'.

Gone are the days when a composer was expected to produce a rich variety of original works, to be a master craftsman for all kinds of instrumentariums, to boil over with inventive ideas, instead of variations. But shouldn't a composer create models that could help others assimilate new developments in the areas of form, harmony, rhythm, dynamics, coloration, topology? Should he not demonstrate how it's possible to balance logical development against surprising ideas, or to pit the intimacy of calmness against youthful stormy temperament? Do we no longer expect a composer to create a rich, diversified work that confronts a variety of challenges for the benefit of not only the musical life of his own nation or continent, but of the whole planet?

It is hard for people in the Nordic countries to comprehend the influence of Adorno in the 1950s. We read his texts, but they do not explain all . . .

Hmm.

... but how ... ? Am I right in believing that he was crucial to the understanding of the necessity for constant renewal of musical material and so forth? Did you experience that in the 1950s?

Indeed! From 1947 to 1951 I studied musicology as a subsidiary subject at the University of Cologne, but I took time to read thoroughly Adorno's *Philosophy of New Music* and to give a lecture on it at the Musicological Institute. I also took part in discussions of the book. You know, the language is extremely complicated, and one needs to analyse critically what he is actually saying. One provocation presented by Adorno's book—the one that made it famous— was obviously that he took the then current consensus about the world-famous Stravinsky and the not-so-famous Schoenberg and turned it around: 'Look at Schoenberg! Stravinsky is really just an overrated folk-musician who writes entertainment music.' That was about the extent of his thesis.

His other provocation consisted of his protest against the political patronization of art. Now, this was in the wake of Nazism with its grand theory to the effect that art must serve politics (like in the Soviet Union to this day): the arts were required to subject themselves to the ideology of the people's party *(Volkspartei)*. Actually, this attitude is widely held, even in our times. In the USA, in the opera houses as well as in the concert halls, there exists an influential wealthy society (with the power of a political party) that subscribes to the taste of the old, Viennese emigrants. Their aesthetic preferences end with Mahler. It is not the communists' 'social realism', but the capitalist emigrants' outdated taste.

Adorno openly attacked this ideology. In the face of slogans like 'music for the working class' and 'music for the masses', he pointed out that music, like all other spiritual realms, has its own inner dynamics, its own evolutionary process, and that it consequently must be free of intervention. He made it clear that Schoenberg had liberated himself from the slave mentality that has been at the root of the European tradition of art music since it was first created and made to serve the social prestige and entertainment of clerical and secular rulers.

However, this liberation has brought about its own serious problems. Whether masterpieces of the past were sponsored by early religious and secular potentates or by nineteenth-century rich bourgeois Maecenases, the fact remained that a wealthy, aristocratic, elitist society supported European art right up to the end of the previous century. In the twentieth century there has been virtually nobody to support art, particularly not after World War I, and definitely not after World War II. For a while, radio stations followed traditional lines and tried to continue support of new musical works, but that's no longer the case. And then this political moloch, the state, became increasingly inflated.

Adorno was right to point out that we have to be more alert than ever before to the dangers of socialist administration of music and the other arts, and that art must be free. Of course, we were in agreement on this point. Then, as he got older (sadly, he died too young), he was brought to despair by confrontation with his own theories. Regrettably, the students at the University of Frankfort made him feel dishonoured, offended and ridiculous. He actually wanted a sympathetic relationship with the 'revolutionary' students, the ones who demanded freedom in all corners of society and who proclaimed, 'We will no longer serve capitalism and those people who are manipulating us with their Coca-Cola art'. Essentially, those students devoured their own father, ruined him. He didn't expect that to happen. At the end he was saddened, because it was all a huge misunderstanding. His ambition was no less than to torpedo such authoritarian systems as Nazism and International Socialism, but he didn't succeed. After Adorno's death, the dominating attitude here in West Germany was to curtail the dependency that was inflicted on serious music by society, not least by the democratic majority parties. It really seemed as if his students and followers were taking his ideology a step forward.

Schoenberg's great achievement with the establishment of his Society for Private Musical Performances *(Verein für musikalische Privataufführungen)* in Vienna was to claim freedom for composers: freedom *from* the prevailing taste of society and its media; freedom *for* music to evolve without interference. In other words, here was a composer who made it clear to society that he would not allow himself to be kicked about like Mozart who was kicked in the backside by a court official of the Archbishop at Salzburg when he was eight days late returning from a vacation in Vienna. In the twentieth century, for the first time, the treatment of composers as servants has been put in perspective. It took an outstanding individual to make people aware that a composer could no longer be the slave of institutions, of a patronizing upper class, of society's prevailing tastes and, least of all, of politicians and publishers who dictate ideologies. His star still shines.

We should never lose sight of this star. We must recognize the effect of the irrational fear of a permanent revolution of the arts, the fear of persistent efforts to develop and evolve reflected in discoveries and inventions. We can see the consequences of this fear everywhere. The belief in eternal progress is like a lost dream, instead we look backwards to the treasures of the past and mix up all that it has given us, from Indian music, over all of European art music, to present day pop music. I mentioned my experience with the new opera by York Höller. According to the publicity, the work is meant to be a 'perspectival reminiscence'. Well, 'recycling' is the fashionable slogan of the 'environmentalists'. The great majority of composers have adopted that concept. This epidemic began with the neoclassicism of Stravinsky and Hindemith, not to mention Milhaud. A bunch of stale tricks! To compose something that never existed before, something that reveals the creative powers of man, this is the utopian vision of the liberated artist. This is the artist who calls to others: 'Prick up your ears, stop talking! If you have really listened, then we may jointly eavesdrop on the next work. But let no one dictate what I should do!'

That vision is the beginning of a new movement. This is something entirely new in the history of this planet. For the first time in the twentieth century, this freedom shines forth, precisely at a time when the taste of the masses seems to be totally dominant—not even the elitist aristocratic taste anymore, but the taste of the masses determined by population research. Quotas based on how many viewers or listeners or buyers there were, are taken as evidence of what is best on the radio, on television, on records, in films and in books. Yet at this critical moment, there are very few artists—are there any at all?—who would suffer death rather than submit to the new feudal system, and who would proclaim: 'No! I am free. I invent what I want and what I am inspired to. It's your problem whether you understand it or not'. We must insist on the unconditional freedom of the arts. At the age of 63, I am no longer in the mood to participate in discussions that question the freedom of art. Many have stated the view both aloud and in writing that Stockhausen is 'the last composer', and that his kind of 'freedom' is no longer feasible.

I would like to talk a bit about critics. We have spoken about Adorno. Now, he held the opinion that the critic should be on the same level as the composer and be able to critique his compositions; he should be as skilful as the composer and actually be able to assist him.

Hmm . . .

Of course, many composers say, 'I don't care what the critics come up with; it makes no difference to me'! But I get the impression that you find it important to establish a counterbalance to the critics' statements. In our initial telephone conversation, you even mentioned one of the worst critics and his false statements. I assume that you are willing to discuss the situation. Can you say something about it? What should a critic be like?

There is a long tradition of writing books about such issues as the conflicts between composers and critics, so we know about this particular relationship right back through the classics. Now, the first critics were also composers or well-trained musicians. They were in close touch with the taste of their period. Critics today are paid by newspapers, publishing houses and other media agencies, who are concerned with the selling of papers, books, records and radio programmes. Therefore, critics can't just write something that goes against the opinion of a lot of people who then would cancel their newspaper subscriptions and stop buying the books and records or switch to other stations. Naturally, that puts the critic in a difficult situation.

When Adorno demands that a critic must be on a level with the composer, he is expressing an idealistic concept. Think of Robert Schumann writing for his *Neue Zeitschrift für Musik* and promoting Chopin and Brahms. The Society of Artists and Art Lovers *(Verein von Künstlern und Kunstfreunden)*, which Schumann organized, called itself the *Davidsbündler* (Davidian fellows) to express the ideal of fighting the philistines in the manner of the biblical singer, David. This is a most unusual example, for it is generally assumed that a composer should compose and not write music criticism. It was Adorno's luck that he found a publishing house that would print what he wrote, obviously because he was very good at arguing his points and brilliant at articulating them, so his books had no problem selling. He was quite simply a good writer. But such a career is only possible when a person is free. That's simply not possible for a critic at the *Kölner Stadt-Anzeiger* (a metropolitan Cologne paper, *ed.*). Here is somebody who hasn't even studied musicology, not to say learned the composer's craft. In Cologne music reviewers are people who have to cover all kinds of activities: concerts of wind ensembles, jazz-bands, symphony orchestras, opera performances, choral societies, men's choruses, virtuosi, contemporary music, and so on. The critics never get a chance to study anything in any depth in order to support their evaluations; they don't listen to any piece repeatedly, they don't study scores, they don't sit in at rehearsals. They are paid very little, and in order to keep their job at a paper, they rush from one concert to the next. What can the poor devils do? They don't have a chance to write anything but the most superficial stuff. Most of the time they are dead tired and leave the concert half-way through. It is not a dignified profession anymore, if ever it was.

In the previous century, and still at the beginning of this one, first performances were described over whole pages. Now it is down to a small column. Editors shorten paragraphs, alter texts, add headlines — all without the critic's consent. The critic is in a miserable situation, and since this often puts him in a bad mood he usually writes something negative. When, on top of that, he is poorly informed, he causes composers and performers much frustration. If he forgets to mention a performer, then the performer raises hell. Essentially, the critic's position is impossible. A critic who was worth his name would have to be adequately informed. A music journalist should write pre-concert announcements or features to give relevant information to his readers, listeners, or viewers *before* a concert, even quite a long time in advance. The story of the music critic is a closed chapter in history.

However, there is the need for a new profession within the media, namely the 'music informant'. That's a person with a musical education who can make listeners and readers aware of what is going to be performed at upcoming concerts and what scores are available, and so forth. This would be very helpful to audiences by providing otherwise inaccessible information to help them prepare for a particular event, learn what other events are going on, discover where they can hear first performances of new works and who the performers are, learn about the background for a work, in short, everything that those interested need in order to make their own judgments. The traditional concept is that a critic must inform the uninformed and must educate fellow citizens with poor taste so that they may improve their taste, but that's a remnant of an age when the prevailing view of culture assumed that most people were blockheads, that only a few were educated, and that those with education must elevate the ignorant to their own level. This process, from the top down, has mostly had the result that people have become even more stupid than they already were.

A new period of enlightenment *(Aufklärung)* must begin with the realization that everybody is intelligent enough to make an individual judgment. Thus, a 'music informant' could help individuals reach their conclusions. It is true that selective information entails the exercise of influence. The solution is to be as careful and inclusive as possible in providing information about available recordings, broadcastings, concerts and lectures, so that people can educate themselves and form their own judgments. This would be the future role of the mediator between composer and audience.

When one considers the wide scope of your compositions, the six volumes of TEXTE *zur* MUSIK, *your* LICHT *project, your correspondence, which fills more than 300 ring binders, your activity as a publisher as well as your many tours, then one wonders how you manage all of it. It seems impossible to maintain this ambitious level of involvement and creativity without running into some crisis. Have you experienced crises?*

Naturally I have. In 1982, for instance, there was a serious crisis over a confrontation with the three main representatives of Deutsche Grammophon Gesellschaft. That year I received the German Record Prize for the recording of JAHRESLAUF. I travelled to Hamburg for the occasion and just before the prize ceremony, I was invited into the office of Deutsche Grammophon-Polygram International. Sitting there were President Holzschneider, Production Director Breest and Marketing Director Pedersen. These gentlemen informed me without further formality that this was the end of the cooperation between Stockhausen and Deutsche Grammophon—after twenty years and around eighty records. First I was told, 'Although you have been the only contemporary composer whose recorded works have never under sold, in fact, have sold very well, that's no longer enough for us. We now need much higher sales figures, at least 50,000 records per year per release, and your works don't quite make that much with the exception of GESANG DER JÜNGLINGE. Therefore, we will no longer produce your recordings'. (This notwithstanding the fact that I had for some years been paying for recording sessions myself, and that I had written liner notes without a fee, and so on.) Suzanne Stephens was present at this conversation. She asked Mr. Pedersen if he had ever heard a single note of Stockhausen's music. He answered, 'No need to, the sales numbers are all I care about'. There was silence from the funny triumvirate. Suzanne said again politely, 'It is really important to know if you are familiar with any of Stockhausen's music'. Mr. Breest cut her short, 'Who in the world has asked you to speak here?'

For a while, there were attempts at a limited cooperation, but eventually it came to an end. Since then there have been no recordings of Stockhausen from Deutsche Grammophon and that did, indeed, constitute a crisis. It was the end of twenty years' work on the creation of an idealistic edition. I had conducted the works, participated as performer, made recordings as sound projectionist, been sound mixer in the studio, designed covers, written and corrected liner notes in three languages, selected photos and, finally, checked the master plates for days on end in order to control the pressings until each record was released. Multiply this by eighty times: each record must have cost me between one-and-a-half months and two years (as in the case of SIRIUS) of work. The European version of MOMENTE demanded six weeks of rehearsals, a tour with seven performances, a week of recording and six weeks of mixing in a studio in Hannover, sitting from morning to night in a narrow air-conditioned room with windows that couldn't be opened so that I developed strep throat. Finally, this resulted in two records. After all that, a couple of years later, I am told, 'As of today, your records will not be produced any more'. I have been through such crises again and again, as in the Electronic Music Studio where, one fine day, there were no more collaborators, equipment was no longer repaired or replaced, and everything went down the drain after I had worked for decades to set it up.

One horrible crisis involved Universal Edition. They published all of my works until 1969. Director Alfred Schlee was higly esteemed by me and at the time I thought of him as a friend, so I had for years been giving him my works virtually free. I received practically nothing for all the works they published although I produced a number of the scores in my own house with a hand press and with the help of collaborators, none of whom were professional graphic artists (they were an architecture student, a painter, my assistants Cornelius Cardew and Joachim Krist, a postman and a fugitive from Hungary). I drew many of the printer's copies myself, and others were drawn by students (Makoto Shinohara, Rolf Gelhaar and Peter Eötvös, to mention a few). Certain scores, such as ZYKLUS, REFRAIN, MIKROPHONIE I, and MIKROPHONIE II, I had printed in Cologne and shipped to Vienna in a container. The printer's copies of virtually all the Stockhausen scores published by Universal Edition were prepared in my house under my supervision, then printed in Cologne or Vienna.

All of that came to an end when the owner, Alfred Kalmus, died in London and the new Director, Stephan Harpner (his son-in-law) came to Vienna. Some time in 1974 he called me in for a conversation, on which occasion Alfred Schlee, the current Vice Director, and Suzanne Stephens also were present. Harpner proclaimed, 'We can no longer publish all of your new works. You will remain under exclusive contract with the U.E. and offer us new scores, but we will only accept what is of interest to us and what has commercial interest. Works that we don't want, you are free to submit to other publishers'. I was totally shocked and was staring at Alfred Schlee, who said nothing, but looked aside and avoided coming to my defence. I said, 'If you reject even one of my children, you shall have none at all. This is the end of Universal Edition'. Then I left.

That was a hard and very difficult time. It led to years of uncertainty when I was at a loss about what to do. I asked other publishers' advice. Mr. Vötterle of Bärenreiter Verlag came to visit me, as well as the Directors of Schott, of Chapell International, Faber & Faber in London and Boosey & Hawkes. All had nothing but money and percentages on their minds. They all wanted to produce simple photocopies of my scores, they would offer nothing before all the costs of production were covered, and so on.

Finally, in 1975, I decided to produce the scores myself since I had done that earlier for U.E. Since then there has been the Stockhausen-Verlag. Very few scores are bought. There are but a few especially interested people who order them, and most scores I give away as presents. But they are printed! I pay the cost of printing with the money that I earn as a conductor and from commissions, or from various activities as sound projectionist, recording director, recording supervisor during sound mixing, and with whatever I earn through GEMA. That leaves me a very small income. Lately, I have also started producing recordings of my works, since no Stockhausen recordings have been issued for many years and none are available in the shops. Just this week, I have begun to press CDs.

So, there have been many crises. They are like natural catastrophes; once they are over, a new and more beautiful landscape emerges.

So, what about the large LICHT *project? You said that it must be finished by year 2002.*

2003, yes.

2003 . . . is that still the goal?

Yes, I will achieve it.

Honestly?

I'm now finished with DIENSTAG AUS LICHT. So, by 1995 at the latest, I must finish FREITAG, and then, by 1998 or 1999, MITTWOCH. After that, I have four or five years until 2003 in which to finish composing SONNTAG AUS LICHT.

This year's Frankfurt Festival, at which you were the featured composer, had the motto, 'Beauty—a utopia'? What is your position on that? Do you understand it as a rhetorical question or as a dialectic statement? In what sense does your music answer that question?

For the opening of the Frankfurt Festival, I gave a lecture with the title *Fremde Schönheit* (Alien Beauty) in which I explained to the audience that the word *fremde* (alien) was originally associated with the meaning of 'far', or 'far from'. The English word 'from', which reflects the original meaning of *fremde*, indicates not only 'from' far, as in 'he comes from', but also away 'from' here, as in 'he goes forth from'. So, *fern*, 'far', and *fremd* are related, just as a *Fremder*, 'an alien', comes from afar.

Schönheit, 'beauty', is derived from *schôn, scono* or *skaun*. It is related to the English 'sheen', which means shine. The earliest source for the word *Schönheit* is the courtly poetry of the thirteenth century. What was called *schön*, was already *schon*, 'finished', 'perfect'. So, *schön*, 'beautiful', implies something both perfect and shiny. This remains true, and it presupposes that we are sensitive to that which is finished and perfect. And there is yet another implication: since Old Norse *skyn* means 'good order' and Old German *skaun* means something 'graceful' to behold, there are indications that *Schönheit* also implies something graceful. So it is not only perfect and shining but also graceful. It denotes luminous spirituality, it shines. *Fremde Schönheit* thus defines the essence of art.

I went on to explain that in this sense, the truly free artist will create incessantly manifestations of the longing for this *fremde Schönheit*. By way of an example, I mentioned my work XI. The word, XI, means 'unknown quantity', 'unknown beauty'. This composition is for any instrument that can produce microtones. There are already two worked-out versions for flute and for basset-horn. Suzanne Stephens plays XI in darkness with a fantastic costume that consists of 700 tiny light sources in wing-like plexiglass tubes. The piece is developed from the nuclear formula of LICHT which is just a couple of notes; it is the skeleton of MONTAG AUS LICHT, and also the source of MONTAGS-GRUSS (MONDAY GREETING). All the tiny intermediary steps that the performer can possibly find between these notes are to be played.

In that way, each instrumentalist may find different numbers; the flute finds a certain number, while the basset-horn finds many more. The number of these steps is the unknown factor in XI. Suzanne Stephens has played the work with a wonderful resolution into small intervals, with changing timbres for each interval, and not just with the use of tones but also with noises.

Expanding on this, I spoke about the possibility of working within a very narrow range. Suzanne Stephens' version of XI spans three octaves, but it is possible to operate within an even smaller space. This is what happens in the work, YPSILON, which is Y in the Greek alphabet and stands for a 'variable quantity', as in mathematics. Herein lies, again, something that's alien. In the case of an instrument with microtones, the unknown is the number of micro-steps one can find between the usual steps of the chromatic scale. In the score of YPSILON it is indicated that the player must find sixteen steps clustering, as closely as possible, around an A-flat in the second octave. For different instruments the distance between these steps varies. They also produce different timbres. Kathinka Pasveer has fittingly performed YPSILON in a marvellous costume in the shape of a Y. The score prescribes that the performer's body must be hung with tiny bells, and that the player from time to time must shake all over.

XI and YPSILON were the two examples of *fremde Schönheit*. At the end of the lecture, I summed it all up and mentioned that the criteria in question have been applied to all aspects of the new sound articulation in the work AVE for basset-horn and alto flute. After my explanations of the new possibilities for sounds and the new language for instrumentalists, the two players performed AVE. That, then, was my answer to the question, is beauty a utopia? At issue is the eternal and unlimited expansion of our concept of beauty in terms of the alien, the perfect and new experiences.

I have no more questions. Can you think of any areas that we should talk about? Of course, we haven't covered everything. However, I have yet another request, namely that you send a message to my students. My idea is to start one of my first class presentations by playing a cassette recording of your voice telling these Danish students how they should work with your music, and do it right. Is that feasible?

Dating from 1950 to the present, there are around 225 individually performable works written by me. If anybody takes an interest in what I have created so far, it must be with the understanding that each individual work represents only a 225th of my total output, and that it consequently cannot give a complete answer to the question about the meaning of my music. One work is one small fruit from a large tree. Students ought to try, as quickly as possible, to become familiar with many different works in order to obtain a musical image of the world that is the real subject of inquiry. Contrary to composers of earlier periods, I don't have the time to write variants of works so that they essentially speak *one* language, like for example, a series of symphonies nos. 1 through 9, or string quartets nos. 1 through 6, and so forth. Of course, there can be significant changes within such categories of works, with respect to themes, developments and formal divisions, but essentially it sounds like a typical language, like a personal style. My time is very limited; I am aware of far too many tasks that are all parts of my role in history. This is something that cannot be done by somebody else at another time, but which is determined by the great changes in the cultural history of Europe and of the planet at large. An electronic revolution is not just something that occurs every hundred years. I emerged as a composer precisely at the boundary between two great epochs of cultural history, and my work has been realized under these conditions. Consequently, I can only make the prototype of each project I undertake, it isn't possible to make a second, third and fourth version in addition for each jump ahead; I must go further and constantly realize new projects for as long as I live. I see many new challenges that I should meet in order to expand my craft and widen the scope of composition. The array of new challenges is seemingly unlimited, certainly far greater than ever before, and that is reflected in the radically different appearance of each of my many works.

So, a person who listens to two works of mine, for example, first PRO-ZESSION and then MOMENTE, can hardly believe that they are interrelated and composed by the same man; if you hear MANTRA and compare it with an excerpt from a recording of AUS DEN SIEBEN TAGEN, then you might deny that they are by the same composer. That's also true of MIKROPHONIE I, if followed by KONTRA-PUNKTE, and so on. Therefore, one has to be cautious about forming a judgment about this Stockhausen or one of his works. So, listen to a lot!

Now, if you ask me *how* one is to listen, I will reply by repeating what I have often said before, that it is best to find a room with fresh air, where it is really quiet, where you are alone (and can't make conversation) and where nobody will make noises or smoke or drink or eat; you'll only be listening. Don't try to use speakers or record players that are less than optimal. Good earphones might be a help. Eventually, you should get to know the music not only through your ears, but also through your eyes; in other words, learn to read scores. Even though you initially won't understand much, frequent use of scores will gradually help you to learn more about the music and the graphic image will improve your listening. You hear more the longer you spend with the written notes and still more as you learn to read them. That's my second point.

Furthermore, it is imperative to hear as many live performances as possible, particularly by musicians who have worked with me, and if at all possible some in which I take part. Not that this can never go wrong, but that rarely happens, because I do not accept any engagements which do not allow for sufficient rehearsals. If the technical side is weak, I will not accept an engagement. I almost always bring technicians and equipment along with me.

So, you should get hold of information about performances and do your utmost to attend, even if you have to hitch-hike, as many young people do, or ride your bike or take the train. At our concerts there are always musicians who follow us around, no matter where we perform, whether it be in Switzerland or in Dresden where we were two weeks ago. Those musicians whom I saw after the concert in Dresden and who waved and smiled at me and asked questions, were the same ones I met a week later in Berlin, so there are numerous musicians and music lovers in Europe who travel to my concerts. I could mention a supervisor of the Royal Stables in The Hague, who shows up at every concert we give. He has simply been fascinated by my music for years, but he also travels to classical concerts in various European cities. He told me that he spends what he earns on this form of musical education. In this way a true music lover might experience a great number of live performances of my music, which is something quite different from recorded versions.

Records are really, as I always say, small acoustical postcards with two-dimensional images of three-dimensional musical structures that are actually performed in large spaces by live interpreters. Records are usually made in studios and lack the spirit *(Esprit)* that comes with an audience. Our live performances are something unique, and this is reinforced by those very elements that recordings entirely fail to render: the rituals that surround performances, the lights, the superb electro-acoustical installation, the movement of sounds around the audience. One can only hope that young people actively try to discover the real music.

Thanks!

Some important concerts that would be good for young people to attend might be a matinee concert at the Cologne Philharmonic Hall on the 5th of April 1992 at 11 a.m., and again on the 6th and 7th at 8 p.m. I will be conducting the Gürzenich Orchestra. Markus Stockhausen and Kathinka Pasveer are soloists, my son Simon plays the synthesizer. The programme will consist of GESANG DER JÜNGLINGE with four-track space projection, then LUZIFERs TANZ, which lasts about 50 minutes.

This is followed by some interesting performances of the entire DIENSTAG AUS LICHT at the Gulbenkian Foundation in Lisbon, Portugal, on the 10th, 11th and 12th May 1992. I mentioned this earlier, but would like to repeat it for your students. We will be rehearsing there from the 7th of May. The Foundation is situated in a very beautiful park and the auditorium is splendid. The sponsor is Carlos de Pontes-Leça. I'll give you the telephone number and address. Rehearsals will be on the 7th, 8th and 9th of May, followed by performances. This is an important event, two-and-a-half hours of music with the student choir of the University of Cologne and, as mentioned, thirty-one instrumentalists and singers.

Following this, we will go to the Holland Festival and rehearse DIENSTAG AUS LICHT at the *Musiktheater* in Amsterdam, with performances scheduled for the 25th and 26th of June. Write to the Director Jan van Vlijmen about reservations. Next, on the 14th of July, there will be an interesting performance of STERNKLANG in England, in Cannon Hill Park at Birmingham. That night there will be a full moon.

Then we enter an important period. I would be very interested if young musicians from Scandinavia could participate—young conductors, particularly. Starting on 7 August, I will be conducting the Ensemble Modern in Frankfurt for ten hours every day; this is in the so-called Orchestra Academy. Then I am going to conduct seven concerts, from the 20th to 27th of August, in the *Alte Oper*, Frankfurt. For this project, I have developed a new concept according to which each concert will have only one work in *live* performance, so that I can explain the work, have the musicians illustrate crucial sections, and finally perform it straight through. At the beginning of each programme, a composition for multi-track tape is going to be played, followed by a work performed live, then there will be a break, to be followed by another composition for tape. In these seven concerts I will present ZEITMASZE, KONTRA-PUNKTE, KREUZSPIEL, STOP, YLEM, ADIEU and DER JAHRESLAUF. At the rehearsals there will be the opportunity for young musicians to come to Frankfurt and participate. Young conductors, in particular, could experience my approach to conducting these works. Each day there will be around ten hours of rehearsals. Write to the Ensemble Modern, Frankfurt, for details.

Is that Karsten Witt?

No, Karsten Witt is not there anymore. Now there is a new person in charge. I'll give you that address, too. Even if only three or four musicians from Scandinavia were to come, that would be good. I am eager to have musicians observe my rehearsals with the Ensemble Modern. I have a rather idiomatic style of conducting. For KREUZSPIEL and ZEITMASZE, I sit on a piano bench, for ADIEU, on the floor. In ZEITMASZE, the musicians stand and play. I prepare DER JAHRESLAUF and YLEM so that I stay out of sight during the performance and instead take over the sound control in the centre of the auditorium. It would be valuable if there were a few young conductors who had witnessed this and could continue from there. It would also be good to have interpreters come and hear how we prepare the work. There are fine musicians in the Ensemble Modern. The opportunity to experience something like that for twenty days can be a great learning experience. Details are available from the *Alte Oper*, where a very nice lady, Aimee Paret, is responsible for the organization and Dr. Rexroth is in charge of programming. Young people may, if they so wish, stay in cheap, plain beds-and-breakfasts or youth hostels.

Can students go?

Where to? To Lisbon?

Yes.

Certainly!

And rehearse with you?

Yes! We will be rehearsing all day long, from morning to evening, with only a short break. You are talking about Lisbon are you not?

Yes.

That would be fine! They should arrive on the 6th of June and stay to the 13th.[2]

That would be . . .

In the end, one learns more about the music from a *staged* performance because then everything is also through-formed for the eyes. But for that, you would have to go to the 1993 stage performance of DIENSTAG AUS LICHT. I'll let you know when that will be.

The interview took place at the composer's home in Kürten in November 1991. An abbreviated version, 'På sporet af en fremmed skønhed: Interview med komponisten Karlheinz Stockhausen' was published in *Dansk Musik Tidsskrift* 67, 1 (1992/93): 2–10.

1. 'Anekdoten und Zeichnungen', *Essays*, ed. by W. Zimmermann. (Kerpen: Beginner Press, 1985), p. 159.
2. Actually, a large group of Danish students and their teacher went to the rehearsals and performances in Lisbon. Stockhausen gave an introductory speech when they arrived and participated in a question-and-answer session.

Edison Denisov

MUSIC MUST BRING LIGHT

As a part of the ISCM World Music Days in Switzerland, a concert was held in the church of the small country town, Boswil. Although only a small provincial town, Boswil has a particular significance in music, for every year it holds composition seminars with participants from all over the world. This year's seminars were scheduled to coincide with the World Music Days. The Soviet composer Edison Denisov was invited to take part in the seminars and also had the opportunity to attend several ISCM concerts.

Internationally the threesome, Sofia Gubajdulina, Alfred Schnittke and Edison Denisov, are considered to be the leading lights of Soviet composition. I met the composer and asked him about conditions at home after the political shake-up. For many years, the ideological and political relationship has made interaction between Soviet composers and others difficult. It was almost impossible for composers to travel out of the country. Denisov reports on these difficult conditions:

It has been possible to travel for quite a while now. But in Breshnev's time everything was run by the communist party and we had a kind of mafia in the composers' union that was strong and had real power. They were convinced that *only* they represented Soviet music, because all the members had received honours. So these people, this mafia, held power for forty years. They often supported mediocre artists in order to get more support, more power, and they fought against composers who had a different way of thinking because the latter group had the talent. I don't believe that there was any political reason for banning performances, recordings or publications of our music, or for preventing us from travelling very often. I received numerous invitations from abroad to attend first performances of my music. For example, I was forbidden to go to the first performance of my Concerto for Cello and Orchestra in Leipzig in East Germany. I was also forbidden to travel to Bulgaria, Czechoslovakia, Yugoslavia and Poland. It had, as I said, nothing to do with politics, but rather with rivalry.

I was never close to this mafia; there are several of us who made a conscious effort to remain independent. I have always tried to retain my integrity with respect to art, I've never tried to write conformist music, but have composed music that I was convinced I had to write. I never wanted to take part in that game and I have never been a double-dealer. Naturally our lives have been quite difficult. Not least it has been a major problem to earn enough money simply to support ourselves. I have a family of four children.

That was before the political changes. Denisov spoke about the conditions that started to change about ten years ago.

They couldn't continue to refuse to perform new works and we were able to travel more and more. Almost everything changed with Gorbachev. Since he came to power we have had no difficulty travelling. Now I accept invitations when I can or want to; I don't have to make up an excuse. That said, however, I refuse three-quarters of all invitations; I only go when it is important. I am here in Switzerland, for example for two months, where I will, among other things, hold masterclasses. In addition, Radio Swiss Romande in Geneva has prepared five broadcasts of my music. And I will go to Fribourg where I will be on an international jury for church music. This is something I have been preparing for for a long time, so I accepted the invitation to work in Switzerland for two months.

But for most of the year Denisov stays in Moscow. He teaches at the conservatory where he has a large group of young students. But how do they regard new music in Russia?

Interest in new music has always been great in our country. The concert halls are always nearly full when we play new music. For example, a year and a half ago Boulez went there for the first time with the Ensemble InterContemporaine to give five concerts. Two of the concerts took place in the large 1300-seat auditorium at the conservatory. The concerts were sold out, not one ticket was left and the audiences were fantastic. Boulez was happy with the warm reception; even when he conducted *Le Marteau sans Maître*—it's a difficult work at first hearing—none of the 1000 strong audience left the hall. They shouted 'bravo' and 'encore'. And when the French electro-acoustic music was played, IRCAM's music, there were no seats available, people even sat on the stairs. The young people, in particular, are interested.

Denisov explains that the reason the public likes good, interesting music, is that it has been banned in the Soviet Union for decades. Only music from the classical period and 'official' music was played. Naturally the public never accepted that; they wanted 'live', new music. And they are very interested in what's happening in the rest of the world.

If one looks at the history of music in Soviet Russia, there were outstanding composers in the 1920s whose works were banned for more than fifty years.

They simply were not to be found in music history books. I am thinking of composers such as Nikolai Roslawez and Alexander Mossolov. It is only now that these composers are beginning to be recognized. Recently the editor of the music journal, *Musica*, published two works for piano by Roslawez, but a large part of his music has been lost; scores have been lost for all time. It is annoying because these composers are more important to me than Prokofiev and Shostakovich.

In the West we hear a lot about the three composers, Sofia Gubaidulina, Alfred Schnittke and Edison Denisov. There are many other composers who seldom have works performed outside of Russia. Doesn't this conflict with the new openness?

I don't know. It's not our business; we—the three that you mention—don't determine the conditions. Naturally we were together when the movement for new music was started and then together in the fight against the 'official' music. But there were others, for example Andrei Volkonsky. He is a very good musician, but unfortunately he has emigrated. He couldn't get anywhere in the Soviet Union and now lives in Aix-en-Provence. Volkonsky is actually unknown, but he is nonetheless a very important figure in Soviet music. I could also name a composer like Valentin Silvestrov, who lives in Kiev, and I wonder why his name isn't mentioned together with ours? Or a composer who I think is one of the most important, Alexander Knaifel, who lives in Leningrad. He is a composer who has still to be recognized. For me he is a great personality and an extremely important Soviet composer. If we consider the younger generation, then I would name Dmitri Smirnov, Victor Jekimovsky, Ashot Zograbiam, Peteris Vasks, Alexander Wustin, Wladislav Schut, and the youngest ones, namely Alexander Raskatov, Vladimir Tarnapolsky and Juri Kasparov. This very interesting new generation is as yet unknown, even among the Soviets.

This was one of the reasons that Denisov founded a society for new music. He is doing everything possible to ensure that music written by composers who have personality, talent and sincerity, will be published, performed and recorded.

At the moment we have sixteen performers in our new music ensemble. I think that it's a very decent ensemble and we give numerous concerts. The ensemble has also begun to record; the first CD has already been produced and published in England. On it are works by Jelena Firsova, Wladisław Schut, my own chamber symphony, and works by Juri Kasparov who is the ensemble's artistic director. The ensemble has just finished recording four additional CDs which will be released soon. This work is very important. We intend to produce a whole series, a kind of anthology of the best composers.

Furthermore, the ensemble often plays music from the 1920s, for example, works by Nikolai Roslawez and Alexander Mossolov. It is important that we do everything possible to gain exposure for this suppressed music.

One of the places where Soviet composers can get their works performed is at the ISCM festivals. This year Denisov has prepared an appeal to the ISCM delegates. He is asking them to recognize the new society in Moscow and to accept it as an ISCM member. The Soviet Union was actually part of the ISCM from 1923 to 1931, but the country's ISCM section was dissolved on ideological and political grounds, and the creative people in the section were removed from official musical life.

At the festival in Zurich, Denisov had the opportunity to attend several concerts. Why is it so important for him to be a member of ISCM, an organization that is considered by many to have no future?

This is the first time I have attended an ISCM concert. The three works I heard indicate that the choice of works performed is not always based on quality. There are some works that aren't good enough to be played at the festival. Possibly it's the fault of the jury, I don't know, but some of those works should not have been there—they were quite simply too poor. Nevertheless I do think that all musicians and sincere composers who work with new music should come together. We can be informed about what our colleagues in other countries are doing and I think that such cooperation can produce many good ideas.

At this moment many exciting things that could benefit the ISCM festival are happening in my country. We could not only inform others about what is happening there, but could also learn how to appreciate the human and musical values in the music that is composed in Russia by non-Russians such as Armenians, Azerbaijanis, Latvians, and so on. I know from attending so many concerts of our music in Holland, England, France and Germany that there is great interest in what is happening there just now.

But the structure of the festival has been criticized and many say that the quality of the music is poor. Could you envisage a different kind of festival with a new structure?

I think that all festivals of this type, for example the Warsaw Autumn Festival or the one in Donaueschingen, all these festivals age with time and die. They cannot continue to exist, inevitably they all become a bit old hat and have to fold. It *isn't* every day that we get music of genius or high quality. In each

Photo: Edison Denisov.

century, and especially in the twentieth century, there has been a lot of mediocre music that will not survive. It is played once and then it's forgotten forever. But that's normal; it's time that makes the best choice. For example, Bach's music was not nearly as well-known as Handel's in their lifetimes. These days we think of Handel as a fine composer, but we all recognize that Bach was much greater and more important musically speaking than Handel, even though the latter was much more admired by his contemporaries. If we compare Mahler and Richard Strauss, the latter was better known and admired at the time, while Mahler was not always taken seriously. But today we recognize that Mahler held much greater importance for music history and that Strauss was mediocre in comparison.

I think it's good to have festivals where music is performed and where composers can meet each other; there should be contact between them. But you should not expect to find music of great value in every concert. I think it is most important that the jury exercises strict judgement in its choice of music. I think that the choices made are not always very good. I don't really know why. But I think that if there were a more rigorous search for new music in the participating countries new names would be found.

To my request for a more detailed description of Denisov's own music, the composer was quiet for a moment. He finds it very difficult to speak about his own music. He hates writing programme notes and refuses as a rule to do so. The music should speak for itself in its own language. He says:

I cannot compose all the time, but rather prefer to think for several months and then work from morning to night. I work best when I have really good soloists. I have, for example, worked a lot with Heinz Holliger. It is an advantage when the composer has the opportunity to work with great interpreters; in any case, it has been very important to me. I have to say honestly that I am very attracted to working with vocal music and particularly with dramatic music. In the future I would really like to compose more music for opera, but it is very difficult to compose in that genre unless one has a commission.

When it comes to the fundamental relationship to composition, Denisov has a number of doubts about the general attitudes of composers.

There are many things that worry me. I think that every artist has to maintain a life-long sense of integrity and not bow to fashion. I have spent my whole life resisting what's fashionable. But what bothers me especially—and this relates to what we talked about before with respect to this festival—is that there are so many composers who work without a real sense of responsibility. I think that a composer is required to exercise strict self-control: to think, to doubt and not to compose automatically. Music shouldn't be composed of clichés. The only music that has any value is that which has a message, a human one.

I, too, work with technical aspects, with constructs—it's essential. If one wants true freedom in composition one must understand the newest compositional techniques. But writing technically perfect music doesn't necessarily work. If the music has no human qualities, if it has no message, then it has no musical value.

But what does the composer mean by saying that the music should have a message? Does it indicate a religious point of departure for the compositional process as is the case with Schnittke?

I don't agree that Schnittke's starting point is religion. His music is not religious at all, but anti-religious. I really like his music, he is a good musician and a good composer. But I don't like his way of thinking which is modelled too much on Bruckner, Mahler and Haydn. I oppose models. It is always difficult to speak about contemporary music, about music by one's friends. I am very interested in what happens, but I don't want to be tough on my friends. I think that others' thoughts and points of view have to be appreciated. But what I don't like about Schnittke's music is that there is no light, there are only shades of grey, and a deformed and uncomfortable view of the world.

The musical aesthetic that is closest to mine is Glinka's, Schubert's and Mozart's. I really like clarity in thought; I don't like 'heavy' music. That's probably why I don't like the music of Richard Strauss. The clarity of the composition is important to me. It certainly is no accident that the most important opera for me is Mozart's *Magic Flute*. Perhaps I am conservative, but that's the way I am.

'Musik skal give lys: Et møde med den sovjetiske komponist Edison Denisov', *Dansk Musik Tidsskrift* 66, 3 (1991/92): 74–78.

Ingvar Lidholm

MY GREAT NEED FOR EXPRESSION

I was born so late in the century that I am only able to read about the time when the composers of your generation were young. For that reason it is interesting to hear from you about your experience of Swedish music in the first decades of the century, and more exciting to hear from one who was there than to read about it in books. In his book on contemporary Nordic music (Vår tids musik i Norden: från 20-tal til 60-tal, 1968), Bo Wallner quotes the indefatigable supporter of the ISCM, Sten Broman, who, from his home in Lund, called the capital city 'Stock-conservative-holm'. You were born in 1921 and experienced a period of music that was called 'Stock-conservative'. Do you agree with that label?

Sten Broman spoke from his point of view, from Skåne (across the channel from Denmark, *ed.*), and from the contacts he had in Denmark. I suppose at that time Copenhagen was much more advanced. In spite of everything that happened during World War I, people in Copenhagen were much more familiar with the new repertoire. And yes, it is true that musical life in Stockholm was very static. In the 1930s national romanticism was still very much in the air and neo-classicism was, well, truly dominant—we actually knew very little about what was happening in the world of new music on the continent and in America. There wasn't much new music performed even though there were performances of both Schoenberg and Bartók. Remember, I grew up in the countryside and had no real contact with Stockholm before 1940 when I moved to the city.

But then you had another source of inspiration, the radio. You listened to it in the 1930s, and later, to night-time broadcasts from Germany . . .

My chief source of information was the radio—even in the 1930s. That was the way that I heard Sibelius and Stravinsky—*Symphony of Psalms* and such things—and I began to orientate myself a bit towards new music—Stravinsky, Bartók and Hindemith.

And you also studied their works?

Yes. Very early I got hold of scores and became familiar with them. So when I went to secondary school, four miles south of Stockholm, I travelled occasionally to Stockholm for concerts and the opera. Then I began to study instrumentation with Nathanael Berg, one of the real nationalists whose strength was his treatment of the orchestra. He knew the orchestra like Richard Strauss knew the orchestra. That was the school I was familiar with even during my secondary school years.

Did national romanticism dominate music at that time?

Yes, you could say that. Of course, personally I did not know much about new music before the 1940s.

The work usually referred to as your debut composition, Toccata E Canto *from 1944, has been described as inspired by Hindemith and Nielsen. Does that mean that you wrote in that style? It is also said that Hindemith's text,* Unterweisung im Tonsatz, *was used. Were you influenced by it?*

It is obvious that I was influenced by the music I heard and Hindemith was clearly a source of inspiration, and Nielsen, naturally. But quite simply it is something that was in the air. One collects, it is available material, and of course one uses it.

In the 1940s it seems that much of your time was taken up with issues of 'workmanship', such as studying Palestrinan counterpoint which was written about by Jeppesen, and also in studying Stravinsky's compositional technique.

Yes, naturally. For me, the first five years of the 1940s were taken up with education and study. I studied Palestrinan counterpoint and common practice counterpoint with Hilding Rosenberg. And we had a study group—we were called the 'Monday Group'.

Was the 'Monday Group' outside the regime of the Music High School?

Yes, it had nothing to do with the Music High School even though several of us were students there. I began at the conservatory—as it was called at that time—in 1940, in all the studies you could think of, for example, violin, viola and conducting. At the same time Karl Birger Blomdahl and Sven Erik Bäck were students of conducting and violin, respectively. We all got that kind of basic instruction.

With Blomdahl, Bäck and yourself in the Monday Group, it must have been significant. Did you take over the scene, so to speak?

Actually we were simply unusually good friends who met regularly. We had an intensive communication, exchanging thoughts and ideas. We debated what we were doing and brought out our scores for discussion and critique. These discussions were often challenging, we were quite critically hard on one another and often there were some very 'sharp' exchanges, but all in all it was done in a friendly spirit. It just so happened that we ended up cooperating in different ways. There was so much we wanted to change in Swedish music. We wanted to renew it, to bring in new repertoire and to shake up the institutions.

And you succeeded very well, for you moved in and took over the key positions.

Yes, because it is true that if you want to accomplish something you have to go out and make it happen. You can't just sit around and complain. You have to take the bull by the horns. We had a chance to accomplish a great deal working within the institutions; later there was some discussion about that. Many felt that they were excluded and the Monday Group was criticized for being dictatorial—that sort of thing. If you have no power, you can do nothing. But when you want to accomplish and renew, you have to create a platform. Otherwise it will just turn into empty rhetoric. The criticism directed toward the Monday Group concerned our work and our positions, among other things. I think that was very unfair. For us it wasn't about having 'power'. We wanted to achieve something; we were motivated by a cause and wished to improve things. In that respect the criticism was very unjust. I would venture to say that without the contribution made by my generation we would not have the richly developed musical life that we have now. We played our part in the development, to quite a significant degree I think.

You became Professor of Composition at the Music High School and you were also involved in radio. You could play and experiment with your music. To what extent then did you leave room for the younger composers to participate?

I think there was a really intense interaction between the generations. We were young ourselves. I believe that we had a clear sense of mission as educators of the public. We wanted above all to spread musical culture everywhere so that it would continually renew itself.

But there were different viewpoints within the Monday Group on that issue. While Blomdahl thought that the composer should follow his personal quest for truth, Bäck pleaded more for the need for contact with the public. Where did you stand on this?

Yes, I was quite in the middle (laughs). It seemed to me like something theoretical that had nothing to do with reality. In the real world you find both

viewpoints fused together, without which fusion you would be working in a vacuum. One or the other? No, I think that both the truthfulness and the contact should be there. And that was actually the way it was. In discussion the viewpoints were exaggerated in an effort to clarify such concepts.

You lived outside of Stockholm and viewed the scene from a distance and yet you placed yourself in that environment. You were the first Swedish composer to go to Darmstadt . . . that was in 1949.

I knew nothing at all about Darmstadt at that time, but I got an invitation to participate in the summer courses. Wolfgang Fortner saw the score for my work, *Toccata E Canto*, and said that there was this Swedish chap who should be invited to Darmstadt. It was an experience that made a deep impression on me, artistically and in other ways. When we arrived in Darmstadt, it was still in ruins, a completely bombed-out city. But in spite of it, in the middle of everything there was an international milieu. The contacts I made there had a strong impact on me.

Did both the philosophers and the composers affect your way of thinking about music?

Mostly it was the composers who did—Messiaen, Fortner, Henze, and so on. I met many who gave me impetus, but obviously I shouldn't exaggerate that. In any case I got a hefty shove forward at Darmstadt.

You were also inspired by the Italian avant-garde; Nono and Berio came a bit later, in the mid-1950s . . .

I was hired by Swedish Radio in 1955 so I could travel a lot and meet many people. That was how I happened to be in Italy.

Was it Nono's humanist outlook as much as his way of thinking about music that inspired you? I ask because the human character and voice and religion has been important for you.

Yes, it is clear that his personality was truly fascinating. But I experienced his music before I met him. I was actually present at the premiere of *Il Canto Sospeso* in Cologne and that was very special. Later I met him. It was an extraordinarily complex experience to be with Nono. There was much in his thinking that I didn't agree with and I always tried to keep a distance from the extremely rigorous speculations and constructivism of the time.

Photo: Ingvar Lidholm (Ulla Lidholm).

Ingvar Lidholm: My Great Need for Expression

You were able to travel in the 1950s and experience the new works of the central European avant-garde. But did you feel in tune with the works of Stockhausen and Boulez?

No, although for some years I consistently adopted a rather strict twelve-tone technique, I didn't preach it. I didn't want it to be dominant and to be the only thing. I felt completely free to use it—or to do something entirely different.

The Monday Group introduced a new kind of work, possibly inspired by modernism. This brings to mind Blomdahl's Faccetter, *Nystroem's* Sinfonia Del Mare, *Bäck's* Chamber Symphony *and your* Ritornel. *How would you characterize* Ritornel?

In the 1950s I wanted to gain fresh ideas and so I travelled and listened to new music. Among other places, I went to London and continued my studies with Mátyás Seiber—I was there, actually, for six months. That was a formative experience because I heard things there that I had never heard before, among them, Dallapiccola's work. There was a lot of new music played in London at that time. My studies with Seiber and contact with his friends and English composers were important. Messiaen, Stravinsky and Dallapiccola were the greatest exponents of that period. Where did I get *Ritornel* from? It could really have been that I wanted to try a bigger form after I had worked with relatively small ones. I wanted to see if I was ready to hold a large form together, and also if I could master a large orchestra, which I hadn't tried. *Ritornel* was actually the first time I tried to think about a piece from conception to realization.

Were you taking stock?

Exactly. I wanted to sum up what I could express at that time.

Now you say 'sum up'. I remember a place where you write, 'Music in its essential form is the spirit doing research'. You go on to say, 'Given this point of departure I decided to search for the sources of the pure beauty of the tone. We have to try to give tones an exact musical content. Emotionally, dynamically and incidentally, to give the rests the same specific weight'.

Yes, that is from an article that I wrote on *Ritornel*. This is the concept behind *Ritornel*, for it is a sonorous and dynamic piece with many rests.

You continue, 'New music does not reject concern for proportion, but I am more and more convinced that neoclassicism has fulfilled its role. Let's turn away from the cult of the traditional and try to formulate a music that speaks directly and strongly to the listener. A music for the people of our time'. What kind of music is that?

That was what I tried to do in *Ritornel*. The new music that streamed forth at that time was completely simple, one could say. This music distanced itself from neo-classicism—the superficial kind. That was my way of thinking at precisely that point in time. It expressed the feeling that we were in a very important phase of development. These were things that had to be carried through, had to be thought through and realized, and simply had to be tried.

Works from that time like Mutanza, *and* Motus-colores, *not forgetting* Poesis, *are modern classics today. Are these the works in which you investigated these possibilities?*

Exactly. I tend to believe that one should not become fixated on techniques of writing and style. It is more important to focus on forms of expression. Quite another question is that of borrowing or trying out different possibilities. For me, the real issue has to do with expression.

So you have, roughly speaking, worked in two main genres, orchestral music and choral music. What do you want to express in music for orchestra? Is there something more to it than the attempt to explore stylistic possibilities?

Now you raise some really big questions. What is it to be a human being? To me, composing is something eminently human. The main thing is to express oneself, one's problems. Next there is, of course, the problem of finding structures—sound structures—that can be used for building large constructions. This issue is inherently complex. One can't just describe it with a few words. As I said, I believe that this really has a lot to do with the basic need to express oneself and that remains the most important part of everything I do.

Why is choral music such an important area for you? Words and choirs seem to give you a particular opportunity to express something quite special. Why?

That's an interesting issue. The voice, and song is such an intimate, or, distinct, part of human beings. It is exciting to work with the unique counterpoint between the various sounds: the voice, the song, and the text. There is an enormous power evoked there. The principal point of composing choral music is to exhaust the text and that is what is engaging about it. Just think of the ingenious structure in a movement by Palestrina, with its vocal counterpoint and the counterpoint between the vowels and consonants in the text, the colours of the vowels as they show up all the time in different combinations. This is purely objective, but added to this are the fantastic emotional powers that emanate from the texts.

Can you describe more precisely what kind of texts arouse your interest?

Preferably those that deal with the big existential issues. Sometimes these texts fascinate me for several years before I tackle them. They should be texts that are both rich human expressions and useful as elements of musical structures. The texts must have their own functional semantic content, and at the same time, they must have a pure abstract sound that allows for decomposition in the process of musical adaptation.

Let us take a concrete example, a choral work like Laudi. *What inspires you to compose such a piece?*

These are extraordinarily complex texts. What makes a person of twenty-six years sit down and write a work like that? You are in the middle of turbulent events and you somehow have to express this and give meaning and order to it. That was probably the case with *Laudi* and the reason that I chose biblical texts. They provided a form. But there was something else: my training. In terms of vocal music, my training was largely by way of Palestrina and was reinforced by the performances of the Eric Ericsson Chamber Choir which projected the incredible beauty crucial to understanding Palestrina's style. This was an impressive balance that we Northerners could benefit from greatly. However the establishment of the choir and the purification of themes notwithstanding, I had the feeling that it wasn't enough. We needed a stronger mode of expression. I simply had a compelling desire to make something other than the radiant pure beauty that we had learned. Modern man had to be represented and I felt myself to be a modern person. I wanted to express myself and I wanted to articulate much more challenging questions than could be answered by the antiquarian musical ideology.

What was the response to works like Four Choruses *from 1953 and subsequently, in the 1960s,* Nausikaa ensam?

I have to say that I have been blessed with a favourable response. *Laudi* got a lot of attention and if I understand correctly what Eric Ericsson and others have said, this work has been important for the development of a modern Swedish choral tradition.

That is to say that a composer like Sven-David Sandström and others interested in choral music have grown up in a tradition that you have helped to make?

Yes, that is probably true in the sense that they are my students and it is not impossible that they have got something out of my instruction. But then all of my students are very independent composers. There are no imitators and that is my standpoint as a teacher: not to mould them in my image. On the contrary, I encourage them to find their own personalities.

Nordic composers who are or have been professors of composition, for example, Per Nørgård, Olav Anton Thommessen and Erik Bergman, warn against cloning composers or being epigones. That is contrary to the norm in southern Europe—or what has been—both in Italy and Germany. I have in mind the Donatoni school, Ferneyhough and so on. Each generation has to go against the previous one, we could call it a revolt against the father figure. Did the generation that followed you and your students say, 'Now we want something completely different'?

I tried to influence them to find their own way, absolutely. That thing with schools, Ferneyhough, and so on, is necessary in one way. Technical discipline, technical ideas and technical systems are very important. One may try to follow a model, but one still has to work constantly against the system. One takes advantage of technical possibilities, but that is not what counts.

Some people think that it is. They think that the structure is the content.

Yes, but I don't agree. Of course, it depends on what we mean by structure, but take something as 'simple' as the twelve-tone technique. That is a structure, but what one can express with it is endlessly varied, purely in terms of expression.

In the development of Nordic choral music, the older composers have contributed new forms. Erik Bergman, for instance, introduced Sprechgesang *to it. Have you made some such contribution?*

I don't know whether I have contributed to any renewal or not. I was never very interested in new techniques in choral music, such as working with new sounds and distortions and so on. Rather I have stayed within the traditional use of the voice.

But still in a new way?

Yes, but I have guarded myself from what could be perceived as external effects. I am very worried about that, and may even add that such things don't constitute a true renewal of vocal music. Possibly if one takes Ligeti and people like that, it has had some importance, but I can't say that development has gone specifically in that direction.

I see the problem: to be expressive, but to avoid superficial effects. Anyway I can trace a development if we move ahead to Ett Drömspel *(A Dream Play) where melody reassumes its predominant role.*

Yes, absolutely. For some reason there was a lot of talk about comprehensibility. I have always thought and said that to write an opera is to make a very direct statement. It is an attempt to reach people in the simplest possible way, but with unlimited nuances. Now, this simplicity has nothing to do with simple-mindedness, and it can just as easily be found in large forms. There must be powerful counterpoint and great complexity in the relationship between the parts. I increasingly feel the need for concrete and direct expression, for reaching people with optimal immediacy and without intellectual entanglement. Complexity, yes, but with an over-arching simplicity—disentanglement.

In your work you have been through many phases.

Yes, that's correct. I have always wanted each piece to be a new venture. I have never wanted to repeat myself. And yet, it is obvious that now I do repeat myself for I feel completely free to take up the old ways as well as the new ones. I do what I feel like doing without any restrictions and that opens my work to criticism. One can accuse me of being conservative, of having lost the sharpness of the avant-garde, but that type of reasoning doesn't interest me any longer.

Have you outgrown your interest in being complex?

What is complexity? A good monophonic melodic structure can be just as complicated as a structure by Ferneyhough, only in another way. Of course I am speaking of real complexity of expression, not about clever technicalities. But it's a difficult issue and it is also a treacherous one because it is so unbelievably hard to get to the core of the matter.

Why did you compose so few works in the 1970s? Most composers experience a crisis at one point or another. Did you come to a point in the 1970s where it was hard to find the way ahead?

Crisis is perhaps the right word for it. Circumstantial problems play a role too: complications in connection with one's job and that kind of thing have an impact. One also writes a lot that isn't published and is merely put to one side. It is true that I have often had major problems, but it's hard to say why. I haven't felt forced to produce something either. I have composed when I have felt the need.

You grew up in a religious environment. This feeling for humanity, communication and religion belong together.

Yes, the big questions are important for me.

Do you have a message?

Yes, it may be hard to formulate the message, but it is there. And it is clear that much of what I have to say is expressed in the texts that I have chosen for my choral music—at least I imagine so.

The Strindberg text is not religious . . .

Strindberg . . . If you take *Drömspelet*, the human being is in focus. Man in all his complexity and his despair, the grotesque disposition and everything, is there. *Drömspelet* focuses on the human condition.

I remember the work as being full of poetry and resonances of life lived, the sustained tradition where the human voice is at the centre. It's been important for you to work with contrasts: intoxicated love and bitter resignation; the personable and the ordinary.

This work is like life itself: the individual sees the isolated details, but from a wider perspective we recognize a search, a yearning for great complexity as you yourself said. I agree with your assessment, so I'll end with taking your words for mine.

'Mit store udtryksbehov – Nordiske komponistprofiler I: Samtale med komponisten Ingvar Lidholm', *Dansk Musik Tidsskrift* 72, 8 (1997/98): 258–264.

Pelle Gudmundsen-Holmgreen

An Established Outsider

Concerning anti-art, cultural pessimism, musical hodge-podge, toe-curling embarrassment, music mobiles, filter composition, absurdity and lions' roars, among other things.

If someone were to draw up a balance sheet on Pelle Gudmundsen-Holmgreen in light of his impending sixtieth birthday, then one of the points would have to be that he has consistently tried to avoid the musical mainstream. When he says his position is on the sidelines of Danish music, it either comes from a lack of self-knowledge or is an affectation, for Pelle Gudmundsen-Holmgreen is one of the most important figures in Danish composition. As befitting his reputation as 'established outsider', he is on bad terms with good taste. Compromises are non-existent for Gudmundsen-Holmgreen; he shows pronounced scepticism towards the possibilities of our culture in general, and an unbending black outlook on life in particular. If one philosophy of life and art approaches that of Gudmundsen-Holmgreen, it must be the absurdism of Samuel Beckett. In his own words:

Pessimism has invaded me completely. There are Utopians who expect a new world if one only does this or that. I consider Utopias strange, captivating, stimulating for our spiritual activities—but completely impossible. One can place man on a pedestal and consider his invention and creativity to be almost divine, or one can look in vain for anything that resembles such a vision. I consider man relatively helpless and at the mercy of forces he can hardly understand. I am a pessimist because we have made so many mistakes. I am a little bit depressed on behalf of mankind. Socrates apparently had no success in convincing us to act sensibly. 'Weaned' in this way, I have become used to a proper scepticism concerning the high-faluting style. I don't sing along with the *Hallelujah* chorus.

I was immediately captivated by Beckett when I saw his *Endgame* at the end of the 1950s. Since then I have read everything that he has written. With his penetratingly black outlook he sees things from the opposite side. Beckett is preoccupied with meaninglessness, which has the strange power of releasing new ways of experiencing the world. By getting rid of all that well-meaning speech one is surrounded by, and knocking it down point by point—

whether it be love of God, mother love, love of children, love of love, all the things we get so crammed full of that finally we don't know what we mean ourselves—then we end up in that catastrophic situation which has something deeply liberating about it. That is one of the reasons, among others, that I am so grateful to Cage who tore the rug out from under everything that we find dear. But the philosophies of these two do not involve complete renunciation as they continue to write. They wished to deal with meaninglessness in order to try to come to grips with it, which is, of course, impossible. But it is the attempt which counts. It reveals their humanity. The problem of form evidently becomes insurmountable. But think about what came out of it: pure, incarnate beauty. Cage said something Beckett could also have said: 'I have nothing to say and I am saying it'.

Pelle Gudmundsen-Holmgreen was born in a house without a piano; music came into his life late. Visual art was at the centre of his childhood home as his father, Jørgen Gudmundsen-Holmgreen, was a sculptor and his grandfather was a painter. The composer's early interest in space and material in art can be heard more or less clearly in his works. Gudmundsen-Holmgreen designs his space by means of a filtering or a grid. Certain notes are chosen to create a symmetrical structure.

The interest in space is also expressed in the composer's fascination with mobiles. It could be said that some of Gudmundsen-Holmgreen's pieces are like musical mobiles: various objects turn around and are seen in different lights and illuminate each other in different ways. The material can have different qualities, it can be rough and obtrusive like scrap from the garbage dump, it can be soft like silk. It's apparent that the composer has been inspired by his father's artistic activities.

I resemble my father. That's not so strange. In addition to being interested in space and material I have also inherited from him a sensuous disposition, a preservation of a childish mind, and hopefully, a certain innocence in my work. I think of that as a cardinal virtue. Even though existence can be unbelievably challenging with experiences that take spontaneity out of people, a certain innocence remains at the bottom of most people's minds. I think that I have, in my association with music, preserved a bit of childish joy.

What I have also inherited from my father is the quest for the perfect form. I know that it isn't possible, but I continue to try. I think that there is a hidden meaning in each piece, a dream that can be reached by gradually peeling away layers. In addition to that I feel the classic need for balance (it has nothing to do with the balance in music of the classical period, but is like a basic need). Balance for me isn't ABA/ternary forms or such, but is comparable to a balancing act. I feel that my pieces are like a tight-rope act. One may be a clown on a tight-rope, 'fall' down innumerable times, wear big shoes and a strange hat. But yet there is something very elegant in the fact that the clown stays on the tight-rope. Among other things, that's the situation in which I find myself with the strange instrumental combinations that I have gradually tried out: we get closer to the offensive or 'embarrassing' part. To write a piece for cello and carhorn is not proper, it just isn't 'done'. This is evident from an English review, which said: 'Performing this kind of music does new music a disservice'.

Instrumentation is important for Pelle Gudmundsen-Holmgreen. To work with a certain gong, a cow bell or a bucket of scrap iron can take time. It's like chewing on timbre. But even though the composer works with putting 'found objects' together, one quickly finds out that it's no pieced-together collage. He wants those subtle timbres and nuances that he himself accentuates by using the old term, Klangfarbenmelodie. *The form of the piece depends on which sound possibilities the instruments offer. Timbre determines form.*

NEW – OLD

Provocation, 'embarrassment', bizarre instrumental combinations, all can be heard in many of the composer's works. But after all one could ask if it really is provocative or embarrassing to combine a cello and a carhorn; after Ligeti's opera, Le Grand Macabre, *it can hardly be said that a car horn is 'painfully new' any longer.*

That's right. But this doesn't have much to do with being 'new'. Moreover my *Plateaux pour deux* is from 1970 and Ligeti's *Le Grand Macabre* is from 1978, Satie's *Parade* is from 1917, and what about Spike Jones? It is more a question of what kind of public one meets; it can be terribly 'embarrassing' to show up with something pretty at a German festival. Embarrassment is a peculiar concept. It occurs when the audience feels out of place and afraid that it has fallen into bad company. I feel that some times I succeed in 'curling the toes' of both laymen and professionals—a very special honour. But it is not that I seek embarrassment, I have simply tried not to be afraid of it.

It's clear that Pelle Gudmundsen-Holmgreen is inspired by such composers as Cage and Varèse. From them he has learned that one can compose with any kind of sound. For example, Gudmundsen-Holmgreen, in the wide Greek landscape, listened to jumping sheep and goats that had small clanging bells hanging on their necks. This polyphonic bell sound is, for example, heard in the work, Mester Jacob (Frère Jacques) *from 1964. The composer explained that the peace and sensation of 'nature' in such a vast landscape meant something special to him, but landscape painting, naturalism, dream music didn't. To him it sounds like Biedermeier wallpaper patterns look. How does the music manage to be a contemporary artistic creation? How do you as a composer manage to counterbalance the idyllic?*

Our world is full of cacophony and infernal machinery. That I can accept: I have composed some of the worst sounding pieces in Denmark. My *Collegium Musicum Concert*, 1964, sounds like a wild traffic jam. I am obsessed with noise and orientate myself in it as a listener. But 'noise' is only one part of the issue and, well, also an old story. Serialism is also an old story, yet still young! Look at Stockhausen. He keeps on working with a way of thinking that was launched with serialism. But I don't believe in the single-minded theory of linear development that lies behind this project, the logic of 'given A, B follows'. I didn't agree with Stockhausen when he made a parallel between music and natural science in an issue of *Dansk Musik Tidsskrift*, imposing the theories of natural science onto music. More than half a century ago Niels Bohr took a different position. He considered art and science to be complementary! That does *not* mean that one should turn a deaf ear to, for example, the electronic possibilities for changing sound, moving sound, spectral analysis, fractals. Personally I follow as best I can and easily find new inspiration, thoughts, etc., but I am perhaps a little lazy, not young anymore, and no longer chasing the 'new'.

I also think that these days there are unfortunate tendencies to become obsessed with technology, hardware and electronics. I am sick and tired of the sound of the synthesizer. There is no programme on Radio Denmark that doesn't have a little pinched synthesizer tune—even the green environment-friendly programmes! I think that the people behind this don't understand that they themselves are being taken for a ride. And in the midst of the concert hall's steadily growing mass of wires and flashing screens, I think of the string quartet as 'alternative energy'. Excuse me for repeating myself; I have said it a few times before, but I feel quite vehement about it. And now that we are on this track: I am quite irritated by the media's restlessness, the way they cut things up into small pieces—and significantly enough at the same time—flattening everything out. We are falling between two stools. But back to the beginning: landscapes, calmness! When I talk about calm, it's not to be free from new situations, disturbances, far from it. For that's what makes it possible to find your own way; it is all the strange and provocative experiences that have forced us to find our way. But calm is just as important. Who doesn't experience a desire for calmness? Just the word, calm. It's a wonderful word, magical, enchanting. It is an endless dream to find a little peace in one's soul. More and more I compose music about this dream. I don't think that it's nostalgia.

Even today there is a steady demand for each work to formulate a new aesthetic. But this has nothing to do with your music?

Photo: Pelle Gudmundsen-Holmgreen (Jeppe Gudmundsen-Holmgreen).

Yes, but only to some extent. I think that each new work has something new in it. But how much? And in what way? The stubborn, idealizing, in many ways 'four-square, modernistic' tradition has had its day. But it did well, for a whole new world emerged out of that way of thinking. Music from the 1950s and 1960s that built on expansion of materials successfully developed a new world. We would not want to have been without a Stockhausen and a Boulez. I myself have been animated by their way of thinking, believed in it. We were seduced by these composers, were so captivated that we lost our heads — and ears!

Was it after a carload of young Danish composers went to the ISCM festival in Cologne in 1960?

Yes, but also earlier. At the end of the 1950s Radio Denmark presented not only these new works, but also Webern and Schoenberg, the old serialists. That was a violent shock. It was not long however, before we developed a healthy scepticism about these ideologies. There is something that characterizes most Danish composers, which is that in this whirlwind of thoughts they have attempted to find a personal solution. Obviously that characterizes any true composer and is naturally nothing particularly Danish. But I must say that this wilfulness has been quite widespread among Danish composers. It is a pluralism that I think is a Danish phenomenon. This must have something to do with the markedly democratic spirit that pervades this little country. Our best composers are individualists who are not tyrannized by a clan of theoreticians and madcaps who demand something specific in music.

In certain large European countries, composers tend to gather together in groups. The French are born fencing masters; they love fencing for its own sake. Germans are idealists by definition so for them it is a matter of honour. That Danish composers can communicate with each other in spite of stylistic differences is possibly a minor miracle. It could also be due to the fortunate fact that we have a pair of open-minded leading figures. For one, Per Nørgård, who has taught generation after generation to open themselves up to whatever they might find, and who is very tolerant towards their individual wishes. In fact, to such an extent that he has been reproached for it. But then he is matched by Karl Aage Rasmussen who represents a counterweight. He disputes a little in the French manner, he's also an admirer of the art of fencing. On the other hand, as Director of the NUMUS festival for contemporary music he allows all kinds of approaches to be heard. It is something of a patchwork festival that contributes to making us all talk to each other — and come to be fond of each other, since no kindness and no disputes are squelched. One gets rid of one's frustrations. There are other examples of tolerance in Danish music. At the Royal Academy of Music in Copenhagen, Ib Nørholm is both obliging and sceptical; Radio Denmark is open-minded, the orchestras happily play the work of young composers, and also the somewhat older generation of composers. Just compare that with the programming of American orchestras! The press is not ideologically fixated, etc. etc. . . . the landscape is open, good to move around in.

Pelle Gudmundsen-Holmgreen has always been open to impressions from all sides, and from many artistic 'directions'. Around 1960 there was a revolutionary period in Danish music that had an effect on Gudmundsen-Holmgreen's music.

In the 1960s we met people working with other art forms and artistic directions alongside new music. Consequently paintings came down from the walls, and music came away from the instruments: Copenhagen was in a state of flux. Art was in a state of upheaval at that time. We looked at the painters and writers around us. Hans-Jørgen Nielsen was editor of *Dansk Musik Tidsskrift* then and he was a spokesman for the new trends. He was himself a 'concrete' poet, as it is called. His work made a strong impression on some of us, Henning Christiansen and me, in particular. 'Fluxus' was fascinating to me, but it wasn't there that I got my real inspiration. I was more on the wavelength of the artist Robert Rauschenberg who, with his installations of 'found objects', created new aesthetic materials. Well-known objects were not only recycled but reborn. You could say that he collected things that one thought couldn't possibly be brought together. But thanks to his clear vision and artistic sensibility, it worked, and not only as a provocation, but as a valid aesthetic statement. I felt in tune with Rauschenberg's methods and his art directly affected my concepts. For instance, as a composer and a user of quotations I have become rather like a collector. That is what I was doing in pieces like *Mester Jacob* and *Repriser* (Recapitulations). They consist of gathered objects, completely finished sound objects, albeit formulated by me. That sounds perhaps unclear, so let's put it in another way: I tried to create some object-like sounds or elements and let them intersect with each other.

Before that, in 1962, I composed *Chronos*, a work that was influenced by Central European modernism. But already you can sense an unwillingness on my part; I couldn't understand why the melody had to progress in large leaps and why moving in scales step by step was a thing of the past. So I resolutely allowed doubled octaves—impossible ever since Webern's time—in my *Collegium Musicum Concerto* (1964). I wrote simple melodies, so already that was in opposition to the German–French coalition. And then came the powerful renewals from the other side of the Atlantic Ocean: minimal art, pop art, Cage. As a composer I don't go down well in continental Europe. The Cage or Varèse mentality does well in Europe because it is so 'uncompromising'. My problem is that I am part European, part Danish and part American: I make a kind of hodge-podge music. This creates difficulties when a foreign audience confuses my intentions with provincialism or rather pure idiocy. They think I am a country bumpkin!

In Denmark too, it happens that my personal solutions are not easily accepted. It feels as awkward as an embarrassing party where people who have nothing to do with each other are invited. I take again the example of the combination of cello and car horn, which sounds like a poor witticism, or like a bar joke, but it is precisely that stupid idea that attracts me. If one thinks more about it, a car horn has its own robust charm, and I have provided the cello and horn with a precise systematic set of social interactions, structured togetherness. I have forced them into a designed 'life style' so that the end result is something more than a joke, namely, a meeting of two worlds that in spite of all their differences are not so incompatible that they can't create something inspiring together. That's the way I have been thinking since 1964. Now, the means are somewhat more discreet, but the structured togetherness is still foremost in my mind. At the same time, I want to consider the musical world as allowing all kinds of sound.

Around a sound

Much of Pelle Gudmundsen-Holmgreen's music rotates; it is non-directional and shows an affinity for a minimalist language that uses a multitude of patterns. But his music distinguishes itself from minimalism in that the hypnotic, transcendental and meditative element is not central. Like concretism in art and poetry his music is concerned with a cleansing process that aims at a music stripped of the artist's personal expressive urges. The listener must find his own way, must be willing to accept standing in one spot and to be forced to turn around and orientate himself in the landscape. This is possibly the most significant feature of music from the 1960s and 1970s. Most recently Gudmundsen-Holmgreen has been extending a helping hand to the listener. For a number of years the composer has been working with so-called 'filter composition', where tones are selected so as to make symmetrical structures. Is it a way of taking the listener by the hand?

Yes, one of the ways! I help the listener with, among other things, arranging the landscape in which we move around. I have worked on it systematically for many years. What's left is a fan of pitches, which unfold from a central note through two semitones (the first one divided into two quarter tones), a whole-tone, a minor third, a major third and then, in the same direction, the same intervals in inversion. A symmetry within our common note system (albeit with the addition of the quarter tones) is made in this way. I can furthermore transpose this structure, so that the system can be spread out from other pitches in the fan. Earlier there were notes that were not found at all in my system; if, for example, I started out from the note D, the notes F and B-natural didn't exist at all. Then I began to transpose, not because I missed these notes, but because I wished to chromaticize the whole field. I needed the possibility of creating melodies in different places—chromatic melodies, at that.

I have a strange, ambiguous, feeling about melody. As I have said, childish simplicity is something desirable, but I feel at the same time that it is elusive; one can be naïve by nature or adopt naïve manners. The latter is conscious and therein lies the problem. I use the childish stuff because I love it, but I am also aware that I do it. When my music sometimes becomes expressive and exploits a pretty melody, it is a 'found' element, and I present it with a wry smile so to speak. There is possibly a 'private' feeling of being naughty in the middle of a world where new music is becoming identified with complexity: Paris, London, Cologne. However, I think that there is a basic attraction to the pure triad, in the same way that it is appealing to write a bold seventh chord. Boogie woogie makes me feel good. In no way should this be understood to mean that I am looking back—I wish to look my times straight in the eye. I'm not interested in ending up like Rued Langgaard—all negative.

THE INNOCENT LAYERS OF CONSCIOUSNESS

When Gudmundsen-Holmgreen begins a work, he listens to multifarious material, rather than beginning with two tones and developing from there.

My problem is that I am never completely sure about what it is I am working with. In such a situation one gets ensnared by *different* ideas. There is disorder in the thought process from the very first; there is disorder in the beginning, the middle and the end. Problems are only augmented if work on one piece takes perhaps half a year: I am not the same person when the work is finished and I have to revise the beginning. If one, on top of that, improvises along the way, then the risk is, that some things sneak in that shouldn't be there. Finally improvisation in itself is problematic, because the composer is limited to what, in actual fact, is often rooted in convention. It is the classic problem: improvisation builds on habitual concepts, on trained instinct. Generally I want to give intuition as much room as possible, and I have all the sympathy in the world for those concepts that are in place right from the beginning of the work's existence—this hazy landscape of the innocent layers of the conscience. When we begin to speculate about it, we have the conflict between the unborn and the all-too-prepared, between intuition and cool calculation. The work can only succeed if there is a beautiful and *miraculous* correspondence between intuition and the thought-out plan for the piece. This is a banal statement but it's nevertheless true.

In an overview of Pelle Gudmundsen-Holmgreen's production, the basic aesthetics are the same as they were thirty years ago, in his first mature works. And yet some-

thing remarkable has happened in the later works: a more organic and flexible procedure is evident, more artistry is included.

The tough period in the 1960s with the anti-art, point-zero search on one side, and serialism on the other, is history. We have now opened doors to new trends, first and foremost, because the musics from the East and from Africa have been drawn into the music of the West and have provided a new range of sensuality. I believe absolutely in musical presence. You can hear it in the string quartet in *Concerto Grosso*; it behaves with artistic refinement, but it is surrounded by some wild bodies of sound, almost a jungle. The phrase 'jungle baroque' has been a key one for me. So a 'raw' lion's roar comes right out of the orchestra. I think it's exciting to combine the raw with the refined, or to put it another way: 'there is rock in baroque and baroque in rock'. Or as I have said about the *Concerto Grosso*: 'Vivaldi on safari, Spike Jones in plaster'. The term, 'jungle-baroque', also points to an increasing interest in rhythm. African music has interested me ever since I saw an African ballet thirty-five years ago. It was one of those life-changing experiences. I was searching for African rhythms long before anyone started talking about them. They didn't suit my work in the 1960s, so I put them on the shelf. In *Kysset, rituelle danse* (The Kiss, Ritual Dances) composed in 1976 for Eske Holm's dance theatre in Pakhus 13, I quoted a number of small motifs taken from a book on African music by the musicologist A.M. Jones. With help from an African master drummer he managed to write down whole pieces in score! A singular achievement at the time the book was published. Since then I have allowed myself to indulge in a more rhythmic 'profile'. In 1977 I wrote *Passacaglia* for tabla and a little ensemble in the African meter *par excellence*, 12/8. In my latest works it pops up again—more rhythmic interest. Most recently I have wanted more 'music', so to speak. I want the musicians to project their musicality to a greater degree, to have more chance to enjoy sounds, rhythms and intervals. That's my dream: to be able to join asceticism and ecstasy.

'En etableret outsider: Om Pelle Gudmundsen-Holmgreen', *Dansk Musik Tidsskrift* 67, 2 (1992/ 93): 38–45.

Hans Gefors
THE WORK OF ART AS A TRUE PRESENCE

Recently various institutions have tried to revive the old idea of a common Nordic identity in music. Such was the theme of the Scandinavian festival held in Berlin in 1994. And in a new music festival—arranged within the framework of the Nordic Music Festival—the organizers want to contribute to an active definition of 'Nordic-ness' as distinct from the rest of the world. According to the festival brochure it seems that it's particularly Nordic to alter the perception of time. The goal is to increase awareness of a supposed 'Nordic way of thinking'.

And then there is the recurrent issue of the Nordic 'sound'. As part of an on-going project, the focal point of a new book on Nordic music history, Musik i Norden, *has been to find common Nordic traits both in the music itself and in music institutions. Personally I find that the common denominator lies in the cooperation between music institutions, rather than seeking common areas of musical expression.*

You have been active in two 'camps', one in Denmark and the other in Sweden. We Danes know that Per Nørgård was inspired by Sibelius and has talked at one point of the 'universe of the Nordic mind'. How do you evaluate the attempt to establish these 'cross references'?

There are only a few instances where it makes sense, and there are preciously few references to other Nordic composers and artists in the history of Swedish music. But if you think back to the turn of the century, there was, in fact, not only a 'Nordic tone' but also close connections between important artists that had not existed before and haven't since. This even influenced artists on the continent, for example, Rilke, Schoenberg, Busoni, and so on. I'm thinking of authors like J.P. Jacobsen, Strindberg and Ibsen. There was a group that met at the *Zum Schwarzen Ferkel* in Berlin consisting of Strindberg, Munch, Obstfelder, Dehmel, Paul, Wedekind, Przybyszewski.

The artists at the turn of the century knew each other; it was natural for Stenhammar to ask Sibelius to conduct his symphonies at Göteborg, just as it was natural for him to invite Nielsen to conduct his symphonies. Stenhammar heard Sibelius's Second Symphony and wrote a letter about the enormous impression the work had on him.

Sibelius was significant for composers from Alfvén and Rosenberg through Åke Hermansson to myself. Nielsen was very familiar with Swedish music and his book, *Living Music,* had an impact on Kallstenius, Nystroem, and the composers in Lars Erik Larsson's generation.

Beyond that, it is the institutional cooperation that has continued; we have some very important organizations like UNM (Young Nordic Music), Nordic Music Days, and NOMUS (Nordic Music Committee/ Nordic Council of Ministers). There is also a tremendous amount of contact between composers and musicians. But there is little in common culturally just now, surprisingly little, in comparison to how often we see each other.

But if we go a bit further back in the century, and look at the development that was spearheaded by various strong personalities in the different countries, would you also say that there was minimal mutual inspiration then?

The 'Monday Group' in Sweden had an enormous importance for music in Stockholm, not least, for the training of composers. They paved the way. When I went there, Ingvar Lidholm was Professor and before him it was Karl Birger Blomdahl. These composers brought the spirit of the 'Monday Group' alive for their students. Daniel Börtz and Sven-David Sandström inherited this view of music. But the Monday Group didn't get their international impulses from Denmark or Norway, but from Hindemith, Honegger, Bartók and from Sacher in Basle. Even at that time the other Nordic countries were uninteresting as sources of inspiration. In Sweden it was the Hindemith tradition that took over and you can trace it even now. Hindemith's is the underlying tradition, a doctrine which dictates that the musical craft must be in order.

Could you name some composers who resonate with this idea? For some, this reference to Hindemith's aesthetic could sound pretty negative.

In the earlier works of Blomdahl, Bäck and Lidholm you can hear from the melodic style that they have studied Hindemith. But the modernist aesthetic also arrived in Sweden via Bengt Hambraeus and Bo Nilsson, who were in Darmstadt very early on, and that influenced the development of the 'Monday Group'. You can see it in Lidholm's *Poesis,* and also in Blomdahl's work, though he was very angry when he heard Xenakis's *Metastaseis,* he said it wasn't music. I know that Lidholm was inspired by Nono's cantata *Il canto sospeso.* It was the Italian treatment of the voice that made the impression. You can hear its influence in Lidholm's *Nausikaa ensam* (Nausika Alone). But again, it is evidently international thought that had an impact on Swedish music.

A little further back there was a group centred around Lars Erik Larsson, de Frumerie and Wirén. I think that in their generation cross-fertilization of ideas was still felt; they knew Holmboe, Riisager and Høffding and were strongly influenced by functionalism in Danish music in the 1930s. Lars Erik

Larsson composed his concertino series consisting of concertos for all the instruments of the orchestra. These were widely used by amateur orchestras, and I am sure that they owed a debt to Nielsen and Høffding. That spirit lived on in Larsson's students.

In the somewhat younger generation there was a personal and, to a certain extent, also a professional connection between Vagn Holmboe and Erik Bergman. They were well acquainted and knew each other's music very well, but their music admittedly does sound different.

AFTER THE WAR

During the isolation of the war, the 'Monday Group' grew from strength to strength. After World War II you didn't travel to Denmark anymore, you travelled further afield. Did the 'Monday Group' develop because it was impossible to get international status and recognition or did they deliberately choose to lock themselves into a local centre?

The 'Monday Group' developed during the war. The members were all very active and all were in their twenties. Blomdahl, the oldest, was twenty-three; when the war was over he was twenty-nine. They couldn't leave the country, they had to stay where they were and figure it all out for themselves. The whole Hindemith influence started when they studied *The Craft of Musical Composition* together. After the war they got in touch with Europe at large. Several of them were fine musicians and scholars: Eric Ericson, Hans Leygraf, Bo Wallner, Ingmar Bengtsson and Nils Wallin. In the 1950s they continued to be absorbed in modernism because there was a strong desire among the group to stay modern and to turn outwards toward the world. It was the beginning of the modernist wave—the optimistic part of it.

But there were other Nordic composers who held similar attitudes: Arne Nordheim from Norway in his earlier days, and the Dane, Gunnar Berg, for example.

Yes, but they were younger and worked entirely on an international basis from the beginning. Nordheim was the first Norwegian to become a real modernist. That generation could turn directly toward Europe. And that's the way it is still. There is no Nordic cultural community, no names that people gather around, nor places where students from different Nordic countries might come to study. There may be initiatives in that direction, but there has not been any real centre to cultivate a common Nordic 'tone'. Conversely, you find national voices surviving within the Nordic countries.

I can remember when I was young reading an interview with Arne Nordheim who had just been in Warsaw in order to produce a tape for one of his pieces.

When his hosts heard the work, they said, 'Oh, that sounds so Norwegian'. Nordheim couldn't understand it because it was simply what he was used to producing in his studio. I think the whole issue is rooted in a *wish* both at home and abroad that a Nordic 'tone' exists. Something along the lines of, 'Wouldn't it be nice if we really had a cultural fellowship and exchanged aesthetic principles instead of just sharing food and socializing'. But when one compares Sweden with, for example, Denmark, it is the differences that strike me most.

We could possibly elaborate on that because you lived in Denmark ten years ago. You studied there for many years, primarily with Nørgård.

Yes, also with Karl Aage Rasmussen, and the entire 'circle' in Århus.

So are you the exception that proves the rule?

Yes, for my part that's the way I feel. That's why I express myself so emphatically (laughter); no one else has such bi-cultural citizenship. There should be more people with insight into Danish composers' way of thinking, and more people in Denmark who understand how the Swedes think when they make music. I saw that clearly when Pelle Gudmundsen-Holmgreen was in Stockholm last year for the Stockholm New Music Festival. He was invited by Göran Bergendal (Producer, Swedish Radio and member of the artistic committee of the Stockholm New Music festival, *ed.*) who knows and appreciates his music very much. There are other Swedes who also like his music very much. He was the featured composer and he *is* a very odd composer. After the performance of his *Concerto Grosso* I spoke with some Swedish composers: they were totally confused. They didn't understand what he wanted to achieve, where he wanted to go, what he had done, and what it meant. They perceived it as complete nonsense. They couldn't interpret the music, they didn't understand how it was put together or why.

Why could you understand it better?

You have to know the whole tradition of 'new simplicity' in Denmark. You have to know certain key works and know how they are put together.

You have named one of the most difficult composers for a foreigner to come in to contact with. In an interview in Dansk Musik Tidsskrift (Danish Music Review) *Gudmundsen-Holmgreen himself said that his music is considered next to impossible for foreigners. Difficult and unmanageable, just like his name which is so long it's impossible to fit it into newspaper columns without ludicrous hyphenations.*

He was also booed at one of the ISCM World Music Days festivals. It's a frequently cited story. Even though you can say that Gudmundsen-Holmgreen is an extreme case he is a good example, because the Swedish composers neither liked what they heard, nor could they understand it.

What kind of discussion did that provoke?

I tried to discuss the idea of 'layer upon layer technique' in which you put different layers together. The layers are phrased independently and thus create relationships that 'rub' against each other. All the while, each layer has its own stylistic identity. The Swedish composers had not heard it that way; they didn't understand the piece in that way. They thought it was too long as they didn't perceive the interaction of the layers. The stylistic references were not interpreted correctly, either. When I tried to explain what I had heard in the piece, it became clear that they hadn't heard the same thing at all.

This idea was confirmed at the last Young Nordic Music Festival in 1994 (Ung Nordisk Musik). Much of the music by young Danish composers, even when they are not directly inspired by Gudmundsen-Holmgreen, is rather odd, compared with that of others.

'Odd'?

Diatonic and constructivist—very Danish. You don't find it in many other places. What you have is a constructivist relationship and then on top of that, a diatonic, naïve or pastoral idea, or whatever you may call it. There is always a pastoral tone—*non espressivo*—but it is structured all the same: rock-hard. This is so peculiarly Danish that others cannot grasp it.

In a panel discussion at the recent Young Nordic Music festival you called Danish music 'freedom-thirsty', Swedish music 'expressive', Finnish 'authoritarian', Icelandic 'traditional' and Norwegian music 'unschooled'. You'll have to explain this in more detail.

With Danish and Swedish composers one can hear who has taught them. With the Norwegians it's as if each one starts anew; there is no common style. In spite of the fact that they have had a Professor of Composition for many years, namely Lasse Thoresen, and a standard institution, there is still no Norwegian school. I'm not saying that that is either good or bad, I'm just making the observation. It is difficult to find a common denominator for Norwegian music. It can be very modernist and it can be unbelievably backward-looking; it can be just about anything. The music of other countries is much more predictable.

So you claim that you can listen to a piece by a young Danish or Swedish composer and afterwards be able to tell who his or her teacher was?

Almost every time. Of course, I'll probably get it wrong if we try this experiment. But when one has read the programme notes and listened to the music, it is much clearer than you would think. To put it differently: the education that young composers receive goes much deeper than they themselves realize.

But in Denmark we pride ourselves on having no school of composition. Only kind and mild-mannered teachers who are very understanding. The recent debate in Dansk Musik Tidsskrift *has brought perspective and nuance to the relationship between teachers and students in Denmark. Moreover, the younger generation is now beginning to write and formulate an independent position on how to proceed.*

Yes, but they work very clearly within the Danish tradition. To put it in perspective I can compare it with my own development, which ended with my going to Denmark—inspired by all the references to Nørgård in Bo Wallner's book *Vår tids musik i Norden*. It was a quite conscious decision; I couldn't stand the music scene in Stockholm. The whole atmosphere, the way people communicated.

Could you be a little more specific?

Yes. There was an episode which proved decisive for me. I was a participant in a workshop for young composers at Fylkingen—the platform for performance of new music—just after I began to study with Ingvar Lidholm. We were supposed to work with Harpans Kraft (Power of the Harp), at that time the most advanced new music ensemble. They were used to having many pieces dedicated to them by former students, for example Daniel Börtz, Sven-David Sandström, Lars-Erik Rosell and Anders Eliasson. So here comes a whole new generation—I was twenty and Lasse Hallnäs and Mikael Edlund were twenty-one, and so on. Suddenly they were presented with four young men who didn't agree with the premise. And the whole thing was a disaster.

What premise?

The premise was that one took over the older generation's position, became conversant with the scene. Just as you had to do your military service, so you had to serve your time in musical life. You began by arranging the chairs in Fylkingen. It was never discussed until this workshop with Harpans Kraft,

Photo: Hans Gefors.

but there it became clear that this was demanded from you without question. But we were twenty and didn't know anything at all. We were unusually young when we started our composition studies; Sven-David Sandström and Daniel Börtz had been older when they set out. So here came a group of people who didn't have the same background as the previous generation.

When you say background, you mean religious background, don't you?

Let's call it a social background with a religious component. Lidholm, Bäck, and Sven-Erik Johansson and most of the others came from religious homes. Blomdahl was actually an engineer and was anti-religious. There is an historical pattern that relates to the migration from the countryside to the cities. In the country villages, music was kept alive by the Fundamentalists, the Pentecostal Church, the Salvation Army and the State Church (Lutheran). This fostered a very strong tradition that had its flowering in art music just as we were becoming involved in music. We were city kids who had played rock and American folk music; we had attended public music schools and had no knowledge of the religious tradition. And they couldn't understand what we were talking about. It was pure nonsense, and possibly also threatening to them. I felt trapped and angry—even though at that time I didn't understand why. We were expected to stand to attention and unquestioningly accept the way music was organized.

So, what about the episode at Fylkingen?

I was young and a little shy. I found it difficult to speak to the musicians and didn't feel at home at that stage. Lidholm hadn't been there to introduce me to the musicians, and don't get me wrong, I was in awe of these famous people. The first thing that happened when we arrived was that we youngsters were scolded, because we didn't understand the blessing and usefulness and the foresightedness of this project. They offered us something and we turned our backs on them. It was a judgement against the young composers, who didn't even know what they had done wrong. It developed into a genuine war of words. People began to attack each other, everyone was against everyone else. It was probably the end of a common cause among Swedish composers. I remember that when I left, I thought that I wanted nothing more to do with the whole thing.

It was a different world when I went to Århus. There I met musicians—I had not met a single musician from the school during my entire first year at the Music School in Stockholm. I hadn't got the basic education I needed either. I got that at Århus. I became involved with AUT (Århus Unge Tone-kunstnere) in a voluntary, uncoerced way. Karl Aage Rasmussen—even though he is only five years older than I—was the strong man there; he was the centre of a group that met, partied and talked about things. We discussed aesthetics till we were blue in the face. It truly stimulated my development, my Swedish reference system was subjected to heavy pressure. Wonderful! We could really be free with each other; you could think what you wanted, and at the same time we could listen to each other's ideas. Implicit in being free is the need to adopt contrary positions and to air your anger.

Was that allowed?

Yes, or perhaps one could say that the culture of the place allowed it; viewpoints were often put forward but you didn't get taken to task because you dared to speak out against the leaders. Unlike the way it had been in Sweden.

The spirit of Århus has been carried on in your work at the Music School in Malmö, where you are Professor of Composition. There is this same desire to engage in dialogue. I experienced it myself when I was a guest lecturer there. Have you succeeded in creating an alternative to the wider musical environment that surrounds you?

I think so, actually, and that thought was confirmed by my good friend Sven-David Sandström just recently at the UNM. He is a Professor in Stockholm and a person with whom I have always kept in touch, even while in Denmark (Sandström is currently Professor of Composition at Indiana University, Bloomington, *ed.*). He said of a performance of a particular piece from Malmö that it could never have been composed in Stockholm. He didn't say why, but I think that I understood what he meant. If you have several working centres, then some things that are acceptable in one place just aren't in another. Some things are possible in Malmö that are not possible in Stockholm and vice versa. I think it's very important, even more important than the national idiom. I don't think that it will be less noticeable in an international culture, but more. Centres of regional style will be created. If you have studied in a certain place, it influences your thinking; it makes some things possible and others impossible.

Now you are speaking of local centres inside national boundaries. But if you as a Swede look at your own generation, and then look at Finland it is very clear that those who influence music these days are those who dared to go abroad. You can't talk about the local, even if we admit that Heininen's influence is something they all experienced. From here it looks like an attempt to become free of Sibelius' spirit, like Hansel and Gretel, who went out to find themselves in the big world. Nevertheless, you call the Finns authoritarian?

Yes, I think it's obvious, particularly at the UNM. I felt that the young Finnish composers had written very competent works, perhaps the best from a technical point of view. But when I spoke with some Danish composers about this they said that they yawned when they listened to these pieces, and so did I. I was really aware of my Danish background; I listen to music in the same way. I was bored by the Finns' desire to make modernism . . .

Towards an ideal?

Yes, and not only that. It's becoming institutionalized in a particular way; it is being raised up to the level of a kind of style that it really didn't set out to be. You can classify all the stylistic traits and there can be different branches to each trait, but in the end they come from one and the same modernist trunk. And all these branches emanate from Schoenberg, never from Stravinsky. It is serialism, the formal part of modernism which becomes institutionalized, never the other. For example, those composers who interested Karl Aage Rasmussen—Ives, the Futurists, Nancarrow and Harry Partch—it is never they who set the tone.

What about this Nordic community that is supposed to include the Finns? Isn't it almost absurd?

What do you mean?

In the work of the Swedish composer Karen Rehnqvist one can clearly trace inspiration from folk songs; in Per Nørgård there are instances of Danish song. In the Norwegian Lasse Thoresen one can trace an attempt to strengthen ties with the folk tradition. But what on earth is the connection between Finland and what the Finns practise at IRCAM?

The Finns say that you can't sit at home at the kitchen table and become international. So they make an extra effort to get exposure, with Heininen's help, of course. They travel abroad, not to the other Nordic countries. This is one of the reasons for the lack of common aesthetic ground. If Swedish composers go abroad they don't go to Denmark. They might go to Finland because of Heininen's success, but they are more likely to go to England or to the USA, to Germany, or to Holland. But then Swedish composers don't travel so much. Personally I'm surprised that not more Nordic composers have come to study with Per Nørgård, I mean he has international stature.

You characterized Swedish composers with the term 'expressive'. Is that due to Hindemith's influence?

I first heard the label 'expressive' from Karl Aage Rasmussen and then suddenly I was in a position to understand it objectively. His comment about Lidholm's music was that it had a special 'espressivo', a violently expressive character. And then I too heard what he meant, particularly in Lidholm's music. Grandiose violent strokes with clear contours. And this tradition is continued with Börtz and Sven-David Sandström. They are both teachers—or have been—in Stockholm. Though as a composer Sven-David is still moving in unexpected directions, he is maintaining his links with the religious tradition of his homeland. And no-one really can understand his music without understanding that dimension.

Although you use the term 'expressive', it is hard to define it because it has so many associations. But, at the very least it implies that expression takes precedence over structure?

Yes, expression is very important. It must be personal, honest and deeply felt. Moreover, expression is bigger than oneself. In Börtz's music it is very clear that it comes close to a collective expression.

Gefors Close-up

I think that what you say is also true for the next generation—not that I would put you into the same category as Anders Eliasson, who expresses a lot of Sturm und Drang in his music. You have a very romantic aesthetic; there are no quotation marks around your music, no parody. Everything is to be taken literally: a sigh is a sigh. But how much of your personal philosophy is embedded in your work? Do you want to see the music as a means of reaching a new understanding of life?

Now you are putting me on the spot. It's a lot easier to talk about other composers. Your questions take me by surprise—do I have a Romantic aesthetic? But if I think about what I want to communicate through my work, I would have to agree with you that it is more than the individual notes. There has to be a reason, you have to dare to do something, and the music has to affect the listener. It is my Swedish legacy that comes through here.

When you say 'affect', we come back to that old problem of construction versus expression. Magnus Lindberg, who, in his early compositions, continued in the modernist tradition, has become more communicative in his new pieces, for example, Coyote Blues. *He sets something in motion and wants the music to reach the listener. Is that what you want, too?*

I have learned to compose following Per Nørgård's way of thinking, so the constructive element is taken for granted. But it can never become the *raison d'être* for writing a piece. On many occasions I have discarded a piece when I realized that I had a structure but that the piece had nothing to say. Therefore I distrust the ability of structure to provide inspiration. So we come to what's even more difficult to talk about: the content.

I visualize an important moment, the starting point, the moment when you decide to be a composer, when you discover that the most important thing in life is to compose music. I'm speaking of an existential moment. As a teenager I was a song-writer. I composed my own songs and sang them at parties in the city and the country. I can trace that background in my operas, even in my orchestral pieces, for the element of song is still there. One way or another, it all comes back to the singer and his guitar. As a composer I am deeply interested in melody in the broadest sense.

Some people talk about being on the trail of a new kind of beauty, one that has never been ventured before, a beauty that isn't kitsch, but rather a valid new expression. Are you on the trail of that kind of beauty?

Yes. That's what I have been doing the whole time. I get very depressed when I read Adorno. Although he wishes that beauty would return, he sees it as lost, and so he tries to construct a world where one talks about the loss. I feel strongly that it's not so. When was beauty lost? On which date? What happened? I don't see any proof that beauty has been lost. Just try to open your eyes and see, not only in music, but also in the theatre, in visual art, in popular music, I mean funk music and so on. If you look at how people live, then you can see that they are always searching for beauty. I think that in art music we have been too willing to accept what Adorno called the negative dialectic. We always come back to the question of authenticity, and, perhaps it's easier to say that beauty isn't authentic and so give up the search. To my mind, that is a kind of laziness. It is considered hard to make something beautiful, and so one makes something ugly—because it's a lot easier to do that.

You don't believe that beauty is a negation, that it is expressed through its absence and that it is beautiful to the degree that it is lacking?

No, that's philosophical twaddle, too smart and too contrived. It's overly intellectual and commonsense dictates that it shouldn't be taken seriously. It is a kind of escape mechanism, an expression for our infinite disappointment that beauty wasn't salvation. I like to communicate. To use an image other than that of the song-writer, I might suggest a good conversation, where one person has an intense dialogue with another. That's where you can really get into some depth; there is a 'you' on the other side.

OPERA COMPOSER

Some years ago you enjoyed real success with the opera Christina. *Recently some scenes have been recorded on CD. My obvious question is: what do you do after success?*

Write another opera. No, seriously, it is a shock, but it brings a kind of experience that can be got no other way. You meet complete strangers who have seen the opera and understand it; composers aren't used to that. Many composers have abandoned the belief that their thoughts can reach the listener. That's when the different escape mechanisms and negative dialectics get going.

I didn't immediately start to compose an opera. Someone suggested that I write an opera on Erik the 14th and become a kind of chronicler. But as I had improved technically as a composer, I wanted to explore and deepen my ability to express myself. There is a song cycle on CD, called *En Obol* (A Penance). I think that in it I was able to reach a new level of expressive power, even though the expression is very introspective compared with *Christina*. Today, as I work towards my third opera, I have simplified my musical language significantly.

For me, composing has something to do with development. There is a lot of talk about the audience and communication, but the important thing is that the individual who is listening is a kind of 'partner'. It should be something like a love relationship. We have to develop together. You receive something from the listener when you reach them, and it is a kind of gift. That has to be developed, and then you must give something back. Perhaps it works and you give thanks to the relationship but it may end in divorce. I can't *think* in terms of buying, selling and management, but today it's difficult not to *talk* in terms of management. Losing the potential for art to awaken understanding is a common mistake.

Are you referring to the attitudes of composers like Górecki and Nyman?

Yes, but I think that there is a big difference between them. Nyman has always wanted success, but Górecki was overwhelmed by it. All you can say is that the possibility for success is always there. I heard a large-scale mass by Górecki in Warsaw in 1983, but I never suspected that he would become a world-famous composer even though I really liked the piece. Composers are perhaps not the best judges when it comes to these things. It is as hard for a composer to calculate what will become successful, as it is for a pop musician to predict what will be a great hit. You cannot compose a successful work on purpose. Afterwards it may be possible to see what made it work, but until then you must make do with being as personable and as good a composer as possible. I am old-fashioned enough to think that we should just be good composers.

BACK IN TIME

We have already spoken about the Nordic character and the claim that a preoccupation with the concept of time is a particular feature of Nordic music. That claim in fact was made by one of the organizers of the Nordic Music Festival, the Swede Anders Hultqvist. He has composed a work called Time and The Bell *and has addressed the question of time in music in various publications, including* Nutida Musik. *What is the point of researching chronometric time as opposed to experienced time? What is it all about? Articles have been written about time, whether it goes backwards and forwards, or whether one can get out of it, or on to it, and even whether one can hear it or not. I don't understand much of it.*

I think that one can only see the 'Nordic spirit' as some kind of idea or metaphysical fellowship. The concept of time is something *all* composers here at the ISCM write about, and whether it concerns getting on or off is an open question. When you hear different pieces, then you distinguish other things more easily—for instance where the composer studied—before you hear the relationship to time. My opera, entitled *The Park* after Botho Strauss, was governed precisely by an exploration of time. But whether that's what ultimately emerges from the work is something I'm not sure about. The drama is built on the action and so the time involved is very concrete. If something is to happen then it takes time. If an action is to be realistic then it takes the time that that action takes, and altering it—to slow motion, or stop-and-go—gives it a completely different expression. Arias are fermatas in the progress of time. In opera you go back and forth, between stepping out of, and back into, time. That's the way it has been since the 1600s. Seen from that viewpoint the exploration of time is not as new as the avant-garde would have it.

What about the Nordic perspective compared with that of the greater world beyond? Right now we are in the midst of the ISCM World Music Days, a festival packed with concerts. I find it amazing that composers from all over the world are still interested in making a glove to fit the hand of 'Central European Modernism'. Pretty shocking, isn't it?

Yes . . . it is quite 'fantastic'. The illusion that modernism is finished is strong both in Sweden and Denmark. Many of my colleagues believe that modernism is a thing of the past, but everything points to that being wrong. Modernism has been institutionalized in a very special way. It has been assured a kind of museum existence. You can give a work a catalogue number and file it under 'Freiburg-Modernism 1994'.

There are young Nordic composers who try to write their way into the Central European tradition.

The Finns do it very successfully through Heininen and by setting up some ideal works that follow the norm according to Schoenberg and to the 'correct' Stravinsky—that is, *Sacre*. Take, for instance, the Norwegian composer, Asbjörn Schaathun. His work *Actions, Interpolations, Analyses* is an example of this phenomenon. I think the piece sounds old-fashioned. Written in the post-Webern idiom, it has the international sound common to all ISCM festivals.

One of my students was at Darmstadt last year. There were 400 young people who went around and practised 7 against 5 all week so that they could play new music. Modern music uses this kind of thing like a fetish. It has been passed on, there has been nothing new in forty years. Modernism is a success. You could write a best seller entitled *The Success of Modernism*.

According to common historical parlance we live in an age of pluralism, and now you say that modernism is stronger than it has ever been.

Yes, that's right. It has become institutionalized. There are some who would put it differently but they are quickly silenced. It is a self-perpetuating system, perhaps because the audience is too small. An audience can change things; there are precedents for that in music history. Mozart was a court composer. And forty years before the *Eroica* Haydn began to invent the symphony. Then along came this new middle-class audience and changed the whole thing. Now we are caught inside an institution in which there is no new audience. Like the ISCM it is a closed system and will probably remain that way until we are told that we are not to use money for that purpose any more. For me it's more valuable to have a good performance at the opera house than at the ISCM World Music Days. I would also rather compose for orchestra than for the ISCM, but most of all I like to work with opera. There you find singers who think that it's really pleasurable to sing the work. There's a whole institution working on your piece. There is enough rehearsal time. It's pleasure.

All of this is missing from the ISCM world of composers who adopt stances with their strong aesthetic statements. That's why it is so easy to write museum modernism, to make such complicated music that it can't be grasped, can't be controlled. We can no longer imagine something that isn't modernism. Several years ago it was post-modernism, but that has now been absorbed by modernism. Not even minimalism has the strength to fight it anymore.

But isn't there a pendulum that swings between historical positions? We have just spoken about a romantic aesthetic nowadays which is a witness to our turning back to historical frames of reference.

Yes. There is nothing to indicate that we are ever going to be finished with anything whatsoever. Although we forget many things they pop up again.

Once something is invented there is always the possibility that it will come back. This goes against the idea that cultural elements are born, grow old and die. The romantic aesthetic is acquiring a new aspect. It has always been present and in the 1800s it became central for various reasons. It's difficult to imagine that there won't always be people who will undergo anything in order to create the perfect work of art, who feel that although what's found there might be illusory, it's worth doing anyway.

The idea that it can be too late or too romantic or too functional stems from idealism and from historical philosophers. I don't believe them and I try to resist their ideas. There will always be aesthetic purists who think that it is crazy that some still think they can afford to be romantic. But the romantic idea wishes to underscore the importance of art. In that way romanticism is in itself almost an ideology and the aesthetic of modernist art is, in fact, romantic because it wants to write off the mindless society that is ruining humanity. In this sense it is a kind of super-romanticism. We want to reach a world where it means something to experience an artwork, though I wonder if institutio-nalized modernism has abandoned even that position. The feeling of together-ness which we can experience in an art work is more powerful than that we can find in anything else—possibly only with the exception of love.

POSTSCRIPT BY HANS GEFORS (JUNE 1999)

At the time of the above interview, I avoided making a clear statement about my views, something I now regret. Since 1994, I have written two more operas, *Vargen Kommar* (Cry Wolf, performed in Malmö, 1997) and *Clara* (performed at the Opéra-Comique in Paris, 1998), and the song-cycle *Lydias sånger* (Songs of Lydia, for mezzo soprano and orchestra, premiered in Stockholm, 1997). These experiences now allow me to articulate my relation-ship to new music more precisely.

These days technical matters are more important than artistic concerns in contemporary music and this has been the case since composers were taken in by scientific ambitions about composition that were supposed to codify the perfect musical work. In reality all that was achieved was a registration of the materials and principles of organization used in any composition. To recog-nize masterpieces you have to make use of a totally different set of human skills and abilities. The codification process has been further escalated through the predominance of computer techniques and the prestige of IRCAM.

Previously it was the concept of the single motif or series permeating every-thing that determined the value of any piece, but now algorithms and spectral analyses occupy the same position. That which should have been a means has become the end. This is a materialistic attitude that is highly problematic from an artistic as well as from a philosophical point of view. I sometimes find artists and works that rise above this world view, but they are exceptional.

Writing about serious music does not at all seem to reflect some of the serious criticism that has been levelled at materialism ('matter over mind') and rationalism by various authors over the last few decades. Also I see no evidence of recent debate about narration and hermeneutics entertained by authors with a humanistic viewpoint. The same is true of contributions from authors who try to see mankind's condition in a new light from the perspective of psychoanalysis or of communication theory. In fact, every day we hear about new avenues to creativity and new techniques of releasing mental energies. None of this has apparently had any influence on the mainstream of compositional activity, which, ever more, has become an enclave for outdated scientific ideals.

Those composers who are enchanted by their craft cannot see beyond the musical materials and do not have the extra energy and ideas needed to look ahead and think about the significance and purpose of music. Consequently, new music is reduced to the level of ornamentation. We squabble about triads or their absence as if *that* were the essence of music. I find this unacceptable. It is crucial that I am able to grow as a human being through the process of composing, and I want the listener to be able to comprehend my intentions and thoughts so that I, in turn, can learn something about myself and about the world from that attentive listener.

Once or twice in the interview I refer to the ideal of a frank conversation and the feeling of presence that it provides. This is not only an abstract idea but a real influence on my work. Thanks to opera I escaped, as if by magic, from the self-imposed limitations of musical compostion that I have just described. Now, almost exclusively, I write large works that last the whole, or at least half, of the evening. The modern standard of a ten-minute long 'aperitif' to a concert of standard repertoire strikes me as incommensurate with essential qualities. The narrative and action that are fundamental to opera have provided me with an unsurpassed starting point for composing. This forces me to articulate my intentions clearly both sensually and conceptually—in a way in which the compositional techniques I use, no matter how ingenious they may be, do not indicate at all. It is as though I have to bring abstract knowledge out into the bright light of the real world with all its desire and resistance. And what satisfaction I feel when it works!

This brings me, finally, to the artificial opposition between absolute music and so-called programme music, something that has poisoned discussion about music for a long time. No composer wants to be accused of writing programme music! The composer of the *Rite of Spring* offers a truly pathetic denial in his *Poetics of Music.* Who really believes that the plot had no significant influence on the composition? What would music be without memories, images, dreams, visions, experiences, situations, meetings, events, gestures?—Merely ornament. It would be just as bad if music lacked consequence, logic, order, form, shape, patterns, style, repetitions, design, traditions, formulas—pure chaos. Genuine music cannot do without both. For me, writing operas has dissolved this opposition, it does not exist.

The listener must be taken into account too. I find it unbearable when young composers reveal that they have absolutely no idea about how the music that's played is to be perceived. Cognitive research explores mutuality (reciprocity) as a fundamental dimension of even the most primitive forms of communication, but composers nevertheless seem unable to throw off those blackboard demonstrations of arrows and connecting squares of the old stimulus–response-type. On a visit to Malmö, British composer Brian Ferneyhough predicted that sometime in the future all listeners would become composers—in other words, a nightmare in which *nobody* listens. Only the serious listener can inform us that we are being understood—not as composers, but as human beings. The last words in Botho Strauss' drama and my opera, *Der Park*, are: 'Haben Sie mich verstanden oder lauschen Sie nur'? which I translate as: 'Do you understand me or are you just registering sounds'? This is precisely the kind of situation to which I am strongly drawn—not to find the right musical motif, but to create a situation in which the spectator responds, 'I understand'!

'Kunstværket som virkeligt nærvær: Samtale med komponisten Hans Gefors', *Dansk Musik Tidsskrift* 65, 4 (1994/95): 146–157.

Alfred Schnittke

BETWEEN HOPE AND DESPAIR

At the Huddersfield Festival in November 1990, Alfred Schnittke celebrated his fifty-sixth birthday with a performance of his Faust Cantata. *At the moment he is composing an opera on the Faust theme and the Cantata will become part of the third act. An outline of his character emerged in the course of the festival through a long series of performances of his works. What Schnittke lacks in outer vitality because of his poor health, he makes up for in his completely masterful musical output. A serious illness in 1985 nearly took his life, but he is recovering slowly. As the composer himself expresses it: 'I have been given a chance to live twice'. Because of his health Schnittke usually does not give interviews. However* Dansk Musik Tidsskrift *succeeded in having a short conversation with him during a rehearsal of his orchestra works.*

Schnittke was born on 24 November 1934 in Engels, in the Soviet Union. His father was a German Jew and worked as a journalist and translator. His mother was a German teacher and a writer for the German newspaper Neues Leben. *Schnittke inherited his parents' interest in writing which has resulted in a series of theoretical articles and essays on Shostakovich, Prokofiev, Stravinsky, Bartók, Webern, Berio and Ligeti, among others. On the musical side, he has written a good number of works in most genres: symphonies, concertos, chamber music, solo works, choral music, ballet, film music (to date, sixty film scores).*

After the Second World War, Schnittke's father was stationed as a journalist in Vienna and his son had the opportunity to become familiar with a whole new artistic tradition and ideology. It was then that he decided to become a composer:

After the war the stay in Vienna meant that I discovered the existence of another contemporary 'world', a very complicated one that, however, cannot be compared with what we are experiencing just now. I discovered the artistic 'relativity' in which nothing was settled beforehand. That made a profound impression on me. Before that, I had worked exclusively from an single thought, in fact, a single-mindedness; now, there suddenly existed a multiplicity. I became preoccupied with Mahler, Schoenberg, Berg and Webern. The most important impression of Vienna came from my work with these composers.

Schnittke visited the West again, in the mid-1970s. He was smuggled in with an orchestra as a pianist in one of his own works. Schnittke went to Germany where he

realized that it was too late for him to contemplate a life of exile in either Western Europe or Israel. It is no exaggeration to say that most of Schnittke's works can be said to be about homelessness. Often this appears to be quite simply his main inspiration for composing. In a restless search for an identity, Schnittke has pursued the development of many different stylistic forms. His music reflects the rootlessness and division of modern life, which points back to the kind of painful and tragic realization that was also expressed in music at the beginning of the century.

In the course of the conversation we quickly came to one of the most important sources of inspiration for Schnittke: Gustav Mahler.

Gustav Mahler was probably the most important for me; the seeds for everything I have composed lie in Mahler's work.

There are several reasons to compare Schnittke with Mahler. In addition to the two composers' comparable approach to purely technical and stylistic elements, there is another important biographical relationship. This is captured in the oft-cited statement by Mahler explaining the reason for his restlessness: 'I am three-times homeless; as a Bohemian among Austrians, as an Austrian among Germans and as a Jew in the whole world', a quotation which finds resonances with Schnittke's experiences as mentioned above; his parents had no Russian citizenship and while he himself grew up in Russia he spoke only German with his family. Does Schnittke feel, like Mahler, homeless in his own country, even though the Russian tradition and culture are a part of his musical upbringing?

Yes, that is very true. For Mahler this sense of homelessness was something central, but at least he spoke German in a German-speaking region. For me Russian means nothing; it is not my mother tongue. When all is said and done, I was possibly born in the wrong place! And it has now become even more complicated for me with the current difficult and unforeseeable development (the collapse of Soviet Union, *ed.*), a development for which there seems to be no solution. I will say it even more emphatically: the enormous problems in Russia which are building up just now will remain and possibly *never* be resolved. At the moment they have been only *apparently* solved.

But even though one can immediately associate Schnittke's music with Mahler's on a stylistic level, for example—in the use of irony and quotations,—these compositional practices do not carry the same meaning for Schnittke as they did for his model.

Photo: Alfred Schnittke.

A Ländler by Mahler is, of course, of quite a different colour from one of mine. I live in another reality, but stand indebted to him because I can use his experiences. One should not just imitate him; it has to go further than that, into something new. However, what 'hangs over' from Mahler is the sense of a complicated life that consists of hope, and not a little despair.

Naturally Schnittke's first musical influences came from composers like Rachmaninov and Shostakovich. He had training but in a tradition with which he had no special relationship. For this reason he drew inspiration from a tradition that he felt he should adhere to, while being cut off from it for historical and political reasons. On top of that he lived (and still lives) like a deeply religious person in a country of atheists. He did not live not under Stalin's terror, but has lived under Brezhnev's stagnation and Gorbachev's perestroika, and now lives with signs that point toward a future of dissolution and chaos. But to write in direct opposition to the system, in sheer defiance, lies far from Schnittke's compositional aesthetic:

When you do something to react *against* a rigid system, the product loses its authenticity. Rather one has to act as though the system doesn't exist at all. That's the only way music continues to be viable in the longer term.

'Mellem håb og fortvivlelse: Et møde med den russiske komponist Alfred Schnittke', *Dansk Musik Tidsskrift* 65, 7 (1990/91): 226–228.

Jukka Tiensuu

Giving Musical Form
to Your Thoughts

The Finnish composer, Magnus Lindberg, told Dansk Musik Tidsskrift *that future composers will be very much occupied with computer music and also with spectral analysis, which is Lindberg's own special interest. Having also worked in these areas, do you agree with Lindberg's evaluation?*

It's an exciting method to work with. A number of composers, including myself, have discovered the benefits of spectral analysis. For this purpose I have conceived computer programs and attempted to incorporate information about sound in various forms. I worked for four years (1978–82) at IRCAM in Paris, which is the foremost place for such research. The study of sound structures—the microcosms of sound—has, indeed, been one of the most important new trends in the 1980s. However, I would say that spectral music and computer music are only part of a larger field, and it is certainly an overestimation to refer to them as *the* future of music. Music isn't simply sound and structure, it is the passing on of ideas.

Which ideas are you concerned with and where does the aesthetic necessity in working with computer music fit into realizing these thoughts?

First of all I have to say that working with the computer is but a small part of my work as a composer. I am not devoted to computer music as such. However, it functions as a very effective tool in certain areas. Computers can manipulate the information that you feed them: calculate, compare, draw logical conclusions. Then they can present the result in different forms: graphically, as sound, as numbers, as written text and so on. Remember, even though you use the computer as a tool, it isn't the same as writing computer music. The machine is of use only in giving form to thoughts. I think that the computer is valuable because it can, for example, produce a composition from one's diverse suggestions: you feed the computer the basic information and it carries out the operations much faster than you could do by hand. For gifted composers, this has resulted in an almost explosive development because you can try out things that, without a computer, would take more than a lifetime to realize!

I would like to repeat my previous question: you have written an article entitled 'The Shortest Way', where you mention 'searching the music's innermost being' and about having 'crystallized your spiritual vision of the world in a composition', and of 'spreading and collecting spiritual energies'. I am interested to know what is the ontology behind these formulations. Let us look at a concrete example. In one of your recent works, Tokko, *you use the computer and the human voice. I hear a kind of dualism, or yin and yang, between the synthetic and the human. How does this choice of materials match your aesthetic ideas? Why is it necessary for you to use a computer-generated tape in this work?*

I don't think that it's a matter of necessity. Just as it isn't at all necessary for me to play the harpsichord, it's just that I really love to. The use of computer in the case of *Tokko* was not just an experiment but rather a challenge for me, not least because this particular juxtaposition of a computer-generated tape and the long, 'holy' tradition of our amateur male choirs, which, to my knowledge, hadn't been used before.

But it is interesting when you speak of 'necessity' as an aesthetic category. It's said that 'necessity is the mother of invention'. But one can also turn it around and say, 'new inventions become the mother of necessity'. I think that when you *have* a computer, then you feel the necessity to use it. It's the same with instrumental developments: as a musician one has to test and become comfortable with the latest developments in order to see how they can be used in music.

The persistent desire to investigate new material constellations makes me think of the diversity of your work. You don't compose many works that fall into the same categories. As soon as a new combination has been tested you abandon it. You seem to think that each new work should be 'from scratch', in a manner of speaking, so that a new work opens up a new world.

Yes. That, at least, is my ideal. I have no wish to write variations on earlier works. The process of creating a new piece is in itself the most important experience for me. So, when the piece is finished, I lay it aside and don't want to look at it any more. This process cannot be combined with a revival of earlier ideas. I also listen to the performances of my own music only if the musicians think it's necessary.

This reminds me of György Ligeti's situation in the 1970s when he had had enough of using the same ideas in so many pieces. Everyone *expected* him to write the same thing, from *Atmosphères* onwards. He wanted to compose something totally different but simply didn't dare to do it, perhaps because he was worried about disappointing his audiences and losing his 'fame'. It is a very common situation: if a young composer discovers something that 'sells' well, he is tempted to continue in the same style and later it becomes almost impossible for him to change direction. These mechanisms are even stronger in commercial music.

But for example, as an explorer of new musical landscapes Miles Davis kept his fans and his good reputation.

Yes, and it shows that one just has to have the courage. But I am convinced that there is a moment of hesitation before one takes the step. And Ligeti actually did it; he changed his style to a certain degree.

After the Horn Trio . . .

Or rather before. And that's when he again demonstrated that he is a great composer. Of course it's not enough just to change—the quality of what you do is more important than the style.

Have you made such a complete shift as a composer?

Well, not such an abrupt change. But if you look at my whole output you will not find any particular line or direction. All my works point in different ways. Risto Nieminen once wrote that it is easier to list what *isn't* in my scores than what *is*. And indeed there isn't much that I would definitively exclude from my music.

I haven't found any distinct use of quotations.

In 1980 I actually composed a chamber work, 'Tombeau de Beethoven', that consists exclusively of quotes from Beethoven's music.

In the course of our conversation you have referred to 'communicating ideas'. Could you explain what this means?

Many composers draw a thick line between music and what happens outside of it. They say, 'Music begins here and stops there; there is nothing outside, next to it, or behind it'. Even if they realize there is something, they don't want to know about it. I certainly try to cross the boundary between music and what lies behind it. I insist on music being larger than life.

My time at IRCAM was a very important period for me. Not only because of the institution itself, but the experience of living in Paris (1977–82), which is a very inspiring city to work in. Some composers will not listen to other composer's works at all; they claim that it might have a negative influence on their own work. I am just the opposite; I like to absorb and to get inspired by everything from my surroundings, including the work of other composers. Philosophically, I am very inspired by the Eastern way of thinking of the world as one whole. Much of Western science relies on studies of phenomena as if they were separated or independent from the rest of the universe, although chaos theory, which is very popular now, is getting closer to the wisdom of the East. To put it squarely: everything that happens is related to and influences everything else. For me this has the consequence that no matter what I do I don't feel that it's useless or unrelated to my 'main' activities. For example I can study modern physics and then use what I have learned when I play the harpsichord!

In this respect our education system has gone astray. The instrument teacher at the conservatory teaches *only* the instrument, not theory, history or aesthetics—not to mention anything that lies beyond the world of practical music-making. The ideal situation would be if the instrument teacher taught everything, so to speak. Like in the traditional Indian music where music and life are taught by the same 'guru'. In that way one develops a concept of the whole.

If you are familiar with the musical philosophy of the middle ages—up to the Renaissance—then you know that music was considered to be a path to deeper understanding: namely, it can enable us to understand the cosmos, God's creations and His intentions, because music can convey the incomprehensible divine on the more comprehensible human level. Music can bring you to an understanding of the meaning and functioning of the universe in a musical microcosm. These thoughts are close to the philosophies of the East and possibly also to the Western philosophy in the future.

The *meaning* of music for man has concerned me greatly for many years. You don't find any culture or any society that has no music. You can manage without technology, cars and houses, but not without music. I think that's of utmost importance to keep in mind. Many people compose music for concert halls; few dare to insist on writing in order to exercise a positive influence on humanity. It sounds, perhaps, a bit self-aggrandizing to say, but if you write music to alert people, to give them new energy and to inspire them, the role of the composer becomes really important. There is no recipe for doing it but you have to have it in your mind every time you begin to compose or practise music. You have to try to make sure that your influence stays positive.

In this regard Giacinto Scelsi, the Italian composer, is something of a role model for me because he emphasized the spiritual aspect of composition. His music was a revelation in the 1970s because it was somewhat unique in Europe; nothing like it had been heard before. Because Scelsi's music had

Photo: Jukka Tiensuu.

been banned for decades, there were suddenly not only a few new works, but a whole series of unique creations to discover. I wasn't the only one who was deeply moved; more and more people are falling under the spell. Unfortunately Scelsi hasn't composed anything for harpsichord, but I have studied and practised his works for piano for a long time.

In order to tie this into our introduction, Scelsi is, something of a father figure for the French spectral composers, partly on the strength of his microtonal research. You improvise; Scelsi did that too. So there is probably a fascination on several levels.

Yes. He was not just an investigator in sound, not just an architect; he also had a spiritual outlook from which we can learn a lot.

You have mentioned composers like Xenakis, Ligeti and Scelsi all of whom have inspired you. I know that you have also been interested in Brian Ferneyhough, studied his works, and performed his music. You don't take on easy tasks. I know that you practised Xenakis's Khoaï *for three years before you dared to perform it. Is there also an element of mental training in such work?*

I hope so. I get so much from working with different concepts, practising a difficult piece, studying scores, and so on. It is fascinating because it is so different from what I myself would create. It is a whole other world that one gets to enter for a while. It can be music from the so-called primitive cultures, ethnic music, animal music, African music, Indian music, folk music, renaissance masters . . .

As a performer you are something of a specialist in renaissance music. Has working with this music had an influence on you?

Until now I haven't noticed any special impact myself, but recently I have been thinking along these lines. However, you will probably not hear Gesualdo quotations in my work in the future. When I study old music, I try to find the best pieces and especially try to find out *why* they are the best. The point is that in that period everyone used, broadly speaking, the same composition technique. And yet there are works that are clearly better than others. This fascination probably reflects something in one's own mind: one dreams of writing a work that won't simply disappear in the vast sea of works, but can stand up and convince just by its exceptional quality.

You mentioned that you resist listening to your own works, but that you respect musicians who ask for suggestions during the process of preparation. This touches on your double role as a composer and performer. Don't you know, better than anybody, about the benefits of performing new music, namely, that you have the composer at hand when there are questions or problems?

Naturally. But there is also another general problem that I myself have experienced: musicians often believe that if they play a new piece they do something of a service for the composer. That's not so. If they perform a service, it's for the audience. In the same way, you shouldn't compose just to give musicians the possibility of performing a new work. To reach the public is the final goal. When you have that in the back of your mind, even when actually composing, it influences you so that you don't compose 'just something'. You have to have something meaningful and new to say—the audience comes to listen to your work with great expectations! That's an enriching thought for me.

I have the same attitude when I perform; I don't improvise solely in new music. When I play old music I always improvise cadenzas, passages, ornamentation, etc. In that way, in a concert, neither I nor the audience know beforehand what's coming. It would be too predictable and thus 'cheating' to play a written-out cadenza.

Do you want to communicate with the audience so much that you think about it while you are working? Or do you also allow yourself to compose for yourself?

That is a difficult question to answer because the question contains a hidden allusion. It implies: are you egotistical or aren't you? And I believe that it is more complicated than that. I have composed many works just for myself, and I think that's completely legitimate. As a matter of fact you can create musical diaries without thinking of publishing them later. Many people keep diaries without thinking of publishing them as such—we need only think of Sibelius' diaries. I think it is good for a composer to compose works for himself in order to learn more about himself. As soon as you get paid for writing a work for somebody else, it looks different. If you are honest, you must produce something that's worth listening to, and therefore you have to think of the audience. But you also know that the audience doesn't know what is best for it; you can't ask a 'member' of the audience for a definition of a good piece of music. The composer must know beforehand how the piece will work, so that it gives the 'total experience'. People come to a concert in order to experience, and to discover something special.

You mention Sibelius with a tinge of irony. Younger Finnish composers often think that he is something of a millstone in the national heritage. How do you see it?

When you live, work, and compose in Finland, you become almost fed up with Sibelius because you meet him at every turn. He is, so to speak, your daily bread! He is so omnipresent that you almost forget he was just a very good composer. It is also irritating to have him everywhere and it becomes hard to like his music; you can read about his music in all the papers, everyone studies him, there is always someone who is writing a new book about him.

Aside from the Finnish ISCM section, the society Korvat Auki (Open Ears) is the most important organization that supports new music in Finland. It has been run by young Finnish composers like Jouni Kaipainen, Magnus Lindberg, Kaija Saariaho and Tapani Länsiö, all of whom were students of Paavo Heininen. What you have in common with these composers is an attitude that opposes Finnish traditionalism, and, in light of what you have just said, a skepticism about monumental works. But it seems now that the young composers are reconsidering the big symphonic forms. Kaipainen has written his first symphony and Lindberg has composed works in the 'grand style'. Even though you can't speak of the 'heavenly length', the younger generation seems to be mature enough now to undertake large-scale works. Can one identify a turning point for your generation in this regard?

If you think about the large forms in the traditional sense, where tensions span very long periods, I don't think we're talking about a turning point. I'm thinking about the Romantic era when the public was acquainted with the rules of tonality. When the romantic composer initiated a dominant suspension he could hold on to it for as long as he wanted: everyone knew that the tonal resolution would come along sooner or later. It wasn't difficult to play with perception over a long period. In today's music you don't know what's going to happen. Previously the audiences were more uniform. Today the public is a mixture in which you cannot expect to find such consistency. One person might come from a background of Mozart and Beethoven, while another is a rock fan, and a third has, just out of curiosity, come in off the street. There is no common language that you can refer to. So to compose a work that builds on the well-known expectations of the listener is now problematic in the same way that it was impossible to build large forms in the seventeenth century, when there wasn't yet available a fully developed tonal system. Consequently, at the beginning of the seventeenth century, the public didn't know what to expect because so many works didn't follow traditional conventions. You could let any chord follow any other, and no voice-leading rules were necessary. It was impossible to build large forms. Today when you write a symphony you often avoid the problem in the same way. If the work lasts forty minutes, for example, it can be broken up into five segments each of which lasts only eight minutes. But on the other hand, many present-day orchestral works are shorter and consist of only one movement. I think problems start accumulating when the length exceeds, say, half an hour. Just look at the composer Kalevi Aho who composes symphonies that are fifty minutes long. He has to use traditional techniques in order to make things work. If you start from scratch to create your own musical world following your own rules, it is difficult to build up long tensions guaranteed to work for the majority of listeners.

But in Finland something has happened with the *conditions* for newly-composed music in recent decades. In the 1970s, there was virtually no contemporary music culture in Finland. There were of course composers, but there were no concert series, no festivals, no large presentations of new music. But as you mentioned, the Finnish ISCM section and Korvat Auki began to present the international avant-garde at the end of the 1970s and the early 1980s. Even so, Korvat Auki was more like a private club where members supported performances of each other's works. Later came the more internationally orientated Helsinki Biennale in 1981 (now called Musica Nova Helsinki, *ed.*), and I started Time of Music in Viitasari in 1982. If you look at the situation today, you will see contemporary music programmed at nearly every festival in Finland. Directors feel that they *have* to have new music, or it won't be a really decent festival. Also, going to such a concert has become socially important, one wants to experience new music with other people, to talk about it and perhaps to influence it.

'At give sine tanker musikalsk form: Interview med den finske komponist og cembalist Jukka Tiensuu', *Dansk Musik Tidsskrift* 66, 1 (1991/92): 10–14.

Tikhon Khrennikov

My Conscience is Clear

Considering the general state of affairs in Russia, Tikhon Khrennikov, formerly the influential General Secretary of the Soviet Composers Union (SK), is doing well. From his apartment in Moscow he has a view of the monumental building that houses the Department of Foreign Affairs. Under Stalin's orders a copy of the building was erected in Warsaw (the Cultural Palace). Not exactly an architectural gem, this is one of the many reminders of the past that most Moscovites would like to see demolished. As far as they are concerned Tikhon Khrennikov belongs to an era that is a closed chapter.

Amongst his fellow composers, Khrennikov is judged to have been 'a man of the system'. They follow this up with evaluations of his character that cannot be quoted here. In the conservatory where he still teaches, portraits of masters such as Shbalin and Shostakovich hang in the classroom. The proud photo of Khrennikov has been removed. The gap in this 'hall of fame' is a daily reminder that he has become persona non grata *in his lifetime.*

As I walk into Khrennikov's apartment I encounter that part of his long life in music; it remains like a kind of showcase. Press photos decorate the walls and book-cases: the hand-shake with Ronald Reagan; socializing with Igor Stravinsky. There is certainly plenty to show, and perhaps equally much to hide. For a number of years Khrennikov has been working on an autobiography that will come out later this year. It will, according to the author, document the fact that all the accusations against him are pure piggishness and false propaganda, including Solomon Volkov's book on Shostakovich which is mentioned in the following interview.

Would you tell me a little about your background?

This book here, written in English, is a biography of me. It was published in the USA.

(Dansk Musik Tidsskrift's interviewer leafs through the book.) From this biography it seems that you have travelled an incredible amount. You seem to have had no problem in getting permission to travel abroad?

All problems evaporated with Stalin's death. The iron curtain existed under him and it was very hard to make foreign contacts. At that time we knew very little about our Western colleagues and their music. We were cut off from the world.

You didn't get out of the Soviet Union during the Stalinist period?

No. Nobody did. It was only after Stalin's death that composers from the West started coming to visit us. After that time friendly connections between colleagues both in the East and in the West began to develop. A delegation of Soviet composers travelled to America for the first time in 1959. Among them were Kabalevsky and Shostakovich. We were pleased that, after a while, the contact was broadened to include not only friendships between musicians, but also friendships between people. The situation in the 1950s had a negative influence on our musical culture. Some musical works and news from abroad did reach us, but only to a very limited degree.

Did you receive privileges because of your central post in the Composers' Union? I am thinking of the periods both under and after Stalin.

I was General Secretary for five years under Stalin. But I had nothing like a privileged position in the Soviet Composers' Union, though I had an unbelievable amount of work. Naturally, there was less work when our network of contacts was smaller. Increasingly the work with foreign contacts became very important. We developed both official and personal friendships with leading foreign composers in France, America and Italy. It was fantastic for us. Our lives became normal. Under Stalin one was persecuted if one set up those kinds of relationships. Everything from abroad was cut off.

It must have required great diplomacy to remain on a good footing with Stalin and at the same time to respond to the concerns of the members of the Composers' Union. How did you tackle the diplomatic aspect of your job? Were you a kind of liaison point between what the regime wanted and what composers wrote?

Composers were completely immersed in the atmosphere that dominated our country. There were no special connections between composers and the government. They lived as ordinary Soviet citizens. The government used Stalin Prizes to encourage composers. Prokofiev, Shostakovich and Khachaturian received Stalin Prizes in 1949 and 1950. I was Chairman for the commission that gave out the Stalin prizes to musicians.

As a member of the committee did you ask composers to write in the same spirit that motivated the prize?

No, everyone composed as they wished. There were certain trends but nowhere was there a recipe for how one should compose. It sounds downright vulgar today when people say that the party prescribed what should be written. That's ridiculous. I was leader of the Composers' Union, but I never composed a work that praised Stalin or members of the government. Khachaturian and Prokofiev did. Even though I was head of the Composers' Union, I had time to do a lot of composing—many songs—all genres of music. I didn't compose one piece, not a single song, that was dedicated to our leader. There was no pressure at all. Shostakovich composed the song about the woods in 1950, Prokofiev composed a cantata in honour of Stalin, and Khachaturian worked together with Stalin and Voroshilov on a national anthem.

Have historians been fair to you and your achievements? You yourself say that there has been a vulgar distortion of what happened, and that the facts are becoming confused.

I feel it is unfair, but I think it will pass. Currently the predominant attitude goes against me. The avant-garde complains that its works were forbidden, but nothing at all was forbidden. Bans were not a factor for composers. Support for art is based on a love of art. When our avant-garde complained, it was because it was a small clique. They didn't find support from broader musical circles, nor from our great composers. No-one censored them, they were simply performed less than other composers. Today there is complete freedom and their music could be played anywhere, but where is it? It was a small sect and it continues with its sectarian existence.

Russian composers are not often performed in the West. Is that what you are saying? But there has hardly been a festival in the West without performances of Schnittke or Gubaidulina!

They have become martyrs.

Perhaps you don't consider them very great artists?

They are talented, but their martyrdom was created on the strength of the current trends. We have more talented composers. Schnittke and Gubaidulina are in vogue. They are not poor composers, but the attention given to them has been exaggerated. It will fall by the wayside like so much else. Only the truly great remain in the end. In our culture there is more than enough that is great and valuable—it is the foundation of the respect our culture enjoys. I speak of Shostakovich, Prokofiev, Khachaturian, Karaev, Sviridov and others. There are many great composers like them.

You don't think then that Gubaidulina's success will endure? Are there other talented names that should also be known in the West?

I don't want to predict anything (laughs). It is fashionable and trendy. Among living composers, I would name Sviridov, Shchedrin, Eshpai, (Boris) Tchaikovsky. But they have been pushed into the background by current trends. There are works by Schnittke and Gubaidulina that I regard highly, but that's no reason to pronounce them the leaders of our musical culture.

Who has inherited Shostakovich's legacy?

There are many talented young composers among my students at the conservatory. You'll have a chance to listen to some of my students, for example, Valodiya Dubinin. At the moment he is at loggerheads with the conservatory because he has neglected to take some courses in which he has to be examined. I would also suggest Serosha Golubkov. They are both wonderful pianists. They're able to present their 'wares' themselves. They are the youngest ones. Among my older students who have now graduated, I would name Alexander Tchaikovsky, forty-two years old. He is one of the most talented from that generation. There are so many who are talented because we have a long tradition of fine musicians. They are not only talented, but also very highly trained professionals. I look with great optimism to the future even though many musicians are leaving us. We are enjoying the growth of wonderfully well-educated practising artists. Even at the ages of fifteen and sixteen they play fantastically well. I have just had a composition recital of my own orchestral works in the conservatory's large auditorium. A sixteen-year-old cellist played my Cello Concerto. His name is Borisław Strulov, a colossally-gifted cellist. He has just performed in a festival in France and was a great sensation. My Second Piano Concerto was performed by a fourteen-year-old girl, Natasha Zagalaskaya.

I would like to go back to something that we were talking about before, namely the problems before and after Stalin. It sounds as though all problems were eased after Stalin's death? Would I be right in assuming that some problems did in fact persist after his death?

Not all problems were resolved with Stalin's death, but the most difficult ones were. Party rule continued and ceased only four years ago. Even under Gorbachev the party leadership continued. It got better when all the interference that had nothing at all to do with music disappeared. A new irritation is that our current government completely lacks any interest in the arts. So I hardly know what is best: concerned influence or this complete indifference and 'go to hell' mentality.

Photo: Tikhon Khrennikov (Walter Kläy).

Am I right in thinking that you believed in communism as an ideology? Are you still a communist at heart?

Socialist (the Russian translator didn't dare use the word communist, *ed.*) ideology has had no real effect in our country. Socialist ideology is a noble cause, but the corrupt forms that it took in our country, served no purpose whatsoever. Under Stalin it took on gangster-like proportions. What matters are the forms it takes and how ideology matches the reality of everyday life. For us it took on crazy forms. Goodness! Save us from turning back to that. We could continue to discuss the problems facing music for days. I am glad to have met you.

One last question. When you have been as highly placed in the system as you have, one must be prepared for criticism. There are also people who have tried to represent you as a villain—as in Volkov's book, for example.

Everything there is a lie. That book has no connection with Shostakovich. It is a lie for the sake of sensation and money. Nasty. Horrid. Loathsome. I have also written a memoir, it is coming out in the spring, in March or April. It is 300 pages long and contains some sensational things. It is largely based on conversations and reports. Everything is supported with documents. It is actually the history of Soviet music in this period. I'm publishing quite a few secret documents from the Central Committee on the affair in 1948, among other things. I describe my meetings with Stalin. They were very interesting.

How did you obtain these papers?

I was helped by the editor, Mrs Robtjova, who is head of the Composers' publishing house. She was able to gain admittance for me to the archive that holds the documents I am publishing. I write about Shostakovich and Prokofiev exactly as it was because I was around them almost every day at that time. I also write about Stravinsky with whom I became a close friend towards the end of his life. I have had some very interesting experiences, as well as some that were difficult. The book is of particular interest to musicians. An American advised me to write a popular book. I dictated my thoughts to him for ten days, six hours a day. My book will surely be of great interest to you. I don't know if it will appear in English.

I am currently imposing some order on my own huge archive. I have found a letter from Shostakovich. On 30 October 1948 he wrote,

> Dear Tikhon Nikolajevich, I send you my hymn for choir, orchestra and two pianos. I have revised the ending according to your suggestion about the ending of the melody at rehearsal letter 2. Your advice cen-

tered on the idea that I shouldn't repeat a turn that had appeared already two bars earlier. It doesn't work to repeat something so soon. Greetings, Dmitri Dmitrijevich. P.S. I am worried that the orchestra and two pianos will sound bad. Typically, the piano sounds physically weak with a choir.

This friendship continued until Shostakovich's death. When Volkov and others want to represent themselves as being close to him, they come up with all kinds of lies about me because I was at the head of Soviet music. My character is such that I don't let lies affect me. Life will set everything straight. I have a completely clear conscience with respect to all my colleagues.

'Jeg har ren samvittighed: Et interview med Tikhon Khrennikov', *Dansk Musik Tidsskrift* 67, 5 (1992-93): 151–154.

Pawel Szymanski

BETWEEN TRADITION AND RENEWAL

*The term that is used in connection with both your own music and that of Stanisław
Krupowicz is 'surconventionalism'. We're familiar with the word 'surrealism', does
the word 'surconventionalism' cover something comparable?*

Krupowicz and I invented the word about ten years ago. Our object was to
find a word that describes the essence of our music in the same way that the
word 'surrealism' is an apt expression with regard to visual art. In music you
can't use the work 'realism'; it is absurd to speak about the presence of something 'real', or therefore 'surreal', in music. But speak of *musical convention*
does make sense: baroque and classical style are, for instance, concepts that I
understand and perceive as musical conventions.

In visual art one of the principles of surrealism is to use real elements,
but in a broken syntax, for example, in the form of a dream-like representation. It is the same in my music: I use some traditional basic forms and structures, but I break the rules consciously. 'Surconventionalism'—at least for
Krupowicz and me—applies to music that relates to tradition, but at the
same time breaks with it.

*So, the relationship between tradition and renewal creates tension in your music.
That's a description that can be applied to just about all music, except for those
composers who claim to create something absolutely new each time. Can you elaborate further?*

The traditional elements in my music are not difficult to see even though I
often try to hide them, like, for example, in 'Two Pieces for String Quartet'. I
admit that baroque music generally influences my music. My hope is that my
musical reconstructions, transformations, or deformations, if you like, are
audible in the sense that the historically-conscious listener, so to speak, can
listen backwards and forwards in history at the same time.

*It seems that a number of recent works by the older generation of composers sound a
bit old-fashioned, to put it bluntly. I'm thinking of a composer like Kotonski, and
also the latest works of Penderecki and Lutosławski that bask in the warmth of tra-*

dition. Is there a neo-romantic wave on the way? What explains this mild breeze that currently blows through Polish music?

I think there is a trend to rely on what's over and done with, and in fact the later works by Penderecki and Lutosławski are not particularly strong or uncompromising. The latter hasn't renewed his technique for a long time. Perhaps you are right that his latest works have become more consonant, and something similar is happening in the middle generation: Wojciech Kilar, Henryk Mikolaj Górecki and Włodzimierz Kotoński. It's going too far to say that they have become old-fashioned, but they have turned back to tonal music. In my generation—Stanisław Krupowicz, Rafał Augustyn, Eugieniusz Knapik and myself—we are all interested in discovering our own attitudes to tonality and to tradition. We have never been interested in avant-garde ideology. At the conservatory we learned the twelve-tone technique and all the other new ways to compose. We listened to the music of the 'Darmstadt' composers, but for us this avant-garde was already an academic issue. We tried, in other words, to free ourselves from the musical strait-jacket of the 1950s.

If we look at a festival like the ISCM World Music Days, where we are at the moment, with music from nearly forty different countries, you can't fail to notice that melody and tonality have made a comeback, albeit in many different guises. The Americans are here with their contribution: repetition seems to have developed into a collective neurotic obsession with them. More and more composers are turning their backs on what is usually termed modernism: Schoenberg and his school, and further on to Boulez and Stockhausen.

That is also my impression and not just on the basis of the works at this festival—and not only here in Poland. There is a new trend in which the best works are not only an expression of a simple turning-back, but a musical freedom and a wealth of ideas seen against the background of the 1950s avant-garde terrorism. This freedom relies on the notion that each composer can write music as he himself thinks fit and each is free to collect historical elements and insert them into the music. Now, late in the 20th century, we can hear music from the last ten centuries, both live and recorded. It is an amazing situation because it is the first time in history that this is possible. The whole tradition is a part of our consciousness. That doesn't mean that one should compose in the style of Mozart, but it is *possible* to go back to Mozart and find out one's own relative position. This basic attitude has something to do with pluralism, some call it 'postmodernism'.

Photo: Pawel Szymanski.

When you speak about compositional freedom now, you almost sound like a spokesman for the view that everything is now possible. You don't mean that, do you?

No. The past should not become all-important. I want my music to be taken in and understood on a higher level, so that the transformations and deformations of the past become only a small part of the experience. Naturally everything isn't possible now, nor will it become so in the future. We can still talk about a good and a bad work. The aesthetic criteria are still valid, even though the aesthetic judgements have to be based on new premises. Yes, we come with preconceived ideas: this is beautiful or this is ugly, and so forth. It is not my role to state what is good or less good, but what we can conclude is that a great deal more is possible and acceptable now than a few decades ago.

When you use the phrase 'it is beautiful or it is ugly', does this also relate to something in your own music? Do you think in conceptual pairs like pretty/ugly?

It is very difficult to define what lies in the word 'beauty'. What is beautiful and what is ugly? Not every single detail in a painting by Rembrandt is beautiful but the paintings as a whole *are*. I can say that it has never been my intention to write ugly music. On the other hand, it is my intention to make more than 'pretty' sounds.

As individuals we are all interested in what is happening outside of music, in society. You have lived and continue to live in a country where social events have had a political impact on your role as a composer. You live in a country where enormous changes are taking place. Warsaw three years ago was completely different from Warsaw today. It's not only a matter of external changes as represented by the Mercedes Benzes, Coca Cola and fast food outlets. It is the whole mentality, the way of thinking, and the political system that are undergoing drastic changes. That must have consequences for you as a composer. Does your music reflect these events directly or indirectly?

The answer has to be no. My music reflects no 'reality' in any way, for I don't think that it is possible for music to reflect anything outside itself. Music is abstract by nature. But of course, I know that not everyone agrees with that viewpoint. It does happen that people who have listened to my music come and tell me about stories that they have heard in my pieces, about something that I never dreamed of expressing. But I cannot say that people cannot experience this or that. My role is simply to set black dots on a piece of paper.

Let us approach the subject from another angle: the last sentence of President Lech Walesa's opening address in the festival programme book, says that we should bring music to the people, to a much wider audience. What do you say to this idea?

I don't want to say anything derogatory about Lech Walesa, but all the same I want to emphasize that people who work in politics ought to be very careful about indicating where art should go, what it should contain, and to whom it should be directed. I know that the development of art is tied to sociological processes, but personally that issue does not particularly interest me. Audiences, musicologists and critics should address that one. As an *artist* I think that it lies outside my concern; I must create, not explain.

How does the current situation for composers in Poland compare with the situation before the political shift? It looks as though the gangsters have, to a large extent, free play, even in your own small musical world.

The changes in society have had serious implications for Szymanski the person, but hopefully not for Szymanski the artist. Formerly the state supported artists, but the significance of this support should not be exaggerated. It was small change. Now the state is very poor, the economy in general is not doing well, so they are cutting back everywhere. The money available for culture is steadily decreasing. We are in a very sad, and in reality, a dangerous situation just now because they are contemplating substantial cuts to the Philharmonic Orchestra. If that happens, it will be particularly difficult to rebuild the organization.

We are freer people now, but paradoxically it is harder for me to live in the new capitalist society. The key word is 'commissions'. It used to be that when I received a commission from a country in the West, I could live off it for several years! Now I can only live off such a commission for a few months because of the economic situation. In other words, there has been an equalization in many areas between the East and the West.

I try to make a living as a freelance composer; it was easier before. Nonetheless I want to emphasize how very pleased I am with the general changes that have taken place in my country in the last five years, even though my situation has become more difficult. I would rather have less money than less personal freedom.

Has it become more and more important to get commissions from abroad?

Yes, it has become very important. And if the commissions fail to materialize, then you have to teach or try to collaborate with theatre people or film makers. You find ways to survive, but the alternatives are limited because the crisis is felt everywhere. I know that artists have broad support in Scandinavian countries in the form of stipends and grants. It is really peculiar because these state systems are much more socialist than the free market system we have in Poland now. We receive virtually nothing from the state here.

Have you ever thought of moving to the West as many artists from the East are doing these days? It could be combined with a position as a teacher.

I wouldn't mind travelling abroad for several years. I am free and can travel wherever I want, but I have never been interested in teaching. If I received an attractive invitation for a position in a foreign country, I would consider it, no doubt about that. Under the communist regime it was difficult to travel to concerts and festivals in the West. I always had to send requests to the police in order to get permission to travel. I was furious about this and felt as though I was in prison. Now I am free—I have my passport in my pocket and can leave the country whenever I want. It is a wonderful situation.

'Mellem tradition og fornyelse: Interview med den polske komponist Pawel Szymanski'. *Dansk Musik Tidsskrift* 67, 3 (1992/93): 97–99.

Philip Glass

WHEN LANGUAGE FAILS
THE WORLD IS REVEALED

What kind of identity does your music have?

Actually I try to avoid identity in music. There's already too much identity; the demand for it has become too oppressive. I look at things from the opposite viewpoint. First of all you have to go out and find your own voice, then you have to get rid of it. One of the problems is to set about writing a piece of music that has no history, that isn't weighed down with tradition.

But doesn't there have to be some form of identity in the music, in the structure?

This is interesting, for here several different relationships come into play, among them the social conventions of our time. In previous conversations we have talked about the very significant period, historically speaking, of the 60s. That was an important period for my generation. We rejected all the music that had been composed before. We didn't reject it from an aesthetic viewpoint—in fact it was music that we really loved—but we didn't follow the line or the development.

We acted and reacted against many things. The resistance began in the 1960s. I met Ravi Shankar and I travelled to India, Afghanistan and Africa. My music developed from those experiences. It was, from an historical perspective, a decisive situation for we had come to the end of a particular kind of music. Now it was important to determine the way to a new music. Sometimes people ask, 'Who invented this new language'? as if a single person had invented it. Naturally it was not just one person; it grew out of the social situation at that point in time. To try to link this historical moment with a personality or identity ('this person invented the language') is to encumber it with something false. It does not describe it as it actually was.

For me the question of identity is difficult to deal with because it conflicts with the way I think, for example, saying something about who shall emerge as the father of this or that. You cannot look at things in that way; reality is very much more complex. We're contributing to a false view of history when we choose to think in that way. And the struggle for identity is actually a consequence of that kind of thinking.

The desire to create a new musical language such as that which you and others want, means taking some kind of standpoint with respect to musical identity. To wish for a non-identity is, in itself, a form of identity. The term 'minimalism' automatically and instantaneously brings to mind names like Glass, Reich, La Monte Young, Riley. Let us go back a little in your development. I would like to hear about how you created your own company, your own publishing venture, your own orchestra. No-one would play your music, so you set up your own performances.

That's right, but everyone did the same thing in the same way: musicians, painters, dancers, sculptors, authors. We all lived in the same place.

In the Soho district?

Yes, around that area, downtown. We were not part of the 'mainstream', but we didn't feel isolated. Here's a significant anecdote: for a long time the *New York Times* refused to review our concerts. In 1970 I spoke with John Rockwell who was one of the young critics for the newspaper. He had just come to New York and would have liked very much to review the events that took place downtown, but that wasn't possible because the arts editor had set a boundary at one particular place, 34th street.

It sounds strange but this dumb attitude was typical of the journalists who were there. They thought: 'There are so many productions, we're going to drop those that happen downtown'. What was the result? This very productive group of artists had to find their own concert halls and develop their own audiences. We learned to support one another. To my surprise I can see that it is still the case in New York that young composers and theatre people work together. When a young person asks me, 'What should I do?' I always answer, 'Go to New York and find someone to work with. You'll learn nothing in school, or at university. Do the work yourself'. When I set up my first concert, it was for the hundred or so people that I knew. For a long time I produced concerts in my loft in an abandoned building on Bleeker Street.

Who was in the group you mention?

There were many: Sol Lewitt, Don Judd, Richard Sera, Chuck Close, Nancy Graves. The painters were the most helpful, because they earned more money than we did. At that time in the late 1960s there was a visual arts boom and the young painters got their work exhibited in the galleries. Often the painters supported their musician friends, by simply sending them money, buying equipment or by paying to produce a concert. Because the painters supported us, the galleries also began to promote concerts, galleries such as the Whitney Museum and the Guggenheim Museum. So the museums were our first concert halls. I don't believe that this is well documented, but that was actually the way it was. My first concerts were at the Leo Castelli Gallery, the Paul Cooper Gallery, the Whitney Museum and the Guggenheim Museum. For the first three years the galleries were the only available concert halls. The people in the audience therefore were also painters or people who were interested in visual art, in addition to the writers, dancers and theatre people who were part of that milieu.

What we did—with, among others, Jon Gibson, La Monte Young, Terry Riley, Meredith Monk, Charlotte Moorman, Philip Niblock, Terry Jennings—was to create a new art form. Important sources of inspiration at that time were John Cage and Merce Cunningham, both of whom were very active.

In early 1970 we set up a new music venue downtown called The Kitchen. I often had performances there with people like John Cage and Anthony Braxton. We presented dance and video performances. The Talking Heads were first seen at The Kitchen. (They were called Talking Heads because people who appeared on television interviews were called that.) Later they became a famous group. Laurie Anderson also first became known as a sculptor when she exhibited at The Kitchen; later she started to do performances. Many of the painters began to make performances and so the concept of 'performance art' developed. We all worked in the place and became a part of each other's work.

So, to sum up what happened downtown: it was a very active scene, people were positive and helpful, and completely cut off from the mainstream.

What did you consider mainstream?

In the music world it was what we called academic music and dodecaphonic serialism—people like Elliott Carter, Gunther Schuller, Milton Babbitt. Their base was school, the university. They completely controlled the finance of the music world: publishers, fundings, prizes and performances. But the fact was that the New York Philharmonic didn't play very much of their music anyway, so their influence was restricted to certain areas—and as soon as we found out that they didn't have so much to offer musically, it wasn't very difficult completely to disassociate ourselves from their music.

What these composers needed was 'security'. There are always people who need economic security. What happens to music in academic circles is that it brings out the need for a kind of safety net. These academics can't live with insecurity, they can't work without having economic security. When these academics write music, it sounds like that.

These schoolteacher composers rejected our music. We decided that we didn't want to follow their line. It is strange to view it historically; why were they uptown and why were we downtown? I don't know. I was interested in people, in ideas, in John Cage, in Merce Cunningham. I was interested in people who lived their lives independently of institutions and certain aesthetic directions. We didn't have economic problems because money didn't interest us!

On the other hand you must have had a certain flair for making money and a feeling for institutionalization, for you were able to create a whole opera company with all that that entails in terms of finance and marketing.

I learned these things as I went along; it wasn't so difficult. For some composers it is completely out of the question to be both businessman and composer at the same time and to emphasize both equally. But you have to be outgoing if you want to promote the music. Berlioz had the same problem. What did he do? He put his scores under his arm, rented a carriage, went to Germany, hired an orchestra, got the music played and collected the takings. One doesn't think about Berlioz in that way, but that's how it was. Somewhat the same happened for Wagner.

It wasn't hard for me to form a travelling theatre — and it was much more stimulating than teaching counterpoint at a university. If I had to choose between teaching music history to twenty students a week and going out and arranging concerts, then the latter would be much more interesting for me. So I have to live with the fact that I have no future — I live in the present. I can talk about how I will be living one year from now — that's all. I don't know how I will be living in 1999. I imagine that I will do something or other, but I have no idea about what it shall be or how I will earn money. But it isn't a problem for me. Not even when I was younger and had two small children. I once talked to a composer who had taken a job as a music teacher. I asked him why he did it. He said that he wanted to have children and he didn't feel that he had enough security to have them without a steady job. I have never had a steady job and never had trouble earning a bit here and a bit there. I loaded vans, sold newspapers, drove taxis for five years — even while working on the opera *Einstein on the Beach*. Many people have a complicated relationship with money. They make a virtue of having a problem. They are in love with it.

When I had finished the opera *La Belle et la bête*, I couldn't find anyone to finance the performance of the work. We aren't talking about an early work, we are talking about a problem that arose three years ago, after having composed eleven operas and after having achieved status as a famous composer! So I went out and gave twenty concerts, made some money from the sale of CDs, and got together enough to set up the show. It's been like that for the last twenty years.

Berlioz and Wagner wrote for a large orchestra in spite of poor economic conditions. Would you have composed for large orchestra if you had had more money?

I'm not sure. For twenty or thirty years I have worked with musicians who are the best imaginable for my kind of music. I have had contact with orchestras and have composed four symphonies all of which have been performed. There are larger orchestra 'set-ups' in some of the operas. I don't write works that cannot be performed, so the problem has never arisen. I don't have a pile of music lying around that has never been performed.

To me the conditions that I have are the best because I don't have any others. I don't dream of having a double orchestra with two organs, six trumpets and so on. I am fortunate in that I myself am capable of creating the conditions that are necessary to get my music performed. But we still have to fight to get these performances. People think that Bob (Robert Wilson, *ed.*) and I can get everything performed. That's not so. We always fight for every single work. Next year I am going to write an opera with Doris Lessing. We have waited eight years to find the right producer for it.

You have been in Europe for several years. The American mentality can be very different from the European. I have noticed that you don't use the same arguments that some European composers would. When you are asked how you compose, which system you use, you answer like Feldman: 'I am the system'. To my question about musical duration, about how you organize the flow of the music in time, you answer like Cage: 'The work is finished when it stops'. Such statements are provocative for a European schooled in German or French thought. I interpret your style of discussion as a kind of defensive manoeuvre, where you try to avoid talking about what lies behind the expressions. Would you agree with that?

I know the attitude, not least from my studies with Nadia Boulanger. She complained all the time and told me that I had no sense of history. It was hard for me to relate to that criticism.

EAST-WEST

In your book Music of Philip Glass (1987) *you write about your encounter with non-western music, saying interesting things about your meeting with Ravi Shankar, and how you solved notation problems by working with Indian music. For a long time now* Dansk Musik Tidsskrift (Danish Music Review) *has published articles that discuss the use of music from other cultures in western music. It would be interesting to hear about your experience of incorporating non-western music into your own work. We could take as a starting point the statement of the German musicologist, Ulrich Dibelius, which was printed in the last issue of* Danish Music Review:

[T]here is no comprehensive project that encompasses all the specific social, aesthetic, religious, historical and economic relationships within an individual society: the musical elements cannot be freely exchanged,

nor brought together with an artificial common denominator. That is precisely why all the beautiful thoughts about a world music come to nothing. It has nothing to do with the fact that music in one place is primitive and in another is artistic, or that the music in one place is original and natural, and in another highly refined, but old-fashioned.

How do you see it?

Basically I agree with Dibelius, even though his formulation is highly academic. What he says is very simple in reality: you cannot take these sounds out of the context in which they are created; they won't *mean* the same any more. But it *can* happen, it happens all the time: Westerners play the sitar and people in India play the electric guitar. Go into any hotel in India and you will find a piano with a pianist who tries to play hotel piano music. It isn't anything special, but when you see it in India it is unintentionally comical. In English we have the term 'chinoiserie': if you want something Chinese then you make it *look* somewhat Chinese. As a composer you have to go deeper than the material's surface and look at the musical language.

In Western music there are specific relationships between harmony, melody and rhythm. In Eastern music the tensions are not built up in the same way. In South India the musical structure is built on the tensions between melody and rhythm so that melodies fit into a *tal* (a kind of cycle). The adventure of the music consists of getting to the moment where the melody and the tal come together or meet. You can experience it when the people in the audience sitting and listening to a mridangam player sit on the edge of their seats and excitedly *wait* for the melody and the *tal* to meet. And when it happens, an almost audible 'aaah' can be heard. Now you might ask: 'What are these people listening for'? They are listening to the rhythmic and melodic cycles as they temporarily create certain relationships.

In Africa, this happens in a different way. Here it is more that rhythmic patterns overlap each other. But here also you can count the places where the individual patterns 'meet', for after that they become separated. In Balinese and Javanese music it happens according to the same kind of ideas.

In Western music rhythm is not nearly so dominant. It can make one think about what actually constitutes the harmony and functionality of the West. The Renaissance masters composed linear music and after Monteverdi they began to develop tonal centres and substitute chords—all of which ended up with the *Tristan* chord.

What can we learn from that? Personally I spent ten years (from 1965– 1974) experimenting with rhythmic cycles in order to discover new tensions

Photo: Philip Glass (John Bentham).

between melody and rhythm. I studied tabla with Alla Rakha because I wanted to know how Indian music worked, why the structures affected me. Before this I had studied harmony and counterpoint with Nadia Boulanger in Paris. Slowly I began to implement these experiences in my own music, in works like *Music in Fifths, Music in Similar Motion* and *Music in Twelve Parts.*

It was also at this time that you felt the need to establish an ensemble in order to realize your music . . .

Yes, and I travelled a lot with the ensemble. There is one amusing detail: at the time I told no-one that my music was inspired by Indian music because there were so many people in America who played the sitar. Remember that the Beatles had just returned from India in 1967 or 1968. I came home a little before that and had begun to work, but suddenly all of New York was full of tabla- and mridaṅgam-players. They played in rock orchestras, in clubs—it was precisely the kind of *chinoiserie* that I didn't like. So I didn't say a word about my music being inspired by Indian music, and no-one noticed it because on the surface given the amplification and synthesizers, it didn't *sound* Indian. It sounded more like some experimental pop music.

After all of these studies your music began to take shape. You presented your music to a German radio programmer, among others.

Yes. In Cologne I went to the director of new music at the radio station and showed him the score of *Music in Similar Motion.* He was very friendly and from looking at my music he thought that I was an amateur, that I had never studied music, so he said, 'Have you ever thought of studying music seriously'? Remember that I had a master's degree from Juilliard, had studied with Nadia Boulanger—had studied music for twenty years! My music was simply *beyond* what one could imagine was possible at that time. I often had that kind of experience then. My musicians and I were perceived as 'primitive'.

But Cage had been in Darmstadt at that time, the public had heard something other than so-called complex music . . .

Yes, but Cage's music did not have much in common with, for example, *Music in Similar Motion.* We knew Cage and he knew us, but seen and heard with European eyes and ears, my music was something that came *from out of nowhere.* We were perceived as a bunch of people who tried to reinvent a musical language, which was in a way the case. We *wanted* to create a whole new music.

In order to create this new language I used Indian music. In order to reform modern music I used its rhythmic patterns. Then, in 1975, I introduced the combination of functional harmony and rhythmic cycles. That is fundamentally what *Einstein on the Beach* is about. Here you find cycles with two, three, four . . . up to seven chords. This piece was an important resource for me in later work. One could say that *Two Pages* and *Music in Fifths* were the entrance to the rhythmic and cyclic world and *Einstein* was the exit, and therefore, the beginning of something new.

I explored this further in *Satyagraha*, with harmonic sequences and rhythmic cycles and slowly found out how to develop tonal centres. That constituted a move toward a new language.

You have talked about these cyclic structures, the meeting of these rhythmic and melodic layers. Can they be compared with the Western principle that was called color *and* talea *in earlier music?*

Possibly, except that in this earlier music the technique is not audible. When you find these retrograde canons in Renaissance music, it's 'eye music'. You can hear that it is beautiful music, but you can't hear the structure. What interested me was that my structures were audible; non-audible structures are uninteresting for me. Generations of composers before me have dedicated their lives to non-audible structures to such an extent that people have said, 'It actually looks better than it sounds'! You can read analyses in *Perspectives in New Music*—they are fascinating but they are exclusively intellectual stimuli.

It isn't my intention to create the traditional opposition between intellectual and anti-intellectual, because one has misunderstood everything if one looks at a work like Terry Riley's *In C* and calls it anti-intellectual music. Actually the structure in that work is worked out extremely carefully! Terry is no primitive. John Adams and La Monte Young aren't primitive either.

I always ask the question: what music do you take home and listen to? What you listen to at home is what you love. I have a beautiful tape of music by M.S. Subbulakshmi that I listened to this morning. We spoke earlier about how painting is a question of seeing, and writing is a matter of speaking, and music is a question of listening. I don't believe that Schoenberg expected us to count the twelve tones, but when you listen to parts of *Einstein* I expect that you can *hear* how the music is developed.

So in that way your music is demanding to listen to . . .

Very demanding because it requires a new way of listening. However, after having performed the music for over thirty years, we can now see that there is a public that can hear the music without difficulty, even an early piece like *Two Pages*. When I played that piece thirty years ago, people in the audience began to riot, they threw things at the piano, they tried to tear me away from the piano stool. Now the same music is perceived as beautiful, almost innocent, music.

MORE TONAL CENTRES

I would like to hear more about your development after Einstein. *You found a way to develop these tonal centres.*

Yes, that's right. It happened in different ways, first of all through the work with the opera *Akhnaten*. Here I began to think about the possibility of polytonality—a music that had the ability to suggest several tonal centres simultaneously. The 'main tonality' should remain unclear—a bit like those optical illusions where you aren't sure which is the foreground and which is background.

Are you thinking about pictures by Maurits Escher?

No, more like the Romanian painter Josef Albers. So I constructed a kind of ambiguous music that if looked at one way was D-flat major, but if viewed in a different way it was B-flat major. The decisive factor was the note D-flat or D. Focusing on one single note determines whether it is one or the other tonal centre. If we hear it as B-flat major, then D-flat major constitutes a minor version of B-flat major.

For me it wasn't so much the music that changed, it was more our way of experiencing it that changed. The *listening process* became different for me in that way—*the way* we listen became, in itself, a part of the construction. So now it gets really interesting for we can no longer determine the tonality of a work. That depends on how we listen to the music.

It's difficult for me to see what's new in that . . .

What's new is that we see that the listening process itself (the act of listening) becomes one of the definitions of what it is we hear. In a way it is what Ulrich Dibelius is explaining when he writes about independent 'existences'. I think that we can only say that a piece exists when the listening is a part of the composition itself. This is a completely new thought about aesthetics and perception. And for me, it is more important than a new theory about hexachords or polymetre, which are theoretical quantities that are uninteresting in the context of perception.

Now to return to the new development in *Akhnaten*; this is where I began to think about cadences. It struck me that I had not thought about cadences as possible formulas. Obviously I had to have cadences, any intelligent person could have seen that! But cadences are actually an expression of something very conventional. So I began to find new chord sequences on the piano in order to create logical progressions. My problem was to find logical ways out. Many traditional harmonies are resolved by unstable intervals, for example, when the tritone is expanded to a sixth or resolved to a third. So if you begin to look carefully at the intervals you will discover that we have stable and unstable intervals and that many harmonic analyses are concerned with how the stable intervals get to be unstable and vice versa.

Take for example, the augmented triad, C, E, G-sharp—you cannot say that it exists as something 'natural' in tonal music. It's the same when we say that right angles don't exist in nature. In both cases it is something that we have invented. So the question is: what has been invented? is it the augmented triad or the diatonic scale? The two things cannot exist at the same time; you cannot find a diatonic scale that contains two major thirds one after the other. So, it is not the augmented triad that is the 'problem child', but the diatonic scale. We know that intellectually, but we act as though we didn't know it!

So I began to look more closely at the augmented triad. I found two possible explanations in a polytonal situation: that is, C major and E major set together. I hear it shifting between C major and E major, but also as a segment of the whole-tone scale. *The Voyage*, the opera that I composed for the Metropolitan Opera, is based on that.

We have accepted a tonal language that is based on three chords. We hear them in the supermarket, in the elevator, we learn them at school, we sing national anthems based on them. But it is something that we have invented, something that is filled with self-contradiction.

Earlier we spoke about taboos in modern music. One of them is the ornament. That is forbidden. When I discovered that, I began to be interested in ornaments. I have a perverse desire to be interested in forbidden things. I introduced *trills* as ornaments in *Les Enfants terrible*, but not as they are used in baroque music. In the same way I tried to create a new form of cadence, for example, in my fifth string quartet.

MUSICAL LANGUAGE

Even perception becomes a driving force that determines the composition's structure and concept. If it cannot be called 'identity' then can it be called a musical 'language'?

What is language? Read Wittgenstein or any other modern philosopher or linguist: the purpose of language is to describe something, but it cannot do it perfectly. You have a kind of existing reality and you have different tools for describing that reality. But these two are always different, so language is always an inadequate entity. But even though language is inadequate it still reflects the quality of our thought. It is the *way* in which language is insufficient that is interesting. To put it differently: it is the way in which things do not function that is interesting. It is when language fails that we can get a glimpse of reality.

That sounds like some kind of negative dialectic . . .

It is rather a positive dialectic, for through the inadequacies of language we get a glimpse of the real. If the opposite were the case, we would be convinced that language was a true description of the world. Back to music: to create a musical system can almost be perceived as a neurotic attempt at creating a perfect language, which obviously is impossible! As an artist you experience this obsession with creating the perfect, logical language, but we know that in the end it will be shown that it isn't possible to create such a thing. If we accept, however, that it won't turn out well, then we find ourselves in an interesting world: we see the world in a new way. We are ready to see that the world, *in reality*, reveals what music reveals of its own essence. It reveals itself in the way that language fails.

Interesting. Can you point to areas where your music fails?

Well, I fail all the time (laughter). We can talk about it on an abstract level. My language should mirror sentiments. What does it mean when a composer expresses himself? When an artist says that he expresses himself, I don't believe it because in order to express oneself consciously one will probably generate a lie, will create a falsehood. All biographies are lies. People believe that my book about myself is an autobiography. That's not true: it says nothing about how many children I have, where I live, about my daily life. When we speak about ourselves we lie, chiefly because the correct tool for describing the truth does not exist. A biography intends to tell the whole story, but cannot. If you ask people to tell you about themselves then they begin to construct an image that they want you to believe—in the way that they would like to see themselves.

Well now, there *is* on the other hand something beautiful about the expression, 'I express myself'. For example, once when I studied with Boulanger we were discussing the resolution of a certain chord. I had followed the rules, but Boulanger said, 'Wrong'! 'No, it's correct, I have resolved the chord in accordance with the laws of harmony', I answered. She stopped saying that it was incorrect, just opened a page of a Mozart score and pointed to a bar and said, 'That's the way it should be'! Mozart had resolved the third in the soprano, I had done it in the tenor. I was deeply confused. Boulanger didn't care whether Mozart had used the rule or not, she spoke about *style*. There were perhaps 6–8 ways to write the piece, Mozart had chosen *his* way of doing it. That was Mozart's style, that's the way you know his music. It's the same way with Rachmaninov and Beethoven—we now know what identifies their music. All the choices that are made by the individual composer—whether it is Glass, Nielsen or Nørgård—are part of their style.

So style and identity are a matter of the accumulation of technical choices?

Yes, it is a matter of technical choices that are projected so instinctively that we cannot articulate the background for those choices. There's the mystery: these highly subjective moments when we feel that it simply *has* to be a certain way. Therefore I would like to go back to your earlier question about how I know when a piece should end, the one that I answer like John Cage: the work is finished when it wants to finish. It is past, when I *know* that it is past. This knowledge is a mystical knowledge that we artists have. It is not something that we can teach others. I call it the mystery of art because it is here that we find personality or identity, if you will. But to search for the core of identity is hopeless; it's like a dog chasing his tail.

POSITIVE MUSIC

When people ask you how you manage to do all your work, you answer that you get up at five o'clock in the morning and work all day. To me it seems as though your work has been free of crises, but shouldn't one have artistic crises in the course of thirty years? Most composers have had deep crises that force the question as to whether they should continue to compose, or stop.

I haven't had crises, but then I don't look at the composing business in the way most others do. I ask: what do we use music for? why do I compose? how can I create music that fits the world and its people? I think of my music as music with a purpose. As an artist you have the chance to be *positive*. If you were a lawyer, politician or general then you would be involved in both positive and negative things. Being an artist is a good metier because it provides the possibility of being wholly positive.

In your book you say, 'The theatre has always interested me because it challenges my ideas about society, my ideas about order'. Is that also positive thinking?

I think so. Take the opera *Ghandhi*. That was special because it dealt with the belief that society could change through non-violent action. Simple non-violent action. That is like my work, its aim is very simple: to try to avoid the negative. Music should not be composed in order to make people sad. And so I have to believe that it is very stimulating to be able to create for the twenty-four people who work on my tours: lighting people, dancers, choreographers. It is deeply satisfying that I, through my work, can create work for them.

I have never worked for the sake of money. I was a taxi-driver until I was forty-one years old. I could have made easier money, but didn't. I have become as famous as I wish to be. I was famous as a thirty-five-year-old! It has been possible for me to think positively. And now I am old enough not to be concerned about whether the music is modern or postmodern.

Were you concerned earlier?

I knew that *Einstein* was something completely new. I knew that it challenged the twentieth-century 'concept' about new music. That was a great joy for me. I liked the fight, I love controversies. As a young man I loved those kinds of things that I now find less interesting. *Einstein* was radical at that time, but no-one writes music in that style now. I don't anyway. Questions about *style* and *history* become less and less important to me. What occupies me now are the 'specialties' in the musical language that we were delving into earlier, there where the music reveals the world through insufficiencies in language. I work more and more intuitively—is that a normal development?

'Når sproget går under åbenbarer verden sig: Møder med den amerikanske komponist Philip Glass', *Dansk Musik Tidsskrift* 70, 8 (1995–96): 254–263.

Magnus Lindberg

A NEW WORLD OF SOUND

Helsinki, March 1989. The city is full of musicians; the fifth biennale for new music has started. I sit in the smoke-filled bar at the Vakuna Hotel and wait for Magnus Lindberg whose piece for orchestra, Kinetics, *has just been premiered. In Finland he is considered the big new name, and optimists call him Sibelius' heir. At precisely the appointed time he emerges through the smoke and settles into one of the easy chairs. Lindberg has recently moved to Paris, and with his casual dress and constantly burning cigarette he looks more like a French intellectual than a Nordic composer. Of course he is in Paris because that's where IRCAM is, the composers' workshop. That's where his works are created. We come quickly to the topic of IRCAM, the composer, and especially his new work. Lindberg briefs me on the background to* Kinetics.

The story behind the work is a long one. In 1981 I composed *Sculpture II*, a piece for large orchestra that was premiered at the Nordic Music Days in Copenhagen in 1984. It was understood that after this, following the precedent of Debussy's *Trois Nocturnes*, I would write two more orchestral pieces to go with it. I didn't expect my music to have anything to do with Debussy's; it was only that the starting point for his work was also a study in small nuances.

Then two years ago I decided to get on with this project. As I said, the starting point was to have been two works, 'Sculpture I' and 'Sculpture III'. But after some time I realized the material that was used eight years earlier couldn't be used anymore. It had to be a completely new work that did not have anything to do with the old one. I had also begun to work at IRCAM with a project that still continues, namely to develop a language that includes spectral harmony, that is, the type of harmony that is based on acoustic phenomena like overtones. All my French colleagues, especially Gérard Grisey, have worked with these ideas for quite a long time. How could I find an aspect that would be completely my own? That was the main idea behind *Kinetics*: to work with a kind of hybrid material, I was going to use a combination of serial, dodecaphonic harmony—as I had worked with them earlier—and group theory, *or* on the other hand, set theory and a harmony that is based on the laws of acoustics. In other words, linking two ways of looking at material.

There was also the inspiration from one of my favourite works, Bernd Alois Zimmermann's last large orchestral work, *Photoptosis*. I don't know if

Zimmermann himself spoke about the foreground and background in this work, but I have analysed it and found a lot of musical ideas that clearly constitute a kind of layered music with both foreground and background. That interested me because in *Kinetics* I wanted to let the acoustics—overtone harmonies, analyses of different sound objects, instrumentation—create a background harmony. The foreground should be made out of the type of harmony I worked with in earlier works, like for example, *Kraft*.

The major part of *Kinetics* is based on these harmonic ideas and the title is also connected to the harmonic language. My problem with purely spectral music has been that it is static. But by combining the spectral and the serial I could achieve 'movement' on the harmonic level, that is in terms of kinetics. I did this, for example, by using Elliott Carter's technique of metrical modulation, where I use a mechanical, pulsing movement, that continues while tempo and time are changed. This motion or transformation applies not only to the tempo and time-plan, but also to harmony.

Can you go into a bit more detail about the thoughts behind the serial part of the work? When you talk about set theory, I suppose you mean Allen Forte's ideas?

Yes, but it goes beyond the prevailing preoccupation with Forte's theory. I have a sizeable computer program that facilitates working with set theory using a database. This database has a great number of chords that are chosen subjectively and categorized. An analytical method makes possible a precise description of the combinatorial aspects of the chords. The problem with set theory is that it simplifies and is mainly statistical. Although a set theory analysis of a chord is merely a representation, a simplification of the original, this program allows me to make corrections and re-enter the results. This is a really advanced data program that is written in Lisp (Lisp is a programming language that is often used for the development of music programs, *ed.*), a kind of artificial intelligence mechanism that allows me to make any chord whatsoever a part of my database with the help of minute adjustments. That sounds perhaps a little cryptic, but it actually means that I can transfer 'colours' from my own harmonic system to the chords, and generate harmonic processes—chains of chords—using the computer and after that manipulate them with the data program. In this way I have control over the material. I can decide that a process will consist of one kind of chord exclusively, or of one type followed by a certain other kind. For me it's like searching to find something equivalent to functional tonality.

I haven't worked with series or classical dodecaphony for a long time, but rather with set theory, group or primary class theory, which allows me to have complete control over the interval content. This is supplemented by means of the computer and allows me to return to the original point of departure, but with a more precise control over the interval relationships. And much of the set theory I am working with at this time is also based on acoustics: I can give certain tones preference, for example, a segment of an overtone series.

What is interesting in this project is how one can create tension and control with the means that we have at our disposal, establish the rules for connecting chord A and chord B. It's comparable to the way in which tonal music functions. In this way I think I have discovered new possibilities in set theory. The problem with this theory is, as I said before, that it is an abstract model of a theoretical way of thinking. I have added programmatic aspects to this process and found that a combination of set theory and acoustics is a useful hybrid.

What about the data system and program? Have you developed that yourself?

Yes, most of it I have written myself, albeit with the help of some French mathematicians and programmers. Some of the technical procedures are difficult, for instance deriving a variety of combinations from a large body of material.

Do you have training as a programmer or something like it?

I took basic courses in these subjects at the Sibelius Academy in the 1970s. We had basic data programming courses for two years, but I can't say that I am a professional in the field. That is precisely one of the reasons I applied to IRCAM where I could work with people who are professionals in the area. I would say that I have limited understanding and a great deal of practical experience.

I spoke with a musician who performed Kinetics. *He said that the piece is not especially difficult to play. You modified the complex background material so that the musicians could learn the piece in a limited amount of time. Is it your own background as a musician that prevails and determines the composition process?*

When one writes for large orchestra one has to make many compromises. I am very critical of the inclination to compose for large orchestra in the Brian Ferneyhough-style. With works for large orchestra one has to be aware of the fact that at best there will be only three or four rehearsals. What I try to do then, without limiting my musical ideas, is to make the layout as clear and concise as possible. My ideal in this regard is Stravinsky, who, instead of overloading some sections, split up the parts. When there was a difficult passage in the trumpets, for instance, he used two trumpets. He was sensible in dividing the parts.

It is important to be aware of practical solutions to problems that can arise. I have reached a point where I simplify the meters so that they completely 'follow' the music. In this way there is no structure behind my bars. I write the music so that all the demanding elements are given to the conductor. This is due most likely, as you say, to my past as a pianist. Before I left the country I often played the piano in the orchestra. As a composer, I consider it important to become familiar with what it's like to sit in the orchestra and rehearse a work, and it is annoying that I have less and less time for this kind of activity. Playing with the Toimii Ensemble is about all that's left.

And performances of a work like Kraft *that demands such large resources are probably very limited?*

Kraft is an extremely expensive piece to stage. The performance on the third of March with the Radio Symphony Orchestra in Copenhagen was the fourth and most recent one.

Let's go back to Kinetics. *We were at the point where you had processed the basic materials with what you call 'hybrid thinking'. But the work isn't finished yet. What is the next step in the process? Instrumentation?*

I should say first that I made a preliminary study with a seven-minute work for piano, called *Twine*. That naturally kept the instrumentation to a minimum so that I could concentrate on the harmonic material. When that piece was finished I had numerous harmonic ideas to work out in *Kinetics*. In this way these two works have the same harmonic principles.

I used to proceed with strict systems but now I have a somewhat more pragmatic attitude about the process. I find it more interesting now to sit at the piano with these new chords and bash through them, gradually becoming acquainted with them. Besides I can use the synthesizer to help listen to the overtones and get to know the material in that way. Then I begin to work with other levels in the music: form, rhythm.

When overtone-based harmony is used, then we are talking about large chords. I have at times used the first 60 overtones. Naturally, this introduces a number of problems with instrumentation. How can one write these out for strings, winds, and so on. That was one of the reasons I wanted to have the synthesizer in the orchestra. It takes care of the overtones.

But only one electronic instrument? You could have used several synthesizers in order to achieve an extremely accurate realization of the overtone spectrum. You wanted to have the sound and the effects of the acoustical instruments?

Yes, it was a conscious choice not to use more electronics, only an ordinary synthesizer that is almost like an extra piano in the orchestra. Besides, I knew that *Kinetics* would be premiered in the Finlandia Concert Hall which has terrible acoustics. For that reason, you could say, that I wrote an extra acoustical element into the piece. The work contains, in a way, its own acoustic. And I wasn't at all sure how that would work as a solution for the orchestra. I was also unsure about other parts of the instrumentation, for example, the brass section plays fortissimo while the strings have long pianissimo tones that possibly wouldn't be heard very well.

After having heard the work do you have any reason to revise the score?

No, I was quite pleased with it and with the changes in colour that were produced by the overtones. Even though the chords are big and compact, the result is a certain softness or richness of sound because a large number of the tones are based on the overtone series. Even the thickest chord has a transparent, consonant colour when it has the cohesion that binds it to the overtone series.

What you say sounds as though you were inspired by Schoenberg's thoughts on Klangfarbenmelodie.

It is clearly important for me, but *Kinetics* is not only 'colour' music. I would rather talk about it in terms of 'harmonic' music. I *have* worked with pieces that to a greater extent focus on the aspect of timbre, and within that I was especially interested in 'dry' sounds, that is to say, all the rough-grained instruments like sandpaper, Latin American rattles, and to some extent, dry, metallic sounds, not to forget, wooden instruments—drums. So the idea of *Klangfarbe* has implied working with these acoustical materials.

Do you have certain theories or aesthetic ideas behind your use of powerful effects as in Kraft, *or, albeit to a lesser extent, in* Kinetics? *I'm thinking of the conscious balancing act between global control over the material and a desire for powerful discharges of energy, ultimately the relationship between rationality and expression.*

I am not sure it is necessarily an issue of definite aesthetics. As far as the powerful effects are concerned, it is hard to overload an orchestra. It's easier to write a fortissimo outburst for the orchestra than for a string quartet. The orchestra can take a lot.

Are you deliberately playing on the showmanship of the orchestra?

Not consciously, but obviously when someone stands and pounds with a huge mallet, invariably there will be a bit of a show. If anyone finds it too showy and cheap then it's just too bad. That's what I want! If there is an

aesthetic element implied, then it must be the wish to work with extreme expressive means, a kind of 'super' expressionism.

I have never had any doubts about using such disturbing instrumental effects. Moreover, I have a kind of seductive desire to try to reach out to youth—the rock public. *Kraft* has probably become so well-known because it cultivates punk and rock aesthetics. I would like to offer today's rock music an element which has been completely lost: dynamics. Today's rock music constantly drives on zero. A few days ago I listened to an old recording by Genesis that has been transferred to CD. My God! what variation in dynamics they used then. The rock music of the 1980s has no changes in dynamics—only maximum loudness and uniformity.

Speaking of stronger instrumental effects, that applies to your work in progress as well. I understand the piano in your summer house has had rather rough treatment.

Yes, that is the basic material for the piece I am currently working on at IRCAM. I have recorded different special piano sounds, but for the first time in my life I have an instrument that I don't have to be careful with. I tuned, for example, the bass strings an octave lower. When the strings loose their energy, they produce these sub-sub-contra tones, but in what we picked up with high quality microphones, we could come incredibly close to a micro-world of sound. I have a number of hours of material that we have recorded with this instrument. It will be computer processed and will later comprise the electronic part of the work. It is an extreme extension of the piano. And I want to find a kind of bridge between the piano and percussion—the work is written for orchestra and four soloists; two pianos and two percussionists—to create a continuity between them. In the orchestra, which comprises 20–25 musicians, there are no descant instruments: no flutes, oboes, trumpets, or violins, only instruments in the alto and bass ranges, a kind of grunting orchestra.

When will it be premiered?

The piece, which still has no title, is a co-production between the Ensemble Moderne and Ensemble InterContemporain in Paris. The premiere will be in Frankfurt in October 1990. When I get back to Paris I will work with an assistant, so that we can revise the piano sounds with computer equipment. There are wonderful programs to be found at IRCAM, for example, sharp digital filters so that one can get an output of 8 Herz. All the filters can be managed by continuous functions, and you can open and close these banks of filters giving a rich complex sound. I find it terribly fascinating to work in this wondrous world.

Photo: Magnus Lindberg (Maarit Kytöharju).

Let me give you an example. Kaija Saariaho also works with filtering sounds. She takes a low tone on a string bass, looks to see what overtones, which formats, are sounding. Then she opens just the filters for these overtones and takes in a flute tone, and suddenly she has a flute tone that sounds like a string bass. By intelligently revising sounds, one can mix characteristics, putting characteristics from two sources together, to get a kind of cross-synthesis.

That sounds like something approaching sampling.

Not in this case. Sampling is actually quite primitive: you record a sound and then you can play around with it. As far as the practical realization of my new work is concerned, I will use sampling to transfer the sounds when they are reworked so that the pianists can play them.

You are talking about sounds as though your work in the future will come more and more to depend on the possibilities and developments offered by the equipment at IRCAM.

Yes, because there you have the potential for a synthetic approach to thinking that I believe is inevitable for today's composers. In the coming decades this way of thinking will become a principal concern of a composer's work, even for those who do not work with electronic music. At IRCAM there is a fantastic databank of the entire sound spectrum of all instruments. There are, for example, all the tones of the piano, and each tone is available as pianissimo, mezzo-forte and fortissimo, so one can see precisely how the overtone spectra look for these tones. Knowledge about these things is absolutely necessary.

You say that as if you had found the Holy Grail at IRCAM. Would you advise all composers to study there?

Not necessarily at IRCAM. Many acoustical areas have yet to be explored, for example, how to make spectral images and establish accurate information about the acoustical properties of different instruments. I am convinced, based on rational thinking, that with the knowledge gained from this type of research, we can advance musical creativity and gradually develop a more intelligent approach to the use of harmony and timbre.

A field that is incredibly fascinating and one that hasn't seen very much experimentation so far, is evolving physical models. At IRCAM we simulate, for example, the data for the violin. You have a string with the two ends fastened down, you have a bow with a kind of friction that causes the strings to vibrate. If you are in control there is no problem with having a string that is 200 metres long, with a diameter of one metre, and a metre-wide bow that can go 10 kilometres an hour. When you have control over the characteristics you can easily spread them out. This is an extreme example that isn't particularly interesting, but when we can make tones with a bow of different widths and influence the attack, and so on, then all the acoustic limitations are overcome. We are also working at this moment with developing 'Chant', a program based on the human voice. It is quite a complicated synthesizing project to simulate the human voice. It contains 150 different parameters and controls all the glottal functions, all the muscular properties and the different shapes of the mouth cavity. In this way you can precisely produce the acoustical conditions for all the vowels.

All of this knowledge is enormously important. It is not a question of simulating the human voice, but of creating a new world of sound. I would like, in time, to see all composers able to get a library of handbooks with exact descriptions of all the instruments and of the characteristics of their tones. My aesthetic, positivist attitude to music is that with better knowledge we can make more interesting music. Scientific research doesn't turn music into an academic, 'dry' art that has no interest for anyone. On the contrary, insight into this kind of special knowledge will allow us to get more out of music.

Some people may possibly say that you will become too much of a scientist with a lab coat . . .

Yes, that's probably right. But there is now a wealth of information that should be mastered before it is permissible to write music. Anyone can throw a major chord down and say it's art. But to write a chord for an orchestra requires quite a bit of background knowledge. Thus I see no problem maintaining the boundary between scientist and composer. Writing music requires enormous control of detail, finesse, knowledge, information, insight. The more control one has, the freer one can be: consciousness and intuition go together.

That you as composer should be constantly in line with technical developments makes me think of Rimbaud's 'Il faut être absolument moderne', or, Habermas' belief that being modern is an incomplete project. Does it seem to you that your music is a continuation of that idea?

That is a good analysis. As professional composers we should use the freedom we have to investigate our material; one should master the vocabulary completely. This can sound a little superior, but that's the way it is. It is also true that the ones who advance the farthest are those who have consciously attempted to change the attitude toward the material they work with.

You have named Stravinsky and Zimmermann as inspirational sources in the development of your musical language. Are there others from our own century?

Many. I have worked with, among others, the writer Juha Silpanen. Three years ago we made a work for radio, *Faust*, that won the Prix Italia. We started by running around for a half year with a tape recorder collecting material, everything that existed in our surroundings. To that we added texts and music that bound the whole together in a kind of continuum. It was research and it was an incredible experience to make music with, so to speak, a reality based on a microphone.

Bartók travelled around and recorded folk music in the midst of daily noise.

Yes, so Bartók found musicians in the country who played the violin and we found power stations (laughter). When we speak of sources of inspiration, I should mention that I also studied with Vinko Globokar for one year in Paris. His idea about music was that there always had to be an outside element, a reference to something outside of the music. As a result I composed a piece for the Toimii Ensemble that year in which I investigated various natural phenomena: water, earth, fire and so on. And I made another one based on Goethe's colour theory, but it was a disaster and I gave up. That project was significant for me because after that I took an unambiguous position: music does not have to have an extra-musical content. As Stravinsky said, 'Composers write notes'. But much of the work with, for example, *Kinetics* has been intuitive; I have sat at the piano and searched for a certain expression, in the same way that a sculptor works: one has an idea about the form that you want to create. And much of what I do at this moment is intuitive. I have no structure to fall back on, but rather I have an elastic material that needs to be moulded.

When one asks Erik Bergman why he went to central Europe at the end of the 1930s he says that it was to get away from the Sibelius-obsession. Have you settled down in Paris to work at IRCAM in order to escape contemporary Finnish musical thinking?

Indeed. There is a limit to what one can experience here in Finland, there is no doubt about that. It is also important to get some perspective on nationalism by getting away from it. Having said that I also think that the geographical situation has radically altered in recent years. It makes no difference whether you sit in an airplane or in a train for the two hours it takes to get to the city. Distance doesn't mean so much anymore. The structure of Europe will also change, becoming one country without borders in the coming years.

'En ny verden af klange: Interview med Magnus Lindberg'. *Dansk Musik Tidsskrift* 64, no. 1 (1989/90): 3–9.

Iannis Xenakis

A Distinctive Profile in New Music

By way of introduction and in order to build a perspective I would like to know how you developed the musical language that is first heard in your landmark work, Metastaseis *(1953–54). In a composition seminar at The Royal Danish Academy of Music you said that it is important to invent a new world, to see beyond that which has already been created. Your own background as a composer is unusual compared with that of other young composers. You were first trained as an architect and you were about 30 years old when you discovered that music was all-important to you. How did you discover or invent your own language and how did your background as an architect and mathematician influence your composition?*

When I was in Greece—where I studied engineering at the Polytechnic Institute—I began to study music with a professor who came from Russia. He tried to teach me to compose in the traditional manner which I thoroughly disliked. I decided to study in the USA in order to learn more. On my way there I stopped in Paris for a while. Later I went to the USA and worked at Bloomington (Indiana University) for five years (1967–72). After that I returned to Paris where I composed music that was inspired by traditional Greek music which attracted me greatly at that time. Then I suddenly broke with this whole tradition and launched straight into the composition of *Metastaseis*, which was premiered in Germany—Donaueschingen—by Hans Rosbaud. After I finished this work I went on to another, *Pithoprakta*, which was premiered by the conductor Hermann Scherchen in Munich. I had found a new expressive means that had to be tested.

You originally went to Paris for political reasons?

I fled Greece for political reasons. At that time I was a communist and I wanted to leave political problems behind me. And, I wanted to be a musician. I had an uncle in the USA and I wanted to get away and to start afresh.

I want to go back to the opening question about your development as a composer. Was it the meeting with Olivier Messiaen that inspired you to develop your completely individual musical expression?

I met Messiaen and showed him some of my music. I asked for his opinion and asked if I could study with him. He accepted me at the Paris Conservatoire without asking me to take the entrance exam or requesting to see any documentary evidence of my previous studies. That was in 1947–48.

In Nouritza Matossian's book, Xenakis, *there is an account of your meeting with Messiaen. He is quoted as saying: 'I understood immediately that he was not like the others'. It seems that he consequently advised you to skip the study of counterpoint and instead to apply your experience as an architect to music. That takes me back to my introductory question: how did you work to transform these experiences into musical sounds?*

I worked as an architect in the firm of Le Corbusier at that time, but I always thought of music as architecture. It was interesting to create music from my experience in a context that had nothing at all to do with music. I actually worked in both directions: I created music from architecture and architecture from music. I worked with Le Corbusier for twelve years—until the end of the 1950s.

Why did you stop working with Le Corbusier?

Because music took more and more of my time. I would like to have continued to work as an architect on the side while working as a composer, but it was impossible. I met architects later in Paris, but I had nothing in common with them and realized that I couldn't take up that work again, so I never went back to working as an architect.

Did you integrate all the experience you had as an architect—of form, volume, surface and proportions—into music?

Yes, but only to a certain extent, because architecture is not the same as music. I have experienced both and I have sometimes tried to combine them. Music is much more abstract than architecture which is based on what you can see and is experienced in several dimensions. Music, on the other hand, is abstract because it treats only the dimension of sound. In itself, the material of sound exists a long way from the experience of everyday life.

Once, at least, you managed to go from architecture to music and from there back to music. I am thinking of the Philips Pavilion at the Brussels World's Fair (1958).

Yes, that's correct. It was at the time when I worked with Le Corbusier. I showed him the design I had made for the Philips pavilion and he was interested. My work there was an extension of *Metastaseis*, which is built to a large extent on the idea of glissandi combined in various ways. I thought of these glissandi as straight lines that can be woven together in a defined space—the same as in music. They have elements in common.

There is a story going around about your meeting with the conductor Hermann Scherchen, and the time you wanted to show him the score for Metastaseis. *Can you tell the story in your own words?*

(laughter) Yes, I can. I composed the work for large orchestra and the score was very big—very tall. I met the conductor at 8 a.m. in his hotel room, where he was reading the score lying in bed, or rather, he was reading down the score. When he got part of the way down, the pages began to fall over his nose, at which point I had to take away the pages as soon as they started to tip over. It was very comical. To my great pleasure Scherchen liked the score very much. He said that it was the first time he had seen such radical music. As you know he did not premiere that work, but, rather, the next one, *Pithoprakta*, a Greek word that means 'actions determined by probability'. This is the first piece in which I tried to work with the concept of probability.

DIALECTICAL TRANSFORMATION

You spoke earlier about the glissandi in Metastaseis. *There was a middle section in the work, or rather, there was a central portion that used serial technique. It was not long after the premiere that you took that part out. Why?*

At that time serial music was something very important, something one had to relate to—particularly because of Schoenberg, Berg and Webern. But I never became an adherent of serialism. I borrowed some ideas from serial music, but the work as a whole is based on 'actions determined by probability'.

In the score you describe the musical process as a 'dialectical transformation'. What does that mean?

In this context 'dialectical' means that there are elements that struggle against each other. This struggle has to lead to a new 'place', a new musical situation. In a broader context dialectical transformation as a guiding principle can be seen as a result of my interest in the old classical philosophy, especially Plato.

We shall return to classical philosophy, but now I would like to dwell a bit on the early part of your output. After the two orchestral works, Metastaseis *and* Pithoprakta, *there was a long period (1956–1962) when you refined the formal aspects of your compositional technique. I am thinking particularly about its theoretical foundation. You also began to work with the computer as a tool.*

Yes. I met a generous man who had an IBM computer and he allowed me to use a computer studio. I tried to write computer programs that could carry out the calculations for 'actions determined by probability' which would otherwise have taken a long time to do manually. That was in the early 1960s.

You continued to work with probability, algorithms, statistics and logic as a starting point for composition. What was the real musical advantage in using these approaches? Was it to avoid other ways of determining structure?

The logical principles I used were supposed to help determine logical steps for making a work move forward, but they were also used to avoid the traditional ways of thinking about music. At that time I studied mathematical logic and tried to use mathematical thought processes in my music.

That was about the same time that Boulez did the opposite: he predetermined all the musical parameters in his Structures I *for two pianos. At that time Stockhausen was also working with refining serial techniques. Did your music develop directly or indirectly from discussions with Boulez and Stockhausen at this time? Or did you feel you had to ignore their music completely?*

I did precisely the latter. I couldn't follow the same paths as those two composers simply because I was not interested in working in the same way. I worked with theories of probability and tried to create music from them. I was not at all interested in being 'serial' or anything like that. I met Boulez and Stockhausen but we soon found we disagreed about everything.

Did you have aesthetic and theoretical discussions with Boulez or Stockhausen? This was, after all, the time when Darmstadt was considered the centre for such discussions?

I had discussions with the Italian composer and conductor Bruno Maderna at Darmstadt. He conducted my music there, a short piece for orchestra, *Achorripsis*, which means 'to throw sounds'. This work is also completely based on probability. In *Pithoprakta*, the material was 'richer' because I could much more easily imagine musical sounds without working strictly with probability.

Your later music can sometimes sound as if you are working intuitively with the material. You became more adept at working with algorithms as a technical means, and so the calculated forms do not sound so rigorous any more. One can even hear sound elements that have their origins in folk music. In Jonchaies *from 1977 the melody is based on a Byzantine folksong.*

I do not remember that work any more.

You don't want to remember that work?

No, I quite simply do not remember it.

But isn't it correct that old folk music traditions have been allowed to infiltrate your music?

Maybe. But my goal was not, and is not, to renew music from earlier times, neither old music nor traditional folk music.

It is commonly believed that composers in Darmstadt in the 1950s and 1960s were not interested in having their music played for the public, that they only composed for themselves and each other, that they experimented and just wanted peace in order to compose. This myth is often repeated. What was your experience at Darmstadt?

It was a place where promising young composers could get their works performed and discussed. Among others I met Nono and Maderna there. Perhaps the composers were so involved with their work that they didn't seem interested in the public. As for me, I was never an insider at Darmstadt. I felt most at ease outside, so to speak. I could not agree with the monolithic aspects of musical thinking that issued from Steinecke, who was director of the Darmstadt Institute. The theoretical departure in Darmstadt was serial music. I was no serialist. In that way, I was much freer than the others. I had a job as an architect, was free, and could allow myself to be out of step with the others. I wasn't forced to follow the Darmstadt serialists.

You have said that you feel very close to Brahms. You feel yourself closely bound to his music. Could you explain this relationship?

No, I can't. I can only say that my feelings and thoughts are closer to Brahms's way of creating art than to that of any other composer. There is nothing more to say. Why? I don't know.

Brahms did not compose as you do.

No, I know that. Perhaps it is exactly for that reason that I admire him (laughter). No, I think that his manner of making sound, of creating structure is very stimulating. That does not mean that I want to be like him.

A NEW WORLD

You have also said that a composer must create his own musical universe, a new world in each work. You expounded on these demanding principles at a seminar for young Danish composition students. However, I would maintain that I can recognize a work by Xenakis—there are definite characteristics that make one think, 'This can only be a work by Xenakis'. Perhaps you can elaborate on what you mean by 'completely new' with regard to your own works?

I find that a difficult matter to explain. Each time I write a work, I have to forget the previous one and the experiences I had while composing it. Sometimes I am successful, on other occasions I am not. Some composers try to take things from the past that you can neither see nor hear, expecting them to reveal themselves, to become alive in a contemporary expression. Where does this compulsive behaviour come from? It relates to the concept of 'renewal'. Some people want to retain the past in art, but also want it to be completely new, which is impossible.

So you don't try to create a connection between the past and the present?

No. Aristoxenes's theoretical works were based on musical scales. His relationship to music does not have much to do with contemporary thought. The past belongs to the past.

When I asked, as I did, it was in fact because you actually gave your work Greek titles that come from another time, indeed from the distant past. How does that relate to what you have said about renewal?

The ancient Greek language often contains a condensation of meaning. That's why I use Greek titles, while, for example, 'sonata' says less to me. In all of my titles there is a seed that expresses the music or the principle of the music.

An example of this . . .

Pithoprakta. The title, as I have said, means 'actions determined by probability'. This work was about precisely that. *Metastaseis* dealt with 'changes'. 'Meta' means 'that which comes after' and 'statis' means 'static condition', hence: the movement from something to something else. This was created by means of glissandi. A glissando is perceived in such a way that you cannot experience a single momentary phase, for you are constantly on the way to somewhere else. There is a regulating flow that can be described as a movement. One can say that a row of points is connected and makes a continuum.

You speak of movement and of glissando as contributing to the development of the music. Can you explain the perception of time in music in general and the concept of time in your own music in particular?

When a composer writes music he uses time. That means that he has the possibility of creating time in his own way. In some cases it goes very slowly, and in other cases it is very complex, and time can be full of 'things', multiple layers, for example. Music is something you can repeat, but time is irreversible. The 'problem' with time in music is the notation of it. Time is always there, in every direction—even in the wallpaper we are looking at right now.

Sometimes we speak of 'clock' time as distinct from 'experienced' time. Is that something you also work with in music?

One has to work with clock time, or real time, if one wants several instruments to play together. Aside from this, clock time is in reality changeable, something without boundaries, undefined when you listen to music.

For example, Ligeti's work for orchestra, Atmosphères, *could be an example that shows how the sensation of time is undetermined?*

Yes. One could ask oneself: why do Bach and Mozart repeat themselves all the time? It is to clarify their ideas, but also because they didn't know how to get further in any other way! They were compelled to repeat.

The relationships between rhythm, melody and harmony are the key concerns of the composers that you have named. Is this something that also affects your music?

One might not easily imagine a melody without a sense of passing time, one note follows after the other. Now, you could say that one could repeat the same note. If that were the case, one would be in a different situation—one doesn't move, the music doesn't move from that place. You could possibly say that that is enough, but I am sick and tired of the kind of music that does not move. It's the same with respect to harmony. It is possible to repeat the same material, both with orchestral and computer music. Time and the events in the music, create a number of actions. I experience harmony like a chain of events. It is natural for people to experience change in the course of time. Harmonic changes exist everywhere, not only in music. It would be fantastic if I could discover something that did not already exist. I haven't done that yet.

Do you contemplate discovering something different from that found in nature?

Yes. Different from nature. Everywhere we see repetitions, or the semblance of repetition. The repeated patterns in the wallpaper are not the same even though they look alike. That is the reason that we in the physical sciences are careful to ascertain whether we are speaking of a change or not. Changes can be so small that we cannot distinguish them, but they are there all the same. Nothing in the world is stationary. Heraditos said, 'You cannot cross the same river twice'. He meant that even though it is the same river, it will have changed and as a person you too will be a little different.

So, correspondingly you try to create a constantly developing music?

It is a natural thing to do. Unless you wish to oppose change and try constant repetition, but this gets tedious after a while and the listeners also get bored after some time. They want something else.

A NEW COMPUTER SYSTEM

In 1966 you developed the concept of the UPIC (Unité Polyagogigue Informatique de CEMAMu) which dealt with composing using a graphic notation that could be translated into music. Looking back at this, can you say something about the significance of transferring graphic notation to sound?

Our work with UPIC was aimed at developing a computer system that could transform a written picture or drawing into musical sounds. We built a machine that 'remembered' the drawing. So, if a composer wrote an orchestral piece, the computer could 'record' and repeat it. This was achieved in Paris more than twenty-five years ago. With this tool the composer could test his theories, hear if what he wrote worked, could change it, and so on.

Did this scientific work take place at the same time as the people at IRCAM were working to develop similar systems?

No, they were much later. They were behind with respect to our work!

From the tone of your reply I can imagine that there was no semblance of cooperation between you and those at IRCAM.

No, there wasn't anything like cooperation. Boulez was Director of IRCAM and he did not want to have me there.

Why?

I don't know. Perhaps it was a matter of different personalities, a question of having to determine the profile of IRCAM. Boulez wished to be the one central figure.

Photo: Iannis Xenakis.

OLD AND NEW

Earlier you mentioned classical philosophy. Let's go back to ancient Greece, to Plato, to the theories of possible society. When Horkheimer and Adorno criticized modern civilization in Dialectic of Enlightenment *they wrote, among other things, on the dialectic between myth and enlightenment in* The Odyssey. *They saw it as one of the earliest representative testimonies to bourgeois western civilization. You too have a wide historical perspective in your thinking and you have also criticized western social systems. Is your interest in historical figures like Plato and Lenin purely political?*

No. It is only partly political. I liked reading Plato in ancient Greek because I found his thoughts on the forms of society interesting. I had to think about these things at that time. After the Russian revolution it became an enormous challenge to think in terms of possible new forms of society. Not in Germany because Hitler was there, but elsewhere it was necessary to think about new forms of society, to discuss which structures were the best. Plato had a point of view that interested me at that time. It fascinated me that Plato considered all men equal. It was actually also the primary theoretical idea in Bolshevism before Stalin came to power. I found a connection between very old and very modern thought and I believed that on an ideological level they had something in common.

Your political interests were gradually transformed into an awareness of structure, musical structure. Has your political engagement had any impact on your work as an artist?

No. My music has always been independent of my political and sociological ideas.

What are you working on just now?

I am working closely on developing the sound of strings. It has been the norm to compose for strings one note at a time. But why not have each string player produce two notes at a time? I am working on developing the musical space in order to give a richer sound to the orchestra. If you had a string orchestra with ten musicians then you would suddenly have twenty parts simultaneously. The challenges posed by this enlargement of sound space have occupied me in my latest works and will continue to do so in future.

'Ny musik med profil: Interview med komponisten Iannis Xenakis', *Dansk Musik Tidsskrift* 71, 3 (Nov. 1996/97): 74–81.

Kaija Saariaho

Colour, Timbre and Harmony

I'd like to paint a portrait which describes your background as a composer and traces some threads running through your output, characterizing the style and development. So let's begin with a question about the initial starting-point. Do you come from a musical family?

No, not at all. But I have always imagined music, and been very sensitive to sounds. It has been an important element for me as long as I can remember. My parents are not musicians, and so I didn't take up an instrument until I started school. I started to play the violin when I was six, and when I was eight I also started to play the piano. I have many scattered memories, but I'm not sure when I really started to compose. I had music in my mind when I was very young. I heard music which I thought came from under the bed, so at night I used to ask my mother if she could switch it off. Of course she didn't understand what I was talking about. I tried to compose, to write some things down, but they didn't really work. When I got to the age of about ten or eleven, I had a real crisis because I read Mozart's biography; it was very painful for me to read that he had already written a lot of music at my age. So I concluded that I was not very gifted as a musician because I hadn't yet composed any major works. Of course in my child's mind I couldn't see that it was because nobody was teaching me composition or anything like that. I was very, very shy, so I didn't like playing for other people at all. That was another problem: my parents were of course glad that I played these instruments and when we had guests round they would have liked me to play for them, but I hated it. Later at the conservatory, of all the dozens of times that I had to play publicly, there were maybe only three times when I was happy with my own playing. So that was cut out also. I adored music and it was the most important thing for me, but I felt that I wasn't worthy to serve the great cause, or something like that.

It sounds like quite a psychological problem.

Yes.

Did you then unconsciously choose the composer's role, instead of the more extrovert musician's, because you could hide better?

I don't think so, because I really wanted to be a musician quite early. But I was discouraged because I was not a great interpreter by my own standards, and so I concluded that I couldn't become a very interesting composer either. And what I hated was the idea of being some kind of average composer. I decided very early that I didn't want to join that crowd.

Did you discuss this with your parents or your teachers?

I discussed it with my parents. Sometimes I hinted that I was dreaming about being a composer, and they thought I was absolutely crazy. They really didn't see why it would make any sense, so I kept it like a secret dream. I continued playing these instruments and I studied music theory later, but I didn't think it would lead to anything.

Were you at the Sibelius Academy at that stage?

No, I was at the Helsinki Conservatory. When I finished school, I went to art school, and after that I went to university, to study musicology. I was between all these different things, feeling all the time that I wasn't a good enough musician. Meanwhile, I had started playing the organ, also, so I imagined that I could become an organist in a church, looking for the meaning of life and serving music in a small village somewhere in Finland. That is until I found out about the boring realities of this job, which were very far from my romantic dream. At some point I had a new crisis and I started to feel that I was wasting my life. I became obsessed with the fear that I was living every day for nothing, and I realized that I *had* to try to compose. It was the only thing that had any meaning. I don't know how much it had to do with music. It's really to do with my personality. So I entered the Sibelius Academy and started to study composition with Paavo Heininen.

Did reading about Mozart and this world of composers mainly of the opposite sex increase your self-criticism?

Yes, I'm sure it affected me; it didn't even seem to be possible for me to become a composer.

It was a man's world.

Yes. When I was searching for my identity, many women writers were important: Edith Södergran, Virginia Woolf, Sylvia Plath, Anaïs Nin. I was interested in how women writers and painters had been able to do this creative work for which I didn't find any satisfying examples in music.

When you went to the Sibelius Academy did you already have your own aesthetic viewpoints? You had been studying musicology, and been used to thinking about music; did your teacher, Paavo Heininen, open your mind to a special way of your own?

It was very painful. Again, it was completely psychological. I had heard an enormous amount of music, and I had many capabilities, but for some reason that I don't understand I was locked into writing vocal music all the time. In my visual expression I always needed to have people, I couldn't break into abstraction. Somebody knowledgeable about these things could maybe tell me one day what it all was about. Paavo restricted me from writing vocal music, and I started analysing many different kinds of music. Paavo has a course that all his students go through; I think I did those exercises extremely badly, but somehow his treatment gave me the tools to write abstract music and get away from the handicap of always needing a text. I don't know what that all was about, because when I got back to the colours of instrumental music, I returned to the initial music of my childhood. The ten years in between had been absolutely horrible.

Now we're in the late 1970s. How did the environment affect you in general? You were a generation that seemed to be working together towards a common goal. You travelled abroad with Magnus Lindberg, Jukka Tiensuu and others to the same institution in Paris, and shared some common ideas about the potentials of the new electronic equipment.

I didn't know Jukka so well, and I still don't, even though we are in regular contact. I got to know Magnus and Esa-Pekka very quickly when I was studying, and they became very important colleagues for me. The Korvat Auki Society was also very important. We had a very serious level of activity, presenting lectures and analyses for one another; it was more important to us to prepare and present those things well for each other, than to do it at the Sibelius Academy. It was very inspiring to have people like these around.

Is it reasonable to talk about a new generation suddenly taking the stage, not only composers, but also conductors such as Esa-Pekka Salonen?

Historically speaking, there had been the avant-garde movement—sawing pianos, and so on—and as a reaction to that there was a nationalist wave in

Finland. The only members of that generation who were not part of that nationalism were Paavo and Erik Bergman. It was Paavo who then opened up other possible musics for us, which were non-existent in Finland. And when we heard all that, there was a reaction, that's true.

Did Paavo Heininen and Erik Bergman also seem non-existent within Finnish music, compared with the wave of nationalism?

Paavo was very badly treated in those days. He was regarded as an *enfant terrible* who wrote all this unplayable music. Erik Bergman was played a lot, but he was still on the outside; he was the first modernist.

When I talked with Magnus Linberg in 1989 in Helsinki, he said that his original point of departure was the modernist aesthetic, and was possibly influenced in his first pieces by Paavo's way of thinking. Was that also the case with you?

I don't know. I cannot be very analytical about my aesthetics because I don't feel that I choose them. It always seems to me that I have the only possible aesthetic for my music, and that my music can exist only in one way, which is the synthesis of so many things that I cannot analyse it.

Why did you come to Paris?

After leaving Finland, I went to Freiburg first, and from there I started to visit Paris for concerts. Ensemble Itinéraire had great concerts; I had heard some of this type of music in Darmstadt. I had used amplification in a limited way, and was becoming interested in the idea of musical interpolation when I heard Tristan and Gérard speak in Darmstadt and learned about these courses at IRCAM (Institut de Recherche et de Coordination Acoustique/Musique).

What is musical interpolation?

It's musical metamorphosis; a certain kind of development based on ideas from many different sources, including minimalism, in the sense that there is no dynamic development, but rather a gradual change from one state to another. These things interested me very much in the early 1980s, especially Gérard Grisey's lectures.

You made one of your early pieces at that time: Vers le blanc.

Photo: Kaija Saariaho (Liselotte Nissen).

That's an extreme explosion of the idea of interpolation. For fifteen minutes, all that's going on pitch-wise is these extremely slow glissandi from one pitch to another. The change of pitch is so slow that you can't hear it, but since there are three pitches sliding in different directions, you do perceive that the harmonic structure is changing, gradually.

Who was your teacher in Freiburg—Klaus Huber?

It was Ferneyhough officially, and I also studied orchestration with Klaus Huber. I cannot say so much about those studies, because the most important thing for me at that time was to get away from Finland. I had been working very closely with Paavo, and I planned to go back to continue studying with him, but I wanted to get away for a year or so. Finland seemed so small. I had written a couple of pieces and the newspapers and audiences started to get interested in this young woman who was composing; it was somehow irritating, because I was just a student and I felt that the interest was ungrounded.

You were put into the spotlight . . . ?

Because I was a young woman. I needed some distance from that attention. I also needed some distance from Paavo, because he was giving me so many new things all the time that I felt my studies would be never-ending. It was rather stressful because I wasn't able to write my own music; he doesn't like his students to compose while they're studying with him, so every piece that I wrote because of inner necessity went against his agenda.

Did Grisey's Darmstadt lectures on harmony and the spectral way of thinking take you forward in a particular direction?

It was the first time I had heard about spectral music, and it was fantastic compared with the post-serial aesthetics that were dominant everywhere, and which didn't really suit my ideas. When all my fellow students in Freiburg saw fantastically complicated systems on the blackboard, I didn't see any of that or hear anything in the music, so I didn't like this approach at all. I wanted to make music for the ears, and when I first heard Gérard's and Tristan's music it seemed so fresh.

How did that resound with your own ideas? People write about the colour, timbre and harmony in your music.

Those things were there already. On my application form for IRCAM, I wrote that I wanted to learn more about sound, and how to analyse it. And so I did gain some structures for analysing sound and for using these analyses to create harmony. Those skills came step by step, a little at a time, and that's why it was so painful. Maybe learning is painful for everybody anyway, but in my case it's that I need to rediscover a way of doing things. It doesn't help me to know that the way exists already. I needed to discover all these things for my own purposes, so that took some years.

How did you actually spend those years doing computerized spectral analysis?

First I learned the sound synthesis program, Chant. Unlike other sound-synthesis programs, Chant doesn't work with oscillators. I never understood oscillators; it's so far from my reality to make sound that way. With Chant you deal with musical and physical parameters directly; this I found extremely interesting because I just wanted to know more about sound itself. I started building sounds by computer, and the next step was of course to ask myself how I could organize them by computer. That turned into a rather long period in which I was trying to understand how I compose, and some parts of that process I tried to program into the computer. The results of that were very mediocre, as I don't have any special talent for programming, and I often needed help with it. But what was interesting was that I was trying to understand how I work, and through the parts of that working process which I did program, I understood that, in fact, even when you think you are creating certain rules for yourself, the process is very rudimentary. You are constantly moderating the issues intuitively, and it's that intuition which makes the music interesting, not the basic rules, which are in fact quite boring. It's not interesting if the computer gives you back music consisting of nothing but the rules which you programmed yourself. So after realizing that, I wanted to come back to instrumental work and I started to analyse instrumental sounds, especially cello sounds, with Anssi Karttunen who happened to be living here at that time. I worked little by little, from the creation of compositional material to ways of finding harmonic structures, and then I had my basic tools. *Lichtbogen* is the first piece where I used these harmonic ideas, exploring them through the cello.

Are your pieces from the mid-1980s a result of your interest in harmonic and spectral analyses?

Yes, certainly. *Lichtbogen, Io, Nymphéa. Du cristal, ...à la fumée* is from the end of that period, but it still comes from the same source.

Could you talk about the transition from that period to the 1990s where your music takes a new departure?

When I started to plan *Du cristal*, I felt that it would be the last piece of that period. That's why I forced myself to write another piece with the same musical material, using it completely differently. That piece became *...à la fumée*.

After all this harmonic and spectral analysis, the crucial point is of course transferring it into real sound. Could you talk about how you approach instrumentation?

That's completely intuitive. I have no rules on instrumentation, although I do have very clear ideas about the kinds of textures, degrees of luminosity in various instruments, and degrees of pigment. I use all these parameters to organize instruments. It's important for me when building a musical form to create contrasting textures, for example, contrasting dark rough-surfaced textures with smooth textures full of bright pigments. I use such general ideas when orchestrating, but as for the actual instruments themselves, I use them very intuitively.

Do you think in terms of colours, or of paintings, or other kinds of visual images?

When I think about colours, it's more about degrees of luminosity than about reds and greens. It's very much combined with a certain atmosphere, which I can't quite define with reference to music, but which is connected with a certain tempo or character. It's important for me to write *dolce* or *con violenza*, or whatever, because the character of the music exists from the beginning; it's not something I invent afterwards.

You give the listener a kind of hint with your titles, which often describe an atmosphere.

To start with, the titles are for my own sake. When I feel that I have the right title, I can focus my material.

So you come up with the title first?

Sometimes. At least very much before the end of the piece, always. It's very important for feeding my imagination. Maybe afterwards I could even remove it, or change it, but it belongs to the music in some way.

You sometimes re-use material from earlier works . . .

Even if I were to use similar structural solutions in several pieces, I would need to find them again each time. I can never look at something I did in an earlier piece, and say, well, I could do the same thing here, it would do just fine. Even if I end up doing something similar, I need to feel the necessity again. I am struggling with this problem right now: in my opera I'm re-using some music from *Oltra mar*, because that was actually my initial plan. That material has a direct connection to certain parts of the opera.

Musical structures?

Yes. Certain parts of the music, and harmonies and so on. I know that I don't need to re-invent this music. It's my own music, so I'm free to use it if I want to, but still it's very painful.

Why?

I find it so boring, somehow, to take pre-existing music. That's often the issue in post-modernism where people make collages. I just don't understand the idea.

Are you caught up in the idea that everything should be absolutely new?

No, I don't care if it's new or not. But it must be new for me.

But still you do it too; you have re-used material from Oltra mar.

It would have been stupid not to take it, because that's why I wrote it that way. It was really written for this purpose, but I still have a hard time copying.

Is Oltra mar *a study for your opera?*

No.

But you had already started your opera when you wrote it?

I was waiting for my libretto. There is a direct link; the musical material is partly the same. But actually everything I've written since 1993 is directly connected to my opera, so this is a really long project.

So you already knew many years ago that you would write an opera?

Yes. I found the subject, and a story which I liked very much, but it took many years before I finally found a writer to make a libretto out of it. The writer's name is Amin Maalouf, a French-Lebanese writer, who has written many books about that period in history, and is a very well-known writer in France.

The importance of your titles is also demonstrated by the title L'amour de loin. *It caused confusion, because suddenly the title changed.*

This is a separate matter, because there are many people working on this project, so there are many opinions concerning the title.

So what is it called now?

Now it's back to *L'amour de loin* again. At some point it was *Clémence*, and there have been other proposals too. I'm not sure that *L'amour de loin* will be the final title, because it points so much to the history and to the period, which are not actually the most important aspects of the opera.

Could you tell me about the subject, and about how you discovered the text?

It's a story, which was written at the beginning of the twelfth century, about one of the first troubadours, Jaufré Rudel, and his distant love. He took to sea to go to see his love who was a countess living in Tripoli, but he fell ill on the boat, and finally died in the arms of this lady. I wondered myself for many years why this story interested me so much. I knew I wanted to write an opera about love and death, because they are the great mysteries remaining to us. We are living in the year 2000 and we have achieved so many things, but advanced so little with these two subjects which concern all of us in that they are the basics of our life. I like the way these things are handled in this story. Later, I understood that the story concerns me personally. There are these two main characters—the troubadour who wants to express his love through writing music, and the lady who was sent to a foreign continent; I realized that they are like the two parts of myself. When I heard about this troubadour's life-story, I wanted to see some of his texts. I got permission to go and see some of them in the national library in Paris, and I especially liked this text, which then became *Lonh*. I have a photo of that page of the manuscript. Coming from a young culture, and being able to hold a book which was written by hand in the twelfth century, was very impressive to me. I couldn't exactly read the music, because it's written in four-line staves, so I just interpreted it my own way. Since then, I've seen more accurate transcriptions of it, but it was just a starting-point for me. I didn't want to use his music, but my interpretation served as a basic material. I also wanted to write the opera for Dawn, with whom I had already been working on *Chateau de l'âme*.

After working on this opera for so many years, would you describe the final work as constituting an end to that period, or will you be able to go further with the same ideas?

I hope it's the end of something! It has been such a long process. I feel that I've been preparing this opera since 1992, with all the vocal music I've been writing. So I hope that after producing all that paper something else will appear out of it!

And has something appeared?

Not yet! Because I'm still composing this piece, my mind is completely absorbed in it. I find it difficult to think about anything else.

You didn't have a commission for the opera at the beginning of the '90s. When did you actually get the commission?

It was in fact Walton Grönroos at The Finnish Opera who first wanted to commission an opera from me, and that's when I started thinking seriously about writing it. I had had many problems approaching the text, and I really didn't know how I would do it. Later Walton left The Finnish Opera and it became rather complicated, because I had this French subject. At that point I was already in contact with Salzburg; they had commissioned *Chateau de l'âme*. I was starting to look into where my opera could be produced, and there was a lot of interest. Some people said to me, why don't you try Salzburg, if they like your music there? I thought it was a crazy idea to start at the top with my first opera, but anyway I sent the project to Gérard Mortier, and he was immediately enthusiastic and took on the whole production. It was an enormous stroke of luck.

Why?

Because he offered me such good conditions. He offered me a commission, which means I can write without having any financial problems. He offered me the possibility of working with all these fantastic musicians and the director Peter Sellars, whom I admired a lot. In fact it was Sellars' production of Messiaen's *Saint François d'Assis* that finally convinced me that I could write my own opera. I was always worried that I should have more dramatic turns, something going on on the stage, and when I saw that in Peter's direction, I felt I could write opera too. So Salzburg has very much been a gift in this respect.

Taking a bird's-eye view of what you have been saying, it looks like one long string of successes, and yet at the same time you have this attitude toward yourself as not being successful enough. Have you gained any self-confidence during these years, which might indicate to you that you have had a rather mistaken view of your own creativity?

I don't know. One can always develop.

But isn't it difficult to retain a dark view of your abilities?

Well, I don't have such a black view of myself, but I'm rather surprised. I don't listen to my music very often, but sometimes when I hear it nicely interpreted, I find myself thinking, this is beautiful music; how was I able to write it? I don't understand. I think I have had a lot of luck; so many good things happened to my music that, of course, it makes me feel good.

Looking back on your output, would you identify some uncertain pieces where you would say, this is where I was trying to do something, and other more successful pieces where you would say, this is where I did it.

I think it goes in phases; I'm not happy with much of my music.

Just a couple of pieces?

The first piece that I feel is entirely mine is the flute piece *Laconisme de l'aile* and I still recognize it as being completely my own music. *Lichtbogen* can be badly performed, but when it's well performed I think it's really mine too. So is *Du cristal, …à la fumée* much less. *Amers* (1992) for solo cello and ensemble really has something to do with me. And maybe some parts of *Chateau de l'âme* and *Oltra mar* as well.

And, I guess, the opera?

Yes, I hope so!

You will receive the Nordic Music Council Prize in March 2000 for your work Lonh *for soprano and electronics. What does it mean for you to receive the Nordic Music Council Prize? Do you feel an affinity with Nordicism? Having achieved so much attention already, it may mean nothing for you, but on the other hand it's a kind of recognition which might affect you.*

I'm Nordic. I don't feel that I became French just because I live in Paris. I feel a very strong Finnish and Nordic identity in the way I have decided to live my life and the way I want to raise my children and so on. Nordic culture is strong, and sometimes very different from French culture. I want to keep up the positive aspects of it in my everyday life. My music has had a lot of recognition, but in fact not so much from the Nordic countries, so for that reason I'm really very happy about this prize. And another reason I'm happy about it is that it's for this chamber music piece which uses technology, and not my opera or my orchestral *Diptych*, or something like that. Even just the decision to award the prize for a chamber piece is a very healthy idea. Everything is going in the direction of mega-concerts. If you really think about important *musical* experiences, they don't happen—for me, at least, in these mega-concerts. Those big events don't have so much to do with music; they have more to do with feeling a connection with 3000 other people. But when we think about important musical experiences, they are more often found in very small venues with one or two musicians, and those are the really important musical exchanges. For some years now I've been dreaming about home concerts, reacting against this mega-thinking. We are small people, and I am less and less able to tolerate this mega-thinking which comes from United States, where most things are measured in terms of money. What has it got to do with our music? For this reason, I was so happy that it was decided to award this prize for a chamber work. When I heard that *Lonh* was one of the pieces, I thought it would have no chance, so I was very glad that it was chosen.

What do you take from Nordic culture? What have we to offer here in France?

A certain healthy straightforward way of dealing with things. Of course, what we Nordic people think of as healthy doesn't have so much to do with the French way of thinking, but I like things to be clear, I like to express myself clearly, and I would like my children to do so too. I like to have a very straightforward relation to my body, also. It's part of this totality which is me, and I would like to keep things simple, not complicate them. I would like to keep things profound, not superficial, and this is what I try to pass on in my music, and in bringing up my children, and in my communication with people. These are typically Nordic features, some of the good sides of our culture. Of course, the culture of where I'm living, here in Paris, has different virtues, which I'm trying to learn, and which have been good for me; for example, not to be so Protestant and strict with myself, to be a little more tender, and to accept oneself as one is.

What has been most difficult to achieve or accept in French culture?

Verbal communication, which is very complicated. In French, you hint at things, you don't say things directly. You have to understand many things between the lines, which I often just don't understand.

Entering an institution like IRCAM, with these guys who are so expert at handling all the technological equipment, you might feel a bit lost to begin with. Was that the case for you, entering a man's world where there were such an extremely advanced way of thinking and of handling machines?

That's true. It was a crazy thing to do. First to go into this man's profession, and then to stick my head into that place, where at that time, ten to fifteen years ago, there were really no women at all, except for the secretaries. So it was completely hopeless, particularly combined with the language and everything. But it also made me understand how over-estimated rational logical thinking is. It's such a small part of our lives, and of course that's the type of thinking that computers understand, but computers are also very limited, and when we speak about art, it's such a small part of it. There are other much more complex ways of thinking and feeling. This kind of apparently quick intelligence, which works with computers, doesn't always work so well with people.

You talked about taking care of your body as much as your mind and inner life. You seem to be expressing a kind of holistic view of living, without being in any way religious. Is that right?

I'm sure that if I didn't have children, and didn't live in this very concrete day-to-day world of small children, I would certainly be radically pursuing a much more ascetic direction, but in this period of my life I appreciate the importance of the totality of each of us as whole beings.

So you might perhaps turn to a more ascetic way of life later on?

Maybe, we'll see. You never know. Maybe I feel this way now precisely because I cannot do otherwise.

Have you considered going back to your home country, as Magnus has done, back to the church in the village, or is that impossible now?

I went with my family a year and a half ago. I was Visiting Professor at the Sibelius Academy, and I taught with Paavo as my colleague—it was great. So we stayed there one winter, nearly a whole year.

What did your husband say to that move?

It was much easier for him than for me, I think. I found the same uniformity, which can be both good and bad, and which is so opposite to the diversity we have in this city, for example. I don't know how life will be when I'm older, it might be very different. Right now, I'm very happy here. My children liked Finland very much.

Can they speak Finnish?

Yes. I speak only Finnish with them. But I was happy to come back to Paris; there's one practical aspect, and that is that I'm too well recognized in Finland as a person.

It's difficult to live a normal life?

Yes, it sounds funny. When I say this to colleagues in America, they think it's fantastic that there is a country where contemporary composers can be esteemed public personalities. In a way it is fantastic, it's true, but that doesn't suit my personality at all. There are people who take it well and handle it wonderfully, like Esa-Pekka; he's not disturbed by being the centre of attention—he seems to love it—but I'm not that kind of person.

Do you enjoy walking through the streets here in Paris, where nobody knows you?

Yes, it's very nice. I often feel as if I'm in a jungle, or a forest. I'm free, in that sense.

'Storslået enkelt: Interview med den finske komponist Kaija Saariaho'. *Dansk Musik Tidsskrift* 74, 6 (1999/00): 182–193.

Biographies: Composers

ERIK BERGMAN (b. 1911, Finland) is the 'grand old man' of Finnish modernism. In the 1940s the romanticism of his early works gave way to a highly chromatic style and in 1952 Bergman experimented with the twelve-tone method. After studies with Wladimir Vogel in Switzerland, Bergman began to use speech in his choral works and further developed his style to include aleatoric and improvisatory techniques. As a composer and as a teacher at the Sibelius Academy he has paved the way for a new generation of composers in Finland. Bergman's scores are published by Boosey & Hawkes and Novello. His works can be heard on recordings from the Ondine label, among others.

EDISON DENISOV (1929–1996, Russia) was a native of Tomsk in Siberia. He first studied mathematics and music at the Moscow Conservatory where he completed his studies in composition with Vissarion Shebalin, orchestration with Nikolai Rakov, analysis with Viktor Zuckerman and piano with Vladimir Below in 1956. From 1959 he taught formal analysis and composition at the same conservatory and in 1990–91 he was invited by Boulez to work at IRCAM in Paris. For almost 30 years Denisov worked with Juri Ljubimov, Director of the Moscow Taganka Theatre, on theatrical performances in Russia and in various European countries. Denisov's scores are published by Internationale Musikverlage Hans Sikorski. Recordings of his music can be found on the Sonora, Accord, Berlin classics, Pierre Varany, Accord and Triton labels.

HANS GEFORS (b. 1952, Sweden) studied composition with Per-Gunnar Alldahl and Maurice Karkoff, and then with Ingvar Lidholm at the State College of Music in Stockholm. He eventually moved to Denmark to study with Per Nørgård at the Royal Academy in Århus. An experienced teacher, music critic and editor, he has been Professor of Composition in Lund. A long-term interest in literature and psychology coupled with a sure dramatic sense have resulted in a number of operas that have appealed to general audiences, first in Sweden and now abroad. Scores can be obtained from the Swedish Music Information Centre. BIS, dacapo and Phono Suecia are labels on which his recordings can be found.

PHILIP GLASS (b. 1937, USA) graduated from the University of Chicago at the age of 19, and then studied composition at the Juilliard School. In search of his own voice, he moved to Paris in the 1960s to work with Nadia Boulanger. He transcribed the Indian music of Ravi Shankar into standard notation and researched music in North Africa, India and the Himalayas before returning to New York to explore the integration of Eastern techniques into his own work. By 1976 he had composed a large body of new music, predominantly for theatre companies and for his own performing group, The Philip Glass Ensemble. His music is published by Chester Music Ltd., and recordings may be found on the Nonesuch label, Sony Music, Deutsche Grammophon, Point, Catalyst and Materiali Sonori.

SOFIA GUBAIDULINA (b. 1931, Russia) comes from Tschistopol in the Tartar region of Russia, a fact that may explain the intense nature of her music. In 1954 she completed her studies in piano and composition at the conservatory in Kasan and continued her work with Nikolai Peiko, a former student of Dmitry Shostakovich, and Vissarion Shebalin at the Moscow Conservatory. Since 1963 she has been a freelance composer. In 1975, together with composers Vyacheslav Artyomov and Viktor Suslin, she founded 'Astraea', a group devoted to improvisation using rare Russian, Caucasian and Central Asian folk instruments. Gubaidulina left Russia for the first time in 1986 when she was invited to the Lockenhaus Festival in Austria. She has lived in Hamburg since 1992. Gubaidulina's scores are published by Internationale Musikverlage Hans Sikorski. Recordings of her music can be found on the Deutsche Grammophon, Chandos, Sonora, col legno, BIS, Berlin Classics, Wergo, Koch International and CPO labels.

PELLE GUDMUNDSEN-HOLMGREEN (b. 1932, Denmark) studied at the Royal Danish Academy of Music in Copenhagen where his principal teachers were Finn Høffding and Svend Westergaard. Gudmundsen-Holmgreen's enduring contribution to present-day Danish music, principally his dedicated individualism and masterly treatment of form, have been constantly to the fore since the early 1960s when he played a significant part in the rejuvenation of Danish Music. His music is published by Edition Wilhelm Hansen and is recorded on dacapo and PAULA, BIS, among others.

VAGN HOLMBOE (1906–96, Denmark), the most important Danish composer and teacher in the period between Carl Nielsen (d. 1931) and the post-war generation of composers, studied with Finn Høffding and Knud Jeppesen at the Royal Danish Academy of Music in Copenhagen. Inspired by the folk music of Romania and influenced by Bartók, Stravinsky and Haydn, Holmboe strove to achieve clarity in his musical expression. The style of his music owes much to his own 'metamorphosis technique', his term for his approach to melodic trans-formation. His large output is published by Edition Wilhelm Hansen; record-ings are to be found on BIS and Marco Polo. Dacapo is currently engaged in recording all of Holmboe's symphonies, string quartets and chamber concertos.

TIKHON KHRENNIKOV (b. 1913, Russia) first studied composition in the Gnessin Institute in Moscow, but later transferred to the Moscow Conserva-tory where he worked with Vissarion Shebalin. From 1941 to 1955 he was Director of Music at the Soviet Army's Central Theatre, and from 1948 to 1991 he was the First Secretary of the USSR's Composers' Society. In his various roles (for instance, as a member of the Control Commission of the Central Committee), he was an important link between the political establishment and his artistic colleagues. Khrennikov's scores are published by the Internationale Musikverlage Hans Sikorski and recordings can be found on Russian Disc.

INGVAR LIDHOLM (b. 1921, Sweden) studied composition in his native Swe-den with Hilding Rosenberg, although he also made short study trips abroad. An influential organizer of music at the Swedish Broadcasting Company, Lidholm spent several years as editor of *Nutida Musik* and in 1960 became a Member of the Royal Academy of Music where he served as Vice President. He also chaired the Swedish ISCM section. Lidholm's varied musical inter-ests include early vocal polyphony as traced in his *Laudi*, pre- and post-war modernism as found in his *Music for Strings 1952* and *Ritornell*, and post-mod-ern exploration of musical sound-scapes as heard in his *Poesis*. The character of his musical thought is marked by his abiding concern for human values. Lidholm's scores are published by Nordiska Musikförlaget, and recordings can be found on the Chandos, Caprice, Consonance and BIS labels.

GYÖRGY LIGETI (b. 1923, Transylvania) ignored his 70th birthday on 28 May 1993, stating that such celebrations are a convention of society and totally unimportant. Ligeti has been one of the most influential composers of the twentieth-century. His ground-breaking works from his 'micro-polyphonic' period satisfied the demands in the late 1950s and early 1960s for a renewal of musical material, and his so-called return to tonality in the 1970s with the Horn Trio first startled, then charmed the musical world. His inventive use of inter-locking rhythmic patterns—only one of the compositional ideas in his *Etudes*—has set its mark on the music of his contemporaries. Schott Music Interna-tional publishes Ligeti's scores and recordings can be found on Wergo, Sony Classical, Phillips, BIS, and Deutsche Grammophon, among others.

MAGNUS LINDBERG (b. 1958, Finland) studied at the Sibelius Academy be-fore continuing private study with Gérard Grisey and Vinko Globokar in

Paris in addition to attending courses given by Franco Donatoni (Siena) and Brian Ferneyhough (Darmstadt). Lindberg's fruitful association with Toimii, an ensemble that he founded with Esa Pekka Salonen, which is dedicated to experimentation in composition, led to a significant engagement with electro-acoustic music, complex scores and work at IRCAM in Paris. More recently he has concentrated on harmonic sonorities. Lindberg has received numerous commissions and prizes and has been the featured composer at many international music festivals. His scores are available from Chester Music Ltd., Edition Fazer, Modus Musiikki. Recordings can be found on the Ades, Ondine, Montaigne and Sterling labels, among others.

ARNE NORDHEIM (b. 1931, Norway) has written works in most genres, but principally for the orchestra. At one time very active in electronic music, but with *Eco* for soprano, two choirs and orchestra he began to explore the post-electronic world of sound in extended instrumental and vocal techniques. In 1994 his music drama *Draumkvædet* was premiered at Oslo's Norwegian Theatre as part of the official cultural programme of the Winter Olympics at Lillehammer. A recent Violin Concerto was followed by *Nidaros*, a large work for soloists, choir and orchestra commissioned for the 1000th anniversary of the city of Trondheim and premiered in the Nidaros Cathedral. Nordheim's scores are published by Edition Wilhelm Hansen and recordings can be found on the Norwegian Hemera and Aurora labels, among others.

PER NØRGÅRD (b. 1932, Denmark) studied composition with Vagn Holmboe and Finn Høffding at the Royal Danish Academy of Music (1952–55), and with Nadia Boulanger in Paris (1956–57). Since his return to Copenhagen in 1957, Nørgård has been in the vanguard of music development as a composer, essayist and theorist, teacher and motivator—in Denmark and the other Nordic countries, and increasingly in the international arena. Already highly regarded as a teacher, his move from Copenhagen to Århus in 1965 led to the consolidation of that city as a centre for contemporary music. Nørgård is currently a full-time composer. His scores are available from Edition Wilhelm Hansen and recordings of his music can be found on dacapo, PAULA, Danacord, Kontrapunkt, Chandos and BIS.

KARL AAGE RASMUSSEN (b. 1947, Denmark) studied composition with Nørgård and Gudmundsen-Holmgreen at the Århus Academy of Music where he now teaches. In addition to being a widely-published essayist and active as editor of journals and Danish Radio programmes, Rasmussen occupies a central role in Danish music. He is artistic director of the annual NUMUS Festival—famous as an arena for discussion and the exchange of ideas. The concise and penetrating critical thought that characterizes his music is also evident in his other work. Edition Wilhelm Hansen publishes his music and dacapo, Bridge Records and PAULA have issued recordings with performances by ensembles such as the Arditti Quartet, Speculum Musicae, Capricorn, and the ensemble founded by Rasmussen, The Elsinore Players.

KAIJA SAARIAHO (b. 1952) studied painting before she began to work in musical composition with Paavo Heininen at the Sibelius Academy in 1976. In 1981–82 she was in Freiburg where Brian Ferneyhough and Klaus Huber were her mentors. Since 1982 Saariaho has resided in Paris where her work at IRCAM (Institut de Recherche et de Coordination Acoustique/Musique) has given rise to her reputation as a pace-setter in the field of electro-acoustic music among the Nordic composers. Her first opera, *L'amour de Loin*, was premiered at the Salzburg Festival in August 2000. Chester Music in London publishes Saariaho's music and recordings can be found on the Finlandia and Ondine labels.

ALFRED SCHNITTKE (1934–1998, Russia) was born in the German region of the Volga Republic. After an initial period in Vienna, he continued his studies in Moscow where his first degree was in choral conducting. He then studied composition and counterpoint with Jevgeni Golubev and instrumentation with Nikolai Rakov at the Moscow conservatory. He also studied with Philipp Herschkovitch, a former student of Webern. For ten years Schnittke taught at the Moscow Conservatory and then became a freelance composer. For the last eight years of his life he lived in Hamburg where he taught composition at the Musikhochschule. Right up to the end of his life Schnittke's rigorous and uncompromising objectivity in his approach to composition never overwhelmed his concern for the human condition. Schnittke's scores are published by Internationale Musikverlage Hans Sikorski, and the complete recordings are due for release on the BIS label. Schnittke's music can also be found on Nonesuch, BIS, Deutsche Grammophon, EMI classics, Sony Music, Marco Polo, Collins Classics and Chandos labels.

ÞORKELL SIGURBJÖRNSSON (b. 1938, Iceland) was born into an Icelandic family of Bishops, and become a composer, teacher and promoter of music following his studies with R.G. Harris at Hamline University and Kenneth Gaburo and Lejaren Hiller at the University of Illinois, Champaign-Urbana. His extensive catalogue includes both sacred and secular works in all genres. Practical, direct and sensitive to the minute as well as to the spectacular in the Icelandic landscape, Sigurbjörnsson has been the most significant advocate for the development of a vital musical life in Iceland since the war. Scores can be obtained from the Icelandic Music Information Centre and recordings are available on the ITM and BIS labels.

KARLHEINZ STOCKHAUSEN (b. 1928, Germany) is one of the foremost composers of the post-war era. In the 1950s after studying with Messiaen and Frank Martin, he developed a highly personal style as evidenced by his *Kreuzspiel* and *Kontra-Punkte*. As a teacher and composer at Darmstadt he was an important exponent of post-war serialism. Since 1977 he has concentrated on the *Licht*-project, a cycle of seven operas each based on one day of the week. Stockhausen's scores are available from Universal Edition and from the Stockhausen Verlag, 5057 Kürten, Germany. Since 1991, the complete recordings of his works have been released on his own label, and are also found on ECM, Nonesuch, Deutsche Grammophon, Accord and Wergo.

PAWEL SZYMANSKI (b. 1954, Poland) studied at the Chopin Academy of Music in Warsaw and gained early encouragement from Tadeusz Baird and Roman Haubenstock-Ramati. Szymanski's work draws inspiration from the old in expressing the new. *Gloria* for women's chorus and orchestra performed at the Warsaw Autumn Festival in 1974, established him as one of the most talented composers of his generation. Szymanski's work is published by Moeck Verlag and Chester Music, among others. Recordings are available from Polskie Nagrania.

OLAV ANTON THOMMESSEN (b. 1946, Norway) first studied composition in the USA at Westminster Choir College, and then at Indiana University with Bernhard Heiden and Iannis Xenakis. He completed his studies in Poland with Piotr Perkowski and in Utrecht with Werner Kaegi and Otto Laske. Currently Professor of Composition at the Norwegian State Academy of Music, Thommessen has lectured widely on music history and film music, and in 1980 initiated a course in auditive analysis (sonology) at the State Academy. Early in the 1980s Thommessen began incorporating quotations from earlier music into some of his compositions. His prodigious output has been widely performed. He has written operas *(A Glass Bead Game, The Hermaprhodite)*, orchestral works *(Beyond Neon)*, many chamber works as well as incidental music for the theatre. The Norwegian Music Information Centre publishes Thommessen's scores and his music is recorded on the Caprice, Hemera and Aurora labels, among others.

JUKKA TIENSUU (b. 1948, Finland) is a harpsichordist, pianist, conductor, teacher and essayist, in addition to being a composer and founder of the festival for contemporary music in Viitasaari. A forerunner of the young modernist generation of 1980s Finland, he studied at the Sibelius Academy under Paavo Heininen, and in Freiburg under Klaus Huber and Brian Ferneyhough. Relinquishing development in the conventional meaning of the word, Tiensuu concentrates on timbre and harmony to achieve the characteristic 'lucid clarity' of his work. His *Tokko* (1987) for male chorus and computer-synthesized tape won first prize at the 1988 Unesco International Composers' Rostrum in Paris. Tiensuu's scores are available from the Finnish Music Information Centre and his music is recorded on the Montaigne, Finlandia and Ondine labels.

IANNIS XENAKIS (b. 1922, Romania) studied mathematics, physics, law, archeology and music in his native Greece. In 1947 because of political difficulties he fled his country and established himself in Paris where he studied with Boulanger and Messiaen, among others. At the same time he worked as an engineer with the famous architect Le Corbusier. Xenakis's music reflects his interest in spatial dimensions; many of his works are inspired by probability and its application to architectural design. The first general recognition of Xenakis's work came with *Metastaseis* (1954) and since then he has been at the forefront of the development of new musical thought in the post-war period. His scores are available from Edition Salabert and recordings of his music can be found on a variety of labels, including Mode, Neuma, Accord, Vandenburg, Hyperion, BIS and Caprice.

BIOGRAPHIES: AUTHORS

ANDERS BEYER (b. 1958, Denmark) editor, author and critic, graduated in musicology from the Institute of Musicology, University of Copenhagen. In addition to his work as a critic for the national daily newspaper, *Information*, he edits *Dansk Musik Tidsskrift* (Danish Music Review) and *Nordic Sounds*. He has taught twentieth-century music history at the University of Copenhagen, and he is a consultant and writer for *The New Grove Dictionary of Music and Musicians* and *Musik in Geschichte und Gegenwart* (MGG). Beyer is editor of the book *The Music of Per Nørgård. Fourteen Interpretative Essays*, Scolar Press, 1996.

JEAN CHRISTENSEN (b. 1940, USA) has been interested in Danish music since the 1970s when she first travelled to Copenhagen to work on her dissertation, 'Arnold Schoenberg's Oratorio, *Die Jakobsleiter*'(UCLA, 1979), with Professor Jan Maegaard. In 1994 she founded a Center for the Study of Danish Music at the University of Louisville where she is Professor of Music History, specializing in twentieth-century music.

INDEX

Page numbers in *italics* refer to illustrations

Y

Z